W9-AWH-665

550 AP®
CALCULUS AB & BC
Practice Questions

The Staff of the Princeton Review

PrincetonReview.com

Random House, Inc. New York

The Princeton Review
111 Speen Street, Suite 550
Framingham, MA 01701
E-mail: editorialsupport@review.com

ISBN: 978-0-8041-2445-4
eBook ISBN: 978-0-8041-2446-1
ISSN: 2330-5614

Editor: Calvin S. Cato
Production Editor: Jesse Newkirk
Production Coordinator: Deborah A. Silvestrini

Printed in the United States of America on partially recycled paper.

10 9 8 7 6 5 4 3 2 1

Editorial

Rob Franek, Senior VP, Publisher
Mary Beth Garrick, Director of Production
Selena Coppock, Senior Editor
Calvin Cato, Editor
Kristen O'Toole, Editor
Meave Shelton, Editor
Alyssa Wolff, Editorial Assistant

Random House Publishing Team

Tom Russell, Publisher
Nicole Benhabib, Publishing Director
Ellen L. Reed, Production Manager
Alison Stoltzfus, Managing Editor
Erika Pepe, Associate Production Manager
Kristin Lindner, Production Supervisor
Andrea Lau, Designer

Acknowledgments

The Princeton Review would like to give a very special thanks to Bikem Polat and Chris Knuth for their hard work on the creation of this title. Their intimate subject knowledge and thorough fact-checking has made this book possible. In addition, The Princeton Review thanks Jesse Newkirk for his hard work in copy editing the content of this title.

About the Authors

Bikem Ayse Polat has been teaching and tutoring through The Princeton Review since 2010. She came to TPR as an undergraduate at the University of California, San Diego from which she graduated in 2011 with two Bachelors of Science degrees in Bioengineering: Pre-Med and Psychology. After graduation, she moved to Cincinnati, OH for a year where she certified to tutor online and was promoted to Master Tutor. She is currently residing in Philadelphia, PA where she is a graduate student at Temple University, working on her Ph.D. in Urban Education. She is certified to teach and tutor numerous Advanced Placement courses as well as the PSAT, SAT, ACT, LSAT, GRE, and MCAT. In her spare time, Bikem enjoys spending time with her dog, Gary, and her nieces, Laila and Serra.

Chris Knuth have been with the Princeton Review for 9 years and has been teaching Math since the 5th grade through various tutoring organizations and classes. He is certified to teach various Advanced Placement courses as well as SAT, ACT, GMAT, GRE, LSAT, DAT, OAT, PSAT, SSAT, and ISEE. He considers Calculus to be his favorite level of Math. Chris would like to thank his family for their unwavering support and always being the "wind in my sail" and give a very special thank you to the teachers who made math fun, Gai Williams and Anita Genduso.

Contents

Part I
Using This Book to Improve Your AP Score

- Preview: Your Knowledge, Your Expectations
- Your Guide to Using This Book
- How to Begin
- AB Calculus Diagnostic Test
- AB Calculus Diagnostic Test Answers and Explanations
- BC Calculus Diagnostic Test
- BC Calculus Diagnostic Test Answers and Explanations

PREVIEW: YOUR KNOWLEDGE, YOUR EXPECTATIONS

Your route to a high score on the AP Calculus Exam depends a lot on how you plan to use this book. Start thinking about your plan by responding to the following questions.

1. Rate your level of confidence about your knowledge of the content tested by the AP Calculus Exam:

    A. Very confident—I know it all
    B. I'm pretty confident, but there are topics for which I could use help
    C. Not confident—I need quite a bit of support
    D. I'm not sure

2. If you have a goal score in mind, circle your goal score for the AP Calculus Exam:

    5   4   3   2   1   I'm not sure yet

3. What do you expect to learn from this book? Circle all that apply to you.

    A. A general overview of the test and what to expect
    B. Strategies for how to approach the test
    C. The content tested by this exam
    D. I'm not sure yet

YOUR GUIDE TO USING THIS BOOK

This book is organized to provide as much—or as little—support as you need, so you can use this book in whatever way will be most helpful for improving your score on the AP Calculus Exam.

*   The remainder of **Part One** will provide guidance on how to use this book and help you determine your strengths and weaknesses.

*   **Part Two** of this book will
    o   provide information about the structure, scoring, and content of the AP Calculus Exam.
    o   help you to make a study plan.
    o   point you towards additional resources.

- **Part Three** of this book will explore various strategies:
  - o   how to attack multiple choice questions
  - o   how to write a high-scoring free response answer
  - o   how to manage your time to maximize the number of points available to you

- **Part Four** of this book contains practice drills covering all of the AB Calculus and BC Calculus concepts you will find on the exams.

- **Part Five** of this book contains practice tests.

You may choose to use some parts of this book over others, or you may work through the entire book. This will depend on your needs and how much time you have. Let's now look how to make this determination.

HOW TO BEGIN

1. **Take a Test**

   Before you can decide how to use this book, you need to take a practice test. Doing so will give you insight into your strengths and weaknesses, and the test will also help you make an effective study plan. If you're feeling test-phobic, remind yourself that a practice test is a tool for diagnosing yourself—it's not how well you do that matters but how you use information gleaned from your performance to guide your preparation.

   So, before you read further, take the AP Calculus AB Diagnostic Test starting at page 7 of this book or take the AP Calculus BC Diagnostic Test starting on page 51. Be sure to do so in one sitting, following the instructions that appear before the test.

2. **Check Your Answers**

   Using the answer key on page 34 (for Calculus AB) or page 78 (for Calculus BC), count how many multiple choice questions you got right and how many you missed. Don't worry about the explanations for now, and don't worry about why you missed questions. We'll get to that soon.

3. **Reflect on the Test**

   After you take your first test, respond to the following questions:

   - How much time did you spend on the multiple choice questions?

   - How much time did you spend on each free response question?

- How many multiple choice questions did you miss?

- Do you feel you had the knowledge to address the subject matter of the essays?

- Do you feel you wrote well organized, thoughtful essays?

- Circle the content areas that were most challenging for you and draw a line through the ones in which you felt confident/did well.

  o Functions, Graphs, and Limits

  o Differential Calculus

  o Integral Calculus

  o Polynomial Approximations and Series (for BC Calculus Students)

  o Applications of Derivatives

  o Applications of Integrals

4. **Read Part Two and Complete the Self-Evaluation**

As discussed in the Goals section above, Part Two will provide information on how the test is structured and scored. It will also set out areas of content that are tested.

As you read Part Two, re-evaluate your answers to the questions above. At the end of Part Two, you will revisit and refine the questions you answered above. You will then be able to make a study plan, based on your needs and time available, that will allow you to use this book most effectively.

5. **Engage with the Drills as Needed**

Notice the word *engage*. You'll get more out of this book if you use it intentionally than if you read it passively, hoping for an improved score through osmosis.

The drills are designed to give you the opportunity to assess your mastery of calculus concepts through test-appropriate questions.

6. **Take Test 2 and Assess Your Performance**

    Once you feel you have developed the strategies you need and gained the knowledge you lacked, you should take one of the practice exams at the end of this book. You should do so in one sitting, following the instructions at the beginning of the test. When you are done, check your answers to the multiple choice sections.

    Once you have taken the test, reflect on what areas you still need to work on, and revisit the drills in this book that address those topics. Through this type of reflection and engagement, you will continue to improve.

7. **Keep Working**

    As you work through the drills, consider what additional work you need to do and how you will change your strategic approach to different parts of the test.

    If you do need more guidance, there are plenty of resources available to you. Our *Cracking the AP Calculus AB & BC Exams* guide gives you a comprehensive review of all the calculus topics you need to know for the exam and offers 5 practice tests (3 for AB and 2 for BC). In addition, you can go to the AP Central website for more information about exam schedules and calculus concepts.

AB Calculus
Diagnostic Test

AP® Calculus AB Exam

DO NOT OPEN THIS BOOKLET UNTIL YOU ARE TOLD TO DO SO.

At a Glance
Total Time
1 hour and 45 minutes
Number of Questions
45
Percent of Total Grade
50%
Writing Instrument
Pencil required

Instructions

Section I of this examination contains 45 multiple-choice questions. Fill in only the ovals for numbers 1 through 45 on your answer sheet.

CALCULATORS MAY NOT BE USED IN THIS PART OF THE EXAMINATION.

Indicate all of your answers to the multiple-choice questions on the answer sheet. No credit will be given for anything written in this exam booklet, but you may use the booklet for notes or scratch work. After you have decided which of the suggested answers is best, completely fill in the corresponding oval on the answer sheet. Give only one answer to each question. If you change an answer, be sure that the previous mark is erased completely. Here is a sample question and answer.

Sample Question   Sample Answer

Chicago is a
(A) state
(B) city
(C) country
(D) continent
(E) village

Use your time effectively, working as quickly as you can without losing accuracy. Do not spend too much time on any one question. Go on to other questions and come back to the ones you have not answered if you have time. It is not expected that everyone will know the answers to all the multiple-choice questions.

About Guessing

Many candidates wonder whether or not to guess the answers to questions about which they are not certain. Multiple choice scores are based on the number of questions answered correctly. Points are not deducted for incorrect answers, and no points are awarded for unanswered questions. Because points are not deducted for incorrect answers, you are encouraged to answer all multiple-choice questions. On any questions you do not know the answer to, you should eliminate as many choices as you can, and then select the best answer among the remaining choices.

THIS PAGE INTENTIONALLY LEFT BLANK.

CALCULUS AB

SECTION I, Part A

Time—55 Minutes

Number of questions—28

A CALCULATOR MAY NOT BE USED ON THIS PART OF THE EXAMINATION

Directions: Solve each of the following problems, using the available space for scratchwork. After examining the form of the choices, decide which is the best of the choices given and fill in the corresponding oval on the answer sheet. No credit will be given for anything written in the test book. Do not spend too much time on any one problem.

In this test: Unless otherwise specified, the domain of a function f is assumed to be the set of all real numbers x for which $f(x)$ is a real number.

1. $\lim\limits_{x \to 0} \dfrac{\sin 2x}{\cos x} =$

   (A) 1
   (B) 2
   (C) 0
   (D) nonexistent
   (E) 2

---

2. $\lim\limits_{x \to \infty} \dfrac{x^4 + x^2 + 1}{3x^4 - x^3 + 2x^2 + 5x - 5} =$

   (A) $\dfrac{1}{3}$

   (B) 0

   (C) ∞

   (D) 3

   (E) The limit does not exist.

GO ON TO THE NEXT PAGE.

3. At what point does the following function have a removable discontinuity?

$$f(x) = \frac{x^2 + x - 2}{x^2 + 7x + 10}$$

(A) $(-5,-1)$
(B) $(-2,-1)$
(C) $(-2,1)$
(D) $(1,1)$
(E) $(1,-1)$

4. Which of the following functions is NOT continuous at $x = -3$?

(A) $f(x) = \begin{cases} \dfrac{x^3 + x - 2}{x^2 - 6x + 9}, & x < -3 \\ 3x^3 + 2x, & x \geq -3 \end{cases}$

(B) $g(x) = \begin{cases} x^2, & x < -3 \\ 9, & x = -3 \\ |3x|, & x > -3 \end{cases}$

(C) $h(x) = \dfrac{2x^2 - 8x + 6}{x^2 + x - 2}$

(D) $j(x) = \sqrt{x - 2}$

(E) $k(x) = (x + 3)^2$

GO ON TO THE NEXT PAGE.

5. Which of the following functions is continuous at $x = -3$?

(A) $f(x) = \begin{cases} \dfrac{x^3 + x - 2}{x^2 - 6x + 9}, & x < 0 \\ 3x^3 + 2x, & x \geq 0 \end{cases}$

(B) $g(x) = \begin{cases} x^2 + 1, & x < -3 \\ 9, & x = -3 \\ |3x|, & x > -3 \end{cases}$

(C) $h(x) = \dfrac{x^2 + x - 2}{2x^2 + 4x - 6}$

(D) $j(x) = (x - 2)^{\frac{3}{2}}$

(E) $k(x) = \left(\sqrt[3]{x + 2} \right)^2$

6. What is $\displaystyle \lim_{h \to 0} \dfrac{\sec\left(\dfrac{\pi}{2} + h\right) - \sec\left(\dfrac{\pi}{2}\right)}{h}$?

(A) $\dfrac{\pi}{2}$

(B) 0

(C) $\dfrac{\sqrt{2}}{2}$

(D) 1

(E) The limit does not exist.

GO ON TO THE NEXT PAGE.

7. If $f(x) = (2x^3 + 33)(\sqrt[5]{x} - 2x)$, then $f'(x) =$

(A) $(2x^3 + 33)\left(\dfrac{1}{5\sqrt[5]{x^4}} - 2\right) + 6x^2\left(\sqrt[5]{x} - 2x\right)$

(B) $(2x^3 + 33)\left(\dfrac{1}{5\sqrt[5]{x^4}} - 2\right) + 6x^3\left(\sqrt[5]{x} - 2x\right)$

(C) $(2x^3 + 33)\left(\dfrac{1}{5}\sqrt[5]{x^4} - 2\right) + 6x^2\left(\sqrt[5]{x} - 2x\right)$

(D) $(2x^3 + 33)\left(\dfrac{1}{5\sqrt[5]{x^4}} - 2\right) + 66x^2\left(\sqrt[5]{x} - 2x\right)$

(E) $(2x^3 + 33)\left(5\sqrt[5]{x^4} - 2\right) + 6x^2\left(\sqrt[5]{x} - 2x\right)$

8. If $y = \left(\dfrac{x^3 - 1}{x^2 + x}\right)^4$, then $\dfrac{dy}{dx} =$

(A) $4\left(\dfrac{x^3 - 1}{x^2 + x}\right)^5 \left(\dfrac{3x^2(x^2 + x) - (x^3 - 1)(2x + 1)}{(x^2 + x)^2}\right)$

(B) $\left(\dfrac{3x^2(x^2 + x) - (x^3 - 1)(2x + 1)}{(x^2 + x)^2}\right)$

(C) $4\left(\dfrac{3x^2(x^2 + x) - (x^3 - 1)(2x + 1)}{(x^2 + x)^2}\right)$

(D) $\left(\dfrac{x^3 - 1}{x^2 + x}\right)^3 \left(\dfrac{3x^2(x^2 + x) - (x^3 - 1)(2x + 1)}{(x^2 + x)^2}\right)$

(E) $4\left(\dfrac{x^3 - 1}{x^2 + x}\right)^3 \left(\dfrac{3x^2(x^2 + x) - (x^3 - 1)(2x + 1)}{(x^2 + x)^2}\right)$

GO ON TO THE NEXT PAGE.

9. Find the second derivative of $x^2 y^2 = 2$ at (2,1).

    (A)   1

    (B) -2

    (C) $\dfrac{1}{2}$

    (D)   2

    (E) $-\dfrac{1}{2}$

10. If the line $y = ax^2 + bx + c$ goes through the point (2,1) and is normal to $y = \dfrac{1}{3}x + 2$ at the point (0,2), then $a = ?$

    (A) $-\dfrac{5}{4}$

    (B) $\dfrac{5}{4}$

    (C) $\dfrac{4}{5}$

    (D) $-\dfrac{4}{5}$

    (E)   2

11. If $\dfrac{d}{dx} f(x) = 2g(x)$ and if $h(x) = x^3$, then $\dfrac{d}{dx} f(h(x)) =$

    (A) $6x^2 g(x^3)$
    (B) $2g(x^3)$
    (C) $2x^2 g(x^3)$
    (D) $6g(x^3)$
    (E) $2x^3 g(x^3)$

GO ON TO THE NEXT PAGE.

12. Which of the following statements about the function given by $f(x) = \frac{6}{5}x^5 - 2x^3$ is true?

    (A) The function has no relative extrema.
    (B) The graph has one point of inflection and two relative extrema.
    (C) The graph has three points of inflection and one relative extremum.
    (D) The graph has three points of inflection and two relative extrema.
    (E) The graph has two points of inflection and two relative extrema.

---

13. $\int (2x-5)^3 \, dx =$

    (A) $\dfrac{(2x-5)^4}{8} + C$

    (B) $\dfrac{(2x-5)^4}{4} + C$

    (C) $\dfrac{(2x-5)^4 x^2}{4} + C$

    (D) $\dfrac{(2x-5)^4}{2} + C$

    (E) $\dfrac{(2x-5)^4}{6} + C$

---

14. $\int 4x^2 \left(\frac{4}{3}x^3 - 6 \right)^9 \, dx =$

    (A) $4x^{20} + C$

    (B) $\dfrac{\left(\frac{4}{3}x^3 + 6 \right)^{10}}{10} + C$

    (C) $9\left(\frac{4}{3}x^3 + 6 \right)^8 + C$

    (D) $10\left(\frac{4}{3}x^3 + 6 \right)^{10} + C$

    (E) $\left(\frac{4}{3}x^3 + 6 \right)^{10} + C$

GO ON TO THE NEXT PAGE.

15. Find the average value of $f(x) = 3x^2 \sin x^3$ on the interval $\left[0, \sqrt[3]{\dfrac{\pi}{2}}\right]$.

(A) $\dfrac{1}{\sqrt[3]{\dfrac{\pi}{2}}}$

(B) $2\sqrt[3]{\dfrac{\pi}{2}}$

(C) $\sqrt[3]{\dfrac{\pi}{2}}$

(D) $\dfrac{\pi}{2}$

(E) 1

16. Find $\dfrac{d}{dx} \displaystyle\int_0^{3x^2} t^2 + 4t \, dt$.

(A) $9x^4 + 12x^2$
(B) $6x(9x^3 + 12x^2)$
(C) $6x^2(9x^4 + 12x^2)$
(D) $90x^3$
(E) $54x^5 + 72x^3$

GO ON TO THE NEXT PAGE.

17. $\int \dfrac{\sec x}{\csc x} dx =$

    (A) $-\ln|\cos x| + C$

    (B) $\ln|\sin x| + C$

    (C) $\ln|\sec x + \tan x| + C$

    (D) $-\ln|\csc x + \cot x| + C$

    (E) $-\ln|\sin x| + C$

18. What is the area between $y = x^3$ and $y = x$?

    (A) 0

    (B) 1

    (C) $\dfrac{1}{4}$

    (D) $\dfrac{3}{4}$

    (E) $\dfrac{1}{2}$

19. Find the volume of the region bounded by $y = (x-5)^3$, the x-axis, and the line $x = 10$ as it is revolved around the line $x = 2$. Set up, but do not evaluate the integral.

    (A) $2\pi \int_5^{10} x(x-5)^3 dx$

    (B) $2\pi \int_5^{10} (x-2)(x-5)^3 dx$

    (C) $2\pi \int_2^{10} x(x-5)^3 dx$

    (D) $2\pi \int_2^{10} (x-2)(x-5)^3 dx$

    (E) $2\pi \int_0^{10} (x-2)(x-5)^3 dx$

GO ON TO THE NEXT PAGE.

20. $\int 3x^2(x^3-3)^7\,dx =$

   (A) $8(x^3-3)^8 + C$

   (B) $\dfrac{(x^3-3)^8}{8} + C$

   (C) $(x^3-3)^8 + C$

   (D) $x^3 + C$

   (E) $x^3(x^3-3)^8 + C$

21. Find the equation for the normal line to $y = 3x^2 - 6x$ at $(2,0)$.

   (A) $y = -6x - \dfrac{1}{3}$

   (B) $y = -\dfrac{1}{6}x + \dfrac{1}{3}$

   (C) $y = \dfrac{1}{6}x + \dfrac{1}{3}$

   (D) $y = 6x + 3$

   (E) $y = -\dfrac{1}{6}x - \dfrac{1}{3}$

22. $\lim\limits_{x \to \infty} \dfrac{\sin x \cos x + \sin x}{x^2} =$

   (A)   0
   (B) −1
   (C) $-\infty$
   (D) ∞
   (E)   1

GO ON TO THE NEXT PAGE.

23. $\dfrac{d}{dx}\displaystyle\int_3^{x^3}\left(2-t^2\right)dt =$

(A) $6x^2 + 3x^8$

(B) $6x^2 - 9x^4$

(C) $2 - x^2$

(D) $6x^2 - 3x^8$

(E) $2 - x^6$

---

24. $\displaystyle\int \dfrac{dx}{\sqrt{9-x^2}} =$

(A) $\dfrac{1}{9}\sin^{-1}\left(\dfrac{x}{3}\right)+C$

(B) $\sin^{-1}\left(\dfrac{x}{3}\right)+C$

(C) $\dfrac{1}{3}\sin^{-1}\left(\dfrac{x}{3}\right)+C$

(D) $\tan^{-1}\left(\dfrac{x}{3}\right)+C$

(E) $\dfrac{1}{9}\tan^{-1}\left(\dfrac{x}{3}\right)+C$

---

25. Find $f'(x)$ for $f(x) = x^3 + 2x$ when $x = 1$.

(A) 2

(B) 3

(C) 4

(D) 5

(E) 6

GO ON TO THE NEXT PAGE.

26. $\dfrac{d^2}{dx^2}\left(x^3+2x^2-14\right)=$

   (A) $6x$
   (B) $6x+4$
   (C) $3x^2+4x$
   (D) $3x^2$
   (E) $4x$

27. Find the absolute maximum on the interval $[-2, 2]$ for the curve $y = 4x^5 - 10x^2 - 8$.

   (A) -2
   (B) -1
   (C) 0
   (D) 1
   (E) 2

28. Find $\dfrac{d^2y}{dx^2}$ at $(-1,-2)$ if $3x^3 - 2x^2 + x = y^3 + 2y^2 + 3y$.

   (A) $\dfrac{10}{7}$

   (B) 2

   (C) $-\dfrac{10}{7}$

   (D) -2

   (E) 0

END OF PART A, SECTION I

**IF YOU FINISH BEFORE TIME IS CALLED, YOU MAY CHECK
YOUR WORK ON PART A ONLY.**

DO NOT GO ON TO PART B UNTIL YOU ARE TOLD TO DO SO.

CALCULUS AB

SECTION I, Part B

Time—50 Minutes

Number of questions—17

A GRAPHING CALCULATOR IS REQUIRED FOR SOME QUESTIONS ON THIS PART OF THE EXAMINATION

Directions: Solve each of the following problems, using the available space for scratchwork. After examining the form of the choices, decide which is the best of the choices given and fill in the corresponding oval on the answer sheet. No credit will be given for anything written in the test book. Do not spend too much time on any one problem.

In this test:

1. The **exact** numerical value of the correct answer does not always appear among the choices given. When this happens, select from among the choices the number that best approximates the exact numerical value.

2. Unless otherwise specified, the domain of a function f is assumed to be the set of all real numbers x for which $f(x)$ is a real number.

29. If $f(x) = x^{-3} + 3\sqrt{x} + 5\pi - e^2$, then $f'(x) =$

(A) $\dfrac{3}{2\sqrt{x}} - 3x^4$

(B) $\dfrac{3}{2}x^{\frac{1}{2}} - 3x^{-4}$

(C) $3x^{-4} + \dfrac{3}{2\sqrt{x}}$

(D) $-\dfrac{3}{x^4} + \dfrac{3}{2\sqrt{x}}$

(E) $3x^2 + \dfrac{3}{2\sqrt{x}}$

GO ON TO THE NEXT PAGE.

30. Find the value of c that satisfies Rolle's theorem for $f(x) = 2x^4 - 16x$ on the interval $[0,2]$.

    (A) 2

    (B) $(-2)^{-\frac{1}{3}}$

    (C) $2^{-\frac{1}{3}}$

    (D) $(-2)^{\frac{1}{3}}$

    (E) $2^{\frac{1}{3}}$

31. Find the absolute maximum of $y = \dfrac{5}{3}x^3 - x^2 - 7x$ on the interval $[-2,2]$.

    (A) $\dfrac{10}{3}$

    (B) $\dfrac{14}{3}$

    (C) 0

    (D) $\dfrac{13}{3}$

    (E) $-\dfrac{539}{75}$

32. Approximate the area under the curve $y = x^2 + 2$ from $x = 1$ to $x = 2$ using four right-endpoint rectangles.

    (A) 4.333
    (B) 3.969
    (C) 4.719
    (D) 4.344
    (E) 4.328

GO ON TO THE NEXT PAGE.

33. Approximate the area under the curve $y = x^2 + 2$ from $x = 1$ to $x = 2$ using four inscribed trapezoids.

(A) 4.333
(B) 3.969
(C) 4.719
(D) 4.344
(E) 4.328

34. Evaluate $\int_{-\pi}^{\pi} \frac{x\cos x^2}{4}\,dx$.

(A) 1
(B) 2
(C) −1
(D) $\frac{1}{8}$
(E) 0

35. Suppose $F(x) = \int_0^x t^3 + t\,dt$. What is the change in $F(x)$ as t increases from 1 to 4.

(A) 72
(B) 71.25
(C) 24.75
(D) 6
(E) 0.75

GO ON TO THE NEXT PAGE.

AB Calculus Diagnostic Test | 23

36. In the xy-plane, $2x + y = k$ is tangent to the graph of $y = 2x^2 - 8x + 14$. What is the value of k?

(A) $\dfrac{3}{2}$

(B) $\dfrac{13}{2}$

(C) 5

(D) $\dfrac{19}{2}$

(E) $\dfrac{25}{2}$

GO ON TO THE NEXT PAGE.

37. The function *f* is continuous on the closed interval [0,4] and twice differentiable over the open interval, (0, 4). If $f'(2) = -5$ and $f''(x) > 0$ over the interval (0, 4), which of the following could be a table of values for *f*?

(A)

x	f(x)
0	10
1	7.5
2	6
3	4.5
4	2

(B)

x	f(x)
0	10
1	7.5
2	6.5
3	3.5
4	2

(C)

x	f(x)
0	10
1	7
2	4.5
3	3
4	2.5

(D)

x	f(x)
0	10
1	8
2	6
3	4
4	2

(E)

x	f(x)
0	10
1	8.5
2	5.5
3	3.5
4	2.5

GO ON TO THE NEXT PAGE.

38. When is the particle whose path is described by $x(t) = 2t^3 - \frac{21}{2}t^2 + 9t - 16$, from $t > 0$, slowing down?

(A) $0 < t < 3$

(B) $\frac{7}{4} < t < 3$

(C) $\frac{1}{2} < t < \frac{7}{4}$

(D) $t > 3$

(E) $\frac{1}{2} < t < 3$

39. What is the are enclosed by the curve $f(x) = 4x^2 - x^4$ and the x-axis.

(A) $\frac{128}{15}$

(B) $\frac{64}{15}$

(C) $\frac{64}{5}$

(D) $\frac{64}{3}$

(E) 0

40. Which of the following is an asymptote for the curve $y = \frac{3x}{x+7}$?

(A) $x = 7$
(B) $y = 3$
(C) $y = -7$
(D) $x = 3$
(E) $x = -3$

GO ON TO THE NEXT PAGE.

41. $\int \dfrac{x}{x^2-7}\,dx =$

   (A) $\ln\left|\dfrac{x}{x^2-7}\right|+C$

   (B) $2\ln\left|x^2-7\right|+C$

   (C) $\ln\left|x^2-7\right|+C$

   (D) $\dfrac{1}{2}\ln\left|x^2-7\right|+C$

   (E) $\ln|x|+C$

---

42. What is the area between the curves $y = x^3 - 2x^2 - 5x + 6$ and $y = x^2 - x - 6$ from $x = -2$ to $x = 3$?

   (A) 30

   (B) $\dfrac{367}{12}$

   (C) 32

   (D) $\dfrac{401}{12}$

   (E) 34

---

43. Find the average value of $f(x) = (3x-1)^3$ on the interval from $x = -1$ to $x = 3$.

   (A) 10.667
   (B) 12
   (C) 9.333
   (D) 15
   (E) 18

GO ON TO THE NEXT PAGE.

44. The curve $y = ax^2 + bx + c$ passes through the point (1,5) and is normal to the line $-x + 5y = 15$ at (0,3). What is the equation of the curve?

(A) $y = 7x^2 - 0.2x + 3$
(B) $y = 2.2x^2 - 0.2x + 3$
(C) $y = 7x^2 + 5x + 3$
(D) $y = 7x^2 - 5x + 3$
(E) $y = 5x^2 - 7x + 3$

45. $\lim\limits_{x \to 1}\left(\left(x^3 + 2x^2 - 3\right)\left(x^{-2} + 7x\right)\right) =$

(A) -1
(B) 0
(C) 1
(D) 8
(E) ∞

STOP
END OF PART B, SECTION I
IF YOU FINISH BEFORE TIME IS CALLED, YOU MAY CHECK YOUR WORK ON PART B ONLY.
DO NOT GO ON TO SECTION II UNTIL YOU ARE TOLD TO DO SO.

SECTION II
GENERAL INSTRUCTIONS

You may wish to look over the problems before starting to work on them, since it is not expected that everyone will be able to complete all parts of all problems. All problems are given equal weight, but the parts of a particular problem are not necessarily given equal weight.

A GRAPHING CALCULATOR IS REQUIRED FOR SOME PROBLEMS OR PARTS OF PROBLEMS ON THIS SECTION OF THE EXAMINATION.

- You should write all work for each part of each problem in the space provided for that part in the booklet. Be sure to write clearly and legibly. If you make an error, you may save time by crossing it out rather than trying to erase it. Erased or crossed-out work will not be graded.

- Show all your work. You will be graded on the correctness and completeness of your methods as well as your answers. Correct answers without supporting work may not receive credit.

- Justifications require that you give mathematical (noncalculator) reasons and that you clearly identify functions, graphs, tables, or other objects you use.

- You are permitted to use your calculator to solve an equation, find the derivative of a function at a point, or calculate the value of a definite integral. However, you must clearly indicate the setup of your problem, namely the equation, function, or integral you are using. If you use other built-in features or programs, you must show the mathematical steps necessary to produce your results.

- Your work must be expressed in standard mathematical notation rather than calculator syntax. For example, $\int_1^5 x^2\, dx$ may not be written as fnInt (X^2, X, 1, 5).

- Unless otherwise specified, answers (numeric or algebraic) need not be simplified. If your answer is given as a decimal approximation, it should be correct to three places after the decimal point.

- Unless otherwise specified, the domain of a function f is assumed to be the set of all real numbers x for which $f(x)$ is a real number.

GO ON TO THE NEXT PAGE.

SECTION II, PART A
Time—30 minutes
Number of problems—2

A graphing calculator is required for some problems or parts of problems.

During the timed portion for Part A, you may work only on the problems in Part A.

On Part A, you are permitted to use your calculator to solve an equation, find the derivative of a function at a point, or calculate the value of a definite integral. However, you must clearly indicate the setup of your problem, namely the equation, function, or integral you are using. If you use other built-in features or programs, you must show the mathematical steps necessary to produce your results.

---

1. A cylindrical drum is filling with water at a rate of 25π in³/sec.

    (a) If the radius of the cylinder is 1/3 the height, write an expression for the volume of water in terms of the height at any instance.
    (b) At what rate is the height changing when the height is 10 in?
    (c) What is the height of the water when it is increasing at a rate of 12 in/sec?

---

2. The function f is defined by $f(x) = \left(9 - x^2\right)^{\frac{3}{2}}$ for $-3 \leq x \leq 3$.

    (a) Find $f'(x)$.
    (b) Write an equation for the line tangent to the graph of f at $x = -2$.

    (c) Let g be the function defined by $g(x) = \begin{cases} f(x), \text{for} -3 \leq x \leq -2 \\ 2x + 9, \text{for} -2 < x \leq 3 \end{cases}$. Is g continuous at $x = -2$? Use the definition of continuity to explain your answer.

    (d) Find the value of $\int_{0}^{3} 3x\left(9 - x^2\right)^{\frac{3}{2}} dx$.

GO ON TO THE NEXT PAGE.

SECTION II, PART B
Time—1 hour
Number of problems—4

No calculator is allowed for these problems.

During the timed portion for Part B, you may continue to work on the problems in Part A without the use of any calculator.

---

3. A particle moves with velocity $v(t) = 9t^2 + 18t - 7$ for $t \geq 0$ from an initial position of $s(0) = 3$.

    (a) Write an equation for the position of the particle.
    (b) When is the particle changing direction?
    (c) What is the total distance covered from $t = 2$ to $t = 5$?

---

4. Let f be the function given by $f(x) = -2x^4 + 6x^2 + 2$.

    (a) Find the equation for the line normal to the graph at $(1,6)$.
    (b) Find the x and y coordinates of the relative maximum and minimum points.
    (c) Find the x and y coordinates of the points of inflection.

---

5. Consider the curve given by $x^3y^2 - 5x + y = 3$.

    (a) Find $\dfrac{dy}{dx}$.

    (b) Find $\dfrac{d^2y}{dx^2}$.

    (c) Find the equation of the normal lines at each of the two points on the curve whose x-coordinate is -1.

GO ON TO THE NEXT PAGE.

6. Let *f* be the function given by $f(x) = 3x^3 - 6x^2 + 4x$.

   (a) Find an equation for the normal line at $x = 2$.
   (b) Where are the relative maxima and minima of the curve, if any exist? Verify your answer.
   (c) Where are the points of inflection? Verify your answer. If there are none, explain why.

STOP

END OF EXAM

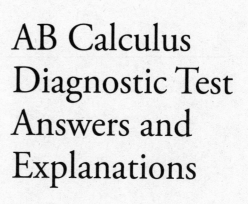

AB Calculus
Diagnostic Test
Answers and
Explanations

ANSWER KEY

Section I

1. C
2. A
3. B
4. D
5. E
6. E
7. A
8. E
9. C
10. B
11. A
12. D
13. A
14. B
15. A
16. E
17. A
18. E
19. B
20. B
21. B
22. E
23. D
24. B
25. D
26. B
27. E
28. A
29. D
30. E
31. D
32. C
33. D
34. E
35. B
36. D
37. E
38. B
39. A
40. B
41. D
42. B
43. B
44. D
45. B

EXPLANATIONS

Section I

1. **C** Use the double angle formula for sine, $\sin 2\theta = 2\sin\theta\cos\theta$, to rewrite the limit and then solve:

$$\lim_{x\to 0}\frac{\sin 2x}{\cos x} = \lim_{x\to 0}\frac{2\sin x\cos x}{\cos x} = \lim_{x\to 0} 2\sin x = 0$$

2. **A** If the highest power of x in a rational expression is the same in both the numerator and the denominator then the limit as x approaches infinity is the coefficient of the highest term in the numerator divided by the coefficient of the highest term in the denominator. The coefficient of the highest term in the numerator is 1 and the coefficient of the highest term in the denominator is 3, so the limit is $\dfrac{1}{3}$.

3. **B** A removable discontinuity occurs when a rational expression has common factors in the numerator and the denominator. The reduced function has the factor $(x + 2)$ in the numerator and denominator, hence there is a removable discontinuity when $x = -2$. The y-coordinate of the discontinuity is found by plugging $x = -2$ into the reduced function, $f(x) = \dfrac{x-1}{x+5}$. Thus, the point where a removable discontinuity exists is $(-2,-1)$.

4. **D** There are three conditions a function must fulfill for it to be continuous at a point $x = c$: 1) $f(c)$ exists, 2) $\lim\limits_{x\to c} f(x)$ exists, and 3) $\lim\limits_{x\to c} f(x) = f(c)$. All of the functions above satisfy all three conditions, except $j(x)$. $j(-3)$ does not exist (and the other two conditions are not met either).

5. **E** There are three conditions a function must fulfill for it to be continuous at a point $x = c$: $f(c)$ exists, $\lim\limits_{x\to c} f(x)$ exists, and $\lim\limits_{x\to c} f(x) = f(c)$. Answer choice E is the only one that satisfies all three. $F(c)$ does not exist in answer choice D. $\lim\limits_{x\to c} f(x)$ does not exist in answer choices A or C. $\lim\limits_{x\to c} f(x) \neq f(c)$ in answer choice B.

6.   E   Recall the definition of the derivative says: $\lim\limits_{h\to 0}\dfrac{f(x+h)-f(x)}{h}=f'(x)$ and the derivative of

sec x is tan x sec x. Thus, $\lim\limits_{h\to 0}\dfrac{\sec\left(\dfrac{\pi}{2}+h\right)-\sec\left(\dfrac{\pi}{2}\right)}{h}=\tan\left(\dfrac{\pi}{2}\right)\sec\left(\dfrac{\pi}{2}\right)=\left(\dfrac{1}{0}\right)\left(\dfrac{1}{0}\right)=\dfrac{1}{0}$. Therefore,

the limit does not exist.

7.   A   Using the Product Rule, $u\dfrac{dv}{dx}+v\dfrac{du}{dx}$, take the derivative of $f(x)$ and you get A.

8.   E   Using the Chain Rule, $\dfrac{dy}{dx}=\dfrac{dy}{dv}\dfrac{dv}{dx}$, take the derivative of $f(x)$ and you get E.

9.   C   First, use implicit differentiation to find $\dfrac{dy}{dx}$:

$$2x^2 y\frac{dy}{dx}+2xy^2 = 0$$

Isolate $\dfrac{dy}{dx}$ and simplify:

$$\frac{dy}{dx}=\frac{-2xy^2}{2x^2 y}=\frac{-y}{x}$$

Next, take the second derivative via implicit differentiation:

$$\frac{d^2 y}{dx^2}=\frac{x\left(-\dfrac{dy}{dx}\right)+y}{x^2}=\frac{-x\dfrac{dy}{dx}+y}{x^2}$$

Plug in $\dfrac{dy}{dx}$:

$$\frac{d^2 y}{dx^2}=\frac{-x\left(\dfrac{-y}{x}\right)+y}{x^2}$$

There is no need to simplify, just plug in the point (2,1):

$$\frac{d^2 y}{dx^2}=\frac{-2\left(\dfrac{-1}{2}\right)+1}{2^2}=\frac{1+1}{4}=\frac{2}{4}=\frac{1}{2}$$

10. **B** Start by plugging (0,2) into $y = ax^2 + bx + c$. Then, $c = 2$. Next, take the derivative of $y = ax^2 + bx + c$:

$\dfrac{dy}{dx} = 2ax + b$. Given that $y = \dfrac{1}{3}x + 2$ is normal to $y = ax^2 + bx + c$, the slope of $y = ax^2 + bx + c$, or

$\dfrac{dy}{dx}$, is –3. Thus, by plugging $x = 0$ into $\dfrac{dy}{dx} = 2ax + b$, $b = -3$. Finally, plug the point (2,1) and the

values of c and b into $y = ax^2 + bx + c$. Therefore, $a = \dfrac{5}{4}$.

11. **A** Plug $h(x)$ in as x into $g(x)$ and take the derivative using the Chain Rule, so $\dfrac{d}{dx}\left(2g\left(x^3\right)\right) = 6x^2 g\left(x^3\right)$.

12. **D** In order to determine the number of relative extrema, the derivative of $f(x)$ must be set equal to zero and the critical points found. When this is done, $f'(x) = 6x^4 - 6x^2$ and the critical points are located at $x = -1$, $x = 0$, and $x = 1$. Therefore, there are three possible relative extrema for this curve, and answer choices A and C can be eliminated. Next, in order to determine the points of inflection, set the second derivative of $f(x)$ equal to zero and solve. When this is done, $f''(x) = 24x^3 - 12x$ and the points of inflection are located at $x = 0$, $x = -\sqrt{\dfrac{1}{2}}$ and $x = \sqrt{\dfrac{1}{2}}$. Thus, there are three points of inflection and the answer is D.

13. **A** Use u-substitution. Here, $u = 2x - 5$ and $du = 2\,dx$. Then,

$$\int (2x-5)^3\,dx = \frac{1}{2}\int u^3\,dx = \frac{1}{2}\left(\frac{u^4}{4}\right) + C = \frac{u^4}{8} + C.$$ Replace u for the final solution: $\dfrac{(2x-5)^4}{8} + C.$

14. **B** Use u-substitution. Here, $u = \dfrac{4}{3}x^3 - 6$ and $du = 4x^2\,dx$. Then,

$$\int 4x^2\left(\frac{4}{3}x^3 - 6\right)^9 dx = \int u^9\,du = \frac{u^{10}}{10} + C.$$ Replace u for the final solution: $\dfrac{\left(\frac{4}{3}x^3 + 6\right)^{10}}{10} + C.$

15. **A** Use the mean value theorem for integrals, $f(c) = \dfrac{1}{b-a}\int_a^b f(x)\,dx$. Thus, for this problem,

$$f(c) = \frac{1}{\sqrt[3]{\frac{\pi}{2}}}\int_0^{\sqrt[3]{\frac{\pi}{2}}} 3x^2 \sin x^3\,dx = \frac{1}{\sqrt[3]{\frac{\pi}{2}}}.$$

16. **E** Use the Second Fundamental Theorem of Calculus: $\dfrac{dF}{dx} = \dfrac{d}{dx}\int_a^x f(t)\,dt = f(x)$. Thus, for this

problem, $\dfrac{dF}{dx} = \dfrac{d}{dx}\int_0^{3x^2} t^2 + 4t\,dt = 6x\left(\left(3x^2\right)^2 + 4\left(3x^2\right)\right) = 54x^5 + 72x^3.$

17. **A** First, rewrite the integral: $\int \dfrac{1/\cos x}{1/\sin x} dx = \int \dfrac{\sin x}{\cos x} dx = \int \tan x\, dx$. You can either derive the integral from $\dfrac{\sin x}{\cos x}$ using u-substitution, or you should have memorized that $\int \tan x\, dx = -\ln|\cos x| + C$.

18. **E** Using vertical slices, the area between the curves follows the general formula: $\int_a^b \left[f(x) - g(x) \right] dx$.

First, it is important to determine where these two curves intersect and which curve is "on top."

The two curves intersect at $x = -1$, $x = 0$, and $x = 1$. Over the interval $[-1, 0]$, the curve $y = x^3$ is "on

top." Therefore, the integral is $\int_{-1}^0 \left(x^3 - x \right) dx = \dfrac{1}{4}$. Over the interval $[0, 1]$, the curve $y = x$ is "on top."

Therefore, the integral is $\int_0^1 \left(x - x^3 \right) dx = \dfrac{1}{4}$. Thus the area between the curves is the sum of these

two areas: $\dfrac{1}{2}$.

19. **B** Since you are not told which method to use to find the volume you must decide, a big hint is the

answer choices. However, if you didn't have this hint, then you can use the rule of thumb that it

is TYPICALLY (but not always) better to use cylindrical shells, if the region is bound by more

than two curves (including an axis) or if one or more curves are given as $y =$ and the others are

given as $x =$. Both conditions are satisfied in this problem, so cylindrical shells is probably best.

The general formula for cylindrical shells is $2\pi \int_a^b x[f(x) - g(x)] dx$. First, the points of intersec-

tion between all these curves must be found, where the region is bound, to establish the limits of

integration. The bounds are $x = 5$ and $x = 10$. Next, determine which curve is "on top" or "more

positive." In this case, the curves in question are $y = (x - 5)^3$ and $y = 0$. Since $y = (x - 5)^3$ is always

more positive than $y = 0$, $y = (x - 5)^3 = f(x)$ and $y = 0 = g(x)$. Finally, the general formula is for a

region that is rotated about the y-axis, or $x = 0$. Since our curve is shifted to be rotated around

$x = 2$, the radius of the cylinder, x, is now $x - 2$ to account for the shift. Thus, the final integral is:

$2\pi \int_5^{10} (x - 2)(x - 5)^3\, dx$.

20. **B** Use *u*-substitution in which $u = x^3 - 3$ and $du = 3x^2 \, dx$. Thus, the integral is:

$$\int u^7 \, du = \frac{u^8}{8} + C = \frac{\left(x^3 - 3\right)^8}{8} + C$$

21. **B** In order to determine the equation for the normal line, take the derivative with respect to *x* at (2,0): $\frac{dy}{dx} = 6x - 6$ which is 6 at (2,0). Since this is the slope of the tangent line, and the slope of the normal line is the opposite reciprocal, the slope of the normal line is $-\frac{1}{6}$. Plug this information into the point-slope formula of a line and simplify to slope-intercept form: $y - 0 = -\frac{1}{6}(x - 2)$ or $y = -\frac{1}{6}x + \frac{1}{3}$.

22. **E** Either use L'Hôpital's rule or recall that $\lim_{x \to \infty} \frac{\sin x}{x} = 1$ and $\lim_{x \to \infty} \frac{\cos x + 1}{x} = 1$. In this case, $\lim_{x \to \infty} \frac{\sin x \cos x + \sin x}{x^2}$ can be rewritten as $\lim_{x \to \infty} \frac{\sin x}{x} \cdot \frac{\cos x + 1}{x} = 1 \cdot 1 = 1$.

23. **D** Following the Second Fundamental Theorem of Calculus,

$$\frac{d}{dx} \int_3^{x^3} \left(2 - t^2\right) dt = [2 - \left(x^3\right)^2]\left(3x^2\right) = \left(2 - x^6\right)\left(3x^2\right) = 6x^2 - 3x^8.$$

24. **B** Use *u*-substitution and recognize that the solution will be an inverse sine function.

$$\int \frac{dx}{\sqrt{9 - x^2}} = \int \frac{dx}{\sqrt{9\left(1 - \frac{x^2}{9}\right)}} = \frac{1}{3} \int \frac{dx}{\sqrt{1 - \frac{x}{9}}}.$$ Thus, the final solution is: $\sin^{-1}\left(\frac{x}{3}\right) + C$.

25. **D** $f'(x) = 3x^2 + 2$ and $f'(1) = 5$.

26. **B** The first derivative is $\frac{d}{dx} = 3x^2 + 4x$. The second derivative is $\frac{d^2}{dx^2} = 6x + 4$.

27. **E** For an absolute maximum, find the first derivative and set it equal to zero to determine the critical points. $\frac{dy}{dx} = 20x^4 - 20x = 0$. The critical points are at *x* = 0 and *x* = 1. Find the second derivative to determine which of these points are maxima and which are minima. Maxima are located where the second derivative is negative; minima where the second derivative is positive. $\frac{d^2y}{dx^2} = 80x^3 - 20$. From here, *x* = 0 corresponds with maximum points. Finally, plug in this value into the original equation to determine which has a higher *y*-value. At *x* = 0, *y* = −8. However, you must remember when determining absolute maxima and minima on a closed interval to always check the endpoints. So, plug in

$x = -2$ and $x = 2$ into the original equation and determine if they have y-values that are more positive than at $x = 0$. At $x = -2$, $y = -176$ and at $x = 2$, $y = 80$. Therefore, $x = 2$ is the absolute maximum.

28. **A** Using implicit differentiation, find the first derivative of the equation and solve for $\dfrac{dy}{dx}$:

$\dfrac{dy}{dx} = \dfrac{9x^2 - 4x + 1}{3y^2 + 4y + 3}$. Next, determine the second derivative, but don't simplify the equation:

$\dfrac{d^2 y}{dx^2} = \dfrac{\left(3y^2 + 4y + 3\right)\left(18x - 4\right) - \left(9x^2 - 4x + 1\right)\left(6y\dfrac{dy}{dx} + 4\dfrac{dy}{dx}\right)}{\left(3y^2 + 4y + 3\right)^2}$. Finally evaluate the first and sec-

ond derivative at $(-1,-2)$. The first derivative at $(-1,-2)$ is 2. The second derivative at $(-1,-2)$ is $\dfrac{10}{7}$.

29. **D** Using the Power and Addition Rules, take the derivative of $f(x)$ and you get D. Remember that π and e are constants.

30. **E** Rolle's Theorem states that if $y = f(x)$ is continuous on the interval $[a, b]$, and is differentiable everywhere on the interval (a, b), and if $f(a) = f(b) = 0$, then there is at least one number c between a and b such that $f'(c) = 0$. $f(x) = 0$ at both $x = 0$ and $x = 2$. Then, solve $f'(c) = 8x^3 - 16 = 0$. $c = 2^{\frac{1}{3}}$.

31. **D** An absolute maximum or minimum occurs when the derivative of a function is zero or where the derivative fails to exist or at an endpoint. First, find the derivative of y, set it equal to zero and solve for x. $\dfrac{dy}{dx} = 5x^2 - 2x - 7 = 0$, then $x = -1$ and $x = \dfrac{7}{5}$. Determine the y-values corresponding to each of these x-values and at the endpoints, $x = -2$ and $x = 2$. The resulting points are $\left(-1, \dfrac{13}{3}\right)$, $\left(\dfrac{7}{5}, -\dfrac{539}{75}\right)$, $\left(-2, -\dfrac{10}{3}\right)$, and $\left(2, -\dfrac{14}{3}\right)$. The maximum is occurs at $\left(-1, -\dfrac{13}{3}\right)$.

32. **C** The formula for the area under a curve using right-endpoint rectangles is:

$A = \left(\dfrac{b - a}{n}\right)\left(y_1 + y_2 + y_3 + \ldots + y_n\right)$, where a and b are the x-values that bound the area

and n is the number of rectangles. Since we are interested in the right-endpoints, the

x-coordinates are $x_1 = \dfrac{5}{4}$, $x_2 = \dfrac{3}{2}$, $x_3 = \dfrac{7}{4}$, and $x_4 = 2$. The y-coordinates are found by plugging

these values into the equation for y, so $y_1 = 3.5625$, $y_2 = 4.25$, $y_3 = 5.0625$, and $y_4 = 6$. Then,

$A = \left(\dfrac{2 - 1}{4}\right)(3.5625 + 4.25 + 5.0625 + 6) = 4.71875$.

33. **D** The formula for the area under a curve using inscribed trapezoids is:

$$A = \left(\frac{1}{2}\right)\left(\frac{b-a}{n}\right)\left(y_0 + 2y_1 + 2y_2 + \ldots + 2y_{n-1} + y_n\right),$$ where a and b are the x-values

that bound the area and n is the number of rectangles. The x-coordinates are

$x_0 = 1$, $x_1 = \frac{5}{4}$, $x_2 = \frac{3}{2}$, $x_3 = \frac{7}{4}$, and $x_4 = 2$. The y-coordinates are found by plugging these val-

ues into the equation for y, so $y_0 = 3$, $y_1 = 3.5625$, $y_2 = 4.25$, $y_3 = 5.0625$, and $y_4 = 6$. Then,

$$A = \left(\frac{1}{2}\right)\left(\frac{2-1}{4}\right)\left(3 + 2(3.5625) + 2(4.25) + 2(5.0625) + 6\right) = 4.34375.$$

34. **E** Use the Fundamental Theorem of Calculus: $\int_a^b f(x)\,dx = F(b) - F(a)$ and u-substitution. For this

problem, $u = x^2$ and $du = 2x\,dx$. Then:

$$\int_{-\pi}^{\pi} \frac{x \cos x^2}{4}\,dx = \int_{-\pi}^{\pi} \frac{\cos u}{8}\,du = \frac{\sin u}{8}\Big|_{-\pi}^{\pi} = \frac{\sin x^2}{8}\Big|_{-\pi}^{\pi} = \frac{\sin \pi^2}{8} - \frac{\sin(-\pi)^2}{8} = 0$$

35. **B** This is an accumulation problem, so use the Second Fundamental Theorem of Calculus,

$$\frac{dF}{dx} = \frac{d}{dx}\int_a^x f(t)\,dt = f(x). \text{ Thus, } F(x) = \int_1^4 t^3 + t\,dt = \left(\frac{t^4}{4} + \frac{t^2}{2}\right)\Big|_1^4 = 72 - 0.75 = 71.25.$$

36. **D** First, rewrite $2x + y = k$ in slope-intercept form: $y = -2x + k$; thus, the slope of the tangent, or

the first derivative of y, is -2. Next, take the derivative of $y = 2x^2 - 8x + 14$ and set it equal to -2:

$\frac{dy}{dx} = 4x - 8 = -2$. Use this equation to solve for the x-value that corresponds to the first derivative

of -2; the x-coordinate is $\frac{3}{2}$. Use this x-coordinate to solve for the corresponding y-coordinate;

plug $x = \frac{3}{2}$ into the equation for the curve y. The y-coordinate equals $\frac{13}{2}$. Finally, go back to the

equation for the tangent line and plug in the x and y values found. Solve for k: $k = \frac{19}{2}$.

37. **E** Since, $f'(x) < 0$, the curve is decreasing, which is true in all answer choices. In addition, because

$f''(x) > 0$, the curve is concave up. The best way to determine which curve is concave up is to

make a quick sketch of the graphs from the data points. When this is done, E is concave up.

38. **B** The particle slows down when the velocity and acceleration have different signs. First, take the first derivative of $x(t)$ and set it equal to zero to solve for the times when the velocity is changing sign: $x'(t) = 6t^2 - 21t + 9 = 0$ when $t = \dfrac{1}{2}$ and $t = 3$. Next, take the second derivative of $x(t)$, and determine when that is changing sign: $x''(t) = 12t - 21 = 0$ when $x = \dfrac{7}{4}$. Since there are three different values for which either the velocity or acceleration equals zero, there are four intervals to check the signs of both the velocity and acceleration:

Time	Velocity	Acceleration
$0 < t < \dfrac{1}{2}$	+	−
$\dfrac{1}{2} < t < \dfrac{7}{4}$	−	−
$\dfrac{7}{4} < t < 3$	−	+
$t > 3$	+	+

Since the velocity and acceleration have different signs over the intervals $0 < t < \dfrac{1}{2}$ and $\dfrac{7}{4} < t < 3$, the correct answer is B.

39. **A** First, determine where $f(x)$ and the x-axis intercept, i.e., solve $f(x) = 0$ for x. Thus, $x = 0$, $x = -2$, and $x = 2$. In order to determine the area under the curve, we must set up and solve two integrals:

$$\int_{-2}^{0} \left(4x^2 + x^4\right) dx + \int_{0}^{2} \left(4x^2 + x^4\right) dx = \frac{128}{15}.$$

40. **B** The line $y = c$ is a horizontal asymptote of the graph of $y = f(x)$ if the limit of the function as x approaches positive and negative infinity equals c. Similarly, the line $x = k$ is a vertical asymptote of the graph of $y = f(x)$ if the limit of the function as x approaches k from the left and right is positive or negative infinity. First, check for a horizontal asymptote, $\lim\limits_{x \to -\infty} \dfrac{3x}{x+7} = 3$ and $\lim\limits_{x \to \infty} \dfrac{3x}{x+7} = 3$, so there is a horizontal asymptote at $y = 3$. Next, check for a vertical asymptote; always check the point where the denominator is undefined, in this case, $x = -7$: $\lim\limits_{x \to -7^-} \dfrac{3x}{x+7} = \infty$ and $\lim\limits_{x \to -7^+} \dfrac{3x}{x+7} = -\infty$. Thus, there is a vertical asymptote at $x = -7$.

41. **D** Use u-substitution in which $u = x^2 - 7$ and $du = 2x\,dx$. Thus, the integral is:

$$\frac{1}{2}\int \frac{du}{u} = \frac{1}{2}\ln|u| = \frac{1}{2}\ln|x^2 - 7| + C$$

42. **B** The formula for the area between two curves is $\int_a^b (f(x) - g(x))\,dx$, where a and b are the x-coordinates that bind the region and $f(x)$ is the more positive curve. Be careful to check if the curves cross the x-axis because multiple integrals will be required if this happens. In this case, the curves intersect on the x-axis at $x = 2$. Therefore, the area between the curves will be:

$$\int_{-2}^{2} (x^3 - 2x^2 - 5x + 6) - (x^2 - x - 6)\,dx + \int_{2}^{3} (x^2 - x - 6) - (x^3 - 2x^2 - 5x + 6)\,dx = 32 + \frac{-17}{12} = \frac{367}{12}.$$

43. **B** Using the MVTI, $\dfrac{1}{3+1}\displaystyle\int_{-1}^{3}(3x-1)^3 = 12$.

44. **D** Plug in the given point, $(0,3)$, into the equation for the curve, $y = ax^2 + bx + c$, thus $c = 3$. Next, rewrite the equation for the normal line in slope-intercept form, $y = \dfrac{1}{5}x + 3$. Since this line is normal to the curve, the slope of the tangent line is the opposite reciprocal to the slope of the normal line. The slope of the tangent line is -5 to evaluate it at $(0,3)$. Take the derivative of y and set it equal to -5: $\dfrac{dy}{dx} = 2ax + b$ and $\dfrac{dy}{dx}\Big|_{x=0} = 2(a)(0) + b = -5$. Therefore, $b = -5$. Finally, solve for a by plugging the second point $(1,5)$ into the equation for the curve. Also, plug in b and c, so: $5 = a + b + c$ or $a = 7$, when $b = -5$ and $c = 3$. Finally, the equation of the curve is $y = 7x^2 - 5x + 3$.

45. **B** $\displaystyle\lim_{x\to 1}\left((x^3 + 2x^2 - 3)(x^{-2} + 7x)\right) = \lim_{x\to 1}(x^3 + 2x^2 - 3) \cdot \lim_{x\to 1}(x^{-2} + 7x) = 0 \cdot 8 = 0$

Section II

1. A cylindrical drum is filling with water at a rate of 25π in³/sec.

   (a) If the radius of the cylinder is $\frac{1}{3}$ the height, write an expression for the volume of water in terms of the height at any instance.

   (a) $V = \pi r^2 h$ and $r = \frac{h}{3}$. Thus, the volume can be found by solving $V = \frac{\pi h^3}{9}$.

   (b) At what rate is the height changing when the height is 10 in?

   (b) The rate the height is changing can be found by taking the first derivative with respect to time. $\frac{dV}{dt} = \frac{\pi h^2}{3} \frac{dh}{dt}$. Plug in the values given and solve for $\frac{dh}{dt}$. $\frac{dh}{dt} = \frac{3}{4}$ in/sec.

   (c) What is the height of the water when it is increasing at a rate of 12 in/sec?

   (c) Use the derivative from part (b) and plug in the values to solve for h, so $h = \frac{5}{2}$ in.

2. The function f is defined by $f(x) = \left(9 - x^2\right)^{\frac{3}{2}}$ for $-3 \leq x \leq 3$.

   (a) Find $f'(x)$.

   (a) $f'(x) = \frac{3}{2}\left(9 - x^2\right)^{\frac{1}{2}}(2x) = 3x\left(9 - x^2\right)^{\frac{1}{2}}$

   (b) Write an equation for the line tangent to the graph of f at $x = -2$.

   (b) Use the equation for $f'(x)$ from part (a) to find the slope of the tangent at $x = -2$: $f'(-2) = -6\sqrt{5}$. Determine the y-coordinate that corresponds with $x = -2$ by plugging it into $f(x)$: $f(-2) = 5\sqrt{5}$. Finally, the equation for the tangent line is: $y - 5\sqrt{5} = -6\sqrt{5}(x + 2)$.

   (c) Let g be the function defined by $g(x) = \begin{cases} f(x), \text{ for} -3 \leq x \leq -2 \\ 2x + 9, \text{ for} -2 < x \leq 3 \end{cases}$. Is g continuous at $x = -2$? Use the definition of continuity to explain your answer.

   (c) The definition of continuity states a function is continuous if three conditions are met: $f(c)$ exists, $\lim_{x \to c} f(x)$ exists, $\lim_{x \to c} f(x) = f(c)$. The first condition is met, $f(-2)$ exists, from part (b). The second condition is violated; the left and right hand limits as x approaches -2 are not equal, so the limit does not exist and the function is not continuous: $\lim_{x \to -2-} g(x) = 5\sqrt{5}$ and $\lim_{x \to +2-} g(x) = 5$.

(d) Find the value of $\int_0^3 3x\left(9-x^2\right)^{\frac{3}{2}} dx$.

(d) Solve using u-substitution, in which $u = 9 - x^2$ and $du = 2x\,dx$. Thus,

$$\int_0^3 3x\left(9-x^2\right)^{\frac{3}{2}} dx = 145.8.$$

3. A particle moves with velocity $v(t) = 9t^2 + 18t - 7$ for $t \geq 0$ from an initial position of $s(0) = 3$.

(a) Write an equation for the position of the particle.

(a) The position function of the particle can be determined by integrating the velocity with respect to time, thus $s(t) = \int v(t)\,dt$. For this problem, $s(t) = \int (9t^2 + 18t - 7)dt = 3t^3 + 9t^2 - 7t + C$. Since we are given the initial position, $s(0) = 3$, plug that in to solve for C. Thus, $C = 3$ and the equation for the position of the particle is $s(t) = 3t^3 + 9t^2 - 7t + 3$.

(b) When is the particle changing direction?

(b) The particle changes direction when the velocity is zero, but the acceleration is not. In order to determine when those times are, set the velocity equal to zero and solve for t. $v(t) = 9t^2 + 18t - 7 = 0$ when $t = \dfrac{1}{3}$ and $t = -\dfrac{7}{3}$. Since, the time range in question is $t \geq 0$, we can ignore $t = -\dfrac{7}{3}$. Then, take the derivative of the velocity function to find the acceleration function, as $\dfrac{d}{dt}\big(v(t)\big) = a(t)$. For the given $v(t)$, $a(t) = 18t + 18$. Check that the acceleration at time $t = \dfrac{1}{3}$ is not zero by plugging into the acceleration function: $a(t) = 30$. Therefore, the particle is changing direction at $t = \dfrac{1}{3}$ because $v(t) = 0$ and $a(t) \neq 0$.

(c)   What is the total distance covered from $t = 2$ to $t = 5$?

(c)   The distance covered is found by using the position function found in part (a). Determine the position at $t = 2$ and subtract it from the position at $t = 5$. From part (b), we know that the object does not change direction over this time interval, so we do not need to find the time piecewise. Thus, $s(5) - s(2) = 568 - 49 = 519$.

4.   Let f be the function given by $f(x) = -2x^4 + 6x^2 + 2$.

(a)   Find the equation for the line normal to the graph at $(1, 6)$.

(a)   The line normal to the graph will have a slope that is the opposite reciprocal of the tangent line at that point. Therefore, begin by finding the slope of the tangent line, i.e., the first derivative. $f'(x) = -8x^3 + 12x$ and $f'(1) = 4$. The slope of the normal line is $-\dfrac{1}{4}$. So, the equation of the normal line is: $y - 6 = -\dfrac{1}{4}(x - 1)$.

(b)   Find the x and y coordinates of the relative maximum and minimum points.

(b)   The relative maximum and minimum will occur at the points when the first derivative is zero or undefined. In this case, set the first derivative to zero and solve for x: $f'(x) = -8x^3 + 12x = 0$, and $x = 0$, $x = \sqrt{\dfrac{3}{2}}$, and $x = -\sqrt{\dfrac{3}{2}}$. To determine which of these is a relative maximum and which is a relative minimum, find the second derivative at each of these critical points. $f''(x) = -24x^2 + 12$, and $f''(0) = 12$, $f''\left(\sqrt{\dfrac{3}{2}}\right) = -24$, and $f''\left(-\sqrt{\dfrac{3}{2}}\right) = -24$. By the second derivative test, $x = 0$ corresponds with a relative minimum because $f''(0) > 0$ and $x = \sqrt{\dfrac{3}{2}}$, and $x = -\sqrt{\dfrac{3}{2}}$ correspond with relative maximums because $f''\left(\sqrt{\dfrac{3}{2}}\right)$ and $f''\left(-\sqrt{\dfrac{3}{2}}\right) < 0$. To determine the y coordinates of these points, plug them back into $f(x)$: $f(0) = 2$, $f\left(\sqrt{\dfrac{3}{2}}\right) = \dfrac{13}{2}$ and $f\left(\sqrt{\dfrac{3}{2}}\right) = \dfrac{13}{2}$. So, a relative minimum occurs at $(0,2)$ and relative maximums occur at $\left(\sqrt{\dfrac{3}{2}}, \dfrac{13}{2}\right)$ and $\left(\sqrt{\dfrac{3}{2}}, \dfrac{13}{2}\right)$.

(c)   Find the x and y coordinates of the points of inflection.

(c)   Points of inflection occur when the second derivative equals zero. Take the second derivative from part (b) and solve for the x values when $f''(x) = 24x^2 + 12 = 0$. So, $x = \dfrac{\sqrt{2}}{2}$ and $x = -\dfrac{\sqrt{2}}{2}$. To determine the y-coordinates for these points of inflection, determine $f(x)$ at each of these points:

$f\left(\dfrac{\sqrt{2}}{2}\right) = \dfrac{9}{2}$ and $f\left(-\dfrac{\sqrt{2}}{2}\right) = \dfrac{9}{2}$. So the points of inflection occur at $\left(\dfrac{\sqrt{2}}{2}, \dfrac{9}{2}\right)$ and $\left(-\dfrac{\sqrt{2}}{2}, \dfrac{9}{2}\right)$.

5.   Consider the curve given by $x^3 y^2 - 5x + y = 3$.

(a)   Find $\dfrac{dy}{dx}$.

(a)   Use implicit differentiation: $2x^3 y \dfrac{dy}{dx} + 3x^2 y^2 - 5 + \dfrac{dy}{dx} = 0$. Simplify and isolate $\dfrac{dy}{dx}$:

$\dfrac{dy}{dx} = \dfrac{5 - 3x^2 y^2}{2x^3 y + 1}$.

(b)   Find $\dfrac{d^2 y}{dx^2}$.

(b)   Use the derivative from part (a) and differentiate again using implicit differentiation:

$\dfrac{d^2 y}{dx^2} = \dfrac{(2x^3 y + 1)\left(-6x^2 y \dfrac{dy}{dx} - 6xy^2\right) - (5 - 3x^2 y^2)\left(2x^3 \dfrac{dy}{dx} + 6x^2 y\right)}{(2x^3 + 1)^2}$. Replace the value for $\dfrac{dy}{dx}$

from part (a) for the final solution:

$\dfrac{d^2 y}{dx^2} = \dfrac{(2x^3 y + 1)\left(-6x^2 y \left(\dfrac{5 - 3x^2 y^2}{2x^3 + y + 1}\right) - 6xy^2\right) - (5 - 3x^2 y^2)\left(2x^3 \left(\dfrac{5 - 3x^2 y^2}{2x^3 + y + 1}\right) + 6x^2 y\right)}{(2x^3 + 1)^2}$.

No need to simplify.

(c)   Find the equation of the normal lines at each of the two points on the curve whose x-coordinate is –1.

(c)   From the original equation, at $x = -1$, $y = -2$ or $y = 1$. Plug those values into $\dfrac{dy}{dx}$ from part (a) to get the slope of the tangents at those points: $-\dfrac{7}{5}$ and –2, respectively. The slopes of the normal lines are the opposite reciprocals of those slopes, so $\dfrac{5}{7}$ and $\dfrac{1}{2}$, respectively. The equations for the normal are then found by using the point-slope formula. The equations are $y+2=\dfrac{5}{7}(x+1)$ and $y-1=\dfrac{1}{2}(x+1)$.

6.   Let f be the function given by $f(x) = 3x^3 - 6x^2 + 4x$.

(a)   Find an equation for the normal line at $x = 2$.

(a)   First determine what $f(2)$ equals: $f(2) = 8$. Next, take the first derivative of $f(x)$: $f'(x)=9x^2-12x+4$. At $x = 2$, $f'(x) = 16$. The slope of the normal line would then be $-\dfrac{1}{16}$. The equation of the normal line is $y-8=-\dfrac{1}{16}(x-2)$.

(b)   Where are the relative maxima and minima of the curve, if any exist? Verify your answer.

(b)   Relative maxima and minima exist where the first derivative is zero or does not exist. Set the first derivative equal to zero and solve or x, $f'(x) = 0$ at $x = \dfrac{2}{3}$. To determine whether this point is a maximum or minimum, check the second derivative. If the second derivative is negative, the point is a maximum. If the second derivative is positive, the point is a minimum. However, if the second derivative is zero, the point is a point of inflection. At $x = \dfrac{2}{3}$, $f''(x) = 0$, so the point is a point of inflection. This curve has no maxima or minima.

(c)   Where are the points of inflection? Verify your answer. If there are none, explain why.

(c)   It was discovered in part (b) that the point of inflection is at $x = \dfrac{2}{3}$. Plug that into $f(x)$ to find the corresponding y-value, which is $\dfrac{8}{9}$. Thus, the point of inflection is located at $\left(\dfrac{2}{3}, \dfrac{8}{9} \right)$. Justification is the same as the justification in part (b).

BC Calculus
Diagnostic Test

The Exam

AP® Calculus BC Exam

SECTION I: Multiple-Choice Questions

DO NOT OPEN THIS BOOKLET UNTIL YOU ARE TOLD TO DO SO.

At a Glance

Total Time
1 hour and 45 minutes
Number of Questions
45
Percent of Total Grade
50%
Writing Instrument
Pencil required

Instructions

Section I of this examination contains 45 multiple-choice questions. Fill in only the ovals for numbers 1 through 45 on your answer sheet.

CALCULATORS MAY NOT BE USED IN THIS PART OF THE EXAMINATION.

Indicate all of your answers to the multiple-choice questions on the answer sheet. No credit will be given for anything written in this exam booklet, but you may use the booklet for notes or scratch work. After you have decided which of the suggested answers is best, completely fill in the corresponding oval on the answer sheet. Give only one answer to each question. If you change an answer, be sure that the previous mark is erased completely. Here is a sample question and answer.

Sample Question   Sample Answer

Chicago is a
(A) state
(B) city
(C) country
(D) continent
(E) village

Use your time effectively, working as quickly as you can without losing accuracy. Do not spend too much time on any one question. Go on to other questions and come back to the ones you have not answered if you have time. It is not expected that everyone will know the answers to all the multiple-choice questions.

About Guessing

Many candidates wonder whether or not to guess the answers to questions about which they are not certain. Multiple choice scores are based on the number of questions answered correctly. Points are not deducted for incorrect answers, and no points are awarded for unanswered questions. Because points are not deducted for incorrect answers, you are encouraged to answer all multiple-choice questions. On any questions you do not know the answer to, you should eliminate as many choices as you can, and then select the best answer among the remaining choices.

THIS PAGE INTENTIONALLY LEFT BLANK.

CALCULUS BC

SECTION I, Part A

Time—55 Minutes

Number of questions—28

A CALCULATOR MAY NOT BE USED ON THIS PART OF THE EXAMINATION

<u>Directions</u>: Solve each of the following problems, using the available space for scratchwork. After examining the form of the choices, decide which is the best of the choices given and fill in the corresponding oval on the answer sheet. No credit will be given for anything written in the test book. Do not spend too much time on any one problem.

<u>In this test</u>: Unless otherwise specified, the domain of a function f is assumed to be the set of all real numbers x for which $f(x)$ is a real number.

1. $\lim\limits_{x \to 3} \dfrac{x^2 - x - 6}{x^2 - 5x + 6} =$

   (A) 0
   (B) 1
   (C) 3
   (D) 5
   (E) The limit does not exist.

2. $\lim\limits_{x \to 0} \dfrac{\sec x}{\csc x} =$

   (A) 0
   (B) 1
   (C) 2π
   (D) ∞
   (E) The limit does not exist.

GO ON TO THE NEXT PAGE.

3. $\dfrac{d}{dx}\left(\dfrac{2x+3}{(x-4)^2}\right)=$

(A) $\dfrac{x-7}{(x-4)^3}$

(B) $\dfrac{-2x-14}{(x-4)^3}$

(C) $\dfrac{2x+14}{(x-4)^3}$

(D) $\dfrac{-2x-14}{(x-4)^4}$

(E) $\dfrac{x+14}{(x-4)^4}$

4. $\lim\limits_{x\to0}\left(\dfrac{2\sin 3x}{3\sin 2x}\right)=$

(A) -1
(B) 0
(C) 1
(D) ∞
(E) The limit does not exist.

5. What type(s) of discontinuity/ies does the function, $f(x)=\dfrac{x^2-7x-18}{x^2-12x+27}$, have?

(A) jump
(B) point
(C) essential
(D) jump and removable
(E) essential and removable

GO ON TO THE NEXT PAGE.

6. Find the fourth derivative of $f(x) = \dfrac{x^4 - 4x^3 + 3x^2 - 4x}{x^3}$.

    (A) $\dfrac{x^3 - 3x + 8}{x^3}$

    (B) $\dfrac{6x - 24}{x^4}$

    (C) $\dfrac{-18x + 96}{x^5}$

    (D) $\dfrac{x^3 - 12x^2 + 3x - 4}{x^2}$

    (E) $\dfrac{7x - 480}{x^6}$

7. $\dfrac{d}{dx}\left(\dfrac{\sec 5x}{5} \right) =$

    (A) $\tan 5x$
    (B) $\sec 5x$
    (C) $\csc 5x$
    (D) $\sec 5x \tan 5x$
    (E) $5\sec 5x \tan 5x$

8. What is the volume of the solid formed by rotating the region between the curves $y = 6x^2 - x$ and $y = x^2 - 6x$ about the y-axis?

    (A) $\dfrac{70\pi}{12}$

    (B) 5π

    (C) $\dfrac{3\pi}{2}$

    (D) π

    (E) $\dfrac{5\pi}{6}$

GO ON TO THE NEXT PAGE.

9. $\int x^3 \ln 2x\, dx =$

(A) $\dfrac{x^4}{16}\left(4\ln 2x - 1\right) + C$

(B) $\dfrac{x^4}{4}\left(\ln 2x + 1\right) + C$

(C) $x^4\left(\ln 2x - 1\right) + C$

(D) $\dfrac{x^4}{4}\left(\ln 2x - 1\right) + C$

(E) $\dfrac{x^4}{16}\left(4\ln 2x + 1\right) + C$

10. $\int \dfrac{x+10}{2x^2 - 5x - 3}\, dx =$

(A) $3\ln|x+3| - \dfrac{1}{2}\ln|2x-1| + C$

(B) $\ln|x+3| - 3\ln|2x-1| + C$

(C) $\ln|x+3| - \dfrac{3}{2}\ln|2x-1| + C$

(D) $3\ln|x+3| + \dfrac{3}{2}\ln|2x-1| + C$

(E) $-\ln|x+3| + \dfrac{3}{2}\ln|2x-1| + C$

GO ON TO THE NEXT PAGE.

11.

x	-2	-1	0	1	2
$f''(x)$	4	1	0	-2	3

The polynomial function f has selected values of its second derivative, f'', given in the table above. Which of the following could be false?

A) The graph of f changes concavity in the interval $(-2, 1)$.
(B) There is a point of inflection on the graph of f at $x = 0$.
(C) The graph of f has a point of inflection at $x = 1.5$.
(D) The graph of f is concave down at $x = 1$.
(E) The graph of f changes concavity in the interval $(1, 2)$.

---

12. If $y = \sqrt[3]{\dfrac{(x+2)^2 (x-4)^3}{x^3 - 1}}$, $\dfrac{dy}{dx} =$

(A) $y\left(\dfrac{2}{3(x+2)} + \dfrac{1}{x-4} - \dfrac{x^2}{x^3-1} \right)$

(B) $y\left(\dfrac{2}{x+2} + \dfrac{3}{x-4} - \dfrac{3x^2}{x^3-1} \right)$

(C) $y\left(\dfrac{2}{3(x+2)} - \dfrac{1}{x-4} - \dfrac{x^2}{x^3-1} \right)$

(D) $y\left(\dfrac{2}{3(x+2)} - \dfrac{1}{x-4} + \dfrac{x^2}{x^3-1} \right)$

(E) $y\left(\dfrac{2}{x+2} - \dfrac{3}{x-4} + \dfrac{3x^2}{x^3-1} \right)$

GO ON TO THE NEXT PAGE.

13. If $y = x^3 + 3x^2 + 5$, then $\dfrac{dy}{dx} =$

    (A) $3x^3 + 6x^2 + 5$

    (B) $3x^2 + 6x$

    (C) $\dfrac{x^4}{4} + x^3 + 5x$

    (D) $15x^5$

    (E) $3x^2 + 6x + 5$

---

14. If $f(x) = \dfrac{x^3 + 2x - 1}{x^2 + x}$, then $f'(x) =$

    (A) $\dfrac{(x^2 + x)(3x^2 + 2) - (x^3 + 2x - 1)(2x + 1)}{(x^2 + x)}$

    (B) $\dfrac{(x^2 + x)(3x + 2) - (x^3 + 2x - 1)(2x + 1)}{(x^2 + x)^2}$

    (C) $\dfrac{(x^2 + x)(3x^2 + 2) - (x^3 + 2x - 1)(2x + 1)}{(x^2 + x)^2}$

    (D) $\dfrac{(x^2 + x)(3x^2 + 2) - 2x(x^3 + 2x - 1)}{(x^2 + x)^2}$

    (E) $\dfrac{(x^2 + x)(3x^2 + 2) + (x^3 + 2x - 1)(2x + 1)}{(x^2 + x)^2}$

GO ON TO THE NEXT PAGE.

15. If $f(x) = 2 \sin(\cos x)$, then $f'(x) =$

    (A) $-2 \sin x \cdot \cos(\cos x)$
    (B) $-2 \cos x \cdot \sin(\sin x)$
    (C) $2 \sin x \cdot \cos x$
    (D) $-2 \sin x \cdot \cos x$
    (E) $2 \sin x \cdot \cos(\cos x)$

16. Find $\dfrac{dy}{dx}$ if $x^3 + 3x^2y + 3xy^2 + y^3 = 27$.

    (A) 27

    (B) $\dfrac{3x^2 + 3y^2}{6x}$

    (C) 1

    (D) $\dfrac{-3x^2 - 3y^2}{6x}$

    (E) -1

17. Water is filling a conical cup at a rate of $\dfrac{2}{3}\pi$ in^3/sec. If the cup has a height of 18 in and a radius of 6 in, how fast is the water level rising when the water is 6 in deep?

    (A) $\dfrac{1}{6}$ in/s

    (B) 6 in/s

    (C) $\dfrac{1}{4}$ in/s

    (D) $\dfrac{8}{3}$ in/s

    (E) $\dfrac{1}{12}$ in/s

GO ON TO THE NEXT PAGE.

18. Find the derivative of $\log_8 \left(x^2+2\right)^3$

    (A) $\dfrac{6x}{\left(x^2+2\right)^3 \ln 8}$

    (B) $\dfrac{6x}{\left(x^2+2\right)\ln 8}$

    (C) $\dfrac{6x\left(x^2+2\right)^3}{\ln 8}$

    (D) $\dfrac{6}{\left(x^2+2\right)\ln 8}$

    (E) $\dfrac{6x\ln 8}{\left(x^2+2\right)}$

---

19. What curve is represented by $x = \cos^2 t$ and $y = \sin^2 t$?

    (A) $y = x + 1$
    (B) $y = -x + 1$
    (C) $y = -x - 1$
    (D) $y = x - 1$
    (E) $y = x$

---

20. Given the position function $x(t) = t^3 - 18t^2 - 84t + 11$ for $t \geq 0$, for what values of t is speed increasing?

    (A) $0 \leq t < 14$
    (B) $0 \leq t < 6$ and $t > 14$
    (C) $0 \leq t < 6$
    (D) $t > 6$
    (E) $6 < t < 14$

GO ON TO THE NEXT PAGE.

21. Find the derivative of $f(x) = e^{\sin^2 x}$

    (A) $2e^{\sin^2 x} \sin x \cos x$

    (B) $e^{\sin^2 x}$

    (C) $e^{\sin^2 x} \sin^2 x$

    (D) $2e^{\sin^2 x} \sin x$

    (E) $e^{\sin^2 x} \sin x \cos x$

22. Given:

x	0	2	6	7	9	12	16
$f(x)$	1	3	7	5	3	6	9

Use a left-hand Riemann sum with the six subintervals indicated by the data to approximate $\int_0^{16} f(x)\,dx$.

    (A) 63
    (B) 99
    (C) 40
    (D) 64
    (E) 100

23. $\int \dfrac{18x^2 + 9}{3x^3 + x}\,dx =$

    (A) $2\ln\left|x^2 + 1\right| + C$

    (B) $\dfrac{1}{2}\ln\left|3x^3 + x\right| + C$

    (C) $\ln\left|3x^3 + x\right| + C$

    (D) $\ln\left|x^2 + 1\right| + C$

    (E) $2\ln\left|3x^3 + x\right| + C$

GO ON TO THE NEXT PAGE.

24. $\int e^x \sin x \, dx =$

    (A) $\dfrac{e^x \sin x - e^x \cos x}{2} + C$

    (B) $\dfrac{e^x \sin x + e^x \cos x}{2} + C$

    (C) $e^x \sin x - e^x \cos x + C$

    (D) $e^x \cos x - e^x \sin x + C$

    (E) $\dfrac{e^x \cos x - e^x \sin x}{2} + C$

---

25. Which of the following integrals converges?

    I. $\displaystyle\int_0^\infty \dfrac{dx}{1 + x^2}$

    II. $\displaystyle\int_0^\infty \dfrac{dx}{\sqrt{1 - x^2}}$

    III. $\displaystyle\int_1^\infty \dfrac{dx}{x}$

    (A)   I
    (B)   II
    (C)   III
    (D)   I & II
    (E)   I, II, & III

---

26. Find the area of the region in the plane enclosed by $r = 5 + 2 \cos \theta$.

    (A) 23π
    (B) 24π
    (C) 25π
    (D) 26π
    (E) 27π

GO ON TO THE NEXT PAGE.

27. If $\dfrac{dy}{dx} = \dfrac{\cos x}{y^2}$ and $y = -1$ when $x = 0$, then the equation for the curve is

    (A) $y^3 = 3\sin x - 1$
    (B) $y^3 = 3\cos x - 1$
    (C) $y = \sin x - 1$
    (D) $y = 3\sin x + 1$
    (E) $y^3 = \sin x$

28. Which of the following series converges?

    I. $\displaystyle\sum_{n=1}^{\infty} 2\left(\dfrac{1}{3}\right)^{n-1}$

    II. $\displaystyle\sum_{n=1}^{\infty} \dfrac{n}{3^n}$

    III. $\displaystyle\sum_{n=1}^{\infty} \dfrac{6n^2}{n^3 + 1}$

    (A) I
    (B) II
    (C) III
    (D) I & II
    (E) I & III

END OF PART A, SECTION I

IF YOU FINISH BEFORE TIME IS CALLED, YOU MAY CHECK YOUR WORK ON PART A ONLY.

DO NOT GO ON TO PART B UNTIL YOU ARE TOLD TO DO SO.

CALCULUS BC

SECTION I, Part B

Time—50 Minutes

Number of questions—17

A GRAPHING CALCULATOR IS REQUIRED FOR SOME QUESTIONS ON THIS PART OF THE EXAMINATION

<u>Directions</u>: Solve each of the following problems, using the available space for scratchwork. After examining the form of the choices, decide which is the best of the choices given and fill in the corresponding oval on the answer sheet. No credit will be given for anything written in the test book. Do not spend too much time on any one problem.

<u>In this test:</u>

1. The **exact** numerical value of the correct answer does not always appear among the choices given. When this happens, select from among the choices the number that best approximates the exact numerical value.

2. Unless otherwise specified, the domain of a function f is assumed to be the set of all real numbers x for which $f(x)$ is a real number.

29. A spherical balloon is losing air at a rate of -24π in^3/sec. How fast is the balloon surface area of the balloon shrinking when the radius of the balloon is 2 in?

(A) -20π in^2/sec
(B) -24π in^2/sec
(C) -48π in^2/sec
(D) -12π in^2/sec
(E) -60π in^2/sec

GO ON TO THE NEXT PAGE.

30. Find $\lim\limits_{x \to 0} \dfrac{(3+2x)^{\frac{3}{2}} - 7x}{2x^2}$.

(A) $\dfrac{\sqrt{3}}{4}$

(B) $\dfrac{4\sqrt{3}}{3}$

(C) $\dfrac{3}{4}$

(D) $\dfrac{1}{4}$

(E) $\dfrac{1}{3}$

31. When are the horizontal and vertical components of the velocity of a curve whose motion is given by $x = \dfrac{5}{2}t^2 + 6$ and $y = 2t^3 - t^2 + t$ equal?

(A) $t = -1$

(B) $t = 2$

(C) $t = \dfrac{1}{6}$

(D) $t = 6$

(E) $t = -2$

GO ON TO THE NEXT PAGE.

32. Find the derivative of $x^2 + 3x^2y + 3xy^2 + y^3 = 2$ at (3,2).

(A) 7

(B) $\dfrac{19}{25}$

(C) $\dfrac{75}{54}$

(D) $-\dfrac{18}{25}$

(E) $-\dfrac{25}{18}$

---

33. A kid on a bike is riding home in the woods on a straight path that is 50 m from the nearest point on the road. His home is 1500 m from the nearest point on the road. If the kid rides at 3 m/s in the woods and 5 m/s on the road, how far from his house should the kid cross to the road to get home in the shortest time?

(A)   37.5 m
(B) 1500 m
(C)   300.5 m
(D) 1200 m
(E) 1462.5 m

---

34. A shoe company determined that its profit equation (in millions of dollars) is given by $P = 2x^3 - 105x^2 + 1500x - 1200$, where x is the number of thousands of pairs of shoes sold and $0 \le x \le 50$. Optimize the manufacturer's profit.

(A) $5.3 billion
(B) $61.3 billion
(C) $1.925 billion
(D) $1.2 billion
(E) $65 billion

GO ON TO THE NEXT PAGE.

35. If the function $f(x) = x^4$ has an average value of 5 on the closed interval $[0, k]$, then $k =$

(A) 5

(B) $\sqrt{5}$

(C) 1

(D) $\sqrt{3}$

(E) $\sqrt{2}$

36. $\int 3x(7^{3x^2+2})dx =$

(A) $\dfrac{49 \cdot 343^{x^2}}{\ln 49} + C$

(B) $\dfrac{343^{x^2}}{2\ln 7} + C$

(C) $\dfrac{49^{x^2}}{\ln 49} + C$

(D) $\dfrac{49 \cdot 343^{x^2}}{\ln 7} + C$

(E) $\dfrac{7^{3x^2+2}}{\ln 7} + C$

37. A rectangle with one side on the x-axis has its upper vertices on the graph of $y = \cos x + 1$. What is the minimum area between the rectangle and the graph of $y = \cos x + 1$ on the interval $(-\pi \leq x \leq \pi)$?

(A) 6.283

(B) 2.988

(C) 1.307

(D) 3.296

(E) 5.022

GO ON TO THE NEXT PAGE.

38. $\int \dfrac{dx}{x^2 + 6x + 10} =$

    (A) $\cot^{-1}(x + 3) + C$
    (B) $\sin^{-1}(x + 3) + C$
    (C) $\sec^{-1}(x + 3) + C$
    (D) $\tan^{-1}(x + 3) + C$
    (E) $\cos^{-1}(x + 3) + C$

---

39. If the path of the particle is given by $x(t) = 2t^2 - 3t + 1$, how far does the particle travel between $t = 0$ and $t = 4$?

    (A) 20

    (B) 21

    (C) $\dfrac{169}{8}$

    (D) 22

    (E) $\dfrac{89}{4}$

---

40. Given the following values for x and $f(x)$, what is the area under $f(x)$. Use a left-hand Riemann sum to approximate.

x	0	1	3	7	8	10	13	15
$f(x)$	2	6	3	4	8	9	12	13

    (A) 46
    (B) 57
    (C) 116
    (D) 207
    (E) 253

GO ON TO THE NEXT PAGE.

41. Find the length of the curve given by $y = \frac{1}{3}(x^2 - 2)^{\frac{3}{2}}$ from $x = 0$ to $x = 4$.

    (A) 12
    (B) 16

    (C) $\frac{64}{3} - 4$

    (D) $\frac{64}{3}$

    (E) $\frac{64}{3} + 4$

42. Find $\frac{d}{dx} \int_1^x (t - t^4) dt$.

    (A) $x - x^4 + 1$
    (B) $x^4 - x + 1$
    (C) $x^4 - x$
    (D) $x - x^4 - 1$
    (E) $x - x^4$

43. A cylindrical pool is filling at a rate of $96\pi \frac{\text{ft}^3}{\text{hr}}$. If the radius of the pool is 4 feet, how fast is the height changing?

    (A) 3 ft/hr
    (B) 4 ft/hr
    (C) 5 ft/hr
    (D) 6 ft/hr
    (E) 7 ft/hr

GO ON TO THE NEXT PAGE.

44. A child jumps on a trampoline and rises at a rate of 10 ft/min. The child's mother is watching from the patio 40 ft away. How fast, in rad/sec, is the angle of elevation between the trampoline and the mother's line of sight of her child increasing when the child is 30 ft in the air?

    (A) $\dfrac{1}{70}$ rad/sec

    (B) $\dfrac{1}{375}$ rad/sec

    (C) $\dfrac{1}{13}$ rad/sec

    (D) $\dfrac{1}{180}$ rad/sec

    (E) $\dfrac{1}{3}$ rad/sec

---

45. Find the derivative of $y = \dfrac{\ln\left(2x^3\right)}{e^{2x}}$.

    (A) $\dfrac{3 + 2\ln\left(2x^3\right)}{e^{2x}}$

    (B) $\dfrac{3 - 2\ln\left(2x^3\right)}{e^{2x}}$

    (C) $\dfrac{3}{xe^{2x}} - \dfrac{2\ln\left(2x^3\right)}{e^{2x}}$

    (D) $\dfrac{3}{xe^{2x}} + \dfrac{2\ln\left(2x^3\right)}{e^{2x}}$

    (E) $\dfrac{3 + \ln\left(4x^9\right)}{e^{2x}}$

STOP

END OF PART B, SECTION I

IF YOU FINISH BEFORE TIME IS CALLED, YOU MAY CHECK YOUR WORK ON PART B ONLY.

DO NOT GO ON TO SECTION II UNTIL YOU ARE TOLD TO DO SO.

SECTION II
GENERAL INSTRUCTIONS

You may wish to look over the problems before starting to work on them, since it is not expected that everyone will be able to complete all parts of all problems. All problems are given equal weight, but the parts of a particular problem are not necessarily given equal weight.

A GRAPHING CALCULATOR IS REQUIRED FOR SOME PROBLEMS OR PARTS OF PROBLEMS ON THIS SECTION OF THE EXAMINATION.

- You should write all work for each part of each problem in the space provided for that part in the booklet. Be sure to write clearly and legibly. If you make an error, you may save time by crossing it out rather than trying to erase it. Erased or crossed-out work will not be graded.

- Show all your work. You will be graded on the correctness and completeness of your methods as well as your answers. Correct answers without supporting work may not receive credit.

- Justifications require that you give mathematical (noncalculator) reasons and that you clearly identify functions, graphs, tables, or other objects you use.

- You are permitted to use your calculator to solve an equation, find the derivative of a function at a point, or calculate the value of a definite integral. However, you must clearly indicate the setup of your problem, namely the equation, function, or integral you are using. If you use other built-in features or programs, you must show the mathematical steps necessary to produce your results.

- Your work must be expressed in standard mathematical notation rather than calculator syntax. For example, $\int_1^5 x^2 \, dx$ may not be written as fnInt (X^2, X, 1, 5).

- Unless otherwise specified, answers (numeric or algebraic) need not be simplified. If your answer is given as a decimal approximation, it should be correct to three places after the decimal point.

- Unless otherwise specified, the domain of a function f is assumed to be the set of all real numbers x for which $f(x)$ is a real number.

GO ON TO THE NEXT PAGE.

SECTION II, PART A
Time—30 minutes
Number of problems—2

A graphing calculator is required for some problems or parts of problems.

During the timed portion for Part A, you may work only on the problems in Part A.

On Part A, you are permitted to use your calculator to solve an equation, find the derivative of a function at a point, or calculate the value of a definite integral. However, you must clearly indicate the setup of your problem, namely the equation, function, or integral you are using. If you use other built-in features or programs, you must show the mathematical steps necessary to produce your results.

---

1. Let y be the function satisfying $f'(x) = -x(1 + f(x))$ and $f(0) = 5$.

   (a) Use Euler's method to approximate $f(1)$ with a step size of 0.25.

   (b) Find an exact solution for $f(x)$ when $x = 1$.

   (c) Evaluate $\int_0^\infty -x\left(1 + f\left(x\right)\right)dx$.

---

2. Let R be the region enclosed by the graphs of $y = x^2 - x - 6$ and $y = x^3 - 2x^2 - 5x + 6$ and the lines $x = -2$ and $x = 2$.

   (a) Find the area of R.
   (b) The horizontal line $y = 0$ splits R into two parts. Find the area of the part of R above the horizontal line.
   (c) The region R is the base of a solid. For this solid, each cross section perpendicular to the x-axis is an equilateral triangle. Find the volume of this solid.
   (d) What is the volume of the solid generated by the region R when it is revolved about the line $x = -3$.

GO ON TO THE NEXT PAGE.

SECTION II, PART B
Time—1 hour
Number of problems—4

No calculator is allowed for these problems.

During the timed portion for Part B, you may continue to work on the problems in Part A without the use of any calculator.

---

3. The derivative of a function f is $f'(x) = (2x + 6)e^{-x}$ and $f(2) = 15$.

    (a) The function has a critical point at $x = -3$. Is there a relative maximum, minimum, or neither at this point on f? Justify your response.
    (b) On what interval, if any, is the graph of f both increasing and concave down? Explain your reasoning.
    (c) Find the value of $f(5)$.

---

4. Consider the equation $x^3 - 2x^2y + 3xy^2 - 4y^3 = 10$.

    (a) Write an equation for the slope of the curve at any point.

    (b) Find the equation of the normal line to the curve at the point $x = 1$.

    (c) Find $\dfrac{d^2y}{dx^2}$ at $x = 1$.

---

5. Given that $f(x) = \sin x$:

    (a) Find the 6th degree Maclaurin series.
    (b) Use the polynomial to estimate $\sin 0.2$.
    (c) Estimate the remainder of the approximation.

GO ON TO THE NEXT PAGE.

6. Two particles travel in the *xy*-plane for time $t \geq 0$. The position of particle A is given by $x = 2t - 3$ and $y = (2t + 1)^2$ and the position of particle B is given by $x = t - 1$ and $y = t + 23$.

   (a) Find the velocity vector for each particle at $t = 3$.
   (b) Set up, but do not evaluate, an integral expression for the distance traveled by particle A from $t = 3$ to $t = 5$.
   (c) At what time do the two particles collide? Justify your answer.

STOP

END OF EXAM

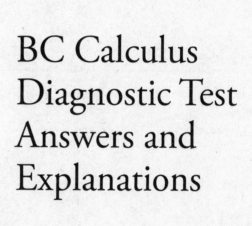

BC Calculus
Diagnostic Test
Answers and
Explanations

ANSWER KEY

Section I

1. D
2. A
3. B
4. C
5. E
6. E
7. D
8. E
9. A
10. E
11. C
12. A
13. B
14. C
15. A
16. E
17. A
18. B
19. B
20. B
21. A
22. D
23. E
24. A
25. A
26. E
27. A
28. D
29. B
30. A
31. C
32. D
33. E
34. B
35. B
36. A
37. B
38. D
39. E
40. E
41. C
42. E
43. D
44. B
45. C

EXPLANATIONS

Section I

1. **D** $\lim\limits_{x \to 3} \dfrac{x^2 - x - 6}{x^2 - 5x + 6} = \lim\limits_{x \to 3} \dfrac{(x+2)(x-3)}{(x-2)(x-3)} = \lim\limits_{x \to 3} \dfrac{x+2}{x-2} = \dfrac{5}{1} = 5$.

2. **A** $\lim\limits_{x \to 0} \dfrac{\sec x}{\csc x} = \lim\limits_{x \to 0} \dfrac{\sin x}{\cos x} = \lim\limits_{x \to 0} \tan x = 0$.

3. **B** $\dfrac{d}{dx}\left(\dfrac{2x+3}{(x-4)^2} \right) = \dfrac{2(x-4)^2 - 2(2x+3)(x-4)}{(x-4)^4} = \dfrac{2(x-4) - 2(2x+3)}{(x-4)^3} = \dfrac{-2x-14}{(x-4)^3}$

4. **C** $\lim\limits_{x \to 0}\left(\dfrac{2\sin 3x}{3\sin 2x} \right) = \left(\dfrac{2}{3} \right)\lim\limits_{x \to 0}\left(\dfrac{\sin 3x}{\sin 2x} \right) = \dfrac{2}{3}\left(\dfrac{3}{2} \right) = 1$.

5. **E** Jump discontinuities exist when the left and right hand limits of the function are not equal at a certain value. A point discontinuity exists when the limit of the function at a certain value does not equal the function at that value. An essential discontinuity is a vertical asymptote. A removable discontinuity occurs where a canceled factor in a rational expression existed. For this function, $f(x) = \dfrac{(x+2)(x-9)}{(x-9)(x-3)}$, since the factor $(x-9)$ can be factored out, there will be a removable discontinuity at $x = 9$. Also, since the function does not exist at $x = 3$, there is a vertical asymptote there, so there is both a removable and an essential discontinuity on this function's graph.

6. **E** First, the function can simplify to $f(x) = \dfrac{x^3 - 12x^2 + 3x - 4}{x^2}$. Use the quotient rule and be prepared to simplify to make the multiple derivatives easier to evaluate. The first derivative is $f'(x) = \dfrac{x^2(3x^2 - 24x + 3) - 2x(x^3 - 4x^2 + 3x - 4)}{x^4} = \dfrac{x^3 - 3x + 8}{x^3}$. The second derivative is $f''(x) = \dfrac{(x^3)(3x^2 - 3) - (3x^2)(x^3 - 3x + 8)}{x^6} = \dfrac{6x - 24}{x^4}$. The third derivative is $f'''(x) = \dfrac{6x^4 - 4x^3(6x - 24)}{x^8} = \dfrac{-18x + 96}{x^5}$. Finally, the fourth derivative is $f^{(4)}(x) = \dfrac{-18x^5 - 5x^4(-18x + 96)}{x^{10}} = \dfrac{72x - 480}{x^6}$.

7. **D** Use u-substitution and remember your derivatives of trig functions.

$\dfrac{d}{dx}\left(\dfrac{\sec 5x}{5} \right) = \dfrac{1}{5}(5)(\sec 5x \tan 5x) = \sec 5x \tan 5x$.

8. **E** First, determine where the two curves intersect. Set them equal to each other and solve for x. Thus, $x = 0$ and $x = -1$ at the points of intersection that bind the area. (Determine which curve is "on top" in order to solve properly.) Next, integrate using cylindrical shells from $x = 0$ to $x = -1$: $2\pi \int_0^1 x\left(6x^2 - x - \left(x^2 - 6x\right)\right) dx = \dfrac{70\pi}{12}$. The washer method would have worked, but you would have had to convert the equations into "$x =$" form. Recall, it is generally best to use the cylindrical shells method when the axis of rotation is in "$x =$" form and the equations in "$y =$" form. When everything is in "$y =$" form the washer method is generally better.

9. **A** Since u-substitution will not work, you must integrate by parts. Recall, the formula is $\int u\, dv = uv - \int v\, du$. For this problem, $u = \ln 2x$, $du = \dfrac{dx}{x}$, $dv = x^3 dx$, and $v = \dfrac{x^4}{4}$. (If you are unsure of the derivative of $\ln 2x$, remember the product rule of logarithms and then differentiate.) Now, the integral is $\int x^3 \ln 2x\, dx = \dfrac{x^4}{4} \ln 2x - \dfrac{1}{4} \int x^3 dx = \dfrac{x^4}{16}\left(4\ln(2x) - 1\right) + C$.

10. **E** Use partial fractions to solve this problem. When this is done, the fraction in the integrand becomes $\dfrac{x + 10}{2x^2 - 5x - 3} = \dfrac{-1}{x + 3} + \dfrac{3}{2x - 1}$. If those two fractions are used as integrands, via u-substitution, the solution is $-\ln|x + 3| + \dfrac{3}{2} \ln|2x - 1| + C$.

11. **C** By the second derivative test, when the second derivative equals zero, there is a point of inflection at that point. A point of inflection signifies a change in the concavity of the graph of the original function. In addition, if the second derivative is negative over an interval, the graph of the original function is concave down over that interval. If the second derivative is positive, the graph is concave up.

12. **A** Rather than deal with the chain, product, and quotient rules, use logarithmic differentiation:

$$\ln y = \frac{1}{3}\left(2\ln(x + 2) + 3\ln(x - 4) - \ln(x^3 - 1)\right)$$
$$= \frac{1}{y}\frac{dy}{dx} = \frac{2}{3(x + 2)} + \frac{1}{x - 4} - \frac{x^2}{x^3 - 1}$$
$$= \frac{dy}{dx} = y\left(\frac{2}{3(x + 2)} + \frac{1}{x - 4} - \frac{x^2}{x^3 - 1}\right)$$

13. **B** Using the Power and Addition Rules, take the derivative of $f(x)$ and you get B. Be careful, C is the integral.

14. **C** Using the Quotient Rule, $\dfrac{v\dfrac{du}{dx} - u\dfrac{dv}{dx}}{v^2}$, take the derivative of $f(x)$ and you get C.

15. **A** Using the Chain Rule, $\dfrac{dy}{dx} = \dfrac{dy}{dv}\dfrac{dv}{dx}$, and $d(\sin x) = \cos x$ and $d(\cos x) = -\sin x$, the answer is A.

16. **E** Use implicit differentiation to find $\dfrac{dy}{dx}$:

$$3x^2 + 6xy + 3x^2\frac{dy}{dx} + 3y^2 + 6xy\frac{dy}{dx} + 3y^2\frac{dy}{dx} = 0$$

Isolate terms containing $\dfrac{dy}{dx}$ by moving all terms that don't contain $\dfrac{dy}{dx}$ to the right side of the equals sign:

$$3x^2\frac{dy}{dx} + 6xy\frac{dy}{dx} + 3y^2\frac{dy}{dx} = -3x^2 - 6xy - 3y^2$$

Factor out $\dfrac{dy}{dx}$:

$$\frac{dy}{dx}\left(3x^2 + 6xy + 3y^2\right) = -3x^2 - 6xy - 3y^2$$

Isolate $\dfrac{dy}{dx}$ and simplify:

$$\frac{dy}{dx} = \frac{-3x^2 - 6xy - 3y^2}{3x^2 + 6xy + 3y^2} = \frac{-\left(3x^2 + 6xy + 3y^2\right)}{3x^2 + 6xy + 3y^2} = -1$$

17. **A** The volume of a cone is found from the formula $V = \dfrac{1}{3}\pi r^2 h$. Because we are told the radius of the cup is 6 in and the height is 18 in, then at any level, the height of the water will be three times the radius, thus, $h = 3r$. Using this relationship, r can be replaced with $\dfrac{h}{3}$ in the formula for volume, so $V = \dfrac{1}{3}\pi\left(\dfrac{h}{3}\right)^2 h = \dfrac{\pi h^3}{27}$. Then, to determine the rate that the water level is rising, we must differentiate both sides with respect to t: $\dfrac{dV}{dt} = \dfrac{\pi h^2}{9}\dfrac{dh}{dt}$. Insert the rate of the cup filling $\left(\dfrac{dV}{dt} = \dfrac{2}{3}\pi \text{ in}^3/\text{sec}\right)$ and the water level at the instant of interest, 6 in, and solve for $\dfrac{dh}{dt}$. Thus, $\dfrac{dh}{dt} = \dfrac{1}{6}$ in/s.

18.	**B**	When $y = \log_a u$, $\dfrac{dy}{dx} = \dfrac{1}{u \ln a} \dfrac{du}{dx}$. For this problem, $u = \left(x^2 + 2\right)^3$ and $\dfrac{du}{dx} = 6x\left(x^2 + 2\right)^2$ (from the

Chain Rule). Therefore, $f'(x) = \dfrac{6x\left(x^2+2\right)^2}{\left(x^2+2\right)^3 \ln 8} = \dfrac{6x}{\left(x^2+2\right)\ln 8}$.

19.	**B**	Since you are relating a sine function and a cosine function, look for a trig identity that easily relates those. In this case, $\cos^2 t + \sin^2 t = 1$. When you replace $\cos^2 t$ and $\sin^2 t$ with x and y, respectively, the equation becomes $x + y = 1$. Solve for y to get $y = -x + 1$.

20.	**B**	Recall that the velocity function is the first derivative of a position function with respect to time and the acceleration function is the second derivative of a position function with respect to time. Further, when the velocity and acceleration of a particle have the same sign, the speed is increasing. Thus, to solve this problem, first the position function must be differentiated with respect to time: $v(t) = 3t^2 - 36t - 84$. This function is set equal to zero and the critical values, or the times when velocity is equal to 0, are found: $t = -2$ and $t = 14$. As the problem states, we are only interested in $t \geq 0$, so we can ignore $t = -2$. Next, find the sign of the velocity over the time ranges of interest: $0 \leq t < 14$ results in $v(t) < 0$, and $t > 14$ results in $v(t) > 0$. Now to determine when the speed is increasing, differentiate the velocity with respect to time to get the acceleration function: $a(t) = 6t - 36$. Determine when the acceleration is 0 ($t = 6$) and then find the sign of the acceleration around that time: $0 \leq t < 6$ has $a(t) < 0$ and $t > 6$ has $a(t) > 0$. The times when both the velocity and the acceleration have the same sign is when $0 \leq t < 6$ and when $t > 14$.

21.	**A**	When $y = e^u$, $\dfrac{dy}{dx} = e^u \dfrac{du}{dx}$. For this problem, $u = \sin^2 x$ and $\dfrac{du}{dx} = 2\sin x \cos x$ (from the Chain Rule). Therefore, $f'(x) = 2e^{\sin^2 x}\sin x \cos x$.

22.	**D**	The formula for the area under a curve using a left-hand Reimann sum is: $A = \left(\dfrac{b-a}{n}\right)\left(y_0 + y_1 + y_2 + y_3 + \ldots + y_n\right)$, where a and b are the x-values that bound the area and n is the number of rectangles. Since we do not have evenly spaced subintervals, we must find the width of each subinterval individually and multiply it by the left-endpoint y-value, so $A = 1(2) + 3(4) + 7(1) + 5(2) + 3(3) + 6(4) = 64$.

23.	**E**	Recall, $\displaystyle\int \dfrac{du}{u} = \ln|u| + C$, so using u-substitution, $u = 3x^3 + x$ and $du = \left(9x^2 + 1\right)dx$. Then, $2\displaystyle\int \dfrac{du}{u} = 2\ln|u| + C = 2\ln\left|3x^3 + x\right| + C$.

24.   **A**   This is a complicated integral and integration by parts is the best way to go for solving it. Recall, the formula for integration by parts is $\int u\,dv = uv - \int v\,du$. For this problem, let $u = e^x$ and $dv = \sin x\,dx$. From these, $du = e^x\,dx$ and $v = -\cos x$. When you input these using the integration by parts formula you get: $\int e^x \sin x\,dx = -e^x \cos x + \int \cos x\,e^x\,dx$. Since we cannot readily integrate $\int \cos x\,e^x\,dx$, we must use integration by parts again. In this case, $u = e^x$ and $dv = \cos x\,dx$. From these, $du = e^x\,dx$ and $v = \sin x$. Insert these in to the equation in place of $\int \cos x\,e^x\,dx$ and you get: $\int e^x \sin x\,dx = -e^x \cos x + e^x \sin x - \int e^x \sin x\,dx$. We are back to where we started. However, we are in a good position now, because we can add $\int e^x \sin x\,dx$ to both sides and we end up with $2\int e^x \sin x\,dx = -e^x \cos x + e^x \sin x$. In order to solve for $\int e^x \sin x\,dx$, just divide both sides by 2: $\int e^x \sin x\,dx = \dfrac{e^x \sin x - e^x \cos x}{2} + C$.

25.   **A**   All the options are improper integrals and they will converge if their limits as they approach infinity exist. So, check them one at a time and POE. I. $\lim\limits_{a \to \infty} \int_0^\infty \dfrac{dx}{1 + x^2} = \lim\limits_{a \to \infty} \tan^{-1} a - \tan^{-1} 0 = \dfrac{\pi}{2}$, so I. converges. II. $\lim\limits_{a \to \infty} \int_0^\infty \dfrac{dx}{\sqrt{1 - x^2}} = \lim\limits_{a \to \infty} \sin^{-1} a - \sin^{-1} 0 = undefined$, so II. diverges. III. $\lim\limits_{a \to \infty} \int_1^\infty \dfrac{dx}{x} = \lim\limits_{a \to \infty} \ln a - \ln 1 = infinity$, so III. diverges.

26.   **E**   Area under polar curve is found by using: $A = \int_a^b \dfrac{1}{2} r^2\,d\theta$. This curve repeats after 2π, thus the region is bound by 0 and 2π. The area is then found from: $A = \int_0^{2\pi} \dfrac{1}{2}(5 + 2\cos\theta)^2\,d\theta$. Solve this and the area is found to be 27π.

27.   **A**   Solve the differential equation by separating the variables and integrating. The equation would then become: $\int y^2\,dy = \int \cos x\,dx$. From here, $y^3 = 3 \sin x + C$. Next, use the initial condition $(0, -1)$ to get the exact equation: $y^3 = 3 \sin x - 1$.

28. **D** A series converges to L when $\lim_{n \to \infty} a_n = L$. There are many tests that can be used to test whether a series will converge. The test depends on the type of series. So, check each series in this problem one at a time and POE. I. is a geometric series. Geometric series converge if $|r| < 1$ and the general form of the series is $\sum_{n=1}^{\infty} ar^{n-1}$. The r in I. is $\frac{1}{3}$, so the series converges. II. can be tested using the ratio test which states that a series in the form $\sum a_n$ converges if $\lim_{n \to \infty} \frac{a_{n+1}}{a_n} < 1$. Then II. can be tested as follows, $\lim_{n \to \infty} \frac{\frac{n+1}{3^{n+1}}}{\frac{n}{3^n}} = \frac{1}{3}$. Since $\frac{1}{3}$ is less than 1, the series converges. For III., the integral test can be used. The integral test states $\sum a_n$ and $\int_1^{\infty} f(x)\,dx$ either both converge or both diverge, for $a_n = f(n)$. Therefore, evaluate the improper integral $\int_1^{\infty} \frac{6x^2}{x^3+1}\,dx$. This integral diverges (it equals infinity), so the series diverges.

29. **B** The balloon losing air at a rate of $-24\pi \text{ in}^3/\sec$ means the volume is shrinking at that rate, but it does not directly relate to surface area. Therefore, we must find an intermediate rate to relate the two formulas, $V = \frac{4}{3}\pi r^3$ and $A = 4\pi r^2$. The common value is r, so the common rate will be $\frac{dr}{dt}$. To solve for $\frac{dr}{dt}$, differentiate the formula for V with respect to t: $\frac{dV}{dt} = 4\pi r^2 \frac{dr}{dt}$. Insert the values for $\frac{dV}{dt}$ and r and solve for $\frac{dr}{dt}$. Thus, $\frac{dr}{dt} = -\frac{3}{2}$ in. Next, differentiate the formula for A with respect to t: $\frac{dA}{dt} = 8\pi r \frac{dr}{dt}$. Insert the values for $\frac{dr}{dt}$ and r to solve for $\frac{dA}{dt}$. Then, $\frac{dA}{dt} = -24\pi \text{ in}^2/\sec$.

30. **A** When you insert 0 for x, the limit is $\frac{0}{0}$, which is indeterminate. Use L'Hôpital's Rule to evaluate the limit: $\lim_{x \to 0} \frac{3(3+2x)^{\frac{1}{2}} - 7}{4x}$. Since this limit is also indeterminate, use L'Hôpital's Rule again: $\lim_{x \to 0} \frac{3(3+2x)^{-\frac{1}{2}}}{4}$. This limit exists and equals $\frac{\sqrt{3}}{4}$.

31. **C** The horizontal and vertical components of the velocity of a curve are found parametrically as the derivatives with respect to time of the x and y components of the motion, respectively. For this curve, $\dfrac{dx}{dt} = 5t$ and $\dfrac{dy}{dt} = 6t^2 - 2t + 1$. When those two expressions are set equal to each other and solved for t, $t = 1$ and $t = \dfrac{1}{6}$. Since $t = 1$ is not an answer choice, C is the correct answer.

32. **D** Use implicit differentiation to find $\dfrac{dy}{dx}$:

$$2x + 6xy + 3x^2 \frac{dy}{dx} + 3y^2 + 6xy\frac{dy}{dx} + 3y^2\frac{dy}{dx} = 0$$

Do not rearrange the terms to isolate $\dfrac{dy}{dx}$. Instead, plug in (3,2) immediately, solve for the derivative, and simplify:

$$2(3) + 6(3)(2) + 3(3)^2\frac{dy}{dx} + 3(2)^2 + 6(3)(2)\frac{dy}{dx} + 3(2)^2\frac{dy}{dx} = 0$$

$$6 + 36 + 27\frac{dy}{dx} + 12 + 36\frac{dy}{dx} + 12\frac{dy}{dx} = 0$$

$$54 + 75\frac{dy}{dx} = 0$$

$$\frac{dy}{dx} = -\frac{54}{75} = -\frac{18}{25}$$

33. **E**

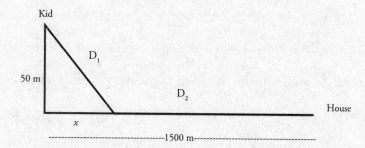

From the diagram, it is clear $D_1 = \sqrt{50^2 + x^2} = \sqrt{2500 + x^2}$ and $D_2 = 1500 - x$. Since distance = rate • time and $r_1 = 3$ and $r_2 = 5$, the times for each leg of the trip are $t_1 = \dfrac{\sqrt{2500 + x^2}}{3}$ and $t_2 = \dfrac{1500 - x}{5}$. Therefore, the total time to ride home is $T = \dfrac{\sqrt{2500 + x^2}}{3} - \dfrac{x}{5} + 300$. To minimize the time, the derivative of T is taken and set equal to zero. $\dfrac{dT}{dx} = \dfrac{1}{3} \cdot \dfrac{1}{2} \cdot 2x \cdot \left(2500 + x^2\right)^{-\frac{1}{2}} - \dfrac{1}{5} = 0$

and $x = \pm \dfrac{75}{2}$. The negative value can be ignored. Because the derivative is ugly, it will take too much time to check the second derivative. (Don't make skipping this a habit, though!) Therefore, the time is minimized when $x = \dfrac{75}{2}$ m. The kid should cross at 1462.5 m from his house.

34. **B** The profit is maximized at the values that make the derivative of the profit equation equal to zero or at the end points of the range. The derivative of the profit equation is $\dfrac{dP}{dx} = 6x^2 - 210x - 1500 = 0$. This equation is true when $x = 10$ or 25. Then, those values and the endpoints, $x = 0$ and $x = 50$ are used to solve for P. The resulting points are $(0, -1200)$, $(10, 5300)$, $(25, 1925)$, and $(50, 61300)$. Since the profit equation is maximized at $x = 50$, and the profit is in millions of dollars, the final result is \$61.3 billion.

35. **B** Use the mean value theorem for integrals, $f(c) = \dfrac{1}{b-a} \displaystyle\int_a^b f(x)\,dx$. Thus, for this problem,

$5 = \dfrac{1}{k-0} \displaystyle\int_0^k x^4\,dx$. Using the Fundamental Theorem of Calculus and solving the equation for k,

$k = \pm\sqrt{5}$.

36. **A** Recall, $\displaystyle\int a^u\,du = \dfrac{a^u}{\ln a} + C$. In this problem, $u = 3x^2 + 2$ and $du = 6x\,dx$.

Thus, $\dfrac{1}{2} \displaystyle\int 7^u\,du = \dfrac{7^u}{2\ln 7} + C = \dfrac{7^{3x^2+2}}{\ln 49} + C = \dfrac{49 \cdot 343^{x^2}}{\ln 49} + C$.

37. **B** The area of a rectangle is $A = lw$. In this case, the width is $2x$ and the length $\cos x + 1$, so $A = 2x\,(\cos x + 1)$. To minimize the area between the rectangle and the graph, the area of the of the rectangle will be maximized. To maximize the area of the rectangle, you must take the derivative of the area and set it equal to zero: $\dfrac{dA}{dx} = 2\cos x - 2x \sin x + 2 = 0$. When you solve this with your calculator, there will be four critical points: $-\pi, -1.30654, 1.30654, \pi$. Plug the points into the formula to determine the area at each point. At $-\pi$ and π, the area is 0. At -1.30654 and 1.30654, the area is 3.29559. (You can confirm this is the maximum by taking the second derivative and checking that it is negative at 1.30654.) Next, determine the area under the curve by using a defi-

nite integral. $\int_{-\pi}^{\pi} \cos x + 1 \, dx = 2\pi$. To determine the area between the rectangle and the curve, subtract the area of the rectangle from the area under the curve: $A_{\text{between}} = 2\pi - 3.29559 = 2.98759$.

38. **D** The current state of the integral makes it appear very difficult to solve. However, notice that there is an x^2 term and no square root. So, think inverse tangent! First, complete the square: $x^2 + 6x + 10 = (x+3)^2 + 1$. Thus, you can rewrite the integral as $\int \dfrac{dx}{(x+3)^2 + 1}$. Now, $u = x + 3$ and $du = dx$. Use the pattern $\int \dfrac{dx}{1+u^2} = \tan^{-1} u + C$. Therefore, $\int \dfrac{dx}{(x+3)^2 + 1} = \tan^{-1}(x+3) + C$.

39. **E** In order to find the distance the particle travels, set the first derivative equal to zero to determine, when, if at all, it changes direction over the time interval: $x'(t) = 4t - 3 = 0$, hence $t = \dfrac{3}{4}$. Since the particle changes direction at $t = \dfrac{3}{4}$, we must find the position of the particle at $t = 0$, $t = \dfrac{3}{4}$, and $t = 4$. $x(0) = 1$, $x\left(\dfrac{3}{4}\right) = -\dfrac{1}{8}$, and $x(4) = 21$. The total distance the particle travels is found by $d = \left| x\left(\dfrac{3}{4}\right) - x(0) \right| + \left| x(4) - x\left(\dfrac{3}{4}\right) \right| = \left| -\dfrac{1}{8} - 1 \right| + \left| 21 + \dfrac{1}{8} \right| = \dfrac{89}{4}$.

40. **E** Given a table of values, a left-hand Riemann sum can be calculated by multiplying the size of the intervals (i.e., the difference in x-values), by the left endpoint y-values and summing them all up.

41. **C** Recall $L = \int_a^b \sqrt{1 + \left(\dfrac{dy}{dx}\right)^2} \, dx$. In this case, $\dfrac{dy}{dx} = x\left(x^2 - 2\right)^{\frac{1}{2}}$ and
$L = \int_0^4 \sqrt{1 + \left(x\left(x^2 - 2\right)^{\frac{1}{2}} \right)^2} \, dx = \dfrac{64}{3} - 4$.

42. **E** From the Second Fundamental Theorem of Calculus, $\dfrac{d}{dx} \int_1^x \left(t - t^4\right) dt = x - x^4$.

43. **D** This is a related rates problem. Since the volume of a cylinder is given by $V = \pi r^2 h$, begin by taking the derivative of both sides of the equation with respect to t. Because the radius is constant, treat it as a constant when taking the derivative: $\dfrac{dV}{dt} = \pi r^2 \dfrac{dh}{dt}$. Now, plug in the given values for $\dfrac{dV}{dt}$ and r: $96\pi = \pi 4^2 \dfrac{dh}{dt}$. Solve for $\dfrac{dh}{dt} = 6$.

44. **B** Draw a picture of the situation:

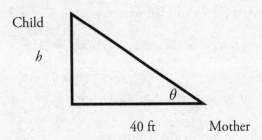

The question is asking about θ in this right triangle and we are given the measurements of the two legs, so set up your equation using tan: $\tan\theta = \dfrac{h}{40}$. As this is a related rates problem, take the first derivative with respect to t: $\sec^2\theta\,\dfrac{d\theta}{dt} = \dfrac{1}{40}\dfrac{dh}{dt}$. Notice the rate of the child rising, $\dfrac{dh}{dt}$, was given in ft/min while the question asks for the solution in rad/sec. Convert $\dfrac{dh}{dt}$ into ft/sec: $\dfrac{dh}{dt} = \dfrac{1}{6}$ ft/sec. Also, note that a height, h, was given in the problem. Plug that into the original equation for tan to solve for θ or directly solve for $\sec^2\theta$: $\tan\theta = \dfrac{30}{40} = \dfrac{3}{4}$. Recall, $1 + \tan^2\theta = \sec^2\theta$, so plug in to solve for $\sec^2\theta$: $\sec^2\theta = \dfrac{25}{16}$. Now, plug in all these values into the derivative of tan and solve for $\dfrac{d\theta}{dt}$: $\dfrac{25}{16}\dfrac{d\theta}{dt} = \dfrac{1}{40}\left(\dfrac{1}{6}\right)$ or $\dfrac{d\theta}{dt} = \dfrac{1}{375}$ rad/sec.

45. **C** Use the quotient rule and recall the derivative of the natural log and e.

$$\frac{dy}{dx} = \frac{\left(e^{2x}\right)\left(\dfrac{6x^2}{2x^3}\right) - 2e^{2x}\ln\left(2x^3\right)}{e^{4x}} = \frac{3}{xe^{2x}} - \frac{2\ln\left(2x^3\right)}{e^{2x}}.$$

Section II

1.   Let y be the function satisfying $f'(x) = -x(1 + f(x))$ and $f(0) = 5$.

(a)   Use Euler's method to approximate $f(1)$ with a step size of 0.25.

(a)   There are two equations you need to know for Euler's method: 1. $x_n = x_{n-1} + h$ and 2. $y_n = y_{n-1} + hy'_{n-1}$. In this case, there will be four steps ($n = 4$) and $h = 0.25$. From the given information, $y' = -x(1 + y)$, so $y'_0 = 0$. It is also given that $x_0 = 0$ and $y_0 = 5$. Then, $x_1 = 0.25$, $y_1 = 5$, and $y'_1 = 1.5$. Next, $x_2 = 0.5$, $y_2 = 4.625$, and $y'_2 = -2.8125$. Once more, $x_3 = 0.75$, $y_3 = 3.92188$, and $y'_3 = -3.69141$. Finally, $x_4 = 1$ and $y_4 = 2.999$.

(b)   Find an exact solution for $f(x)$ when $x = 1$.

(b)   Solve the differential equation: $\dfrac{dy}{dx} = -x(1 + y)$. Then, $y = Ce^{-\frac{x^2}{2}} - 1$. With the initial condition that $f(0) = 5$, $f(x) = 6e^{-\frac{x^2}{2}} - 1$. Therefore, $f(1) = 6e^{-\frac{1}{2}} - 1 \approx 2.639$.

(c)   Evaluate $\int_0^\infty -x(1 + f(x))\,dx$.

(c)   First, remember the Fundamental Theorem of Calculus: $\int_a^b f'(x)\,dx = f(b) - f(a)$. From part (b), $f(x) = 6e^{-\frac{x^2}{2}} - 1$. Notice that $\int_0^\infty -x(1 + f(x))\,dx$ is an improper integral. So, evaluate $\lim_{a \to \infty} f(a)$ and $f(0)$ and find the difference. $\lim_{a \to \infty} f(a) = -1$ and $f(0) = 5$. Therefore, $\int_0^\infty -x(1 + f(x))\,dx = -6$.

2.   Let R be the region enclosed by the graphs of $y = x^2 - x - 6$ and $y = x^3 - 2x^2 - 5x + 6$ and the lines $x = -2$ and $x = 2$.

(a)   Find the area of R.

(a) $Area = \int_a^b [f(x) - g(x)] dx$. We are told the region is bound by $x = -2$ and $x = 2$. Further,

$y = x^3 - 2x^2 - 5x + 6$ is always more positive or "on top" over the entire region, so

$f(x) = x^3 - 2x^2 - 5x + 6$ and $g(x) = x^2 - x - 6$. Now, the integral can be set up:

$A = \int_{-2}^{2} (x^3 - 2x^2 - 5x + 6) - (x^2 - x - 6) dx$. When solved, the area is found to be 32 units squared.

(b)   The horizontal line $y = 0$ splits R into two parts. Find the area of the part of R above the horizontal line.

(b)   The line $y = 0$ divides R so that the area above R is the region enclosed by $y = 0$ and

$y = x^3 - 2x^2 - 5x + 6$. Now, the limits of integration are when these two curves intersect. These

curves intersect at $x = -2$, $x = 1$, and $x = 3$. However, R is bound between $x = -2$ and $x = 2$, so the

limits of integration are $x = -2$ and $x = 1$. The same formula for area can be used from part (a), but

the specific values input would be the ones described here. Thus, $A = \int_{-2}^{1} (x^3 - 2x^2 - 5x + 6 - 0) dx$.

Thus, the area of this portion of $R = \dfrac{63}{4}$.

(c)   The region R is the base of a solid. For this solid, each cross section perpendicular to the x-axis is an equilateral triangle. Find the volume of this solid.

(c)   The volume of the solid is found by integrating the area of the cross-section, so $V = \int_a^b A(x) dx$.

In this case, since the cross-section is an equilateral triangle, $A = (side)^2 \dfrac{\sqrt{3}}{4}$, where the side length

is the length between the curves, i.e., $f(x) - g(x)$. From part (a), we know $f(x) = x^3 - 2x^2 - 5x + 6$

and $g(x) = x^2 - x - 6$ and the limits of integration are $x = -2$ and $x = 2$. The equation for the volume

is then $V = \int_{-2}^{2} \frac{\sqrt{3}}{4} \left[\left(x^3 - 2x^2 - 5x + 6 \right) - \left(x^2 - x - 6 \right) \right] dx = \frac{8576\sqrt{3}}{105} = 141.467$ units cubed.

(d) What is the volume of the solid generated by the region R, when it is revolved about the line $x = -3$.

(d) Since you are not told which method to use to find the volume you must decide. You can use

the rule of thumb that it is typically (but not always) better to use cylindrical shells, if the region

is bound by more than two curves (including an axis) or if one or more curves are given as $y =$ and

the others are given as $x =$. Both conditions are satisfied in this problem, so cylindrical shells is

probably best. The general formula for cylindrical shells is $2\pi \int_{a}^{b} x[f(x) - g(x)] dx$. We know from

part (a) the limits of integration are $x = -2$ and $x = 2$ and we have established which curve is $f(x)$

and which is $g(x)$ in part (a). The only thing left to establish is the radius of the cylinder from the

axis of rotation. Since there is a shift in the axis to $x = -3$, the radius is $x + 3$. Thus, the final inte-

gral is: $V = 2\pi \int_{-2}^{2} (x+3) \left[\left(x^3 - 2x^2 - 5x + 6 \right) - \left(x^2 - x - 6 \right) \right] dx = \frac{6046\pi}{35} = 542.688$ units cubed.

3. The derivative of a function f is $f'(x) = (2x + 6)e^{-x}$ and $f(2) = 15$.

(a) The function has a critical point at $x = -3$. Is there a relative maximum, minimum, or neither at this point on f? Justify your response.

(a) You have two options here: 1) Using the first derivative test: Since $x = -3$ is a critical point, a local minimum will exist when $f'(x) < 0$ for $x < -3$ and $f'(x) > 0$ for $x > -3$. In this case, those two criteria are satisfied, so $x = -3$ is a relative minimum. 2) You can use the second derivative test: Take the derivative of $f'(x)$. $f''(x) = (-2x - 4)e^{-x}$. Plug $x = -3$ into $f''(x)$. From the second derivative test, if $f''(c) < 0$, then c is a relative maximum, but if $f''(c) > 0$, then c is a relative minimum. In this case, $f''(-3) = 2e^{-3}$ which is greater than 0, so $x = -3$ is a relative minimum of f.

(b)   On what interval, if any, is the graph of f both increasing and concave down? Explain your reasoning.

(b)   First, use the second derivative from part (a). Find the points of inflection by setting $f''(x) = 0$. There is a point of inflection at $x = -2$. Now, test the behavior of $f''(x)$ around $x = -2$. When $x < -2$, $f''(x) > 0$, which means the curve is "concave up." When $x > -2$, $f''(x) < 0$, which means the curve is "concave down." To determine when the curve is decreasing, the first derivative must be tested. We already know from the question stem to part (a) that there is a critical point at $x = -3$. So, test the behavior of $f'(x)$ around $x = -3$. For $x < -3$, $f'(x) < 0$, and, thus, falling or decreasing. For $x > -3$, $f'(x) > 0$ and, thus, rising or increasing. When the behaviors of the first and second derivatives of f are combined, $f(x)$ is increasing and concave down over the interval $x > -2$.

(c)   Find the value of a $f(5)$.

(c)   In order to find $f(5)$, you can integrate to find f and then use the initial condition $f(2) = 15$ to find the exact solution. Once the exact solution (the exact equation) is found, then f can be evaluated at $x = 5$. A more direct path would be to integrate $f'(x)$ over the range from $x = 2$ to $x = 5$. The value found can then be added to $f(2)$. So the solution would be

$$f(5) = f(2) + \int_2^5 (2x+6)e^{-x}\,dx = 15 - 18e^{-5} + 12e^{-2}.$$

4.   Consider the equation $x^3 - 2x^2y + 3xy^2 - 4y^3 = 10$.

(a)   Write an equation for the slope of the curve at any point.

(a)   Find the first derivative of this equation using implicit differentiation:

$$3x^2 - \left(2x^2\frac{dy}{dx} + 4xy\right) + \left(6xy\frac{dy}{dx} + 3y^2\right) - 12y^2\frac{dy}{dx} = 0$$

$$3x^2 - 4xy + 3y^2 = \frac{dy}{dx}\left(2x^2 - 6xy + 12y^2\right)$$

$$\frac{dy}{dx} = \frac{3x^2 - 4xy + 3y^2}{2x^2 - 6xy + 12y^2}$$

(b)   Find the equation of the normal line to the curve at the point $x = 1$.

(b)   At $x = 1$, $y = -1$. Plug these values into the equation for $\dfrac{dy}{dx}$ from part (a). Then, the slope of the tangent line is 1. The slope of the normal line is the opposite reciprocal, which is -1. Using point-slope formula, the equation of the normal is $y + 1 = x - 1$ or $y = x - 2$.

(c)   Find $\dfrac{d^2 y}{dx^2}$ at $x = 1$.

(c)   The second derivative follows directly from the first in part (a):

$$\frac{d^2 y}{dx^2} = \frac{(2x^2 - 6xy + 12y^2)\left(6x - 4x\dfrac{dy}{dx} - 4y + 6y\dfrac{dy}{dx}\right) - (3x^2 - 4xy + 3y^2)\left(4x - 6x\dfrac{dy}{dx} - 6y + 24y\dfrac{dy}{dx}\right)}{(2x^2 - 6xy + 12y^2)^2}$$

Rather than trying to simplify the equation, plug in the value for $\dfrac{dy}{dx}$ from part (b) and $x = 1$ and $y = -1$. When simplified using those values, $\dfrac{d^2 y}{dx^2} = \dfrac{1}{2}$.

5.   Given that $f(x) = \sin x$:

(a)   Find the 6th degree Maclaurin series.

(a)   In order to determine the 6th degree Maclaurin series, use the general formula:

$$f(x) = \sum_{k=0}^{\infty} \frac{f^{(k)}(0)}{k!}(x)^k = f(0) + f'(0)(x) + \frac{f''(0)}{2!}x^2 + \ldots + \frac{f^{(n)}(0)}{n!}x^n + \ldots \text{. So, find } f(x) \text{ and the}$$

first 5 derivatives of $f(x)$:

$$f(x) = \sin x,\ f'(x) = \cos x,\ f''(x) = -\sin x,\ f'''(x) = -\cos x,\ f^{(4)}(x) = \sin x,\ \text{and } f^{(5)}(x) = \cos x$$

Then, evaluate each of those equations at $x = 0$:

$$f(0) = 0,\ f'(0) = 1,\ f''(0) = 0,\ f'''(0) = -1,\ f^{(4)}(0) = 0,\ \text{and } f^{(5)}(0) = 1. \ \text{Finally, insert the values}$$

into the formula for a Maclaurin series and simplify: $\sin x = 0 + x + 0 - \dfrac{x^3}{3!} + 0 + \dfrac{x^5}{5!} = x - \dfrac{x^3}{3!} + \dfrac{x^5}{5!}$.

(b) Use the polynomial to estimate sin 0.2.

(b) From part (a), $\sin x = x - \dfrac{x^3}{3!} + \dfrac{x^5}{5!}$. To approximate sin 0.2, plug 0.2 in for x in the equation and simplify: $\sin 0.2 \approx 0.2 - \dfrac{0.2^3}{3!} + \dfrac{0.2^5}{5!} \approx 0.201336$.

(c) Estimate the remainder of the approximation.

(c) The formula for the Lagrange remainder is $R_n(x,a) \le f^{(n+1)}(c)\dfrac{(x-a)^{n+1}}{(n+1)!}$. Use the series you found in part (a) to generalize the series $\sin x = \sum_{k=0}^{\infty}(-1)^k \dfrac{x^{2k+1}}{(2k+1)!}$. From here, $R_{2n}(x,0) \le \dfrac{x^{2n+1}}{(2n+1)!}\sin(c + \dfrac{(2n+1)\pi}{2})$. (in this case, it is R_{2n} not R_n because every other term is 0.) Recall, $|\sin x| \le 1$, so $R_{2n+1}(x,0) \le \dfrac{|x|^{2n+1}}{(2n+1)!}$. Therefore, $R_7(x,0) \le \dfrac{x^7}{(7)!}$. (In general, a good approximation of the remainder/error bound of an nth degree Taylor polynomial is the next nonzero term in a decreasing series.) For the approximation in part (b), plug 0.2 for x into $\dfrac{x^7}{(7)!}$. Therefore, the remainder is $\dfrac{(0.2)^7}{(7)!} \approx 2.540 \times 10^{-9}$.

6. Two particles travel in the xy-plane for time $t \ge 0$. The position of particle A is given by $x = 2t - 3$ and $y = (2t + 1)^2$ and the position of particle B is given by $x = t - 1$ and $y = t + 23$.

(a) Find the velocity vector for each particle at $t = 3$.

(a) The velocity vector of each particle is found by taking the derivative of each particle's motion, so the vector is $\left(\dfrac{dx}{dt}, \dfrac{dy}{dt}\right)$. For particle A, $\dfrac{dx}{dt} = 2$ and $\dfrac{dy}{dt} = 8t - 4$. For particle B, $\dfrac{dx}{dt} = 1$ and $\dfrac{dy}{dt} = 1$. Evaluate each of these derivatives at $t = 3$, so the final velocity vectors are $A = (2,20)$ and $B = (1,1)$.

(b) Set up, but do not evaluate, an integral expression for the distance traveled by particle A from $t = 3$ to $t = 5$.

(b) The formula for the distance travelled parametrically, or the length of the curve, is

$\int_{a}^{b} \sqrt{\left(\dfrac{dx}{dt}\right)^2 + \left(\dfrac{dy}{dt}\right)^2}\, dt$. Since the velocity vector does not equal zero at any time over the interval

from $t = 3$ to $t = 5$, the particle does not change direction and we can plug in the formulas for the

x and y components of the velocity from part (a): $L = \int_{2}^{5} \sqrt{2^2 + (8t - 4)^2}\, dt$, which is simplified to

$L = \int_{2}^{5} \sqrt{64t^2 - 64t + 20}\, dt$.

(c) At what time do the two particles collide? Justify your answer.

(c) The particles will collide when the x and y coordinates of their position functions are equal to each other. Therefore, set the position functions equal and solve for t. Beginning with the x-components: $2t - 3 = t - 1$, so $t = 2$. Plug $t = 2$ into the y-components and confirm they are equal. For particle A: $y = (2 \cdot 2 + 1)^2 = 25$. For particle B: $y = 2 + 23 = 25$. Both the x and y components are equal at $t = 2$, so that is when they collide.

Part II
About the
AP Calculus
Exams

- AB Calculus vs BC Calculus
- The Structure of the AP Calculus Exams
- Overview of Content Topics
- How AP Exams Are Used
- Other Resources
- Designing Your Study Plan

AB CALCULUS VS BC CALCULUS

AP Calculus is divided into two types: AB and BC. The former is supposed to be the equivalent of a semester of college calculus; the latter, a year. In truth, AB calculus covers closer to three quarters of a year of college calculus. In fact, the main difference between the two is that BC calculus tests some more theoretical aspects of calculus and it covers a few additional topics. In addition, BC calculus is harder than AB calculus. The AB exam usually tests straightforward problems in each topic. They're not too tricky and they don't vary very much. The BC exam asks harder questions. But neither exam is tricky in the sense that the SAT is. Nor do they test esoteric aspects of calculus. Rather, both tests tend to focus on testing whether you've learned the basics of differential and integral calculus. The tests are difficult because of the breadth of topics that they cover, not the depth. You will probably find that many of the problems in this book seem easier than the problems you've had in school. This is because your teacher is giving you problems that are harder than those on the AP.

THE STRUCTURE OF THE AP CALCULUS EXAMS

Now, some words about the test itself. The AP exam comes in two parts. First, there is a section of multiple-choice questions covering a variety of calculus topics. The multiple choice section has two parts. Part A consists of 28 questions; you are not permitted to use a calculator on this section. Part B consists of 17 questions; you are permitted to use a calculator on this part. These two parts comprise a total of 45 questions.

After this, there is a free response section consisting of six questions, each of which requires you to write out the solutions and the steps by which you solved it. You are permitted to use a calculator for the first two problems but not for the four other problems. Partial credit is given for various steps in the solution of each problem. You'll usually be required to sketch a graph in one of the questions. The College Board does you a big favor here: You may use a graphing calculator. In fact, The College Board recommends it! And they allow you to use programs as well. But here's the truth about calculus: Most of the time, you don't need the calculator anyway. Remember: These are the people who bring you the SAT. Any gift from them should be regarded skeptically!

OVERVIEW OF CONTENT TOPICS

Topics in italics are BC Topics. This list is drawn from the topical outline for AP calculus furnished by the College Board. You might find that your teacher covers some additional topics, or omits some, in your course. Some of the topics are very broad, so we cannot guarantee that this book covers these topics exhaustively.

I. Functions, Graphs, and Limits
A. Analysis of Graphs

- You should be able to analyze a graph based on "the interplay between geometric and analytic information." The preceding phrase comes directly from the College Board. Don't let it scare you. What the College Board really means is that you should have covered graphing in precalculus, and you should know (a) how to graph and (b) how to read a graph.

B. Limits

- You should be able to calculate limits algebraically, or to estimate them from a graph or from a table of data.

- You do **not** need to find limits using the Delta-Epsilon definition of a limit.

C. Asymptotes

- You should understand asymptotes graphically and be able to compare the growth rates of different types of functions (namely polynomial functions, logarithmic functions, and exponential functions).

- You should understand asymptotes in terms of limits involving infinity.

D. Continuity

- You should be able to test the continuity of a function in terms of limits and you should understand continuous functions graphically.

- You should understand the intermediate value theorem and the extreme value theorem.

E. *Parametric, Polar, and Vector Functions*

- *You should be able to analyze plane curves given in any of these three forms. Usually, you will be asked to convert from one of these three forms back to Rectangular Form (also known as Cartesian Form).*

II. Differential Calculus
A. The Definition of the Derivative

- You should be able to find a derivative by finding the limit of the difference quotient.

- You should also know the relationship between differentiability and continuity. That is, if a function is differentiable at a point, it's continuous there. But if a function is continuous at a point, it's not necessarily differentiable there.

B. Derivative at a Point

- You should know the Power Rule, the Product Rule, the Quotient Rule, and the Chain Rule.

- You should be able to find the slope of a curve at a point, and the tangent and normal lines to a curve at a point.

- You should also be able to use local linear approximation and differentials to estimate the tangent line to a curve at a point.

- You should be able to find the instantaneous rate of change of a function using the derivative or the limit of the average rate of change of a function.

- You should be able to approximate the rate of change of a function from a graph or from a table of values.

- You should be able to find Higher-Order Derivatives and to use Implicit Differentiation.

C. Derivative of a Function

- You should be able to relate the graph of a function to the graph of its derivative, and vice-versa.

- You should know the relationship between the sign of a derivative and whether the function is increasing or decreasing (positive derivative means increasing; negative means decreasing).

- You should know how to find relative and absolute maxima and minima.

- You should know the mean value theorem for derivatives and Rolle's theorem.

D. Second Derivative

- You should be able to relate the graph of a function to the graph of its derivative and its second derivative, and vice-versa. This is tricky.

- You should know the relationship between concavity and the sign of the second derivative (positive means concave up; negative means concave down).

- You should know how to find points of inflection.

E. Applications of Derivatives

- You should be able to sketch a curve using first and second derivatives and be able to analyze the critical points.

- You should be able to solve Optimization problems (Max/Min problems), and Related Rates problems.

- You should be able to find the derivative of the inverse of a function.

- You should be able to solve Rectilinear Motion problems.

F. *More Applications of Derivatives*

- *You should be able to analyze planar curves in parametric, polar, and vector form, including velocity and acceleration vectors.*

- *You should be able to use Euler's Method to find numerical solutions of differential equations.*

- *You should know L'Hôpital's Rule.*

G. Computation of Derivatives

- You should be able to find the derivatives of Trig functions, Logarithmic functions, Exponential functions, and Inverse Trig functions.

- *BC students should be able to find the derivatives of parametric, polar, and vector functions.*

III. Integral Calculus
A. Riemann Sums

- You should be able to find the area under a curve using left, right, and midpoint evaluations and the Trapezoidal Rule.

- You should know the fundamental theorem of calculus:

$$\int_a^b f(x)dx = F(b) - F(a)$$

B. Applications of Integrals

- You should be able to find the area of a region, the volume of a solid of known cross-section, the volume of a solid of revolution, and the average value of a function.

- You should be able to solve acceleration, velocity, and position problems.

- *BC students should also be able to find the length of a curve (including a curve in parametric form) and the area of a region bounded by polar curves.*

C. Fundamental Theorem of Calculus

- You should know the first and second fundamental theorems of calculus and be able to use them to find the derivative of an integral, and in analytical and graphical analysis of functions.

D. Techniques of Antidifferentiation

- You should be able to integrate using the power rule and *U*-Substitution.

- *You should be able to do Integration by Parts and simple Partial Fractions.*

- *You should also be able to evaluate Improper Integrals as limits of definite integrals.*

E. Applications of Antidifferentiation

- You should be able to find specific antiderivatives using initial conditions.

- You should be able to solve separable differential equations and logistic differential equations.

- You should be able to interpret differential equations via slope fields. Don't be intimidated. These look harder than they are.

IV. *Polynomial Approximations and Series*
  A. *The Concept of a Series*

  - *You should know that a series is a sequence of partial sums and that convergence is defined as the limit of the sequence of partial sums.*

  B. *Series Concepts*

  - *You should understand and be able to solve problems involving Geometric Series, the Harmonic Series, Alternating Series, and P-Series.*

  - *You should know the Integral Test, the Ratio Test, and the Comparison Test, and how to use them to determine whether a series converges or diverges.*

  C. *Taylor Series*

  - *You should know Taylor Polynomial Approximation; the general Taylor Series centered at x = a; and the Maclaurin Series for e^x, sin x, cos x, and $\frac{1}{1-x}$.*

  - *You should know how to differentiate and antidifferentiate Taylor Series and how to form new series from known series.*

  - *You should know functions defined by power series and radius of convergence.*

  - *You should know the Lagrange error bound for Taylor Series.*

HOW AP EXAMS ARE USED

Different colleges use AP Exams in different ways, so it is important that you go to a particular college's web site to determine how it uses AP Exams. The three items below represent the main ways in which AP Exam scores can be used:

- **College Credit.** Some colleges will give you college credit if you score well on an AP Exam. These credits count towards your graduation requirements, meaning that you can take fewer courses while in college. Given the cost of college, this could be quite a benefit, indeed.

- **Satisfy Requirements.** Some colleges will allow you to "place out" of certain requirements if you do well on an AP Exam, even if they do not give you actual college credits. For example, you might not need to take an introductory-level course, or perhaps you might not need to take a class in a certain discipline at all.

- **Admissions Plus.** Even if your AP Exam will not result in college credit or even allow you to place out of certain courses, most colleges will respect your decision to push yourself by taking an AP Course or even an AP Exam outside of a course. A high score on an AP Exam shows mastery of more difficult content than is taught in many high school courses, and colleges may take that into account during the admissions process.

OTHER RESOURCES

There are many resources available to help you improve your score on the AP Calculus Exam, not the least of which are your **teachers**. If you are taking an AP class, you may be able to get extra attention from your teacher, such as obtaining feedback on your essays. If you are not in an AP course, reach out to a teacher who teaches calculus, and ask if the teacher will review your free response questions or otherwise help you with content.

Another wonderful resource is **AP Central**, the official site of the AP Exams. The scope of the information at this site is quite broad and includes:

- Course Description, which includes details on what content is covered and sample questions
- Sample test questions
- Essay prompts from previous years

The AP Central home page address is: **http://apcentral.collegeboard.com/apc/ Controller.jpf**.

The AP Calculus AB Exam Course home page address is: **http://apcentral.college board.com/apc/public/courses/teachers_corner/2178.html**

The AP Calculus BC Exam Course home page address is: **http://apcentral.college board.com/apc/public/courses/teachers_corner/2118.html**

Finally, **The Princeton Review** offers tutoring and small group instruction. Our expert instructors can help you refine your strategic approach and add to your content knowledge. For more information, call 1-800-2REVIEW.

For a comprehensive review of calculus topics please check out our guide: *Cracking the AP Calculus AB and BC Exams* in stores now!

DESIGNING YOUR STUDY PLAN

As part of the Introduction, you identified some areas of potential improvement. Let's now delve further into your performance on the diagnostic exam, with the goal of developing a study plan appropriate to your needs and time commitment.

Read the answers and explanations associated with the Multiple Choice questions and respond to the following questions:

- Review the Overview of Content Topics on page 4. Next to each topic, indicate your rank of the topic as follows: "1" means "I need a lot of work on this," "2" means "I need to beef up my knowledge," and "3" means "I know this topic well."

- How many days/weeks/months away is your exam?

- What time of day is your best, most focused study time?

- How much time per day/week/month will you devote to preparing for your exam?

- When will you do this preparation? (Be as specific as possible: Mondays & Wednesdays from 3 to 4 pm, for example.)

- What are your overall goals in using this book?

Part III
Test-Taking Strategies for the AP Calculus Exams

- How to Approach Multiple Choice Questions
- How to Approach Free Response Questions
- Derivatives and Integrals That You Should Know
- Prerequisite Mathematics

HOW TO APPROACH MULTIPLE CHOICE QUESTIONS

Cracking the Multiple Choice Questions

Section I of the AP Calculus Exam consists of 45 multiple choice questions, which you're given 105 minutes to complete. This section is worth 50 percent of your grade. This section is broken up into two parts. Part A consists of 28 questions that you will have to answer without the use of calculator. Part B consists of 17 multiple choice questions where you are allowed to use a calculator.

All the multiple choice questions will have a similar format: Each will be followed by five answer choices. At times, it may seem that there could be more than one possible correct answer. There is only one! Remember that the committee members who write these questions are calculus teachers. So, when it comes to calculus, they know how students think and what kind of mistakes they make. Answers resulting from common mistakes are often included in the five answer choices to trap you.

Use the Answer Sheet

For the multiple choice section, you write the answers not in the test booklet but on a separate answer sheet (very similar to the ones we've supplied at the very end of this book). Five oval-shaped bubbles follow the question number, one for each possible answer. *Don't* forget to fill in all your answers on the answer sheet. Don't just mark them in the test booklet. Marks in the test booklet will not be graded. Also, make sure that your filled-in answers correspond to the correct question numbers! Check your answer sheet after every five answers to make sure you haven't skipped any bubbles by mistake.

Should You Guess?

Use process of elimination (POE) to rule out answer choices you know are wrong and increase your chances of guessing the right answer. Read all the answer choices carefully. Eliminate the ones that you know are wrong. If you only have one answer choice left, *choose it,* even if you're not completely sure why it's correct. Remember: Questions in the multiple choice section are graded by a computer, so it doesn't care *how* you arrived at the correct answer.

Even if you can't eliminate answer choices, go ahead and guess. AP exams no longer include a guessing penalty of a quarter of a point for each incorrect answer. You will be assessed only on the total number of correct answers, so be sure to fill in all the bubbles even if you have no idea what the correct answers are. When you get to questions that are too time-consuming, or that you don't know the answer to (and can't eliminate any options), don't just fill in any answer. Use what we call "your letter of the day" (LOTD). Selecting the same answer choice each time you guess will increase your odds of getting a few of those skipped questions right.

Use the Two-Pass System

Do not waste time by lingering too long over any single question. If you're having trouble, move on to the next question. After you finish all the questions, you can come back to the ones you skipped.

The best strategy is to go through the multiple choice section twice. The first time, do all the questions that you can answer fairly quickly—the ones where you feel confident about the correct answer. On this first pass, skip the questions that seem to require more thinking or the ones you need to read two or three times before you understand them. Circle the questions that you've skipped in the question booklet so that you can find them easily in the second pass. You must *be very careful* with the answer sheet by making sure the filled-in answers correspond correctly to the questions.

Once you have gone through all the questions, go back to the ones that you skipped in the first pass. But don't linger too long on any one question even in the second pass. Spending too much time wrestling over a hard question can cause two things to happen: One, you may run out of time and miss out on answering easier questions in the later part of the exam. Two, your anxiety might start building up, and this could prevent you from thinking clearly, which would make answering other questions even more difficult. If you simply don't know the answer, or can't eliminate any of them, just use your LOTD and move on.

HOW TO APPROACH FREE RESPONSE QUESTIONS

Cracking Free Response Questions

Section II is worth 50 percent of your grade on the AP Calculus Exam. This section is composed of two parts. Part A contains two free response questions (you may use a calculator on this part); Part B contains four free response questions where there are no calculators allowed. You're given a total of 90 minutes for this section.

Clearly Explain and Justify Your Answers

Remember that your answers to the free response questions are graded by *readers* and not by computers. Communication is a very important part of AP Calculus. Compose your answers in precise sentences. Just getting the correct numerical answer is not enough. You should be able to *explain* your reasoning behind the technique that you selected and *communicate* your answer in the context of the problem. Even if the question does not explicitly say so, always explain and *justify* every step of your answer, including the final answer. Do not expect the graders to read between the lines. Explain everything as though somebody with no knowledge of calculus is going to read it. Be sure to present your solution in a systematic manner using solid logic and appropriate language. And remember: Although you won't earn points for neatness, the graders can't give you a grade if they can't read and understand your solution!

Use Only the Space You Need

Do not try to fill up the space provided for each question. The space given is usually more than enough. The people who design the tests realize that some students write in big letters and some students make mistakes and need extra space for corrections. So if you have a complete solution, don't worry about the extra space. Writing more will not earn you extra credit. In fact, many students tend to go overboard and shoot themselves in the foot by making a mistake after they've already written the right answer.

Read the Whole Question!

Some questions might have several subparts. Try to answer them all, and don't give up on the question if one part is giving you trouble. For example, if the answer to part (b) depends on the answer to part (a), but you think you got the answer to part (a) wrong, you should still go ahead and do part (b) using your answer to part (a) as required. Chances are that the grader will not mark you wrong twice, unless it is obvious from your answer that you should have discovered your mistake.

Use Common Sense

Always use your common sense in answering questions. For example, on one free response question that asked students to compute the mean weight of newborn babies from given data, some students answered 70 pounds. It should have been immediately obvious that the answer was probably off by a decimal point. A 70-pound baby would be a giant! This is an important mistake that should be easy to fix. Some mistakes may not be so obvious from the answer. However, the grader will consider simple, *easily recognizable errors* to be *very important*.

REFLECT

Respond to the following questions:

- How long will you spend on multiple choice questions?

- How will you change your approach to multiple choice questions?

- What is your multiple choice guessing strategy?

- How much time will you spend on each free response question?

- How will you change your approach to the free response questions?

- Will you seek further help, outside of this book (such as a teacher, tutor, or AP Central), on how to approach the calculus exam?

DERIVATIVES AND INTEGRALS THAT YOU SHOULD KNOW

1. $\dfrac{d}{dx}[ku] = k\dfrac{du}{dx}$

2. $\dfrac{d}{dx}[k] = 0$

3. $\dfrac{d}{dx}[uv] = u\dfrac{dv}{dx} + v\dfrac{du}{dx}$

4. $\dfrac{d}{dx}\left[\dfrac{u}{v}\right] = \dfrac{v\dfrac{du}{dx} - u\dfrac{dv}{dx}}{v^2}$

5. $\dfrac{d}{dx}[e^u] = e^u\dfrac{du}{dx}$

6. $\dfrac{d}{dx}[\ln u] = \dfrac{1}{u}\dfrac{du}{dx}$

7. $\dfrac{d}{dx}[\sin u] = \cos u\dfrac{du}{dx}$

8. $\dfrac{d}{dx}[\cos u] = -\sin u\dfrac{du}{dx}$

9. $\dfrac{d}{dx}[\tan u] = \sec^2 u\dfrac{du}{dx}$

10. $\dfrac{d}{dx}[\cot u] = -\csc^2 u\dfrac{du}{dx}$

11. $\dfrac{d}{dx}[\sec u] = \sec u\tan u\dfrac{du}{dx}$

12. $\dfrac{d}{dx}[\csc u] = -\csc u\cot u\dfrac{du}{dx}$

13. $\dfrac{d}{dx}[\sin^{-1} u] = \dfrac{1}{\sqrt{1 - u^2}}\dfrac{du}{dx}$

14. $\dfrac{d}{dx}[\tan^{-1} u] = \dfrac{1}{1 + u^2}\dfrac{du}{dx}$

15. $\dfrac{d}{dx}[\sec^{-1} u] = \dfrac{1}{|u|\sqrt{u^2 - 1}}\dfrac{du}{dx}$

16. $\int k \, du = ku + C$

17. $\int u^n \, du = \dfrac{u^{n+1}}{n+1} + C; \, n \ne -1$

18. $\int \dfrac{du}{u} = \ln|u| + C$

19. $\int e^u \, du = e^u + C$

20. $\int \sin u \, du = -\cos u + C$

21. $\int \cos u \, du = \sin u + C$

22. $\int \tan u \, du = -\ln|\cos u| + C$

23. $\int \cot u \, du = \ln|\sin u| + C$

24. $\int \sec u \, du = \ln|\sec u + \tan u| + C$

25. $\int \csc u \, du = -\ln|\csc u + \cot u| + C$

26. $\int \sec^2 u \, du = \tan u + C$

27. $\int \csc^2 u \, du = -\cot u + C$

28. $\int \sec u \tan u \, du = \sec u + C$

29. $\int \csc u \cot u \, du = -\csc u + C$

30. $\int \dfrac{du}{\sqrt{a^2 - u^2}} = \sin^{-1}\dfrac{|u|}{a} + C; \, |u| < a$

31. $\int \dfrac{du}{a^2 + u^2} \, du = \dfrac{1}{a}\tan^{-1}\dfrac{u}{a} + C$

32. $\int \dfrac{du}{u\sqrt{u^2 - a^2}} = \dfrac{1}{a}\sec^{-1}\dfrac{u}{a} + C; \, |u| > a$

PREREQUISITE MATHEMATICS

One of the biggest problems that students have with calculus is that their algebra, geometry, and trigonometry are not solid enough. In calculus, you'll be expected to do a lot of graphing. This requires more than just graphing equations with your calculator. You'll be expected to look at an equation and have a "feel" for what the graph looks like. You'll be expected to factor, combine, simplify, and otherwise rearrange algebraic expressions. You'll be expected to know your formulas for the volume and area of various shapes. You'll be expected to remember trigonometric ratios, their values at special angles, and various identities. You'll also be expected to be comfortable with logarithms and exponents.

Powers

When you multiply exponential expressions with like bases, you add the powers.

$$x^a \cdot x^b = x^{a+b}$$

When you divide exponentiated expressions with like bases, you subtract the powers.

$$\frac{x^a}{x^b} = x^{a-b}$$

When you raise an exponentiated expression to a power, you multiply the powers.

$$\left(x^a\right)^b = x^{ab}$$

When you raise an expression to a fractional power, the denominator of the fraction is the root of the expression, and the numerator is the power.

$$x^{\frac{a}{b}} = \sqrt[b]{x^a}$$

When you raise an expression to the power of zero, you get one.

$$x^0 = 1$$

When you raise an expression to the power of one, you get the expression.

$$x^1 = x$$

When you raise an expression to a negative power, you get the reciprocal of the expression to the absolute value of the power.

$$x^{-a} = \frac{1}{x^a}$$

Logarithms

A logarithm is the power to which you raise a base, in order to get a value. In other words, $\log_b x = a$ means that $b^a = x$. There are several rules of logarithms that you should be familiar with.

When you take the logarithm of the product of two expressions, you add the logarithms.

$$\log(ab) = \log a + \log b$$

When you take the logarithm of the quotient of two expressions, you subtract the logarithms.

$$\log\left(\frac{a}{b}\right) = \log a - \log b$$

When you take the logarithm of an expression to a power, you multiply the logarithm by the power.

$$\log(a^b) = b \log a$$

The logarithm of 1 is zero.

$$\log 1 = 0$$

The logarithm of its base is 1.

$$\log_b b = 1$$

You cannot take the logarithm of zero or of a negative number.

In calculus, and virtually all mathematics beyond calculus, you will work with natural logarithms. These are logs with base e and are denoted by ln. Thus, you should know the following:

$$\ln 1 = 0$$

$$\ln e = 1$$

$$\ln e^x = x$$

$$e^{\ln x} = x$$

The change of base rule is: $\log_b x = \dfrac{\ln x}{\ln b}$

Geometry

The area of a triangle is $\dfrac{1}{2}$ *(base)(height)*.

The area of a rectangle is *(base)(height)*.

The area of a trapezoid is $\dfrac{1}{2}$ *(base$_1$ + base$_2$)(height)*.

The area of a circle is πr^2.

The circumference of a circle is $2\pi r$.

The Pythagorean theorem states that the sum of the squares of the legs of a right triangle equals the square of the hypotenuse. This is more commonly stated as $a^2 + b^2 = c^2$ where c equals the length of the hypotenuse.

The volume of a right circular cylinder is $\pi r^2 h$.

The surface area of a right circular cylinder is $2\pi rh$.

The volume of a right circular cone is $\dfrac{1}{3}\pi r^2 h$.

The volume of a sphere is $\dfrac{4}{3}\pi r^3$.

The surface area of a sphere is $4\pi r^2$.

Trigonometry

Given a right triangle with sides x, y, and r and angle θ below:

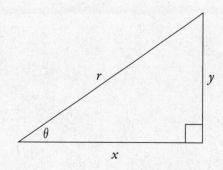

$$\sin\theta = \frac{y}{r}$$

$$\cos\theta = \frac{x}{r}$$

$$\tan\theta = \frac{y}{x}$$

$$\csc\theta = \frac{r}{y}$$

$$\sec\theta = \frac{r}{x}$$

$$\cot\theta = \frac{x}{y}$$

Thus, $\sin\theta = \dfrac{1}{\csc\theta}$

Thus, $\cos\theta = \dfrac{1}{\sec\theta}$

Thus, $\tan\theta = \dfrac{1}{\cot\theta}$

$$\sin 2\theta = 2\sin\theta\,\cos\theta$$

$$\cos 2\theta = \cos^2\theta - \sin^2\theta$$

$$\cos^2\theta = \frac{1 + \cos 2\theta}{2}$$

$$\cos 2\theta = 1 - 2\sin^2\theta$$

$$\cos 2\theta = 2\cos^2\theta - 1$$

$$\sin^2\theta = \frac{1 - \cos 2\theta}{2}$$

$$\sin^2\theta + \cos^2\theta = 1$$

$$1 + \tan^2\theta = \sec^2\theta$$

$$1 + \cot^2\theta = \csc^2\theta$$

$$\sin(A + B) = \sin A \cos B + \cos A \sin B$$

$$\sin(A - B) = \sin A \cos B - \cos A \sin B$$

$$\cos(A + B) = \cos A \cos B - \sin A \sin B$$

$$\cos(A - B) = \cos A \cos B + \sin A \sin B$$

You must be able to work in radians and know that $2\pi = 360°$.

You should know the following:

$\sin 0 = 0$	$\cos 0 = 1$	$\tan 0 = 0$
$\sin\dfrac{\pi}{6} = \dfrac{1}{2}$	$\cos\dfrac{\pi}{6} = \dfrac{\sqrt{3}}{2}$	$\tan\dfrac{\pi}{6} = \dfrac{1}{\sqrt{3}}$
$\sin\dfrac{\pi}{4} = \dfrac{1}{\sqrt{2}}$	$\cos\dfrac{\pi}{4} = \dfrac{1}{\sqrt{2}}$	$\tan\dfrac{\pi}{4} = 1$
$\sin\dfrac{\pi}{3} = \dfrac{\sqrt{3}}{2}$	$\cos\dfrac{\pi}{3} = \dfrac{1}{2}$	$\tan\dfrac{\pi}{3} = \sqrt{3}$
$\sin\dfrac{\pi}{2} = 1$	$\cos\dfrac{\pi}{2} = 0$	$\tan\dfrac{\pi}{2} = \infty$
$\sin \pi = 0$	$\cos \pi = -1$	$\tan \pi = 0$
$\sin\dfrac{3\pi}{2} = -1$	$\cos\dfrac{3\pi}{2} = 0$	$\tan\dfrac{3\pi}{2} = \infty$
$\sin 2\pi = 0$	$\cos 2\pi = 1$	$\tan 2\pi = 0$

Part IV
Drills

Chapter 1
Limits Drill 1

LIMITS DRILL 1

1. $\displaystyle\lim_{x \to \infty} \frac{4x^4 + 5}{\left(x^2 - 2\right)\left(2x^2 - 1\right)} =$

   (A) $-\infty$
   (B) -2
   (C) 0
   (D) 2
   (E) ∞

2. $\displaystyle\lim_{x \to \infty} \frac{x + x^3 + x^5}{1 - x^2 + x^4} =$

   (A) ∞
   (B) $\dfrac{5}{4}$
   (C) 1
   (D) $-\infty$
   (E) Does not exist

3. $\displaystyle\lim_{x \to \infty} \frac{x^2 + 2}{x^3 + x^2 - 1} =$

   (A) $-\infty$
   (B) 0
   (C) 1
   (D) ∞
   (E) Does not exist

4. $\displaystyle\lim_{x \to \infty} \frac{3x^4 + x - 5}{1 - 2x^2 + 6x^4} =$

   (A) 0
   (B) $\dfrac{1}{2}$
   (C) 2
   (D) 5
   (E) Does not exist

5. $\displaystyle\lim_{x \to -3} \frac{x^2 - 9}{x^2 + 2x - 3} =$

   (A) $-\dfrac{3}{2}$
   (B) -1
   (C) 1
   (D) $\dfrac{3}{2}$
   (E) Does not exist

6. $\displaystyle\lim_{h \to 0} \frac{\left(h - 1\right)^3 + 1}{h} =$

   (A) $-\infty$
   (B) -3
   (C) 0
   (D) 3
   (E) ∞

7. $\displaystyle\lim_{x \to 16} \frac{4 - \sqrt{x}}{x - 16} =$

   (A) $-\infty$
   (B) $-\dfrac{1}{8}$
   (C) 0
   (D) $\dfrac{1}{8}$
   (E) Does not exist

8. $\displaystyle\lim_{x \to 0} \frac{1 - \sqrt{\left(1 - x^2\right)}}{x} =$

   (A) $-\infty$
   (B) -1
   (C) 0
   (D) ∞
   (E) Does not exist

9. $\lim\limits_{x \to 1} \dfrac{x^4 - 1}{x^3 + 5x^2 - 6x} =$

(A) 0

(B) $\dfrac{4}{7}$

(C) $\dfrac{7}{4}$

(D) 4

(E) Does not exist

10. $\lim\limits_{x \to 0} \dfrac{(x + 7)^2 - 49}{x} =$

(A) 0
(B) 2
(C) 8
(D) 10
(E) 14

11. $\lim\limits_{x \to \infty} \dfrac{7x^{10} - 4x^3 - 20}{4x^4 - 2x^8 + x^{10}} =$

(A) 7
(B) 1
(C) 0
(D) –7
(E) Does not exist

12. $\lim\limits_{x \to \infty} \dfrac{5x^2 - x + 2}{3x^2 - 3x + 1} =$

(A) $\dfrac{3}{5}$

(B) 1

(C) $\dfrac{5}{3}$

(D) 2

(E) Does not exist

13. $\lim\limits_{x \to \infty} \dfrac{4x^2}{7 + 8x^3} =$

(A) ∞

(B) $\dfrac{1}{2}$

(C) $\dfrac{4}{7}$

(D) 0

(E) Does not exist

14. $\lim\limits_{x \to 3} \dfrac{x^2 - 9}{x^3 - x^2 - 6x} =$

(A) 1

(B) $\dfrac{2}{5}$

(C) $\dfrac{5}{2}$

(D) ∞

(E) Does not exist

15. $\lim\limits_{h \to 0} \dfrac{4h^3 - 2h}{5h + 2h^2 - h^3} =$

(A) Does not exist

(B) 0

(C) 1

(D) –1

(E) $-\dfrac{2}{5}$

16. $\lim_{x \to -2} \dfrac{x+2}{x^2-4} =$

(A)   0

(B) -1

(C) $-\dfrac{1}{4}$

(D) $\dfrac{1}{4}$

(E)   Does not exist

17. $\lim_{x \to 5} \dfrac{25x-5x^2}{x-5} =$

(A) -25
(B)   25
(C)   5
(D) ∞
(E)   Does not exist

18. $\lim_{x \to 7} \dfrac{49-x^2}{x-7} =$

(A) -49
(B) -14
(C)   0
(D)   14
(E)   49

19. $\lim_{x \to \infty} \dfrac{x^{100}-99}{x^{99}} =$

(A)   Does not exist
(B) -1
(C)   0
(D)   1
(E) ∞

20. $\lim_{x \to 3} \dfrac{x^2-7x+12}{x^2-9} =$

(A)   Does not exist

(B)   1

(C) $\dfrac{1}{6}$

(D) $-\dfrac{1}{6}$

(E) -1

21. $\lim_{x \to \infty} \dfrac{x^2-x-6}{x^2-5x+6} =$

(A)   0
(B)   1
(C)   3
(D)   5
(E)   The limit does not exist.

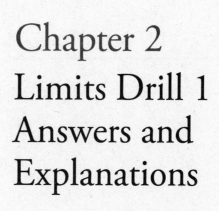

Chapter 2
Limits Drill 1
Answers and
Explanations

ANSWER KEY

1. D
2. A
3. B
4. B
5. D
6. D
7. B
8. C
9. B
10. E
11. A
12. C
13. D
14. B
15. E
16. C
17. A
18. B
19. E
20. D
21. B

EXPLANATIONS

1. **D**   To do this question, we need to remember how to attack limits. These are generally good candidates for the first pass. When the limit approaches infinity, simply divide both top and bottom by the highest power of x in the fraction. Foiling out the bottom produces a $2x^4$ as the leading term, so both top and bottom will be divided by an x^4 term.

$$\lim_{x \to \infty} \frac{\dfrac{4x^4}{x^4} + \dfrac{5}{x^4}}{\dfrac{2x^4}{x^4} - \dfrac{5x^2}{x^4} + \dfrac{2}{x^4}} =$$

Simplify.

$$\lim_{x \to \infty} \frac{4 + \dfrac{5}{x^4}}{2 - \dfrac{5}{x^2} + \dfrac{2}{x^4}} =$$

As x gets larger, the fractional terms approach 0 so all that is left is $\dfrac{4}{2}$ which equals 2.

Also, when limits approach infinity, it is good to keep in mind that when the degrees are the same in the numerator and denominator, then you only need to look to the leading coefficients to find the limits.

2. **A**   When calculating limits approaching ∞, you should pay attention to the highest degree of the numerator and denominator. If the highest degree is in the numerator, then the limit will become infinitely larger without bound, thus making it ∞. The long way is to divide each term by the highest term, in this case, x^5.

$$\lim_{x \to \infty} \frac{\dfrac{x}{x^5} + \dfrac{x^3}{x^5} + \dfrac{x^5}{x^5}}{\dfrac{1}{x^5} - \dfrac{x^2}{x^5} + \dfrac{x^4}{x^5}} =$$

Simplify

$$\lim_{x \to \infty} \frac{\left(\dfrac{1}{x^4}\right) + \left(\dfrac{1}{x^2}\right) + 1}{\left(\dfrac{1}{x^5}\right) - \left(\dfrac{1}{x^3}\right) + \left(\dfrac{1}{x}\right)} =$$

As x approaches ∞, the fractional terms will get smaller and smaller, going to 0. The only value left is in the numerator and as x would get larger and larger, the limit increases without bound, making it ∞.

3. **B** When we look to the highest degree, it is in the denominator, which, when limits approach infinity, automatically means the entire expression will approach 0.

Divide by the highest term throughout the expression.

$$\lim_{x \to \infty} \frac{\dfrac{x^2}{x^3} + \dfrac{2}{x^3}}{\dfrac{x^3}{x^3} + \dfrac{x^2}{x^3} - \dfrac{1}{x^3}} =$$

Simplify.

$$\lim_{x \to \infty} \frac{\dfrac{1}{x} + \dfrac{2}{x^3}}{1 + \dfrac{1}{x} - \dfrac{1}{x^3}} =$$

4. **B** Know the rule: When a limit approaches infinity and the degrees in the numerator and denominator are the same, simply look to the leading coefficients to calculate the limit. In this case, the leading coefficients are the 3 in the numerator and the 6 in the denominator. $\dfrac{3}{6}$ reduces to $\dfrac{1}{2}$, making it your answer.

5. **D** This question tests your knowledge of discontinuity. If you plug in −3 directly, the denominator becomes 0, and thus is undefined. If we factor and cancel the numerator and denominator, the problem becomes solvable.

Factor and cancel out like terms.

$$\lim_{x \to -3} \frac{x^2 - 9}{x^2 + 2x - 3} = \frac{(x+3)(x-3)}{(x+3)(x-1)} = \frac{(x-3)}{(x-1)}$$

Plug in −3 to evaluate the limit.

$$\lim_{x \to -3} \frac{(x-3)}{(x-1)} = \frac{(-3)-3}{(-3)-1} = \frac{-6}{-4} = \frac{3}{2}$$

6. **D** This question tests your knowledge of discontinuity. If you plug in 0 directly, the denominator becomes 0, and thus is undefined. If we expand out the numerator and reduce, the problem becomes solvable.

Expand the numerator.

$$\lim_{h \to 0} \frac{(h-1)^3 + 1}{h} = \frac{h^3 - 3h^2 + 3h - 1 + 1}{h} = \frac{h^3 - 3h^2 + 3h}{h} = h^2 - 3h + 3$$

Plug in 0 to evaluate the limit.

$$\lim_{h \to 0} \ 0^2 - 3(0) + 3 = \ 0^2 - 3(0) + 3 = 3$$

7. **B** This question tests your knowledge of discontinuity. If you plug in 16 directly, the denominator becomes 0, and thus is undefined. If we multiply both the numerator and denominator by $4 + \sqrt{x}$, then the question becomes solvable.

Multiply top and bottom by $4 + \sqrt{x}$.

$$\lim_{x \to 16} \frac{4 - \sqrt{x}}{x - 16} \times \frac{4 + \sqrt{x}}{4 + \sqrt{x}} = \frac{16 - x}{(x - 16)(4 + \sqrt{x})} = \frac{-1}{4 + \sqrt{x}}$$

Plug in 16 to evaluate the limit.

$$\lim_{x \to 16} \frac{-1}{4 + \sqrt{x}} = \frac{-1}{4 + 4} = -\frac{1}{8}$$

8. **C** This question tests your knowledge of discontinuity. If you plug in 0 directly, the denominator becomes 0, and thus is undefined. If we multiply both the numerator and denominator by $1 + \sqrt{(1 - x^2)}$, then the question becomes solvable.

Multiply the top and bottom by $1 + \sqrt{(1 - x^2)}$.

$$\lim_{x \to 0} \frac{1 - \sqrt{(1 - x^2)}}{x} \times \frac{1 + \sqrt{(1 - x^2)}}{1 + \sqrt{(1 - x^2)}} = \frac{1 - (1 - x^2)}{x\left(1 + \sqrt{(1 - x^2)}\right)} = \frac{x}{1 + \sqrt{(1 - x^2)}}$$

Plug in 0 to evaluate the limit.

$$\lim_{x \to 0} \frac{x}{1 + \sqrt{(1 - x^2)}} = \frac{0}{2} = 0$$

9. **B** This question tests your knowledge of discontinuity. If you plug in 1 directly, the denominator becomes 0, and thus is undefined. If you factor and cancel like terms, then the question becomes solvable.

Factor and cancel like terms.

$$\lim_{x \to 1} \frac{x^4 - 1}{x^3 + 5x^2 - 6x} = \frac{(x^2 + 1)(x^2 - 1)}{x(x^2 + 5x - 6)} = \frac{(x^2 + 1)(x + 1)(x - 1)}{x(x + 6)(x - 1)} = \frac{(x^2 + 1)(x + 1)}{x(x + 6)}$$

Plug in 1 and evaluate the limit.

$$\lim_{x \to 1} \frac{(x^2 + 1)(x + 1)}{x(x + 6)} = \frac{(2)(2)}{(1)(7)} = \frac{4}{7}$$

10. **E** This question tests your knowledge of discontinuity. If you plug in 0 directly, the denominator becomes 0, and thus is undefined. If you expand out the numerator and cancel like terms, then the question becomes solvable.

Expand out numerator and cancel like terms.

$$\lim_{x \to 0} \frac{(x + 7)^2 - 49}{x} = \frac{x^2 + 14x + 49 - 49}{x} = \frac{x^2 + 14x}{x} = x + 14$$

Plug in 0 to evaluate the limit.

$$\lim_{x \to 0} x + 14 = 0 + 14 = 14$$

11. **A** To calculate a limit as it approaches infinity, look to the terms in the numerator and denominator to find the highest degrees. In this case, they are both 10, so the limit is simply the coefficients divided by each other, $\frac{7}{1}$, or 7.

12. **C** To calculate a limit as it approaches infinity, look to the terms in the numerator and denominator to find the highest degrees. In this case, they are both 2, so the limit is simply the coefficients divided by each other, $\dfrac{5}{3}$.

13. **D** To calculate a limit as it approaches infinity, look to the terms in the numerator and denominator to find the highest degrees. In the numerator, the degree is 2, where in the denominator, the degree is 3. When the degree in the denominator is greater than the degree in the numerator, the limit will approach 0.

14. **B** The first instinct in limit questions is to try to plug in the value x is approaching. If you plug 3 in, the denominator becomes 0, thus undefined. However, using a little algebra, we are able to remove a term from the numerator and denominator.

$$\lim_{x \to 3} \frac{x^2 - 9}{x^3 - x^2 - 6x} = \frac{(x+3)(x-3)}{x(x+2)(x-3)} = \frac{x+3}{x(x+2)}$$

Now that the numerator and denominator are simplified, you can simply plug 3 in for x to evaluate the limit.

$$\lim_{x \to 3} \frac{3+3}{3(3+2)} = \frac{2}{5}$$

15. **E** If you plug in 0 directly, the value becomes $\dfrac{0}{0}$ and can't be evaluated. However, an h is able to be cancelled out of the denominator by factoring.

$$\lim_{x \to 0} \frac{4h^3 - 2h}{5h + 2h^2 - h^3} = \frac{2h(2h^2 - 1)}{h(5 + 2h - h^2)} = \frac{2(2h^2 - 1)}{5 + 2h - h^2}$$

Now that the numerator and denominator are simplified, you can simply plug 0 in for h to evaluate the limit.

$$\lim_{x \to 0} \frac{2(2(0)^2 - 1)}{5 + 2(0) - (0)^2} = \frac{2(-1)}{5 + 0 - 0} = \frac{-2}{5}$$

16. **C** If you plug in –2, the limit becomes $\dfrac{0}{0}$, which is undefined. By factoring the denominator, the discontinuity can be removed which will allow calculation.

$$\lim_{x \to -2} \frac{x+2}{x^2-4} = \frac{x+2}{(x+2)(x-2)} = \frac{1}{x-2}$$

Now the limit is able to be evaluated by plugging in –2 for x.

$$\lim_{x \to -2} \frac{1}{(-2)-2} = -\frac{1}{4}$$

17. **A** If you plug in 5 immediately, the limit becomes $\dfrac{0}{0}$, which is undefined. By factoring the numerator, the discontinuity can be removed which will allow calculation.

$$\lim_{x \to 5} \frac{25x-5x^2}{x-5} = \frac{5x(5-x)}{x-5} = -5x$$

Now the limit is able to be evaluated by plugging in 5 for x.

$$\lim_{x \to 5} -(5)(5) = -25$$

18. **B** If you plug in 7 directly to the limit, then it becomes $\dfrac{0}{0}$ which is undefined. First, the numerator must be factored to remove the discontinuity.

$$\lim_{x \to 7} \frac{49-x^2}{x-7} = \frac{(7+x)(7-x)}{x-7} = -(7+x)$$

Plug in 7 to evaluate the limit.

$$\lim_{x \to 7} -(7)+(7) = -(14) = -14$$

19.   **E**   When evaluating limits at infinity, you must pay attention to the degrees in both the numerator and denominator. In this case, the degree in the numerator is 100, while in the denominator, it's 99. Since the degree is higher in the numerator, the limit will go to infinity as x approaches infinity.

20.   **D**   If you plug in 3 directly, the limit becomes $\frac{0}{0}$ and is undefined. First, the numerator and denominator must be factored.

$$\lim_{x \to 3} \frac{x^2 - 7x + 12}{x^2 - 9} = \frac{(x-4)(x-3)}{(x+3)(x-3)} = \frac{(x-4)}{(x+3)}$$

Now, plug 3 in for x to evaluate the limit.

$$\lim_{x \to 3} \frac{(x-4)}{(x+3)} = \frac{3-4}{3+3} = \frac{-1}{6}$$

21.   **B** $\lim_{x \to \infty} \frac{x^2 - x - 6}{x^2 - 5x + 6} = \lim_{x \to \infty} \frac{(x+2)(x-3)}{(x-2)(x-3)} = \lim_{x \to \infty} \frac{x+2}{x-2} = \frac{\infty}{\infty} = 1.$

Chapter 3
Limits Drill 2

LIMITS DRILL 2

1. $\lim\limits_{x \to 1} \dfrac{x^2 - 1}{x - 1} =$

   (A) Does not exist
   (B) 2
   (C) 0
   (D) –2
   (E) ∞

2. $\lim\limits_{x \to 0} \dfrac{(3 + x)^2 - 9}{x} =$

   (A) 6
   (B) 3
   (C) 0
   (D) –6
   (E) Does not exist

3. $\lim\limits_{x \to 0} \dfrac{\sqrt{(x^2 + 9)} - 3}{x^2} =$

   (A) Does not exist

   (B) ∞

   (C) 6

   (D) 0

   (E) $\dfrac{1}{6}$

4. $\lim\limits_{x \to 2} \dfrac{x^2 + x - 6}{x - 2} =$

   (A) ∞
   (B) 2
   (C) 5
   (D) 0
   (E) Does not exist

5. $\lim\limits_{x \to -4} \dfrac{x^2 + 5x + 4}{x^2 + 3x - 4} =$

   (A) ∞

   (B) $\dfrac{5}{3}$

   (C) 1

   (D) $\dfrac{3}{5}$

   (E) Does not exist

6. $\lim\limits_{x \to 4} \dfrac{x^2 - 4x}{x^2 - 3x - 4} =$

   (A) ∞

   (B) $\dfrac{5}{4}$

   (C) 1

   (D) $\dfrac{4}{5}$

   (E) Does not exist

7. $\lim\limits_{x \to 7} \dfrac{\sqrt{(x + 2)} - 3}{x - 7} =$

   (A) ∞

   (B) 7

   (C) 6

   (D) 0

   (E) $\dfrac{1}{6}$

8. $\lim\limits_{x \to -1} \dfrac{x^2 + 2x + 1}{x^4 - 1} =$

(A)   0
(B)   –1
(C)   1
(D) ∞
(E)   Does not exist

9. $\lim\limits_{x \to 0} \dfrac{(2 + x)^3 - 8}{x} =$

(A)   0

(B)   12

(C) $\dfrac{1}{12}$

(D)   1
(E) ∞

10. $\lim\limits_{x \to 0} \dfrac{x^3 + 2x^2 - 3x}{x^2 - x} =$

(A) ∞
(B)   3
(C)   0
(D)   –3
(E)   Does not exist

11. $\lim\limits_{x \to -4} \dfrac{x^2 + 2x - 8}{x + 4} =$

(A) ∞
(B)   6
(C)   –4
(D)   –6
(E)   Does not exist

12. $\lim\limits_{x \to -9} \dfrac{81 + 18x + x^2}{x + 9} =$

(A)   Does not exist
(B)   –81
(C)   –18
(D)   –9
(E)   0

13. $\lim\limits_{x \to 2} \dfrac{x - 2}{x^3 - 2x^2} =$

(A)   Does not exist

(B)   0

(C) $\dfrac{1}{4}$

(D)   1

(E) ∞

14. $\lim\limits_{x \to \infty} \dfrac{9x^2 + 4x - 20}{3 + 4x - 5x^2} =$

(A) $-\dfrac{9}{5}$

(B)   –1

(C)   0

(D)   1

(E) $\dfrac{9}{5}$

15. $\lim\limits_{t \to 0} \dfrac{t^4 + 2t^2}{3t^2 - 2t} =$

(A) ∞

(B) 1

(C) $\dfrac{2}{3}$

(D) $\dfrac{1}{3}$

(E) 0

16. $\lim\limits_{y \to -1} \dfrac{y^2 + 2y + 1}{y^2 + y} =$

(A) 0
(B) 1
(C) 2
(D) –1
(E) Does not exist

17. $\lim\limits_{h \to 0} \dfrac{\sqrt{(4 + h)} - \sqrt{4}}{h} =$

(A) –1

(B) 0

(C) $\dfrac{1}{4}$

(D) 1

(E) ∞

18. $\lim\limits_{x \to -7} \dfrac{x^3 + 7x^2}{x^3 + 2x^2 - 35x} =$

(A) $-\dfrac{7}{12}$

(B) $\dfrac{7}{12}$

(C) 1

(D) 7

(E) ∞

19. $\lim\limits_{x \to 0} \dfrac{x}{x^2 - x} =$

(A) Does not exist
(B) 1
(C) 0
(D) –1
(E) $-\infty$

20. $\lim\limits_{x \to 0} \left(\dfrac{\tan 3x}{\sin 2x} \right) =$

(A) 0
(B) 1
(C) 1.5
(D) 2
(E) Does not exist

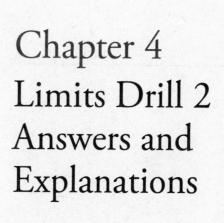

Chapter 4
Limits Drill 2
Answers and
Explanations

ANSWER KEY

1. B
2. A
3. E
4. C
5. D
6. D
7. E
8. A
9. B
10. B
11. D
12. E
13. C
14. A
15. E
16. A
17. C
18. B
19. D
20. C

EXPLANATIONS

1. **B** If you plug $x = 1$ into the limit, it becomes $\frac{0}{0}$, which is undefined. First, a little factoring must be done in the numerator to remove the discontinuity.

$$\lim_{x \to 1} \frac{x^2 - 1}{x - 1} = \frac{(x+1)(x-1)}{x-1} = x + 1$$

Now, you can evaluate the limit in its reduced form.

$$\lim_{x \to 1} (x + 1) = 2$$

2. **A** If you plug $x = 0$ into the limit, it becomes $\frac{0}{0}$, which is undefined. First, the numerator must be expanded so an x term can cancel out.

$$\lim_{x \to 0} \frac{(3 + x)^2 - 9}{x} = \frac{9 + 6x + x^2 - 9}{x} = \frac{6x + x^2}{2} = 6 + x$$

Now, you can evaluate the limit in its reduced form.

$$\lim_{x \to 0} (6 + 0) = 6$$

3. **E** If you plug $x = 0$ into the limit, it becomes $\frac{0}{0}$, which is undefined. First, you must rationalize the expression so the x^2 term can be cancelled out.

$$\lim_{x \to 0} \frac{\sqrt{(x^2 + 9)} - 3}{x^2} \times \frac{\sqrt{(x^2 + 9)} + 3}{\sqrt{(x^2 + 9)} + 3} = \frac{x^2 + 9 - 9}{x^2 \left(\sqrt{(x^2 + 9)} + 3 \right)} = \frac{1}{\sqrt{(x^2 + 9)} + 3}$$

Now, you can evaluate the limit in its reduced form.

$$\lim_{x \to 0} \frac{1}{\sqrt{(0^2 + 9)} + 3} = \frac{1}{6}$$

4. **C** If you plug $x = 2$ into the limit, it becomes $\dfrac{0}{0}$, which is undefined. First, you must factor the numerator to cancel out the like terms.

$$\lim_{x \to 2} \frac{x^2 + x - 6}{x - 2} = \frac{(x+3)(x-2)}{x-2} = x + 3$$

Now, you can evaluate the limit in its reduced form.

$$\lim_{x \to 2} 2 + 3 = 5$$

5. **D** If you plug $x = -4$ into the limit, it becomes $\dfrac{0}{0}$, which is undefined. First, you must factor both the numerator and denominator to cancel like terms.

$$\lim_{x \to -4} \frac{x^2 + 5x + 4}{x^2 + 3x - 4} = \frac{(x+4)(x+1)}{(x+4)(x-1)} = \frac{x+1}{x-1}$$

Now, you can evaluate the limit in its reduced form.

$$\lim_{x \to -4} \frac{(-4)+1}{(-4)-1} = \frac{-3}{-5} = \frac{3}{5}$$

6. **D** If you plug $x = 4$ into the limit, it becomes $\dfrac{0}{0}$, which is undefined. First, you must factor both the numerator and denominator to cancel like terms.

$$\lim_{x \to 4} \frac{x^2 - 4x}{x^2 - 3x - 4} = \frac{x(x-4)}{(x+1)(x-4)} = \frac{x}{x+1}$$

Now, you can evaluate the limit in its reduced form.

$$\lim_{x \to 4} \frac{4}{4+1} = \frac{4}{5}$$

7. **E** If you plug $x = 7$ into the limit, it becomes $\dfrac{0}{0}$, which is undefined. First, you must rationalize the expression to eliminate common terms.

$$\lim_{x \to 7} \frac{\sqrt{(x+2)} - 3}{x - 7} \times \frac{\sqrt{(x+2)} + 3}{\sqrt{(x+2)} + 3} = \frac{x + 2 - 9}{(x-7)\left(\sqrt{(x+2)} + 3\right)} = \frac{1}{\sqrt{(x+2)} + 3}$$

Now, you can evaluate the limit in its reduced form.

$$\lim_{x \to 7} \frac{1}{\sqrt{(7+2)}+3} = \frac{1}{6}$$

8. **A**   If you plug $x = -1$ into the limit, it becomes $\frac{0}{0}$, which is undefined. First, you must factor the numerator and denominator to cancel out like terms.

$$\lim_{x \to -1} \frac{x^2 + 2x + 1}{x^4 - 1} = \frac{(x+1)(x+1)}{(x^2+1)(x^2-1)} = \frac{(x+1)}{(x-1)(x^2+1)}$$

Now, you can evaluate the limit in its reduced form.

$$\lim_{x \to -1} \frac{(-1+1)}{(-1-1)((-1)^2 - 1)} = 0$$

9. **B**   If you plug $x = 0$ into the limit, it becomes $\frac{0}{0}$, which is undefined. First, you must expand out the numerator to cancel out like terms.

$$\lim_{x \to 0} \frac{(2+x)^3 - 8}{x} = \frac{8 + 12x + 6x^2 + x^3 - 8}{x} = \frac{12x + 6x^2 + x^3}{x} = 12 + 6x + x^2$$

Now, you can evaluate the limit in its reduced form.

$$\lim_{x \to 0} 12 + 6(0) + (0)^2 = 12$$

10. **B**   If you plug 0 in directly, the limit becomes $\frac{0}{0}$, which is undefined. First, the numerator and denominator must be factored to cancel out like terms.

$$\lim_{x \to 0} \frac{x^3 + 2x^2 - 3x}{x^2 - x} = \frac{x(x+3)(x-1)}{x(x-1)} = \frac{(x+3)}{1}$$

Now, you can plug 0 in for x to evaluate the limit.

$$0 + 3 = 3$$

11. **D** If you plug -4 directly into the limit, it becomes $\frac{0}{0}$, which is undefined. First, the numerator must be factored to cancel out the like term.

$$\lim_{x \to -4} \frac{x^2 + 2x - 8}{x + 4} = \frac{(x+4)(x-2)}{x+4} = x - 2$$

Now -4 can be plugged in for x to evaluate the limit.

$(-4) - 2 = -6$

12. **E** If you plug -9 directly into the limit, it becomes $\frac{0}{0}$ which is undefined. First, you must factor the numerator and cancel the like term.

$$\lim_{x \to -9} \frac{81 + 18x + x^2}{x + 9} = \frac{(x+9)^2}{x+9} = x + 9$$

Plug -9 in for x to evaluate the limit.

$(-9) + 9 = 0$

13. **C** If you plug 2 in for x, the limit becomes $\frac{0}{0}$ which is undefined. First, you must factor the denominator to cancel out the like term.

$$\lim_{x \to 2} \frac{x - 2}{x^3 - 2x^2} = \frac{x - 2}{x^2(x - 2)} = \frac{1}{x^2}$$

Now, 2 can be plugged in to x to evaluate the limit.

$$\lim_{x \to 2} \frac{1}{(2)^2} = \frac{1}{4}$$

14. **A** When evaluating limits at infinity, you must look to the degrees in the numerator and the denominator, which in this case, are the same at 2. Since you would simply divide each term by the highest degree, you must only look to the coefficients of the highest degree terms. Since in the numerator the leading coefficient is 9 and in the denominator the leading coefficient is -5, you only need to divide them to find the limit. The limit is $\frac{-9}{5}$.

15.   **E**   If you plug zero directly into the limit, the result is $\frac{0}{0}$, which is undefined. You must first factor the numerator and denominator to cancel out like terms.

$$\lim_{t \to 0} \frac{t^4 + 2t^2}{3t^2 - 2t} = \frac{t^2(t^2 + 2)}{t(3t - 2)} = \frac{t(t^2 + 2)}{3t - 2}$$

Now zero can be plugged in to calculate the limit.

$$\lim_{t \to 0} \frac{(0)(0^2 + 2)}{3(0) - 2} = 0$$

16.   **A**   If you plug −1 directly into the limit, the value becomes $\frac{0}{0}$ which is undefined. First, you must factor both numerator and denominator and look for terms to cancel out.

$$\lim_{y \to -1} \frac{y^2 + 2y + 1}{y^2 + y} = \frac{(y + 1)^2}{y(y + 1)} = \frac{y + 1}{y}$$

Now −1 can be plugged in to evaluate the limit.

$$\lim_{y \to -1} \frac{(-1) + 1}{1} = 0$$

17.   **C**   To evaluate this limit, first, you must rationalize the numerator.

$$\lim_{h \to 0} \frac{\sqrt{(4 + h)} - \sqrt{4}}{h} \times \frac{\sqrt{(4 + h)} + \sqrt{4}}{\sqrt{(4 + h)} + \sqrt{4}} = \frac{4 + h - 4}{h\sqrt{(4 + h)} + \sqrt{4}} = \frac{1}{\sqrt{(4 + h)} + \sqrt{4}}$$

Plug 0 into the reduced function to evaluate the limit.

$$\lim_{h \to 0} \frac{1}{\sqrt{(4 + 0)} + \sqrt{4}} = \frac{1}{4}$$

18. **B** If you plug -7 directly into the limit, it becomes $\dfrac{0}{0}$ which is undefined. First, factor the expression on top and bottom and cancel out any like terms.

$$\lim_{x \to -7} \frac{x^3 + 7x^2}{x^3 + 2x^2 - 35x} = \frac{x^2(x+7)}{x(x-5)(x+7)} = \frac{x}{x-5}$$

Now plug -7 in for x to evaluate the limit.

$$\lim_{x \to -7} \frac{(-7)}{(-7)-5} = \frac{7}{12}$$

19. **D** If you plug zero directly into the limit, it becomes $\dfrac{0}{0}$ which is undefined. You must first factor the denominator to cancel any like terms.

$$\lim_{x \to 0} \frac{x}{x^2 - x} = \frac{x}{x(x-1)} = \frac{1}{x-1}$$

Now you can plug in 0 for x to evaluate the limit.

$$\lim_{x \to 0} \frac{1}{(0)-1} = -1$$

20. **C** Begin by separating the functions into sines and cosines to evaluate:

$$\lim_{x \to 0}\left(\frac{\tan 3x}{\sin 2x} \right) = \lim_{x \to 0}\left(\frac{\sin 3x}{\cos 3x \sin 2x} \right) = \frac{3}{(1)(2)} = \frac{3}{2}.$$

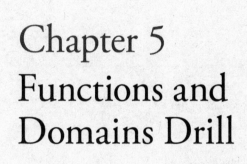

Chapter 5
Functions and
Domains Drill

FUNCTIONS AND DOMAINS DRILL

1. If $f(x) = \sqrt{x}$, $g(x) = x^2 - 36$, and $h(x) = x^3 + 2$, then $f(g(h(2))) =$

   (A) -10
   (B) -8
   (C) 0
   (D) 8
   (E) 10

2. What is the domain of $f(x) = \dfrac{1}{\sqrt[4]{(x^2 - 5x)}}$?

   (A) $0 < x < 5$
   (B) All real numbers; $x \neq 0$
   (C) All real numbers; $x \neq 5$
   (D) All real numbers; $x \neq 0, 5$
   (E) $x < 0$ and $x > 5$

3. Find the domain of $f(x) = \sqrt[4]{(1 - x^2)}$.

   (A) $(-\infty, -1)$
   (B) $(-1, 1)$
   (C) $(1, \infty)$
   (D) $(-\infty, 1)$
   (E) $(-1, \infty)$

4. If $f(x) = 3x + 2$ and $g(x) = (x - 2)^2$, then $g(f(0)) =$

   (A) -14
   (B) -4
   (C) 0
   (D) 4
   (E) 14

5. What is the domain of $\dfrac{1}{x^2 - 4}$?

   (A) All real numbers
   (B) All real numbers ; $x \neq 0$
   (C) All real numbers ; $x \neq 2$
   (D) All real numbers ; $x \neq -2$
   (E) All real numbers ; $x \neq \pm 2$

6. Consider the function, $f(x) = x^3 + \dfrac{5}{2}x^2 - 2x + 6$. Which of the following must be false?

   (A) There is a relative maximum at $x = -2$.
   (B) There is an absolute maximum on the interval $[2,4]$ at $x = 4$.
   (C) There is a relative minimum at $x = \dfrac{1}{3}$.
   (D) There is an absolute minimum at $x = \dfrac{1}{3}$, on the interval $[-4, 1]$.
   (E) There is an absolute maximum at $x = -2$, on the interval $[-4, 1]$.

7. Consider the function $f(x) = \begin{cases} x^3 - 5, & x \leq 2 \\ x^2 + 2, & x > 2 \end{cases}$. What type of discontinuity occurs at $x = 2$?

   (A) point
   (B) essential
   (C) removable
   (D) jump
   (E) There is no discontinuity at $x = 2$.

8. For what value of a is the function $f(x) = \begin{cases} ax^2 + 2, & x < 1 \\ x^3 - 1, & x \geq 1 \end{cases}$ continuous at $x = 1$?

(A) −3
(B) −2
(C) −1
(D) 0
(E) 1

9. Given the function $f(x) = f(x) = \begin{cases} x^3 + 2x^2 - 5, & x < 1 \\ ax^2 + 7x - 4, & x \geq 1 \end{cases}$, at what value of a will the function be continuous?

(A) −10
(B) −7
(C) −5
(D) 1
(E) 5

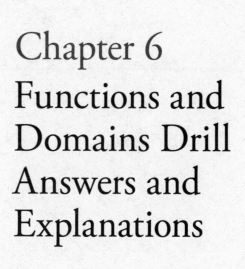

Chapter 6
Functions and Domains Drill Answers and Explanations

ANSWER KEY

1. D
2. E
3. B
4. B
5. E
6. D
7. D
8. B
9. C

EXPLANATIONS

1. **D** We must combine the functions starting from the innermost operation and work outwards.

    Calculate $h(2)$ first.

    $h(2) = 2^3 + 2 = 10$

    Calculate $g(10)$ next.

    $g(10) = (10)^2 - 36 = 64$

    Calculate $f(64)$ next.

    $f(64) = \sqrt{(64)} = 8$

2. **E** To find the domain of this function, we must find where the denominator is equal to zero.

    Set the denominator equal to zero and solve for x.

    $$\sqrt[4]{\left(x^2 - 5x\right)} = 0$$
    $$x^2 - 5x = 0$$
    $$x(x - 5) = 0$$

    $x = 0; x = 5$

    Since the radical is in the denominator, and requires an even root, the values of x must produce a positive radicand, so we must test values to see what yields a result greater than zero. Test values around the x-values.

    $f(-1) = +$ $f(2) = -$ $f(6) = +$

    Therefore, the domain must be $x < 0$ and $x > 5$.

3. **B** Find the domain of $f(x) = \sqrt[4]{\left(1 - x^2\right)}$.

    Since the function has an even root, it must be greater than or equal to zero. But first, we must set it equal to zero to find what x is equal to.

    $$\sqrt[4]{\left(1 - x^2\right)} = 0$$
    $$1 - x^2 = 0$$
    $$1 = x^2$$
    $$\pm 1 = x$$

Test values around the x-values found in step 1.

$$f(-2) = - \qquad\qquad f(0) = + \qquad f(2) = -$$

Therefore, the domain must be $(-1, 1)$.

4. **B** We must calculate the value of the composite function starting with the innermost value. Find $f(0)$ first.

$$f(0) = 3(0) + 2 = 2$$

Find $g(2)$ next.

$$g(2) = (2 - 2)^2 = 0$$

5. **E** Set the denominator equal to zero and solve for x.

$$x^2 - 4 = 0$$
$$x^2 = 4$$
$$x = \pm 2$$

6. **D** Set the first derivative equal to zero to determine the critical points: $f'(x) = 3x^2 + 5x - 2 = 0$. Thus, $x = \dfrac{1}{3}$ and $x = -2$. In order to determine whether these points are maximums or minimums, take the second derivative and evaluate it at each of the critical points: $f''(x) = 6x + 5$, $f''\left(\dfrac{1}{3}\right) = 7$ and $f''(-2) = -7$. Since, the second derivative is positive at $x = \dfrac{1}{3}$, that $x = \dfrac{1}{3}$ is at a minimum. Similarly, because the second derivative is negative at $x = -2$, $x = -2$ is at a maximum. These points are relative minima and maxima over the entire function, because there are no bounds on the function. These points are absolute minima and maxima on closed intervals if there are no other points that are less or greater than those.

7. **D** Graph the function to see the discontinuity. If you cannot, notice that the function shifts position at $x = 2$ and it is not continuous at that point. The limits on either side of $x = 2$ are not equal, so the discontinuity cannot be a point or removable. Furthermore, there is no asymptote, so the discontinuity is not essential. Therefore, it is a jump discontinuity.

8. **B** There are three conditions that must be satisfied for a function to be continuous: 1. $f(c)$ exists. 2. $\lim\limits_{x \to c} f(x)$ exists. 3. $\lim\limits_{x \to c} f(x) = f(c)$. For this function, condition 1 is met because $f(1) = 0$. For the function to be continuous, the left and right hand limits must be equal when approaching $x = 1$. Therefore, we must set $a + 2 = 0$ and $a = -2$. When $a = -2$, the third condition is also met: the limit will equal 0 and $f(1) = 0$.

9.   **C**   For a function to be continuous, three conditions need to be met: $f(c)$ exists, $\lim_{x \to c} f(x)$ exists, and $\lim_{x \to c} f(x) = f(c)$. For a piecewise function, the $f(c)$ and the limit as x approaches c must be equal for both pieces, especially at the point where the pieces meet, in this case, $x = 1$. So, first determine $f(1)$ by plugging 1 into the top piece: $f(1) = -2$. Then, set the second piece equal to that value and solve for a. When this is done, $a = -5$. To verify that the function is truly continuous, take the left and right hand limits of $f(x)$ as x approaches 1. Both the left and right hand limits equal -2, so the limit exists and it is equal to $f(1)$, so the function is continuous when $a = -5$.

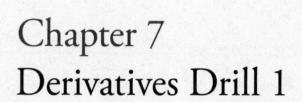

Chapter 7
Derivatives Drill 1

DERIVATIVES DRILL 1

1. If $y = (x^2 + 1)^5$, then $y' =$

    (A) $5(x^2 + 1)^4$
    (B) $10x(x^2 + 1)^4$
    (C) $5x(x^2 + 1)^4$
    (D) $5(2x)^4$
    (E) $(2x)^5$

2. If $y = 4\pi^2 x^2$, then what is y'?

    (A) $8\pi^2 x$
    (B) $8\pi x^2 + 8\pi^2 x$
    (C) $16\pi x$
    (D) $2\pi^2 x^2$
    (E) 0

3. If $f(x) = \sin x \cos x$, then $f'\left(\dfrac{\pi}{2}\right) =$

    (A) -2
    (B) -1
    (C) 0
    (D) 1
    (E) 2

4. If $f(x) = 3x^3 - 2x^2 + x$, then $f'(2) =$

    (A) 39
    (B) 29
    (C) 19
    (D) 9
    (E) -9

5. If $y = x \cos x$, then find y'.

    (A) $\cos x + x \sin x$
    (B) $-\sin x$
    (C) $\cos x - x \sin x$
    (D) $-x \sin x$
    (E) $x \sin x - \cos x$

6. Find y' if $y = x \csc x - \cot x$.

    (A) $\csc x \, (\csc x - \cot x)$
    (B) $\csc x \, (\csc x + 1 - x \cot x)$
    (C) $\csc x \, (\csc x + \cot x)$
    (D) $-\csc x \, (x \cot x - \csc x)$
    (E) $x \csc^2 x - \cot x$

7. What is the derivative of $y = \dfrac{(3x - 4)}{(x^2 + 1)}$?

    (A) $\dfrac{(3 + 8x - 3x^2)}{(x^2 + 1)^2}$

    (B) $\dfrac{3}{2x}$

    (C) $\dfrac{(3 - 8x + 3x^2)}{(x^2 + 1)^2}$

    (D) $\dfrac{(3 + 8x + 3x^2)}{(x^2 + 1)^2}$

    (E) $\dfrac{(3 - 8x - 3x^2)}{(x^2 + 1)^2}$

8. If $f(x) = \sin x \ln x$, then what is $f'(x)$?

(A) $\dfrac{(\cos x)}{x}$

(B) $\dfrac{(\cos x \ln x)}{x}$

(C) $\dfrac{\cos x \ln x - (\sin x)}{x}$

(D) $\dfrac{\cos x \ln x + (\sin x)}{x}$

(E) $\cos x \left(\ln x + \dfrac{1}{x} \right)$

9. If $y = \sin(\ln x)$, then $y' =$

(A) $\cos(\ln x)$

(B) $\sin(\ln x) + \left(\dfrac{1}{x} \right)$

(C) $\dfrac{(\sin(\ln x))}{x}$

(D) $\dfrac{(\cos(\ln x))}{x}$

(E) $\dfrac{-(\cos(\ln x))}{x}$

10. If $f(x) = x^3 - \left(\dfrac{3 \ln 3}{2} \right) x^2$, then what is $f'(x)$?

(A) $3x^2 - 3x \ln 3$

(B) $3x^2 - 3x - 1$

(C) $3x^2 + 3x \ln 3$

(D) $3x^2 - x \ln 3x$

(E) $\dfrac{3x^2 - 3^x}{\ln 3}$

11. If $y = \sqrt{x} \cos x$, find y'.

(A) $x^{-\frac{1}{2}} \left(\left(\dfrac{\cos x}{2} \right) - x \sin x \right)$

(B) $\dfrac{[-\sin x]}{2\sqrt{x}}$

(C) $\dfrac{(\sqrt{x})}{2} - \sin x$

(D) $-x \sin x - \sqrt{x} \cos x$

(E) $x^2 \sin 2 + \left(\dfrac{1}{2\sqrt{x}} \right)$

12. If $y = x^2 \ln(2x)$, then what is the value of y' at $x = \dfrac{1}{2}$?

(A) $-\ln 4$

(B) $-\dfrac{1}{2}$

(C) 0

(D) $\dfrac{1}{2}$

(E) $\ln 4$

13. Find $f'(2)$ if $f(x) = \dfrac{(x^2 + 2)}{(x^4 - 3x^2 + 1)}$.

(A) -4

(B) $-\dfrac{1}{5}$

(C) 0

(D) $\dfrac{1}{5}$

(E) 4

14. If $y = \left(\dfrac{1 - \cos x}{1 + \cos x}\right)^4$, then find y'.

(A) $4\left[\dfrac{(1 - \cos x)}{(1 + \cos x)}\right]^3$

(B) $4\left[\dfrac{(1 + \sin x)}{(1 - \sin x)}\right]^3$

(C) $\dfrac{[8 \sin x\,(1 - \cos x)^3]}{(1 + \cos x)^5}$

(D) $\dfrac{[4 \sin x\,(1 - \cos x)^3]}{(1 + \cos x)^4}$

(E) $\dfrac{[-4 \sin x\,(1 - \cos x)]}{(1 + \cos x)^2}$

15. What is $f'(x)$ if $f(x) = x^3 \cos x$?

(A) $3x^2 \cos x - x^3 \sin x$
(B) $-3x^2 \sin x$
(C) $3x^2 \cos x + x^3 \sin x$
(D) $x^3 \sin x - 3x^2 \cos x$
(E) $3x^2 \sin x$

16. If $y = \dfrac{(\sec x)}{(1 + \tan x)}$, find $\dfrac{dy}{dx}$.

(A) $\dfrac{(\sec x \tan x)}{(\sec^2 x)^2}$

(B) $\dfrac{-(\sec x \tan x)}{(\sec^2 x)}$

(C) $\dfrac{(\tan^2 x)}{(\sec^2 x)^2}$

(D) $\dfrac{\sec x \tan x\,(1 + \tan x) + \sec x\,(\sec^2 x)}{(1 + \tan x)^2}$

(E) $\dfrac{\sec x \tan x\,(1 + \tan x) - \sec x\,(\sec^2 x)}{(1 + \tan x)^2}$

17. If $f(\theta) = \theta \sin \theta$, then what is $f''(\theta)$?

(A) $\theta \sin \theta - 2 \cos \theta$
(B) $\cos \theta - \theta \sin \theta$
(C) $-\sin \theta$
(D) $\theta \cos \theta - 2 \sin \theta$
(E) $2 \cos \theta - \theta \sin \theta$

18. If $y = x^2 \tan x$, then $y' =$

(A) $x^2 \sec^2 x$
(B) $2x \sec^2 x$
(C) $2x \tan x + x^2 \sec^2 x$
(D) $2x \tan x - x^2 \sec^2 x$
(E) $-x^2 \sec^2 x$

19. If $f(x) = 3x^2 - 3x \ln 6$, then $f'(x) =$

(A) $6x + 3 \ln 6$
(B) $66 \ln (x + 3)$
(C) $(x + 3)\,6x + 2$
(D) $63 \ln (x + 3)$
(E) $(x + 3) \ln 6$

20. If $f(x) = \left(\dfrac{(x + 3)}{(x^2 - 4)}\right)$, then $f'(x) =$

(A) $\dfrac{(x^2 - 6x - 4)}{(x^2 - 4)^2}$

(B) $\dfrac{(x^2 + 6x + 4)}{(x^2 - 4)^2}$

(C) $\dfrac{1}{(2x)^2}$

(D) $\dfrac{-(x^2 + 6x + 4)}{(x^2 - 4)^2}$

(E) $\dfrac{-(x + 3)}{(x^2 - 4)^2}$

21. If $y = \ln(4x^2)$, then $y' =$

(A) $8x$

(B) $8x \ln(4x^2)$

(C) $\dfrac{4}{x^2}$

(D) $\dfrac{2}{x^2}$

(E) $\dfrac{2}{x}$

22. If $y = x^3 \sin^2 x$, then $y' =$

(A) $3x^2 \sin^2 x + 2x^3 \sin 2x$
(B) $3x^2 \sin x \cos x$
(C) $3x^2 \sin^2 x + x^3 \sin 2x$
(D) $6x^2 \sin x \cos x$
(E) $6x^2 \sin x + 2x^3 \sin x \cos x$

23. If $f(x) = (x-2)(2x+3)$, then $f'(x) =$

(A) 2
(B) $2x$
(C) $4x$
(D) $4x + 1$
(E) $4x - 1$

24. If $y = \dfrac{1}{2}x^6 - 3x^4 + x$, then $y' =$

(A) $3x^5 - 12x^3 + 1$

(B) $-3x^5 + 12x^3 - 1$

(C) $\dfrac{1}{14}x^7 - \dfrac{1}{5}x^5 + \dfrac{1}{2}x^2$

(D) $\dfrac{1}{2}x(x^5 - 6x + 2)$

(E) $15x^4 - 36x^2$

25. Find $f''(x)$ if $f(x) = \sin 3x + 2\cos x - \sin 2x$.

(A) $9 \sin 3x - 4 \sin 2x + 2 \cos x$
(B) $-9 \sin 3x + 4 \sin 2x - 2 \cos x$
(C) $4 \sin 2x - 9 \sin 3x - 2 \cos x$
(D) $4 \sin 3x - 9 \sin 2x - 2 \cos x$
(E) $-4 \sin 2x + 9 \sin 3x + 2 \cos x$

26. Find y' if $2\sqrt{x} + \sqrt{y} = 10$

(A) $2\sqrt{\dfrac{y}{x}}$

(B) $-2\sqrt{\dfrac{y}{x}}$

(C) $-2\sqrt{\dfrac{x}{y}}$

(D) $2\sqrt{\dfrac{x}{y}}$

(E) $4\sqrt{\dfrac{y}{x}}$

27. What is y' if $2x^3 + x^2y - xy^3 = 9$?

(A) $\dfrac{y^3 - 6x^2 - 2xy}{x^2 - 3xy^2}$

(B) $\dfrac{y^3 + 3x^2 - 2xy}{x^2 - 3xy^2}$

(C) $\dfrac{y^3 - 6x^2 + 2xy}{x^2 - 2xy^2}$

(D) $\dfrac{y^3 - 6x^2 - 2xy}{x^2 + 3xy^2}$

(E) $\dfrac{y^3 + 6x^2 - 2xy}{x^2 - xy^2}$

28. What is the derivative of $y^5 + x^2y^3 = 1 + x^4y$?

(A) $\dfrac{4xy - 2x^2y - 5y}{3x^2y^2 - x^4}$

(B) $\dfrac{3x^2y - 2xy^3 + 5y^4}{3x^2y^2 + x^4}$

(C) $\dfrac{4x^3y - 2xy^3 - 5y^4}{3x^2y^2 - x^4}$

(D) $\dfrac{x^3y - 3xy^3 - 5y^4}{3x^2y^2 - x^4}$

(E) $\dfrac{4x^3y + 2xy^3 + 5y^4}{3x^2y^2 - x^4}$

29. Find y' if $1 + x = \sin(xy^2)$.

(A) $\dfrac{1 - y^2\cos(xy^2)}{2xy\cos(xy^2)}$

(B) $\dfrac{2xy\cos(xy^2)}{1 - y^2\cos(xy^2)}$

(C) $\dfrac{1 + y^2\cos(xy^2)}{2xy\cos(xy^2)}$

(D) $\cos(xy^2) - 1$

(E) $2xy\cos(xy^2) - 1$

30. $\dfrac{d}{dx}\left(2\left(x^2 + 3\right)^3\right) =$

(A) $6\left(x^2 + 3\right)^2$

(B) $4x\left(x^2 + 3\right)^2$

(C) $12x\left(x^2 + 3\right)^2$

(D) $6x\left(x^2 + 3\right)^2$

(E) $4\left(x^2 + 3\right)^2$

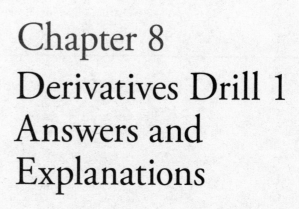

Chapter 8
Derivatives Drill 1
Answers and
Explanations

ANSWER KEY

1. B
2. A
3. B
4. B
5. C
6. B
7. A
8. D
9. D
10. A
11. A
12. D
13. A
14. C
15. A
16. E
17. E
18. C
19. A
20. D
21. E
22. C
23. E
24. A
25. C
26. A
27. A
28. D
29. A
30. C

EXPLANATIONS

1. **B**   Take the derivative using the chain rule.

   $$y' = 5(x^2 + 1)^4 \times (2x)$$

   $$= 10x\,(x^2 + 1)^4$$

2. **A**   Find the derivative.

   $$y' = 4\pi^2 \times 2x$$

   $$= 8\pi^2 x$$

3. **B**   Take the derivative using the product rule and trigonometric derivatives.

   $$f'(x) = \cos x \cos x + \sin x\,(-\sin x)$$

   Don't simplify! Plug in $\dfrac{\pi}{2}$.

   $$f'\left(\frac{\pi}{2}\right) = \cos\left(\frac{\pi}{2}\right)\cos\left(\frac{\pi}{2}\right) - \sin\left(\frac{\pi}{2}\right)\sin\left(\frac{\pi}{2}\right)$$

   $$= (0)(0) - (1)(1)$$

   $$= -1$$

4. **B**   Take the derivative and plug in 2.

   $$f'(x) = 9x^2 - 4x + 1$$

   $$f'(2) = 9(2)^2 - 4(2) + 1$$

   $$= 36 - 8 + 1$$

   $$= 29$$

5. **C**   This question is testing your knowledge of the product rule and derivatives of trigonometric functions.

   Find y'.

   $$y' = (1)\cos x + x(-\sin x)$$

   $$= \cos x - x\sin x.$$

6. **B** This question is testing your knowledge of the product rule and derivatives of trigonometric functions.

   The derivative of $x\csc x$ is $(1)\csc x + x(-\csc x \cot x)$ and the derivative of $\cot x$ is $-\csc^2 x$. That makes the derivative all together $\csc x - x\csc x \cot x + \csc^2 x$.

   Factor out a term of $\csc x$ to match the answer choices.

   $$y' = \csc x (\csc x + 1 - x\cot x)$$

7. **A** This question is testing you on the quotient rule of derivatives.

   Take the derivative of the function.

   $$y' = \frac{(3)(x^2+1)-(3x-4)(2x)}{(x^2+1)^2}$$

   $$= \frac{3x^2+3-6x^2+8x}{(x^2+1)^2}$$

   $$= \frac{3+8x-3x^2}{(x^2+1)^2}$$

8. **D** This question is testing you on the product rule, trigonometric differentiation, and the derivative of the natural logarithm.

   Take the derivative

   $$f'(x) = \cos x \times \ln x + \sin x \times \left(\frac{1}{x}\right)$$

   $$= \cos x \ln x + \frac{\sin x}{x}$$

9. **D** This question is testing you on the chain rule, trigonometric differentiation, and the derivative of the natural logarithm.

   Take the derivative of the function, starting from the outside and working your way in.

   $$y' = \cos(\ln x) \times \left(\frac{1}{x}\right)$$

   $$= \frac{\cos(\ln x)}{x}$$

10. **A** Take the derivative.

    $$f'(x) = 3x^2 - 3x \ln 3$$

11.   **A**   Take the derivative.

$$y' = \frac{1}{2}x^{-\frac{1}{2}}\cos x + x^{\frac{1}{2}}(-\sin x)$$

$$= x^{-\frac{1}{2}}\left(\frac{\cos x}{2} - x\sin x\right)$$

12.   **D**   Take the derivative.

$$y' = 2x\ln(2x) + x^2\left(\frac{1}{2x}\right) \times 2$$

Don't simplify! Just plug in $\frac{1}{2}$ for x.

$$y' = 2\left(\frac{1}{2}\right)\ln(1) + \left(\frac{1}{2}\right)^2\left(\frac{1}{1}\right) \times 2$$

$$= 0 + \frac{1}{2}$$

$$= \frac{1}{2}$$

13.   **A**   Take the derivative using the quotient rule.

$$f'(x) = \frac{(2x)(x^4 - 3x^2 + 1) - (x^2 + 2)(4x^3 - 6x)}{(x^4 - 3x^2 + 1)^2}$$

Don't simplify! Plug in 2 for x.

$$f'(2) = \frac{(4)(5) - (6)(20)}{(5)^2}$$

$$= \frac{20 - 120}{25}$$

$$= -4$$

14.   **C**   Find the derivative using the quotient rule in combination with the chain rule.

$$y' = \frac{4(1 - \cos x)^3}{(1 + \cos x)^3} \cdot \frac{(\sin x)(1 + \cos x) - (1 - \cos x)(-\sin x)}{(1 + \cos x)^2}$$

$$= \frac{4(1 - \cos x)^3(\sin x + \sin x \cos x + \sin x - \sin x \cos x)}{(1 + \cos x)^5}$$

$$= \frac{4(1 - \cos x)^3(2\sin x)}{(1 + \cos x)^5}$$

$$= \frac{8\sin x(1 - \cos x)^3}{(1 + \cos x)^5}$$

15. **A** Find the first derivative using the product rule.

$$f'(x) = (3x^2)(\cos x) + (x^3)(-\sin x)$$

$$= 3x^2 \cos x - x^3 \sin x$$

16. **E** Find the derivative using the quotient rule and trigonometric derivatives.

$$y' = \frac{(\sec x \tan x)(1 + \tan x) - (\sec x)(\sec^2 x)}{(1 + \tan x)^2}$$

17. **E** Find the second derivative.

$$f'(\theta) = \sin \theta + \theta \cos \theta$$

$$f''(\theta) = \cos \theta + \cos \theta - \theta \sin \theta$$

$$= 2 \cos \theta - \theta \sin \theta$$

18. **C** If $y = x^2 \tan x$, then $y' =$

Take the derivative using trigonometric derivatives and the product rule.

$$y' = (2x) \tan x + (x^2) \sec^2 x.$$

19. **A** Take the derivative using the rule of raising a number to a function.

$$f'(x) = 6x + 3 \ln 6.$$

20. **D** Take the derivative using the quotient rule.

$$f'(x) = \frac{(1)(x^2 - 4) - (x + 3)(2x)}{(x^2 - 4)^2}$$

$$= \frac{x^2 - 4 - 2x^2 - 6x}{(x^2 - 4)^2}$$

$$= \frac{-x^2 - 6x - 4}{(x^2 - 4)^2}$$

21. **E** Take the derivative using the derivative of the natural log function and the chain rule.

$$y' = \frac{1}{4x^2}(8x)$$

$$= \frac{8x}{4x^2}$$

$$= \frac{2}{x}$$

22.　**C**　Take the derivative using the product rule, chain rule, and trigonometric derivatives.

$$y' = 3x^2 \sin^2 x + x^3 (2 \sin x \cos x)$$

Use the trigonometric identity $\sin 2x = 2 \sin x \cos x$ to rewrite the derivative.

$$y' = 3x^2 \sin^2 x + x^3 \sin 2x.$$

23.　**E**　Although the product rule could be used to evaluate the derivative, this question is quickly solved if you FOIL out the function first.

$$(x - 2)(2x + 3) = 2x^2 - x - 6$$

Find the derivative.

$$f(x) = 2x^2 - x - 6$$
$$f'(x) = 4x - 1$$

24.　**A**　Calculate the derivative using the power rule for each term.

$$y = \frac{1}{2}x^6 - 3x^4 + x$$

$$y' = 3x^5 - 12x^3 + 1$$

25.　**C**　Calculate the first derivative using the trigonometric derivatives and the chain rule.

$$f(x) = \sin 3x + 2 \cos x - \sin 2x$$
$$f'(x) = 3 \cos 3x - 2 \sin x - 2 \cos 2x$$

Now take the second derivative paying attention to the sign changes when applying the trigonometric derivatives.

$$f'(x) = 3 \cos 3x - 2 \sin x - 2 \cos 2x$$
$$f''(x) = -9 \sin 3x - 2 \cos x + 4 \sin 2x$$
$$f''(x) = 4 \sin 2x - 9 \sin 3x - 2 \cos x$$

26.　**A**　Take the derivative with respect to x.

$$2\sqrt{x} + \sqrt{y} = 10$$

$$2\left[\frac{1}{2}x^{-\frac{1}{2}}\right] + \frac{1}{2}y^{-\frac{1}{2}}\, y' = 0$$

$$x^{-\frac{1}{2}} + \frac{1}{2}y^{-\frac{1}{2}}\, y' = 0$$

$$\frac{1}{2}y^{-\frac{1}{2}}\, y' = \frac{1}{\sqrt{x}}$$

$$y' = 2\sqrt{\frac{y}{x}}$$

27. **A**   Take the derivative with respect to x using the power rule and product rule.

$$2x^3 + x^2 y - xy^3 = 9$$

$$6x^2 + 2xy + x^2 y' - (y^3 + 3xy^2 \, y') = 0$$

$$6x^2 + 2xy + x^2 y' - y^3 - 3xy^2 \, y' = 0$$

$$(x^2 - 3xy^2) \, y' = y^3 - 6x^2 - 2xy$$

$$y' = \frac{y^3 - 6x^2 - 2xy}{x^2 - 3xy^2}$$

28. **D**   Take the derivative with respect to x using the power rule and product rule.

$$y^5 + x^2 y^3 = 1 + x^4 y$$

$$5y^4 + 2xy^3 + 3x^2 y^2 \, y' = 4x^3 y + x^4 y'$$

$$3x^2 y^2 y' - x^4 \, y' = 4x^3 y - 2xy^3 - 5y^4$$

$$(3x^2 y^2 - x^4) \, y' = 4x^3 y - 2xy^3 - 5y^4$$

$$y' = \frac{4x^3 y - 2xy^3 - 5y^4}{3x^2 y^2 - x^4}$$

29. **A**   Take the derivative with respect to x using the product rule, the chain rule, and the differentiation formula for the sine function.

$$1 + x = \sin(xy^2)$$

$$1 = \cos(xy^2) \bullet (y^2 + 2xy \, y')$$

$$1 = y^2 \cos(xy^2) + 2xy \cos(xy^2) \, y'$$

$$1 - y^2 \cos(xy^2) = 2xy \cos(xy^2) \, y'$$

$$\frac{1 - y^2 \cos(xy^2)}{2xy \cos(xy^2)} = y'$$

30. **C** $\dfrac{d}{dx}\left(2\left(x^2 + 3\right)^3\right) = 2\left(3\left(x^2 + 3\right)^2 (2x)\right) = 12x\left(x^2 + 3\right)^2$

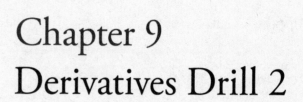

Chapter 9
Derivatives Drill 2

DERIVATIVES DRILL 2

1. If $f(x) = \sin(\csc x)$, then $f'(x) =$

   (A) $\csc x \cot x \cos(\csc x)$
   (B) $-\csc x \cot x \cos(\csc x)$
   (C) $\cot^2 x \cos(\csc x)$
   (D) $-\cot^2 x \cos(\csc x)$
   (E) $\cos(-\csc x \cot x)$

2. If $y = 6x^5 - 5x^4$, then $y^{(4)} =$

   (A) $30x^4 - 20x^3$
   (B) $120x^3 - 60x^2$
   (C) $360x^2 - 120x$
   (D) $720x - 120$
   (E) 720

3. Find the derivative of $f(x) = e^{2x} \sin^2 3x$.

   (A) $2e^{2x} \sin 3x (\sin 3x + 3\cos 3x)$
   (B) $6e^{2x} \sin^2 3x + 2e^{2x} \sin 3x \cos x$
   (C) $2e^{2x} \sin 3x (\sin 3x - 3\cos 3x)$
   (D) $-2e^{2x} \sin 3x (\sin 3x + 3\cos 3x)$
   (E) $2e^{2x} \sin 3x \cos x - 6e^{2x} \sin^2 3x$

4. If $y = e^x (\ln x)^2$, then $y' =$

   (A) $2e^x \ln x$

   (B) $\left(\dfrac{2}{x}\right) e^x \ln x$

   (C) $e^x \ln x \left[\ln x + \dfrac{1}{x}\right]$

   (D) $2xe^x \ln x$

   (E) $\dfrac{2 \ln x}{xe^x}$

5. If $y = \tan^2(3\theta)$, then $y' =$

   (A) $\sec^2(3\theta) - 1$
   (B) $2 \tan(3\theta)$
   (C) $6 \sec^2(3\theta)$
   (D) $6 \tan(3\theta) \sec^2(3\theta)$
   (E) $3 \tan(3\theta) \sec^2(3\theta)$

6. If $f(x) = \sin(\sin(\sin x))$, then what is $f'(x)$?

   (A) $\cos(\cos(\cos x))$
   (B) $\cos x \cos(\sin x) \cos(\sin(\sin x))$
   (C) $\cos(\sin(\cos x))$
   (D) $\cos x + \sin x \cos x + \sin^2 x$
   (E) $\cos(\cos x) \cos x$

7. If $y = \cos^4(\sin^3 x)$, then $y' =$

   (A) $-12 \sin^2 x \cos x \sin(\sin^3 x) \cos^3(\sin^3 x)$
   (B) $4 \cos^3(\sin^3 x)$
   (C) $4 \cos^3(3 \sin^2 x)$
   (D) $\cos^4(3 \sin^2 x)$
   (E) $12 \sin^2 x \cos x \sin(\sin^3 x) \cos^3(\sin^3 x)$

8. What is the derivative of $f(x) = \sin^2 \pi x$?

   (A) $2\pi \sin 2\pi x$
   (B) $2 \cos \pi x$
   (C) $\sin 2\pi x$
   (D) $\pi \sin 2\pi x$
   (E) $\sin \pi x \cos \pi x$

9. If $y = \cos(\tan x)$, then $y' =$

   (A) $\sec^2 x \sin(\tan x)$
   (B) $-\sin(\sec^2 x)$
   (C) $-\sec^2 x \sin(\tan x)$
   (D) $\sec x \tan x \sin(\tan x)$
   (E) $-\sec x \tan x \sin(\tan x)$

10. If $f(x) = (x^{-2} + x^{-3})(x^5 - 2x^2)$, then $f'(x) =$

   (A) $-3x^2 + 2x + 2x^{-2}$
   (B) $3x^2 + 2x - 2x^{-2}$
   (C) $x^3 + x^2 - 2 - 2x^{-1}$
   (D) $x^4 + x^3 - 2x + 2\ln x$
   (E) $-3x^2 - 2x - 2x^{-2}$

11. What is the derivative of $y = \dfrac{2t}{(4 + t^2)}$?

   (A) $\dfrac{(8 + 2t^2)}{(4 + t^2)^2}$

   (B) $\dfrac{(8 - 2t^2)}{(4 + t^2)^2}$

   (C) $\dfrac{1}{2t^2}$

   (D) $\dfrac{-(8 - 2t^2)}{(4 + t^2)^2}$

   (E) $\dfrac{-(8 + 2t^2)}{(4 + t^2)^2}$

12. Find the derivative of $y = \dfrac{(x + 1)}{(x^3 + x - 2)}$

   (A) $\dfrac{(2x^3 + 3x^2 + 1)}{(x^3 + x - 2)^2}$

   (B) $\dfrac{(2x^3 - 3x^2 - 1)}{(x^3 + x - 2)^2}$

   (C) $\dfrac{1}{(3x^2 + 1)}$

   (D) $\dfrac{-(2x^3 - 3x^2 - 1)}{(x^3 + x - 2)^2}$

   (E) $\dfrac{-(2x^3 + 3x^2 + 1)}{(x^3 + x - 2)^2}$

13. If $y = \sqrt{x}\, \sin x$, then $y' =$

   (A) $\dfrac{1}{2}x^{-\frac{1}{2}}[\sin x + 2x \cos x]$

   (B) $\dfrac{1}{2}\sqrt{x}\,[\sin x + 2x \cos x]$

   (C) $\dfrac{1}{2}x^{-\frac{1}{2}}\cos x$

   (D) $\sqrt{x}\cos x$

   (E) $-\dfrac{1}{2}x^{-\frac{1}{2}}[\sin x + 2x \cos x]$

14. If $f(x) = x^2 \sin x \tan x$, then $f'(x) =$

   (A) $2x \cos x \sec^2 x$
   (B) $x^2 (\cos x \tan x + \sin x \sec^2 x) + 2x (\sin x \tan x)$
   (C) $-x^2 (\cos x \tan x + \sin x \sec^2 x) + 2x (\sin x \tan x)$
   (D) $-2x \cos x \sec^2 x$
   (E) $x^2 (\cos x + \sec^2 x)$

15. What is the derivative of $y = \tan (\sin x)$?

   (A) $\sec^2 (\cos x)$
   (B) $\cos x \sec (\sin x) \tan (\sin x)$
   (C) $\cos x \sec^2 (\sin x)$
   (D) $-\cos x \sec^2 (\sin x)$
   (E) $-\sec^2 (\cos x)$

16. If $y = 2 \csc (4x)$, then $y' =$

   (A) $-2 \cot^2 (4x)$
   (B) $2 \cot^2 (4x)$
   (C) $-8 \csc (x) \cot (x)$
   (D) $2\theta \csc (4x) \cot (4x)$
   (E) $-8 \csc (4x) \cot (4x)$

17. What is the derivative of $y = (x^2 + 2x)e^x$?

    (A) $(x+1)e^x$
    (B) $2(x+1)e^x$
    (C) $2x(x+1)e^{x-1}$
    (D) $(x^2 + 4x + 2)e^x$
    (E) $(x^2 - 4x - 2)e^x$

18. If $y = e^2 \ln x$, then $y' =$

    (A) 0

    (B) $\dfrac{e^2}{x}$

    (C) $\dfrac{2e}{x}$

    (D) $2e \ln x + \dfrac{e^2}{x}$

    (E) $2e \ln x - \dfrac{e^2}{x}$

19. Find $f'(x)$ if $f(x) = \tan x + \sec^2 x$.

    (A) $\sec^2 x\,(1 + 2\tan x)$
    (B) $2\sec^2 x + \tan x$
    (C) $\sec^2 x\,(1 - 2\tan x)$
    (D) $\tan x - \sec^2 x$
    (E) $2\sec^2 x - \tan x$

20. If $y = e^{\sin x}$, then $y'(\pi) =$

    (A) -2
    (B) -1
    (C) 0
    (D) 1
    (E) 2

21. Find y' if $y = \ln(4x^2 - 3x + 3)$

    (A) $\dfrac{(8x + 3)}{(4x^2 - 3x + 3)}$

    (B) $\dfrac{(8x + 3)}{(4x^2 + 3x + 3)}$

    (C) $\dfrac{(8x - 3)}{(4x^2 - 3x + 3)}$

    (D) $\dfrac{-(8x - 3)}{(4x^2 - 3x + 3)}$

    (E) $\dfrac{-(8x + 3)}{(4x^2 + 3x + 3)}$

22. What is the derivative of $f(x) = x^4 \tan 5x$?

    (A) $\dfrac{1}{5} x^5 \sec^2 5x$

    (B) $20\, x^3 \sec^2 5x$

    (C) $x^3\,(4 \tan 5x - 5x \sec^2 5x)$

    (D) $-x^3\,(4 \tan 5x - 5x \sec^2 5x)$

    (E) $x^3\,(4 \tan 5x + 5x \sec^2 5x)$

23. If $y = \tan^2(\sin \theta)$, then $y' =$

    (A) $-2 \cos \theta \tan(\sin \theta) \sec^2(\sin \theta)$
    (B) $2 \sec^2(\cos \theta)$
    (C) $2 \tan(-\cos \theta)$
    (D) $\cos \theta \tan(\sin \theta) \sec^2(\sin \theta)$
    (E) $2 \cos \theta \tan(\sin \theta) \sec^2(\sin \theta)$

24. If $y = \sec(1 + x^2)$, then $y' =$

    (A) $\sec(2x) \tan(2x)$
    (B) $2x \sec(2x) \tan(2x)$
    (C) $2x \sec^2(1 + x^2)$
    (D) $2x \sec(1 + x^2) \tan(1 + x^2)$
    (E) $2x \tan^2(1 + x^2) \sec(1 + x^2)$

25. If $y \sin (x^2) = x \sin (y^2)$, then $y' =$

(A) $2 \sec (y^2) - 2 \csc (x^2)$

(B) $\dfrac{\sin (y^2) - 2xy \cos (x^2)}{\sin (x^2) - 2xy \cos (y^2)}$

(C) $2 \cos y - 2 \cos x$

(D) $\dfrac{\sin (y^2) + 2xy \cos (x^2)}{\sin (x^2) - 2xy \cos (y^2)}$

(E) $\dfrac{\sin (x^2) + 2xy \cos (y^2)}{\sin (y^2) - 2xy \cos (x^2)}$

26. If $x^2 \cos y + \sin 2y = xy$, then find y'.

(A) $\dfrac{2x \cos y - y}{x + x^2 \sin y - 2 \cos 2y}$

(B) $x + x^2 \sin y - 2 \cos 2y$

(C) $2x \cos y - y$

(D) $\dfrac{x + x^2 \sin y - 2 \cos 2y}{2x \cos y - y}$

(E) $\dfrac{2x \cos y + y}{x + x^2 \sin y - 2 \cos 2y}$

27. If $\sec y = \sec^2 x$, then $y' =$

(A) $\dfrac{2 \sec^2 x \tan x}{\sec y \tan y}$

(B) $\dfrac{\sec y \tan y}{2 \sec^2 x \tan x}$

(C) $2 \sec^2 x \tan x$

(D) $\tan y - 2 \tan x$

(E) $\sec y \tan y$

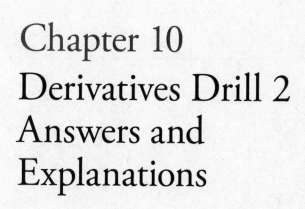

Chapter 10
Derivatives Drill 2
Answers and
Explanations

ANSWER KEY

1. B
2. D
3. A
4. C
5. D
6. B
7. A
8. D
9. C
10. A
11. B
12. E
13. A
14. B
15. C
16. E
17. D
18. B
19. A
20. B
21. C
22. E
23. E
24. D
25. B
26. A
27. A

EXPLANATIONS

1. **B** Take the derivative using trigonometric derivatives and the chain rule.

   $f(x) = \sin(\csc x)$
   $f'(x) = \cos(\csc x)(-\csc x \cot x)$
   $f'(x) = -\csc x \cot x \cos(\csc x)$

2. **D** Start calculating the derivatives to get to the 4th derivative by using the power rule.

   $y = 6x^5 - 5x^4$
   $y' = 30x^4 - 20x^3$
   $y'' = 120x^3 - 60x^2$
   $y'^{(3)} = 360x^2 - 120x$
   $y'^{(4)} = 720x - 120$

3. **A** Take the derivative using the derivative of the exponential function, trigonometric derivatives, the product rule, and the chain rule.

   $f(x) = e^{2x} \sin^2 3x$
   $f'(x) = (2e^{2x})(\sin^2 3x) + (e^{2x})(2 \sin 3x \cos 3x \times 3)$
   $f'(x) = 2e^{2x} \sin^2 3x + 6e^{2x} \sin 3x \cos 3x$
   $f'(x) = 2e^{2x} \sin 3x (\sin 3x + 3 \cos 3x)$

4. **C** Take the derivative using the differentiation rules of exponential functions, natural logarithms, the product rule and the chain rule.

   $y = e^x (\ln x)^2$
   $y' = e^x (\ln x)^2 + e^x \left[2(\ln x)\left(\dfrac{1}{x}\right) \right]$
   $y' = e^x \ln x \left[\ln x + \left(\dfrac{2}{x}\right) \right]$

5. **D** Take the derivative using the trigonometric derivative formula for tangent and the chain rule.

   $y = \tan^2 (3\theta)$
   $y' = 2 \tan (3\theta) \sec^2 (3\theta)\, 3$
   $y' = 6 \tan (3\theta) \sec^2 (3\theta)$

6. **B** Take the derivative using the trigonometric formula for the sine function, as well as the chain rule, starting from the outside and working your way in the parentheses.

$$f(x) = \sin(\sin(\sin x))$$
$$f'(x) = \cos(\sin(\sin x)) \cos(\sin x) \cos x$$
$$f'(x) = \cos x \cos(\sin x) \cos(\sin(\sin x))$$

7. **A** Take the derivative using the trigonometric formula for the sine and cosine functions and the chain rule.

$$y = \cos^4(\sin^3 x)$$
$$y' = 4 \cos^3(\sin^3 x)(-\sin(\sin^3 x)) \, 3 \sin^2 x \cos x$$
$$y' = -12 \sin^2 x \cos x \sin(\sin^3 x) \cos^3(\sin^3 x)$$

8. **D** Take the derivative using the trigonometric formula for the sine function and the chain rule.

$$f(x) = \sin^2 \pi x$$
$$f'(x) = 2 \sin \pi x \cos \pi x \, \pi$$
$$f'(x) = 2\pi \sin \pi x \cos \pi x$$
$$f'(x) = \pi \sin 2\pi x \qquad\qquad (\text{* Note: } \sin 2x = 2 \sin x \cos x)$$

9. **C** Take the derivative using the trigonometric formula for the cosine and tangent functions, as well as the chain rule.

$$y = \cos(\tan x)$$
$$y' = -\sin(\tan x) \sec^2 x$$
$$y' = -\sec^2 x \sin(\tan x)$$

10. **A** Although the product rule can be used to get this derivative, first apply FOIL and then use the power rule of exponents to make it easier.

$$(x^{-2} + x^{-3})(x^5 - 2x^2) = x^3 - 2 + x^2 - 2x^{-1}$$
$$f(x) = x^3 + x^2 - 2 - 2x^{-1}$$
$$f'(x) = 3x^2 + 2x + 2x^{-2}$$

11. **B** Take the derivative using the quotient rule.

$$y = \frac{2t}{(4+t^2)}$$
$$y' = \frac{(2)(4+t^2) - (2t)(2t)}{(4+t^2)^2}$$
$$y' = \frac{8 + 2t^2 - 4t}{(4+t^2)^2}$$
$$y' = \frac{8 - 2t^2}{(4+t^2)^2}$$

12. **E** Take the derivative using the quotient rule.

$$y = \frac{(x+1)}{(x^3 + x - 2)}$$

$$y' = \frac{(1)(x^3 + x - 2) - (x+1)(3x^2 + 1)}{(x^3 + x - 2)^2}$$

$$y' = \frac{x^3 + x - 2 - (3x^3 + x + 3x^2 + 1)}{(x^3 + x - 2)^2}$$

$$y' = \frac{-2x^3 - 3x^2 - 1}{(x^3 + x - 2)^2}$$

$$y' = \frac{2x^3 - 3x^2 + 1}{(x^3 + x + 2)^2}$$

13. **A** Take the derivative using the trigonometric formula for the sine function and the product rule.

$$y = \sqrt{x} \sin x$$

$$y' = \left(\frac{1}{2}x^{-\frac{1}{2}}\right)(\sin x) + \left(x^{\frac{1}{2}}\right)(\cos x)$$

$$y' = \left(\frac{1}{2}x^{-\frac{1}{2}}\right)[\sin x + 2x \cos x]$$

14. **B** Take the derivative by carefully using the product rule, as well as the trigonometric formula for both the sine and tangent functions.

$$f(x) = x^2 \sin x \tan x$$

$$f'(x) = (2x)(\sin x \tan x) + (x^2)(\cos x \tan x + \sin x \sec^2 x)$$

15. **C** Take the derivative of the function using the differentiation rules for the tangent and sine functions, as well as the chain rule.

$$y = \tan (\sin x)$$

$$y' = \sec^2(\sin x) \cos x$$

$$y' = \cos x \sec^2(\sin x)$$

16. **E** Take the derivative of the function using the differentiation rule for the cosecant function, as well as the chain rule.

$$y = 2 \csc (4x)$$

$$y' = -8 \csc (4x) \cot (4x)$$

17.   **D**   Take the derivative of the function using the product rule, the power rule, and the exponential function rule.

$$y = (x^2 + 2x)e^x$$
$$y' = (2x + 2)(e^x) + (x^2 + 2x)(e^x)$$
$$y' = (x^2 + 4x + 2)e^x$$

18.   **B**   Take the derivative of the function using the constant rule, and the derivative of the natural logarithm function. (Remember, e^2 is a constant!)

$$y = e^2 \ln x$$
$$y' = e^2 \left(\frac{1}{x} \right)$$
$$y' = \left(\frac{e^2}{x} \right)$$

19.   **A**   Take the derivative using the rules of differentiation for both the tangent and secant functions, as well as the power rule.

$$f(x) = \tan x + \sec^2 x$$
$$f'(x) = \sec^2 x + 2 \sec x \sec x \tan x$$
$$f'(x) = \sec^2 x \, (1 + 2 \tan x)$$

20.   **B**   Take the first derivative using the rule of exponential functions and of the sine function.

$$y = e^{\sin x}$$
$$y' = e^{\sin x} \cos x$$

Do not simplify! Plug in $x = \pi$ immediately.

$$y' = e^{\sin \pi} \cos \pi$$
$$= e^0 \, (-1)$$
$$= -1$$

21.   **C**   Take the derivative of the function by using the differentiation formula for the natural logarithm function and the chain rule.

$$y = \ln (4x^2 - 3x + 3)$$
$$y' = \left[\frac{1}{(4x^2 - 3x + 3)} \right](8x - 3)$$
$$y' = \frac{(8x - 3)}{(4x^2 - 3x + 3)}$$

22.   **E**   Take the derivative using the product rule, the differentiation formula for the tangent function and the chain rule.

$$f(x) = x^4 \tan 5x$$
$$f'(x) = (4x^3)(\tan 5x) + (x^4)(\sec^2 5x)(5)$$
$$f'(x) = x^3 (4 \tan 5x + 5x \sec^2 5x)$$

23.   **E**   To find this derivative, you must utilize the chain rule and the rules of trigonometric differentiation for the tangent and sine functions.

$$y = \tan^2 (\sin \theta)$$

$$y' = 2 \tan (\sin \theta) \times \sec^2 (\sin \theta) \times \cos \theta$$

So, $y' = 2 \cos \theta \tan (\sin \theta) \sec^2 (\sin \theta)$

24.   **D**   Take the derivative using the trigonometric rule for the secant function and the chain rule.

$$y = \sec (1 + x^2)$$

$$y' = \sec (1 + x^2) \tan (1 + x^2) \times 2x$$

$$y' = 2x \sec (1 + x^2) \tan (1 + x^2)$$

25.   **B**   Take the derivative with respect to x using the product rule, the chain rule, and the differentiation formula for the sine function.

$$y \sin (x^2) = x \sin (y^2)$$
$$\sin (x^2) \, y' + y \cos (x^2) \bullet 2x = \sin (y^2) + x \cos (y^2) \bullet 2y \, y'$$
$$\sin (x^2) \, y' + 2xy \cos (x^2) = \sin (y^2) + 2xy \cos (y^2) \, y'$$
$$\sin (x^2) \, y' - 2xy \cos (y^2) \, y' = \sin (y^2) - 2xy \cos (x^2)$$
$$(\sin (x^2) - 2xy \cos (y^2)) \, y' = \sin (y^2) - 2xy \cos (x^2)$$
$$y' = \frac{\sin (y^2) - 2xy \cos (x^2)}{\sin (x^2) - 2xy \cos (y^2)}$$

26. **A** Take the derivative with respect to x using the product rule, chain rule, and the differentiation rules for the sine and cosine functions.

$$x^2 \cos y + \sin 2y = xy$$
$$2x \cos y - x^2 \sin y \, y' + 2 \cos 2y \, y' = y + xy'$$
$$2x \cos y - y = xy' + x^2 \sin y \, y' - 2 \cos 2y \, y'$$
$$2x \cos y - y = (x + x^2 \sin y - 2 \cos 2y) \, y'$$
$$\frac{2x \cos y - y}{x + x^2 \sin y - 2 \cos 2y} = y'$$

27. **A** Take the derivative with respect to x using the chain rule and the differentiation rule for the secant function.

$$\sec y = \sec^2 x$$
$$\sec y \tan y \cdot y' = 2 \sec x \cdot \sec x \tan x$$
$$y' = \frac{2 \sec^2 x \tan x}{\sec y \tan y}$$

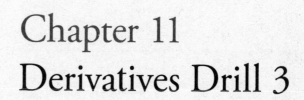

Chapter 11
Derivatives Drill 3

DERIVATIVES DRILL 3

1. Find y' if $x^6 + y^6 = 6$.

    (A) $\dfrac{(6 - 6x^5)}{6y^5}$

    (B) $\dfrac{x^5}{y^5}$

    (C) $\dfrac{y^5}{x^5}$

    (D) $-\dfrac{x^5}{y^5}$

    (E) $-\dfrac{y^5}{x^5}$

2. Given $h(x) = f(g(\sin x))$, what is h' in terms of f' and g'?

    (A) $\cos x \times f'(g(\sin x)) \times g'(\sin x)$
    (B) $f'(g'(\cos x))$
    (C) $f(g'(\sin x)) \times f'(g(\sin x))$
    (D) $\cos x \times f(g'(\sin x)) \times f'(g(\sin x))$
    (E) $-\cos x \times f'(g(\sin x)) \times g'(\sin x)$

3. If $f(x) = x^2 g(x)$, $g(3) = 2$, and $g'(3) = 1$, then what is $f'(3)$?

    (A) 30
    (B) 21
    (C) 3
    (D) −21
    (E) −30

4. If $y = 4x - \tan x$, then $y' =$

    (A) $4 + \sec^2 x$
    (B) $4 - \sec x \tan x$
    (C) $4 - \sec^2 x$
    (D) $4 + \sec x \tan x$
    (E) $4 \sec^2 x$

5. If $y = \cot(3x^2 + 5)$, then $y' =$

    (A) $-\csc^2(6x)$
    (B) $-6x \csc^2(3x^2 + 5)$
    (C) $6x \csc^2(3x^2 + 5)$
    (D) $-6x \csc(3x^2 + 5) \cot(3x^2 + 5)$
    (E) $6x \csc(3x^2 + 5) \cot(3x^2 + 5)$

6. If $y = \csc(\cot x)$, then $y' =$

    (A) $-\csc(\csc^2 x) \cot(\csc^2 x)$
    (B) $-\csc^2 x \csc(\cot x) \cot(\cot x)$
    (C) $-\csc^2 x \cot^2(\cot x)$
    (D) $\csc^2 x \cot^2(\cot x)$
    (E) $\csc^2 x \csc(\cot x) \cot(\cot x)$

7. If $y = \tan(\sec x)$, then $y' =$

    (A) $\sec^2(\sec x \tan x)$
    (B) $\sec x \tan x \sec^2(\sec x)$
    (C) $\sec(\sec x) \tan(\sec x)$
    (D) $-\sec x \tan x \sec^2(\sec x)$
    (E) $-\sec(\sec x) \tan(\sec x)$

8. Let $r(x) = f(g(h(x)))$, where $h(1) = 2$, $g(2) = 3$, $h'(1) = 4$, $g'(2) = 5$, and $f'(3) = 6$. What is the value of $r'(1)$?

    (A) 1
    (B) 3
    (C) 20
    (D) 120
    (E) 720

9. If $y = \cot(\csc x)$, then $y' =$

    (A) $\csc^2(\csc x \cot x)$
    (B) $-\csc^2(-\csc x \cot x)$
    (C) $\csc x \cot x \csc^2(\csc x)$
    (D) $-\csc x \cot x \csc^2(\csc x)$
    (E) $\csc^2(\csc x) \cot(\csc x)$

10. If $y = \sec(\tan x)$, then $y' =$

    (A) $\sec(\sec^2 x)\tan(\sec^2 x)$
    (B) $\tan^2(\sec^2 x)\sec(\tan x)$
    (C) $-\sec^2 x \sec(\tan x)\tan(\tan x)$
    (D) $\sec^2 x \sec(\tan x)\tan(\tan x)$
    (E) $-\sec(\sec^2 x)\tan(\sec^2 x)$

11. If $F(x) = f(3f(4f(x)))$, where $f(0) = 0$ and $f'(0) = 2$, then what is the value of $F'(0)$?

    (A) 96
    (B) 72
    (C) 24
    (D) 2
    (E) 0

12. If $x^3 + y^3 = 1$, then $y' =$

    (A) $\dfrac{x^2}{y^2}$

    (B) $\dfrac{(1-x^2)}{y^2}$

    (C) $-\dfrac{x^2}{y^2}$

    (D) $\dfrac{(1-y^2)}{x^2}$

    (E) $\dfrac{x}{y}$

13. If $x^2 + xy - y^2 = 4$, then $y' =$

    (A) $\dfrac{(4 - 2x - y)}{(2y - x)}$

    (B) $\dfrac{(2x + y)}{(2x - y)}$

    (C) $\dfrac{(2y - x)}{(2x + y)}$

    (D) $\dfrac{(2x + y)}{(2y - x)}$

    (E) $\dfrac{(2x + y)}{(x - 2y)}$

14. Find y' if $x^3 + y^3 = 6xy$.

    (A) $\dfrac{(3x^2 - 6y)}{(6x - 3y^2)}$

    (B) $\dfrac{(6y - 3x^2)}{(3y^2 - 6x)}$

    (C) $\dfrac{(3x^2 + 6y)}{(6x + 3y^2)}$

    (D) $\dfrac{3x^2}{2y^2}$

    (E) $\dfrac{2x^2}{3y^2}$

15. Find y' if $4\cos x \sin y = 1$.

    (A) $\cot x \cot y$
    (B) $\tan x \cot y$
    (C) $\cot x \tan y$
    (D) $1 - \cos x \sin y$
    (E) $\tan x \tan y$

16. If $x^3 + y^3 = xy$, then what is y'?

    (A) $\dfrac{(3y^2 - x)}{(y - 3x^2)}$

    (B) $\dfrac{(y + 3x^2)}{(3y^2 + x)}$

    (C) $\dfrac{(y - 3x^2)}{(3y^2 - x)}$

    (D) $\dfrac{(3y^2 + x)}{(y + 3x^2)}$

    (E) $\dfrac{(y + 3x^2)}{(3y^2 - x)}$

17. Find y' if $x = \ln(x^2 + y^2)$.

(A) $\dfrac{-(2x)}{(x^2 + y^2 - 2y)}$

(B) $\dfrac{(2x)}{(x^2 + y^2 - 2y)}$

(C) $\dfrac{(x^2 + y^2 - 2x)}{(2y)}$

(D) $\dfrac{(2x + 2y)}{(x^2 + y^2)}$

(E) $\dfrac{(2x - 2y)}{(x^2 + y^2)}$

18. $x^4 + y^4 = \pi^4$. Find $\dfrac{dy}{dx}$.

(A) $\dfrac{-x^3}{y^3}$

(B) $\dfrac{-y^3}{x^3}$

(C) $\dfrac{x^3}{y^3}$

(D) $\dfrac{y^3}{x^3}$

(E) $\dfrac{(\pi^3 - x^3)}{y^3}$

19. If $3x^2 \sin y = \tan x$, then $y' =$

(A) $\dfrac{(\sec^2 x)}{(6x \cos y)}$

(B) $\dfrac{(\sec^2 x - 6x \sin y)}{(3x^2 \cos y)}$

(C) $\dfrac{(\sec^2 x + 6x \sin y)}{(3x^2 \cos y)}$

(D) $\dfrac{-(\sec^2 x)}{(6x \cos y)}$

(E) $6x \cos y - \sec^2 x$

20. Find the derivative of y, when $y = \dfrac{(x^3 - 2x^2)\sin^2 x}{(x^2 + 1)^3}$?

(A) $y\left(\dfrac{3x - 4}{x^2 - 2x} + 2\tan x + \dfrac{6x}{x^2 + 1} \right)$

(B) $y\left(\dfrac{3x - 4}{x^2 - 2x} + 2\cot x + \dfrac{6x}{x^2 + 1} \right)$

(C) $y\left(\dfrac{3x - 4}{x^2 - 2x} - 2\tan x - \dfrac{6x}{x^2 + 1} \right)$

(D) $y\left(\dfrac{3x - 4}{x^2 - 2x} + 2\tan x - \dfrac{6x}{x^2 + 1} \right)$

(E) $y\left(\dfrac{3x - 4}{x^2 - 2x} + 2\cot x - \dfrac{6x}{x^2 + 1} \right)$

21. $\dfrac{dy}{dx}$ of $y = \left(\dfrac{3x^2 + 6}{2x - 1} \right)^3 =$

(A) $3\left(\dfrac{3x^2 + 6}{2x - 1} \right)^2 \left(\dfrac{(2x - 1)(6x) - 2(3x^2 + 6)}{(2x - 1)^2} \right)$

(B) $3\left(\dfrac{3x^2 + 6}{2x - 1} \right)^2$

(C) $\left(\dfrac{3x^2 + 6}{2x - 1} \right)^2 \left(\dfrac{(2x - 1)(6x) - 2(3x^2 + 6)}{(2x - 1)^2} \right)$

(D) $3\left(\dfrac{3x^2 + 6}{2x - 1} \right)^2 \left(\dfrac{(2x - 1)(6x) + 2(3x^2 + 6)}{(2x - 1)^2} \right)$

(E) $3\left(\dfrac{3x^2 + 6}{2x - 1} \right)^2 \left(\dfrac{(2x - 1)(6x) - 2(3x^2 + 6)}{(2x - 1)} \right)$

22. Find $\dfrac{dy}{dx}$ if $y^3 + 2y^2 = 4x - 12$.

(A) $\dfrac{4x}{3y^2 + 4y}$

(B) $\dfrac{4}{3y^2 + 4y}$

(C) $\dfrac{4}{y^3 + 2y^2}$

(D) $\dfrac{4x}{y^3 + 4y}$

(E) $\dfrac{4}{y^2 + y}$

23. Find $\dfrac{d^2y}{dx^2}$ if $y^3 + 2y^2 = 4x - 12$ and $y = 1$ at $x = 7$.

(A) $-\dfrac{111}{343}$

(B) $-\dfrac{33}{49}$

(C) $-\dfrac{4}{7}$

(D) $\dfrac{4}{7}$

(E) $\dfrac{33}{49}$

24. What is $\dfrac{dy}{dx}$ if $y = \log_3\left(4x^3 - 2x\right)$?

(A) $\dfrac{12x^2 - 2}{\left(2x^3 - x\right)\ln 3}$

(B) $\dfrac{6x^2 - 1}{\left(2x^3 - x\right)\ln 3}$

(C) $\dfrac{12x^2 - 1}{\left(4x^3 - 2x\right)\ln 3}$

(D) $\dfrac{6x^2 - 1}{\left(2x^3 - x\right)\ln 10}$

(E) $\dfrac{6x^2 - 1}{\left(2x^3 - 1\right)\ln 3}$

25. Find the derivative of the inverse of $y = x^4 - 3$ when $y = -2$.

(A) $\dfrac{1}{32}$

(B) $\dfrac{1}{4}$

(C) $\dfrac{1}{2}$

(D) 1

(E) $\dfrac{3}{2}$

26. Find $\dfrac{dy}{dx}$ for $4x^2 - 2x^2y + 2xy^2 - 3y^2 = x$ at $x = 1$.

(A) -4

(B) 0

(C) $-\dfrac{5}{4}$

(D) 1

(E) $-\dfrac{37}{4}$

27. If $f(x) = 2x^2 - 3x + 6$, find a derivative of $f^{-1}(x)$ at $y = 15$.

(A) $\dfrac{1}{9}$

(B) $-\dfrac{2}{9}$

(C) $\dfrac{2}{9}$

(D) 3

(E) $-\dfrac{3}{2}$

28. Find $\dfrac{dy}{dx}$ if $y = \dfrac{\left(3x^3 + 2\right)^2}{x-2}$.

(A) $\dfrac{y\left(18x^2\right)}{3x^3 + 2}$

(B) $y\left(\dfrac{1}{x-2}\right)$

(C) $y\left(\dfrac{18x^2}{3x^3 + 2} + \dfrac{1}{x-2}\right)$

(D) $y\left(\dfrac{18x^2}{3x^3 + 2} - \dfrac{1}{x-2}\right)$

(E) $\left(\dfrac{18x^2}{3x^3 + 2} + \dfrac{1}{x-2}\right)$

Chapter 12
Derivatives Drill 3
Answers and
Explanations

ANSWER KEY

1. D
2. A
3. B
4. C
5. B
6. E
7. B
8. D
9. C
10. D
11. A
12. C
13. D
14. B
15. E
16. C
17. C
18. A
19. B
20. E
21. A
22. B
23. A
24. B
25. B
26. E
27. A
28. D

EXPLANATIONS

1. **D**   Take the derivative implicitly with respect to x and isolate y'.

    $$x^6 + y^6 = 6$$

    $$6x^5 + 6y^5 \, y' = 0$$

    $$6y^5 \, y' = -6x^5$$

    $$y' = -\frac{x^5}{y^5}$$

2. **A**   You must find the derivative by utilizing the chain rule twice, as well as the trigonometric differentiation formula for the sine function.

    $$h(x) = f(g(\sin x))$$

    $$h'(x) = f'(g(\sin x)) \times g'(\sin x) \times \cos x$$

    $$h'(x) = \cos x \times f'(g(\sin x)) \times g'(\sin x)$$

3. **B**   You must take the derivative using the power and product rules first.

    $$f(x) = x^2 \, g(x)$$

    $$f'(x) = 2x \, g(x) + x^2 \, g'(x)$$

    To find what $f'(3)$ is equal to, you must use the other pieces of information and plug in accordingly.

    $$f'(3) = 2(3) \, g(3) + (3)^2 \, g'(3) = (6)(2) + (9)(1) = 21.$$

4. **C**   Take the derivative using the power rule and the trigonometric rule for the tangent function.

    $$y = 4x - \tan x$$

    $$y' = 4 - \sec^2 x$$

5. **B**   Take the derivative using the trigonometric rule for the cotangent function and the chain rule.

    $$y = \cot (3x^2 + 5)$$

    $$y' = -\csc^2 (3x^2 + 5) \times 6x$$

    $$y' = -6x \csc^2 (3x^2 + 5)$$

6.   **E**   Take the derivative using the trigonometric rules for the cosecant and cotangent functions, as well as the chain rule.

$$y = \csc(\cot x)$$

$$y' = -\csc(\cot x)\cot(\cot x) \times -\csc^2 x$$

$$y' = \csc^2 x \csc(\cot x)\cot(\cot x)$$

7.   **B**   Take the derivative using the trigonometric differentiation rules for the tangent and secant functions, as well as the chain rule.

$$y = \tan(\sec x)$$

$$y' = \sec^2(\sec x) \times \sec x \tan x$$

$$y' = \sec x \tan x \sec^2(\sec x)$$

8.   **D**   First, you must take the derivative using the chain rule twice.

$$r(x) = f(g(h(x)))$$

$$r'(x) = f'(g(h(x))) \times g'(h(x)) \times h'(x)$$

Evaluate the derivative at $x = 1$ using the information provided in the question.

$$r'(x) = f'(g(h(x))) \times g'(h(x)) \times h'(x)$$

$$r'(1) = f'(g(h(1))) \times g'(h(1)) \times h'(1)$$

$$r'(1) = f'(g(2)) \times g'(2) \times (4)$$

$$r'(1) = f'(3) \times (5) \times (4)$$

$$r'(1) = (6) \times (5) \times (4) = 120$$

9.   **C**   Take the derivative using the trigonometric differentiation rules for the cotangent and cosecant functions, as well as the chain rule.

$$y = \cot(\csc x)$$

$$y' = -\csc^2(\csc x)(-\csc x \cot x)$$

$$y' = \csc x \cot x \csc^2(\csc x)$$

10. **D** Take the derivative using the trigonometric differentiation rules for the secant and tangent functions, as well as the chain rule.

$y = \sec(\tan x)$

$y' = \sec(\tan x) \tan(\tan x) \times \sec^2 x$

$y' = \sec^2 x \sec(\tan x) \tan(\tan x)$

11. **A** Take the derivative of $F(x)$ using the chain rule.

$F(x) = f(3f(4f(x)))$

$F'(x) = f'(3f(4f(x))) \times 3 f'(4f(x)) \times 4 f'(x)$

Evaluate the derivative at $x = 0$ using the information provided in the question.

$F'(x) = f'(3f(4f(x))) \times 3 f'(4f(x)) \times 4 f'(x)$

$F'(0) = f'(3f(4f(0))) \times 3 f'(4f(0)) \times 4 f'(0)$

$F'(0) = f'(3f(4(0))) \times 3 f'(4(0)) \times 4(2)$

$F'(0) = f'(0) \times 3(2) \times 4(2)$

$F'(0) = (2) \times 3(2) \times 4(2) = 96$

12. **C** Calculate the derivative with respect to x.

$$3x^2 + 3y^2 \, y' = 0$$
$$3y^2 \, y' = -3x^2$$
$$y' = \frac{-x^2}{y^2}$$

13. **D** Calculate the derivative with respect to x.

$$2x + y \, xy' - 2y \, y' = 0$$
$$(x - 2y) \, y' = -(2x + y)$$
$$y' = \frac{2x + y}{2y - x}$$

14.　**B**　Calculate the derivative with respect to x.

$$3x^2 + 3y^2 \; y' = 6y + 6xy'$$
$$(3y^2 - 6x) \; y' = 6y - 3x^2$$
$$y' = \frac{6y - 3x^2}{3y^2 - 6x}$$

15.　**E**　Calculate the derivative with respect to x.

$$4\left[(-\sin x)(\sin y) + (\cos x)(\cos y) \; y'\right] = 0$$
$$\cos x \cos y \; y' = \sin x \sin y$$
$$y' = \tan x \tan y$$

16.　**C**　Calculate the derivative with respect to x.

$$3x^2 + 3y^2 \; y' = y + xy'$$
$$(3y^2 - x) \; y' = y - 3x^2$$
$$y' = \frac{y - 3x^2}{3y^2 - x}$$

17.　**C**　Calculate the derivative with respect to x.

$$1 = \frac{2x + 2y \; y'}{x^2 + y^2}$$
$$x^2 + y^2 = 2x + 2y \; y'$$
$$x^2 + y^2 - 2x = 2y \; y'$$
$$\frac{x^2 + y^2 - 2x}{2y} = y'$$

18.　**A**　Calculate the derivative with respect to x.

$$4x^3 + 4y^3 \; y' = 0$$
$$4y^3 \; y' = -4x^3$$
$$y' = -\frac{x^3}{y^3}$$

19. **B** Calculate the derivative with respect to x.

$$6x \sin y + 3x^2 \cos y \, y' = \sec^2 x$$
$$3x^2 \cos y \, y' = \sec^2 x - 6x \sin y$$
$$y' = \frac{\sec^2 x - 6x \sin y}{3x^2 \cos y}$$

20. **E** This problem can be solved using the Chain rule, Product rule, and Quotient rule, but that can get especially messy. We are going to use logarithmic differentiation to solve it. First, take the natural log of both sides: $\ln y = \ln\left(\dfrac{\left(x^3 - 2x^2\right)\sin^2 x}{\left(x^2 + 1\right)^3}\right)$. Use logarithmic rules to simplify the equation: $\ln y = \ln\left(x^3 - 2x^2\right) + 2\ln(\sin x) - 3\ln\left(x^2 + 1\right)$. Now, differentiate both sides with respect to x: $\dfrac{1}{y}\dfrac{dy}{dx} = \dfrac{3x - 4}{x^2 - 2x} + 2\cot x - \dfrac{6x}{x^2 + 1}$. Finally, isolate $\dfrac{dy}{dx}$: $\dfrac{dy}{dx} = y\left(\dfrac{3x - 4}{x^2 - 2x} + 2\cot x - \dfrac{6x}{x^2 + 1}\right)$.

21. **A** Use the chain and quotient rules: $\dfrac{dy}{dx} = 3\left(\dfrac{3x^2 + 6}{2x - 1}\right)^2\left(\dfrac{(2x - 1)(6x) - 2\left(3x^2 + 6\right)}{(2x - 1)^2}\right)$.

22. **B** Use implicit differentiation: $\dfrac{3y^2 dy}{dx} + 4y\dfrac{dy}{dx} = 4$. Thus, $\dfrac{dy}{dx} = \dfrac{4}{3y^2 + 4y}$.

23. **A** Via implicit differentiation, $\dfrac{dy}{dx} = \dfrac{4}{3y^2 + 4y}$ and $\dfrac{d^2 y}{dx^2} = \dfrac{\left(3y^2 + 4y\right) - 4(6y + 4)\left(\dfrac{dy}{dx}\right)}{\left(3y^2 + 4y\right)^2}$. Evaluate $\dfrac{dy}{dx}$ at $(7,1)$, to get, $\dfrac{dy}{dx} = \dfrac{4}{7}$. Plug in these points to solve $\dfrac{d^2 y}{dx^2} = -\dfrac{111}{343}$

24. **B** Recall, $\dfrac{dy}{dx} = \dfrac{1}{u\ln a}\left(\dfrac{du}{dx}\right)$. In this problem, $u = 4x^3 - 2x$ and $du = \left(12x^2 - 2\right)dx$. Thus, $\dfrac{dy}{dx} = \dfrac{12x^2 - 2}{\left(4x^3 - 2x\right)\ln 3} = \dfrac{6x^2 - 1}{\left(2x^3 - x\right)\ln 3}$.

25. **B** $\dfrac{d}{dx}f^{-1}(x)\big|_{x=c}=\dfrac{1}{[\frac{d}{dy}f(y)]_{y=a}}$. Here, $y=-2$ when $x=1$ and $\dfrac{dx}{dy}=\dfrac{1}{\frac{dy}{dx}}=\dfrac{1}{4x^3}$. Evaluate this deriva-

tive at $x=1$ to get the solution: $\dfrac{1}{4}$.

26. **E** First, plug $x=1$ into the equation and solve for y. The result will be two y values, $y=-3$ and $y=1$. Next, use

implicit differentiation to find the first derivative: $8x-2x^2\dfrac{dy}{dx}-4xy+4xy\dfrac{dy}{dx}+2y^2-6y\dfrac{dy}{dx}=1$.

Do not simplify because the questions asks for the derivative at $x=1$. Thus, the final step is to plug

$(1,1)$ and $(1,-3)$ into the equation for the first derivative and solve for the derivatives at these points.

At $(1,1)$, $\dfrac{dy}{dx}=\dfrac{5}{4}$. At $(1,-3)$, $\dfrac{dy}{dx}=-\dfrac{37}{4}$. Since the derivative at $(1,-3)$ is an option, the answer is E.

27. **A** The derivative of the inverse is: $\dfrac{d}{dx}f^{-1}(x)\big|_{x=c}=\dfrac{1}{\left[\dfrac{d}{dy}f(y)\right]_{y=a}}$. To begin, determine the x-val-

ue that corresponds to $y=15$. There are two possible x-values: $x=-\dfrac{3}{2}$ and $x=3$. Next, find the

derivative of the function $f(x)$: $f'(x)=4x-3$. Plug this into the left hand side of the formula

by first taking the inverse. Then, evaluate the function at both x-values: $\dfrac{1}{4x-3}\big|_{x=-\frac{3}{2}}=-\dfrac{1}{9}$ and

$\dfrac{1}{4x-3}\big|_{x=3}=\dfrac{1}{9}$.

28. **D** Because the quotient rule and chain rule would get messy here, use logarithmic dif-

ferentiation. First, take the natural log of both sides of the equation and simplify:

$\ln y=\ln\left(\dfrac{(3x^3+2)^2}{x-2}\right)=2\ln(3x^3+2)-\ln(x-2)$. Now, differentiate both sides using implicit

differentiation: $\dfrac{1}{y}\dfrac{dy}{dx}=\dfrac{18x^2}{3x^3+2}-\dfrac{1}{x-2}$. Solve for $\dfrac{dy}{dx}$: $\dfrac{dy}{dx}=y\left(\dfrac{18x^2}{3x^3+2}-\dfrac{1}{x-2}\right)$.

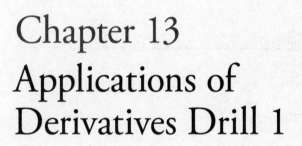

Chapter 13
Applications of
Derivatives Drill 1

APPLICATIONS OF DERIVATIVES DRILL 1

1. Find the equation of the line tangent to $y = \dfrac{2x}{(x+1)}$ at (1,1).

   (A) $x - 2y = -1$
   (B) $2x - y = 1$
   (C) $x - y = 2$
   (D) $x - 2y = 1$
   (E) $2x + y = 1$

2. If $f(x) = \sqrt{4x + 1}$, then find $f''(2)$.

   (A) -8

   (B) $-\dfrac{4}{27}$

   (C) 0

   (D) $\dfrac{4}{27}$

   (E) 8

3. Find the critical numbers of $y = 3x^4 + 4x^3 - 12x^2$.

   (A) 0
   (B) $-2, 1$
   (C) $0, 1$
   (D) $-2, 0, 1$
   (E) $-1, 0, 2$

4. What is the maximum value of $f(x) = 2x^3 - 3x^2 - 12x + 1$ on the interval $[-2,3]$?

   (A) -3
   (B) 0
   (C) 2
   (D) 6
   (E) 8

5. Find the interval(s) on which f is decreasing for $f(x) = 2x^3 + 3x^2 - 36x$.

   (A) $(-\infty,-3)$
   (B) $(-2,3)$
   (C) $(-3,2)$
   (D) $(2,3)$
   (E) $(2,\infty)$

6. Find all critical numbers of $y = 2x^3 - 3x^2 - 12x$.

   (A) -2
   (B) -1
   (C) $-2, -1$
   (D) $-1, \ 2$
   (E) $1, \ 2$

7. Find any points of inflection of $y = x^4 + 4x^3$.

   (A) $(-2,-16)$
   (B) $(0,0)$
   (C) $(2,16)$ and $(0,0)$
   (D) $(0,0)$ and $(-2,-16)$
   (E) $(2,16)$

8. Find the equation of the line tangent to $y = \sin(\sin x)$ at $(\pi, 0)$.

   (A) $x - y = \pi$
   (B) $x + y = \pi$
   (C) $2x - y = \pi$
   (D) $x - 2y = \pi$
   (E) $x + y = 2\pi$

9. Find the minimum value of $f(x) = 2x^3 + 3x^2 - 36x$.

   (A) -44
   (B) -9
   (C) 3
   (D) 9
   (E) 44

10. What is the point of inflection of $f(x) = (x + 1)^5 - 5x - 2$?

(A) $(-3,1)$
(B) $(-1,3)$
(C) $(0,0)$
(D) $(1,3)$
(E) $(3,1)$

11. On what interval(s) is f decreasing if $f(x) = 2 + 2x^2 - x^4$?

(A) $(-1,0)$ only
(B) $(1,\infty)$ only
(C) $(-\infty,-1)$ and $(0,1)$
(D) $(-1,0)$ and $(1,\infty)$
(E) $(0,1)$ only

12. A particle is traveling according to $f(x) = x^3 - 12x^2 + 36x$. What is the velocity at $x = 3$ seconds?

(A) -18
(B) -9
(C) 0
(D) 9
(E) 18

13. If a ball is thrown upward with a velocity of 80 ft/s, then its height after t seconds is $s = 80t - 16t^2$. What is the maximum height of the ball?

(A) 2.5
(B) 80
(C) 100
(D) 180
(E) 270

14. Find the equation of the normal line to the curve $y = \dfrac{\sqrt{x}}{(1 + x^2)}$ at $\left(1, \dfrac{1}{2}\right)$.

(A) $8x + 2y = 7$
(B) $2x + 8y = 7$
(C) $8x - 2y = 7$
(D) $2x - 8y = 7$
(E) $8x - 2y = -7$

15. For what values of x does the graph of $f(x) = x + 2\sin x$ have a horizontal tangent on $[0,2\pi]$?

(A) $\dfrac{\pi}{3}$ and $\dfrac{2\pi}{3}$

(B) $\dfrac{2\pi}{3}$ and $\dfrac{4\pi}{3}$

(C) $\dfrac{4\pi}{3}$ and $\dfrac{5\pi}{3}$

(D) $\dfrac{4\pi}{3}$ only

(E) no values

16. Find an equation of the tangent line to the curve $y = 2x \sin x$ at the point $\left(\dfrac{\pi}{2}, \pi\right)$.

(A) $y = 2x + \pi$

(B) $y = 2x - \pi$

(C) $y = 2x$

(D) $y = 2x + \left(\dfrac{\pi}{2}\right)$

(E) $y = 2x - \left(\dfrac{\pi}{2}\right)$

17. A particle travels in a position governed by the equation $s(t) = 4t^3 - 16t^2$. What is its acceleration at $t = 2$ seconds?

(A) 0
(B) 2
(C) 10
(D) 12
(E) 16

18. If a particle travels along a path according to the equation $s(t) = 6t^2 - 4t + 3$, then what is the velocity at $t = 2$ seconds?

(A) −20
(B) −10
(C) 0
(D) 10
(E) 20

19. Find the absolute maximum value of $f(x) = (x^2 + 2x)^3$ on the interval $[-2,1]$.

(A) − 2
(B) − 1
(C) 0
(D) 1
(E) 27

20. What is the x-coordinate of the point of inflection of $f(x) = 4x^3 + 3x^2 - 6x$?

(A) −4
(B) $-\dfrac{1}{4}$
(C) 0
(D) $\dfrac{1}{4}$
(E) 4

21. On what interval(s) is f decreasing for $f(x) = \dfrac{x^2}{(x^2 + 3)}$?

(A) $(-\infty,\infty)$
(B) $(-\infty,0)$
(C) $(0,\infty)$
(D) $(-\infty,-3)$
(E) $(-3,\infty)$

Questions 22–23 rely on the following information:

Suppose that $h(x) = f(x)\, g(x)$ and $F(x) = f(g(x))$, where $f(2) = 3$, $g(2) = 5$, $g'(2) = 4$, $f'(2) = -2$, and $f'(5) = 11$.

22. What is the value of $F'(2)$?

(A) 44
(B) 22
(C) 2
(D) −22
(E) −44

23. What is the value of $h'(2)$?

(A) 10
(B) 5
(C) 2
(D) −5
(E) −10

24. A particle moves on a vertical line so that its coordinate at time t is given by $y = t^3 - 12t + 3$, where $t \geq 0$. What is its acceleration at time t ?

(A) $\dfrac{1}{4}t^4 - 6t^2 + 3t + 1$
(B) $3t^2 - 12$
(C) $6t$
(D) 6
(E) 0

25. Find the equation of the tangent line to the equation $x^2 + xy + y^2 = 3$ at the point $(1,1)$.

(A) $x - y = -2$
(B) $x + y = -2$
(C) $2x + y = 2$
(D) $x - y = 2$
(E) $x + y = 2$

26. Find the equation of the tangent line to the equation $x^2 + 2xy - y^2 + x = 2$ at (1,2).

    (A) $x - 3y = 1$
    (B) $7x + 2y = 3$
    (C) $7x - 2y = 3$
    (D) $3x + y = 1$
    (E) $3x - y = 3$

27. What is the slope of the equation $\sin(xy) = 0$ at $\left(2, \dfrac{\pi}{2}\right)$?

    (A) $-\pi$
    (B) $-\dfrac{\pi}{2}$
    (C) $-\dfrac{\pi}{4}$
    (D) $-\dfrac{\pi}{6}$
    (E) $\dfrac{\pi}{4}$

Chapter 14
Applications of Derivatives Drill 1 Answers and Explanations

ANSWER KEY

1. A
2. B
3. E
4. E
5. C
6. D
7. D
8. B
9. A
10. B
11. D
12. B
13. C
14. C
15. B
16. C
17. E
18. E
19. E
20. D
21. B
22. A
23. C
24. C
25. E
26. C
27. C

EXPLANATIONS

1. **A**   Utilize the quotient rule to evaluate this derivative.

$$y' = \frac{\left[2(x+1) - 2x(1)\right]}{(x+1)^2}$$

Find the slope at (1,1) by plugging in 1 for x.

$$y' = \frac{\left[2(2) - 2(1)(1)\right]}{(1+1)^2} = \frac{2}{4} = \frac{1}{2}$$

Use the point-slope equation of a line to answer the question.

$$y - y_1 = m(x - x_1)$$
$$y - 1 = \frac{1}{2}(x - 1)$$
$$2y - 2 = x - 1$$
$$x - 2y = -1$$

2. **B**   This question is testing your knowledge of higher order derivatives and the chain rule. Start by calculating the first derivative.

$$f''(x) = \frac{1}{2}(4x+1)^{-\frac{1}{2}}(4)$$

$$= 2(4x+1)^{-\frac{1}{2}}$$

$$f''(x) = 2\left[-\frac{1}{2}(4x+1)^{-\frac{3}{2}}(4)\right]$$

Don't simplify! Plug in 2 for x.

$$f''(2) = 2\left[-\frac{1}{2}(4(2)+1)^{-\frac{3}{2}}(4)\right]$$

$$= -4\left(\frac{1}{27}\right)$$

$$= -\frac{4}{27}$$

3. **E**   This question is testing your knowledge of the first derivative and setting it equal to 0.

Find the derivative.

$$y' = 12x^3 + 12x^2 - 24x$$

Set it equal to 0 and solve for x.

$$y' = 12x(x^2 - x - 2) = 0$$

$$12x = 0 \text{ and } (x^2 - x - 2) = 0$$

$$x = 0 \text{ and } x = 2, -1.$$

4. **E** To find the maximum, you must take the derivative and test values around the critical numbers.

Take the derivative and set equal to 0 to find the critical numbers.

$$f'(x) = 6x^2 - 6x - 12 = 0$$

$$x^2 - x - 2 = 0$$

$$(x - 2)(x + 1) = 0$$

$$x = 2 \; ; x = -1$$

Test values around the critical numbers to determine behavior

$$f'(-2) = + \qquad\qquad f'(0) = - \qquad f'(3) = +$$

This tells us that before -1, f is increasing and after -1, f switches to decreasing, making $x = -1$ a relative maximum. To calculate the value, simply plug -1 into the original $f(x)$.

$$f(-1) = 2(-1)^3 - 3(-1)^2 - 12(-1) + 1$$

$$= -2 - 3 + 12 + 1 = 8.$$

Since we are asked to find the maximum over the closed interval $[-2,3]$, we must test the endpoints as being possible maximums before deciding on $f(-1)$. So,

$$f(-2) = 2(-2)^3 - 3(-2)^2 - 12(-2) + 1 = -3$$

$$f(3) = 2(3)^3 - 3(3)^2 - 12(3) + 1 = -8$$

Since neither of these are greater than $f(-1) = 8$, 8 is the maximum value.

5. **C** Take the derivative and set it equal to 0 to find the critical numbers.

$$f'(x) = 6x^2 + 6x - 36 = 0$$

$$x^2 + x - 6 = 0$$

$$(x + 3)(x - 2) = 0$$

$$x = -3 \; ; x = 2$$

Test values around the critical numbers to find where f is decreasing.

$$f'(-4) = + \qquad\qquad f'(0) = - \qquad\qquad f'(3) = +$$

This tells us the values in between -3 and 2 are where f is decreasing because the first derivative is negative over that interval.

6. **D**   Take the derivative and set it equal to 0. Remember that critical numbers are the x-values corresponding to when the first derivative is equal to zero.

$$y' = 6x^2 - 6x - 12 \ = 0$$

$$x^2 - x - 2 = 0$$

$$(x - 2)(x + 1) = 0$$

$$x = 2 \; ; x = -1$$

7. **D**   Find the second derivative of the function and set it equal to 0. Remember that points of inflection are found when the second derivative is equal to zero and solved; these are the points when the curve is changing concavity.

$$y' = 4x^3 + 12x^2$$
$$y'' = 12x^2 + 24x = 0$$
$$12x(x + 2) = 0$$
$$x = 0 \; ; x = -2$$

Find the points by plugging the x-values into the original function.

$$y = (0)^4 + 4(0)^3 = 0 \quad ; \qquad y = (-2)^4 + 4(-2)^3 = -16$$
$$(0,0) \qquad\qquad\qquad\qquad (-2,-16)$$

8. **B**   Find the derivative using trigonometric formulas and the chain rule.

$$y' = \cos (\sin x) \times \cos x$$

Plug in $x = \pi$ to find the slope.

$$m = \cos (\sin \pi) \times \cos \pi$$
$$= \cos (0) \times (-1)$$
$$= (1) \times (-1)$$
$$= -1$$

Use the point-slope equation of a line to answer the question.

$$y - y_1 = m(x - x_1)$$
$$y - 0 = -1(x - \pi)$$
$$y = -x + \pi$$
$$x + y = \pi$$

9. **A** Find the derivative and set it equal to 0 to find the critical points.

$$f'(x) = 6x^2 + 6x - 36 = 0$$
$$x^2 + x - 6 = 0$$
$$(x - 2)(x + 3) = 0$$
$$x = 2 \; ; x = -3$$

Test values around the critical points to see the behavior of f.

$$f'(-4) = + \qquad\qquad f'(0) = - \qquad\qquad f'(3) = +$$

Since f is decreasing before 2 and increasing after it, $x = 2$ is a relative minimum.

Plug 2 into the original function to find the minimum value.

$$f(2) = 2(2)^3 + 3(2)^2 - 36(2)$$
$$= 16 + 12 - 72$$
$$= -44$$

10. **B** Get the 2nd derivative and set it equal to 0.

$$f'(x) = 5(x + 1)^4 - 5$$
$$f''(x) = 20(x + 1)^3 = 0$$
$$(x + 1)^3 = 0$$
$$x + 1 = 0$$
$$x = -1$$

Plug -1 into the original function to find the y-coordinate.

$$f(-1) = (-1 + 1)^5 - 5(-1) - 2$$
$$= 3$$

11. **D** Find the derivative and set it equal to 0.

$$f'(x) = 4x - 4x^3 = 0$$
$$4x(1-x^2) = 0$$
$$x = 0 \ ; \ x = 1 \ ; \ x = -1$$

Test values around the critical numbers to see the behavior of f.

$$f'(-2) = + \quad f'\left(-\frac{1}{2}\right) = - \quad f'\left(\frac{1}{2}\right) = + \quad f'(2) = -$$

Since f' is negative on two of the four test points, the interval over which f is decreasing is $(-1, 0)$ and $(1, \infty)$.

12. **B** Since the derivative of a position function is the velocity, we must find the first derivative.

$$f'(x) = 3x^2 - 24x + 36$$

Plug in 3 to find the instantaneous velocity.

$$f'(3) = 3(3)^2 - 24(3) + 36 = -9$$

13. **C** To determine where the ball is at a relative maximum, take the first derivative and set it equal to 0.

$$s' = 80 - 32t = 0$$

$$80 = 32t$$

$$\frac{5}{2} = t$$

Test values around $\frac{5}{2}$ to know the behavior of s.

$$s'(2) = + \quad s'(3) = -$$

Since s is increasing before $\frac{5}{2}$ and decreasing after it, $\frac{5}{2}$ is a relative max.

Plug in $\frac{5}{2}$ to the position function to find the maximum height.

$$s\left(\frac{5}{2}\right) = 80\left(\frac{5}{2}\right) - 16\left(\frac{5}{2}\right)^2 = 200 - 100 = 100$$

14. **C** Find the derivative.

$$y' = \frac{\left(\frac{1}{2}x^{-\frac{1}{2}}\right)(1+x^2) - (\sqrt{x})(2x)}{(1+x^2)^2}$$

Don't simplify! Plug in $x = 1$ to find the slope.

$$m = \frac{\left(\dfrac{1}{2}\right)(1)(2) - (1)(2)}{(2)^2}$$

$$= -\frac{1}{4}$$

Find the normal slope by taking the negative reciprocal and use that in the point-slope formula for a line.

$$m_{normal} = 4$$

$$y - y_1 = m(x - x_1)$$

$$y - \frac{1}{2} = 4\,(x - 1)$$

$$2y - 1 = 8(x - 1)$$

$$2y - 1 = 8x - 8$$

$$7 = 8x - 2y$$

15. **B** Take the derivative and set it equal to 0 because a horizontal tangent is a line with the slope of 0.

$$f'(x) = 1 + 2\cos x = 0$$

$$1 = -2\cos x$$

$$-\frac{1}{2} = \cos x$$

$$\frac{2\pi}{3}, \frac{4\pi}{3} = x$$

16. **C** Find an equation of the tangent line to the curve $y = 2x \sin x$ at the point $\left(\dfrac{\pi}{2}, \pi\right)$.

Find the derivative.

$$y' = 2\sin x + 2x\cos x$$

Don't simplify! Plug in $\dfrac{\pi}{2}$ to find the slope.

$$m = 2\sin\left(\frac{\pi}{2}\right) + 2\left(\frac{\pi}{2}\right)\cos\left(\frac{\pi}{2}\right)$$

$$= 2\,(1) + 0$$

$$= 2$$

Use the point-slope formula for a line to find the equation.

$$y - y_1 = m(x - x_1)$$

$$y - \pi = 2\left(x - \frac{\pi}{2}\right)$$

$$y - \pi = 2x - \pi$$

$$y = 2x$$

17. **E** When given the position function, taking the first derivative will yield the velocity and taking the second derivative will yield the acceleration.

Take the second derivative and plug in $t = 2$.

$$s'(t) = v(t) = 12t^2 - 32t$$
$$s''(t) = v'(t) = a(t) = 24t - 32$$
$$a(2) = 24(2) - 32 = 16.$$

18. **E** When given the position function, simply take the first derivative to find the velocity function.

$$s(t) = 6t^2 - 4t + 3$$
$$v(t) = s'(t) = 12t - 4$$

Plug in 2 for t to find the velocity.

$$v(2) = 12(2) - 4 = 20$$

19. **E** Take the derivative using the chain rule and then set it equal to zero to find any critical points of the function.

$$f(x) = (x^2 + 2x)^3$$
$$f'(x) = 3(x^2 + 2x)^2(2x + 2) = 0$$

$3(x^2 + 2x) = 0$	$(2x + 2) = 0$
$x^2 + 2x = 0$	$2(x + 1) = 0$
$x(x + 2) = 0$	$x + 1 = 0$
$x = 0 \; ; x = -2$	$x = -1$

To find the absolute maximum value of a function, you must plug critical points as well as interval endpoints into the original function to find the greatest output. Since –2 is already an endpoint on the interval, you only need to check it once.

$f(-2) = (4 - 4)^3 = 0$	$f(0) = (0 + 0)^3 = 0$
$f(-1) = (1 - 2)^3 = -1$	$f(1) = (1 + 2)^3 = 27$

20. **D** To find the *x*-coordinate of the point of inflection, you must take the second derivative of the function and set it equal to zero. To do this, you must differentiate according to the power rule of derivatives.

$$f(x) = 4x^3 + 3x^2 - 6x$$
$$f'(x) = 12x^2 + 6x - 6$$
$$f''(x) = 24x + 6 = 0$$
$$24x = -6$$
$$x = -\frac{1}{4}$$

21. **B** Take the first derivative using the quotient rule and set it equal to zero.

$$f(x) = \frac{x^2}{(x^2 + 3)}$$
$$f'(x) = \frac{(2x)(x^2 + 3) - (x^2)(2x)}{(x^2 + 3)^2}$$
$$f'(x) = \frac{2x^3 + 6x - 2x^3}{(x^2 + 3)^2}$$
$$f'(x) = \frac{6x}{(x^2 + 3)^2} = 0$$
$$6x = 0$$
$$x = 0$$

Test values of $x = -1$ and $x = 1$ to determine the behavior of *f*.

$$f'(-1) = -$$
$$f'(1) = +$$
f is decreasing on $(-\infty, 0)$

22. **A** You must first take the derivative of $F(x)$ using the chain rule.

$$F(x) = f(g(x))$$

$$F'(x) = f'(g(x)) \times g'(x)$$

To figure out the value of $F'(2)$, you must use the other information provided in the initial given paragraph.

$$F'(2) = f'(g(2)) \times g'(2) = f'(5) \times (4) = (11)(4) = 44$$

23. **C** You must first take the derivative of $h(x)$ using the product rule.

$h(x) = f(x)g(x)$

$h'(x) = f'(x)g(x) + f(x)\, g'(x)$

To figure out the value of $h'(2)$, you must use the other information provided in the initial given paragraph.

$h'(2) = f'(2)\, g(2) + f(2)\, g'(2) = (-2)(5) + (3)(4) = 2$

24. **C** To find the acceleration at time t, you must take the derivative of the given position function twice.

$y = t^3 - 12t + 3$

$y' = 3t^2 - 12$

$y'' = 6t$

25. **E** Take the derivative with respect to x using the power rule and product rule.

$x^2 + xy + y^2 = 3$
$2x + y + xy' + 2y\, y' = 0$

Don't simplify! Plug in the coordinate immediately to solve for the slope.

$$2x + y + xy' + 2y\, y' = 0 \quad \text{at} \quad (1,1)$$
$$2(1) + (1) + (1)\, y' + 2(1)\, y' = 0$$
$$2 + 1 + y' + 2\, y' = 0$$
$$3\, y' = -3$$
$$y' = -1$$

Use the point-slope formula to find the equation of the tangent line at $(1,1)$.

$y - y_1 = m(x - x_1)$
$y - 1 = -1(x - 1)$
$y - 1 = -x + 1$
$x + y = 2$

26. **C** Take the derivative with respect to x using the power rule and the product rule.

$x^2 + 2xy - y^2 + x = 2$
$2x + 2(y + xy') - 2y\, y' + 1 = 0$

Don't simplify! Plug in the coordinate immediately to solve for the slope.

$$2x + 2(y + xy') - 2y \, y' + 1 = 0 \quad \text{at} \quad (1,2)$$
$$2(1) + 2((2) + (1) \, y') - 2(2) \, y' + 1 = 0$$
$$2 + 4 + 2 \, y' - 4 \, y' + 1 = 0$$
$$7 - 2 \, y' = 0$$
$$7 = 2 \, y'$$
$$\frac{7}{2} = y'$$

Use the point-slope formula to find the equation of the tangent line at (1,2).

$$y - y_1 = m(x - x_1)$$
$$y - 2 = \frac{7}{2}(x - 1)$$
$$y - 2 = \frac{7}{2}x - \frac{7}{2}$$
$$2y - 4 = 7x - 7$$
$$7x - 2y = 3$$

27. **C** Take the derivative with respect to x using the differentiation formula for the sine function, the chain rule, and the power rule.

$$\sin(xy) = 0$$
$$\cos(xy) \times (y + xy') = 0$$

Don't simplify! Plug in the coordinate point immediately

$$\cos\left(2 \cdot \frac{\pi}{2}\right) \cdot \left(\frac{\pi}{2} + 2y'\right) = 0$$
$$\left(\frac{\pi}{2}\right)\cos(\pi) + 2\cos(\pi) \, y' = 0$$
$$-\left(\frac{\pi}{2}\right) - 2y' = 0$$
$$-2y' = \frac{\pi}{2}$$
$$y' = -\frac{\pi}{4}$$

APPLICATIONS OF DERIVATIVES DRILL 2

Chapter 15
Applications of
Derivatives Drill 2

APPLICATIONS OF DERIVATIVES DRILL 2

1. What is the equation of a parabola $y = ax^2 + bx + c$ that passes through $(1, 4)$ and whose tangent lines at $x = -1$ and $x = 5$ have slopes 6 and -2, respectively?

   (A) $y = \dfrac{2}{3}x^2 + \dfrac{14}{3}x$

   (B) $y = \dfrac{14}{3}x^2 + \dfrac{2}{3}x$

   (C) $y = \dfrac{2}{3}x^2 - \dfrac{14}{3}x$

   (D) $y = -\dfrac{14}{3}x^2 - \dfrac{2}{3}x$

   (E) $y = -\dfrac{2}{3}x^2 + \dfrac{14}{3}x$

2. At what point(s) on the curve $y = \sin x + \cos x$, $0 \leq x \leq 2\pi$, is the tangent line horizontal?

   (A) $\left(\dfrac{\pi}{4}, \sqrt{2} \right)$

   (B) $\left(\dfrac{\pi}{4}, \sqrt{2} \right)$ and $\left(\dfrac{5\pi}{4}, \sqrt{2} \right)$

   (C) $\left(\dfrac{5\pi}{4}, -\sqrt{2} \right)$

   (D) $\left(\dfrac{5\pi}{4}, \sqrt{2} \right)$

   (E) $\left(\dfrac{\pi}{4}, -\sqrt{2} \right)$ and $\left(\dfrac{5\pi}{4}, \sqrt{2} \right)$

3. The volume of a cube is increasing at a rate of 10 cm³/min. How fast is the surface area increasing when the length of an edge is 30 cm?

   (A) $\dfrac{4}{3}$ cm²/min

   (B) $\dfrac{3}{4}$ cm²/min

   (C) $\dfrac{3}{2}$ cm²/min

   (D) $\dfrac{2}{3}$ cm²/min

   (E) $\dfrac{5}{4}$ cm²/min

4. How long does it take for a ball to reach 35 m/s if it is pushed down a hill and its position at time t, in seconds, is given by $s = 5t + 3t^2$, in meters?

   (A) 2 seconds
   (B) 3 seconds
   (C) 4 seconds
   (D) 5 seconds
   (E) 6 seconds

5. What is the maximum height reached by a ball if it travels according to the function $s = 80t - 16t^2$, in meters?

   (A) 100
   (B) 80
   (C) 60
   (D) 50
   (E) 40

6. What is an equation of the line tangent to $y^2 = x^3 + 3x^2$ at the point $(1, -2)$?

   (A) $4x + 9y = 1$
   (B) $9x - 4y = 1$
   (C) $4x - 9y = 1$
   (D) $4y - 9x = 1$
   (E) $9x + 4y = 1$

7. Find the point on the curve $y = x^{\frac{1}{2}}$ that is a minimum distance from the point (16,0).

(A) $\left(\dfrac{7}{2}, \sqrt{\dfrac{7}{2}}\right)$

(B) $(16,4)$

(C) $\left(\dfrac{31}{2}, \sqrt{\dfrac{31}{2}}\right)$

(D) $\left(\dfrac{33}{2}, \sqrt{\dfrac{33}{2}}\right)$

(E) $\left(2, \sqrt{2}\right)$

8. A cone-shaped funnel has a diameter of 10 m and a height of 12 m. Find the error in the volume if the height is exact, but the diameter is 10.2 m.

(A) $4\pi\, m^3$

(B) $12\pi\, m^3$

(C) $\dfrac{5}{3}\pi\, m^3$

(D) $20\pi\, m^3$

(E) $\dfrac{5}{6}\pi\, m^3$

9. Find the length of the curve $x = t^2 + 3$ and $y = 2t^2 - 7$ from $t = 2$ to $t = 5$.

(A) 156
(B) 78
(C) $75\sqrt{5}$
(D) $39\sqrt{5}$
(E) $21\sqrt{5}$

10. Find a point on the curve $y = x^3 - 4x^2 - 3x + 13$ where the normal is parallel to the y-axis.

(A) $(3,-5)$

(B) $\left(-\dfrac{1}{3}, -\dfrac{365}{27}\right)$

(C) $(0,0)$

(D) $(3,5)$

(E) $\left(\dfrac{1}{3}, \dfrac{365}{27}\right)$

11. Find the slope of the tangent line to the curve $r = 2 + 3\sin\theta$.

(A) $\dfrac{3\sin 2\theta + 2\cos\theta}{3\cos^2\theta - 2\sin\theta - 3\sin\theta\cos\theta}$

(B) $\dfrac{3\sin 2\theta + 2\cos\theta}{3\cos^2\theta - 2\sin\theta + 3\sin\theta\cos\theta}$

(C) $\dfrac{3\sin\theta\cos\theta + 2\cos\theta}{3\sin^2\theta - 2\sin\theta - 3\sin\theta\cos\theta}$

(D) $\dfrac{3\sin\theta\cos\theta - 2\cos\theta}{3\sin^2\theta - 2\sin\theta - 3\sin\theta\cos\theta}$

(E) $\dfrac{3\sin 2\theta + 2\cos\theta}{3\cos^2\theta + 2\sin\theta + 3\sin\theta\cos\theta}$

12. Find the equation of the line tangent to the curve $3x^3 - 2x^2 + x = y^3 + 2y^2 + 3y$ at $y = -2$.

(A) $y = 2x - 1$
(B) $y = 2x$
(C) $y = \dfrac{45}{2}x$
(D) $y = \dfrac{6}{23}x$
(E) $y = 2x - 2$

13. The curve $y = ax^3 + bx^2 + cx + d$ passes through the point $(2, 8)$ and is normal to $y = -\dfrac{1}{3}x - 4$ at $(0, -4)$. If $b = 5$, what is the value of a?

(A) -2

(B) $-\dfrac{7}{4}$

(C) $-\dfrac{3}{2}$

(D) -1

(E) $-\dfrac{1}{2}$

14. At what time does the particle change direction if the position function is given by $x(t) = 2x^4 - 4x^3 + 2x^2 - 8$, where $t > 0$?

(A) $\dfrac{1}{4}$

(B) 1

(C) $\dfrac{3}{2}$

(D) 2

(E) $\dfrac{5}{2}$

15. What is the particle's velocity $\left(\dfrac{dy}{dx}\right)$ at $t = 3$ if $x = 3x^3 - 2x^2 + 4$ and $y = 2x^2 + 3x - 7$?

(A) 69

(B) 15

(C) $\dfrac{5}{23}$

(D) 4

(E) $\dfrac{23}{5}$

16. Use differentials to approximate $(5.2)^3$.

(A) 125
(B) 130
(C) 135
(D) 140
(E) 145

17. The radius of a cylinder is increased from 9 to 9.03 inches. If the height remains constant at 12 inches. Estimate the change in volume.

(A) 0.005π in^3
(B) 3.24π in^3
(C) 6.48π in^3
(D) 9π in^3
(E) 12π in^3

18. Use differentials to approximate $\cos 275°$.

(A) $\dfrac{\pi}{72}$

(B) $\dfrac{\pi}{36}$

(C) $\dfrac{\pi}{18}$

(D) $\dfrac{\pi}{9}$

(E) $\dfrac{\pi}{3}$

19. Find the length of the curve $y = \dfrac{4}{3}x^{\frac{3}{2}}$ from $x = 0$ to $x = 6$.

(A) $\dfrac{59}{3}$

(B) 20

(C) $\dfrac{61}{3}$

(D) $\dfrac{62}{3}$

(E) 21

20. If $x^2 + y^2 = 25$, then find the slope of the tangent that passes through the point(2,4).

(A) -1

(B) $-\dfrac{1}{2}$

(C) 0

(D) $\dfrac{1}{2}$

(E) 1

21. Find the equation of the tangent line to the curve $x^2 + xy + y^2 = 3$ at (1,1).

(A) $3x - y = 2$
(B) $x - y = 2$
(C) $3x + y = 2$
(D) $x + y = 2$
(E) $x - 3y = -2$

22. What is the slope of the line normal to the curve $f(x) = x^4 + 3x^2$ that passes through the point (2,1)?

(A) 44

(B) $\dfrac{1}{44}$

(C) 0

(D) $-\dfrac{1}{44}$

(E) -44

23. What dimensions must a rectangle have to maximize the area and have a perimeter of 100 meters?

(A) 40 m by 10 m
(B) 45 m by 5 m
(C) 35 m by 15 m
(D) 30 m by 20 m
(E) 25 m by 25 m

24. What two positive numbers not only yield a minimum sum, but also produce a product of 100?

(A) 50 and 2
(B) 25 and 4
(C) 10 and 10
(D) 20 and 5
(E) 100 and 1

25. What two numbers both have a sum of 23 and a product that is maximized?

(A) 12 and 11
(B) 11.5 and 11.5
(C) 10 and 13
(D) 9.5 and 13.5
(E) 8 and 15

26. If $y = 4x^3 - 9x^2 + 6x$, then what is the value of the relative minimum, if any?

(A) -1

(B) 0

(C) $\dfrac{1}{2}$

(D) 1

(E) 2

Chapter 16
Applications of
Derivatives Drill 2
Answers and
Explanations

ANSWER KEY

1. E
2. B
3. A
4. D
5. A
6. E
7. C
8. A
9. E
10. A
11. A
12. B
13. B
14. B
15. C
16. D
17. C
18. B
19. D
20. B
21. D
22. D
23. E
24. C
25. B
26. D

EXPLANATIONS

1. **E** First, you must take the derivative of the given function, keeping in mind that a, b, and c all represent constants, not variables.

$$y = ax^2 + bx + c$$

$$y' = 2ax + b$$

Given the 2 coordinates and their respective slopes, you are able to come up with two linear equations relating a and b, which can be solved to determine the individual values.

$$y'(-1) = 2a(-1) + b = 6 \text{ and } y'(5) = 2a(5) + b = -2$$

So, the equations are $-2a + b = 6$ and $10a + b = -2$.

Stack the equations on top of one another to start solving for the constants. You can eliminate b entirely by subtracting the two equations.

$$\begin{array}{r} -2a + b = 6 \\ -(10a + b = -2) \\ \hline -12a = 8 \\ a = -\dfrac{2}{3} \end{array}$$

Plugging the value of a into either equation yields $b = \dfrac{14}{3}$.

Now that you know the values of a and b, you must go back to the original function given and use the given coordinate to determine the value of c.

$$y = ax^2 + bx + c$$

$$y = -\frac{2}{3}x^2 + \frac{14}{3}x + c$$

Now, plug in the coordinate.

$$4 = -\frac{2}{3}(1)^2 + \frac{14}{3}(1) + c$$

$$4 = -\frac{2}{3} + \frac{14}{3} + c$$

$$0 = c$$

So, the equation of the parabola is $y = -\dfrac{2}{3}x^2 + \dfrac{14}{3}x$.

2. **B** You must take the derivative of the function using the trigonometric differentiation rules for the sine and cosine functions, and then set it equal to zero to find the critical points.

$y = \sin x + \cos x$

$y' = \cos x - \sin x = 0$

$\cos x = \sin x$

$1 = \tan x$

$\dfrac{\pi}{4}, \dfrac{5\pi}{4} = x$

To find the points, you must plug the values of x you found in step one into the original given function.

$$y = \sin\left(\dfrac{\pi}{4}\right) + \cos\left(\dfrac{\pi}{4}\right) \quad \text{and} \quad y = \sin\left(\dfrac{5\pi}{4}\right) + \cos\left(\dfrac{5\pi}{4}\right)$$

$$y = \dfrac{\sqrt{2}}{2} + \dfrac{\sqrt{2}}{2} \quad \text{and} \quad y = -\dfrac{\sqrt{2}}{2} - \dfrac{\sqrt{2}}{2}$$

$$y = \sqrt{2} \quad \text{and} \quad y = -\sqrt{2}$$

The points are $\left(\dfrac{\pi}{4}, \sqrt{2}\right)$ and $\left(\dfrac{5\pi}{4}, -\sqrt{2}\right)$.

3. **A** The key to success in any related rates question is to clearly identify what you have and what you need to solve for.

Given: $\dfrac{dV}{dt} = 10 \text{ cm}^3 / \min$ and $s = 30$ cm.

Solve for: $\dfrac{dA}{dt}$.

Recall the formula for volume of a cube ($V = s^3$) and surface area of a cube ($A = 6s^2$). You must take the derivatives of each so you can see what they have in common.

$V = s^3$ $\qquad\qquad\qquad\qquad$ $A = 6s^2$

$\dfrac{dV}{dt} = 3s^2 \dfrac{ds}{dt}$ $\qquad\qquad\qquad$ $\dfrac{dA}{dt} = 12s \dfrac{ds}{dt}$

You must use the volume equation first because you need to calculate a value for $\frac{ds}{dt}$ to use in the surface area equation.

$$\frac{dV}{dt} = 3s^2 \frac{ds}{dt}$$

$$10 \text{ cm}^3 / \text{min} = 3(30 \text{ cm})^2 \frac{ds}{dt}$$

$$10 \text{ cm}^3 / \text{min} = 2700 \text{ cm}^2 \frac{ds}{dt}$$

$$\frac{1}{270} \text{ cm}^3 / \text{min} = \frac{ds}{dt}$$

Use the value calculated for $\frac{ds}{dt}$ in the surface area equation now to solve for $\frac{dA}{dt}$.

$$\frac{dA}{dt} = 12s \frac{ds}{dt}$$

$$\frac{dA}{dt} = 12(30 \text{ cm}) \left(\frac{1}{270} \text{ cm} / \text{min} \right)$$

$$\frac{dA}{dt} = \frac{4}{3} \text{ cm}^2 / \text{min}$$

4. **D** Since the question gives you a velocity, you must take the derivative of the position function to attain the velocity function. When you have that, set the two equal to each other and solve for t.

$s = 5t + 3t^2$

$s' = 5 + 6t = 35$

$6t = 30$

$t = 5$ seconds

5. **A** Take the derivative and set it equal to zero to determine the critical numbers of s.

$s = 80t - 16t^2$

$s' = 80 - 32t = 0$

$-32t = -80$

$t = \frac{5}{2}$

Test values around the critical number to determine the behavior of s and confirm that $t = \frac{5}{2}$ is a maximum.

$s'(2) = +$; $s'(3) = -$

To find the height, plug $\left(\dfrac{5}{2}\right)$ in to the original function given.

$$s\left(\frac{5}{2}\right) = 80\left(\frac{5}{2}\right) - 16\left(\frac{5}{2}\right)^2 = 200 - 100 = 100$$

6. **E** Take the derivative implicitly with respect to x.

$y^2 = x^3 + 3x^2$

$2y\ y' = 3x^2 + 6x$

Do not simplify! Plug in the point immediately to find the slope.

$2(-2)\ y' = 3(1)^2 + 6(1)$

$-4\ y' = 9$

$y' = -\dfrac{9}{4}$

Use the point-slope equation of a line to find the equation.

$y - y_1 = m(x - x_1)$

$y - (-2) = \left(-\dfrac{9}{4}\right)(x - 1)$

$4y + 8 = -9x + 9$

$9x + 4y = 1$

7. **C** The distance between the point (16,0) and the curve is found by using the Pythagorean theorem, specifically the equation for the distance can be set up as: $D^2 = (x - 16)^2 + (y - 0)^2 = x^2 - 32x + 256 + y^2$. When y is replaced with the equation of the curve $y = \sqrt{x}$, the equation becomes $D^2 = x^2 - 32x + 256 + x = x^2 - 31x + 256$. Rename as L, such that $D^2 = L$, then take the derivative of L. Set the derivative equal to zero to minimize (or maximize) the distance and solve for x. $\dfrac{dL}{dx} = 2x - 31 = 0;\ x = \dfrac{31}{2}$. Find the corresponding y-value, $\sqrt{\dfrac{31}{2}}$. To determine whether this point is a minimum or maximum, find the second derivative of L. $\dfrac{d^2L}{dx^2} = 2$. Since the second derivative is positive, the point is a relative minimum.

8. **A** In order to approximate the error in the volume of the cone use the approximation formula: $dy = f'(x)dx$. For this problem, $f(x) = V = \frac{1}{3}\pi r^2 h$, $f'(x) = \frac{dV}{dr} = \frac{2}{3}\pi rh = 40\pi$, and $dx = dr = 0.1$. Recall that the diameter is given, so we need to divide that measure in half to get the radius. When these values are input into the equation is $dy = dV = 40\pi(0.1) = 4\pi \, m^3$.

9. **E** The length of a curve described parametrically is found by using $L = \int_a^b \sqrt{\left(\frac{dx}{dt}\right)^2 + \left(\frac{dy}{dt}\right)^2} \, dt$. In this problem, $a = 2$ and $b = 5$; $\frac{dx}{dt} = 2t$ and $\frac{dy}{dt} = 4t$. So the length of the curve is $L = \int_2^5 \sqrt{(2t)^2 + (4t)^2} \, dt = 2\sqrt{5} \int_2^5 t^2 \, dt = 21\sqrt{5}$.

10. **A** Since the normal is parallel to the y-axis, the tangent to this curve will be perpendicular to the y-axis (opposite reciprocals). Thus, $\frac{dy}{dx} = 0$. Taking the first derivative of y, and setting it equal to zero, we can determine the x-coordinate of the point: $\frac{dy}{dx} = 3x^2 - 8x - 3 = 0$; $x = -\frac{1}{3}$ or $x = 3$. When these x-values are plugged into y, the two possible points are: $\left(-\frac{1}{3}, \frac{365}{27}\right)$ and $(3, -5)$.

11. **A** $\frac{dy}{dx} = \frac{f'(\theta)\sin\theta + f(\theta)\cos\theta}{f'(\theta)\cos\theta - f(\theta)\sin\theta}$. For this problem,

$f'(\theta) = 3\cos\theta$ and $\frac{dy}{dx} = \frac{3\cos\theta\sin\theta + (2 + 3\sin\theta)\cos\theta}{3\cos^2\theta - (2 + 3\sin\theta)\sin\theta}$.

With algebra and trig identities, the final solution is A.

12. **B** First, plug $y = -2$ into the equation: $3x^3 - 2x^2 + x + 6 = 0$. Remember, the AP writers will not give you a very complicated equation that you cannot factor, so always test "easy" values first. For example, test $x = 1$, $x = -1$, $x = 0$, and if necessary, $x = 2$ and $x = -2$. In this case, $x = -1$ works, so the point that the line will be tangent to is $(-1, -2)$. Next, use implicit differentiation to find the first derivative of the equation: $9x^2 - 4x + 1 = 3y^2 \frac{dy}{dx} + 4y \frac{dy}{dx} + 3 \frac{dy}{dx}$. Do not simplify; immediately plug in the point $(-1, -2)$ and solve for $\frac{dy}{dx}$. Thus, the slope of the tangent will be 2. Finally, plug in the point and slope into the equation of the line: $y + 2 = 2(x + 1)$. Simplified, the equation of the line is $y = 2x$.

13. **B** First, plug in the second point, $(0,-4)$, and solve for d: $d = -4$. Next, plug in the first point, $(2,8)$, into the equation along with $d = -4$: $12 = 8a + 4b + 2c$. Now, because the curve is normal to the line $y = -\dfrac{1}{3}x - 4$, the first derivative at $(0,-4)$ is 3. Thus, take the first derivative of the equation for the curve: $\dfrac{dy}{dx} = 3ax^2 + 2bx + c$. Set the first derivative equal to 3 and plug in $x = 0$: $3 = 3a(0)^2 + 2b(0) + c$. This gives you $c = 3$. You were told $b = 5$ in the question stem, so, to solve for a, plug in the values of b, c, and d into the reduced equation, $12 = 8a + 4b + 2c$, and solve for a. Therefore, $a = -\dfrac{7}{4}$.

14. **B** To determine when the particle changes direction, take the first derivative and set it equal to zero; the particle changes direction when the velocity is equal to zero. $x'(t) = 8x^3 - 12x^2 + 4x = 0$. The particle then changes direction at $x = 0$, $x = \dfrac{1}{2}$, and $x = 1$.

15. **C** First take the derivative of each parametric function: $\dfrac{dx}{dt} = 9x^2 - 4x$ and $\dfrac{dy}{dt} = 4x + 3$. Now evaluate each of these derivatives at $t = 3$, $\dfrac{dx}{dt} = 69$ and $\dfrac{dy}{dt} = 15$. Finally, the particle's velocity, $\dfrac{dy}{dx} = \dfrac{\dfrac{dy}{dt}}{\dfrac{dx}{dt}} = \dfrac{15}{69} = \dfrac{5}{23}$.

16. **D** The formula for differentials is $f(x + \Delta x) = f(X) + f'(x)\Delta x$. For this question, $f(x) = x^3, f'(x) = 3x^2, x = 5$, and $\Delta x = 0.2$.

Plug in those values: $(5.02)^3 = 5^3 + 3(5)^2(0.2) = 140$.

17. **C** The formula for the volume of a cylinder is $V = \pi r^2 h$. The first derivative is $\dfrac{dV}{dr} = 2\pi rh$. Use differentials to solve for the approximate change in volume: $dV = 2\pi rh\, dr$. Plug in the given values, where $dr = 0.03$, and solve for dV: $dV = 2\pi(9)(12)(0.03) = 6.48\pi$ in^3.

18. **B** When dealing with trig functions, the formula for differentials, $f(x + \Delta x) = f(x) + f'(x)\Delta x$, will not work in degrees, only radians. So, first determine the values of x and Δx in radians:

$x = 270° = \dfrac{3\pi}{2}$ radians and $\Delta x = 5° = \dfrac{\pi}{36}$ radians. Note, $f(x) = \cos x$ and $f'(x) = -\sin x$. Plug everything into the formula for differentials: $\cos 275° = \cos\left(\dfrac{3\pi}{2}\right) + \left(-\sin\left(\dfrac{\pi}{36}\right)\right)\left(\dfrac{\pi}{36}\right) = \dfrac{\pi}{36}$.

19. **D** The length of a curve can be found by the formula $L = \int_a^b \sqrt{1 + \left(\dfrac{dy}{dx}\right)^2}\, dx$, where a and b are the end-points of the curve. $L = \int_0^6 \sqrt{1 + \left(2x^{\frac{1}{2}}\right)^2}\, dx = \int_0^6 \sqrt{1 + 4x}\, dx$. This integral can be solved by u-substitution and the Fundamental Theorem of Calculus, so the length of the curve is $\dfrac{62}{3}$.

20. **B** Calculate the derivative with respect to x.

$2x + 2y\, y' = 0$

Do not simplify! Plug in the point (2, 4) to find the slope.

$2(2) + 2(4)\, y' = 0$

$4 + 8\, y' = 0$

$8\, y' = -4$

$y' = -\dfrac{1}{2}$

21. **D** Calculate the derivative with respect to x.

$2x + y + x\, y' + 2y\, y' = 0$

Do not simplify! Plug in (1, 1) to find the slope.

$2(1) + (1) + (1)\, y' + 2(1)\, y' = 0$

$2 + 1 + y' + 2\, y' = 0$

$3\, y' = -3$

$y' = -1$

Use the point-slope form of a line to find the equation.

$y - y_1 = m(x - x_1)$
$y - 1 = -1(x - 1)$
$y - 1 = -x + 1$
$x + y = 2$

22. **D** Take the derivative and plug in 2 for x to get the slope.

$$f'(x) = 4x^3 + 6x$$

$$f'(2) = 4(2)^3 + 6(2)$$

$$= 32 + 12$$

$$= 44$$

Take the negative reciprocal of the slope to get the normal slope.

$$m = -\frac{1}{44}$$

23. **E** For optimization problems, you must find two equations to relate to one another. Establish your equations for perimeter and area of a rectangle, keeping in mind that the total perimeter is provided to you.

$$100 = 2x + 2y \qquad\qquad A = xy$$

Take the perimeter equation and isolate one of the variables. Solve it for y and you get

$$100 - 2x = 2y$$
$$50 - x = y$$

Plug the expression from the above into the area formula to gain the new expression in terms of x.

$$A = x(50 - x) = 50x - x^2$$

Take the derivative and set it equal to zero to determine the critical point.

$$A = 50x - x^2$$
$$0 = 50 - 2x$$
$$2x = 50$$
$$x = 25$$

Testing the value of $x = 20$ reveals that the function is increasing and testing the value of $x = 30$ reveals that the function is decreasing, confirming that 25 is a maximum.

Find the y value by plugging in $x = 25$ to the rewritten perimeter expression.

$$50 - x = y$$
$$50 - (25) = y$$
$$25 = y$$

The dimensions are 25 by 25.

24.   **C**   For optimization problems, you must find two equations to relate to one another. Establish your equations for product and sum, keeping in mind that the product is provided to you.

$$S = x + y \qquad 100 = xy$$

Take the product equation and isolate one of the variables. Solving for y yields:

$$\frac{100}{x} = y$$

Plug the expression from the above into the sum formula to gain the new expression in terms of x.

$$S = x + \left(\frac{100}{x}\right)$$

Take the derivative and set it equal to zero to determine the critical point.

$$S = x + \left(\frac{100}{x}\right)$$

$$0 = 1 - \frac{100}{x^2}$$

$$\frac{100}{x^2} = 1$$

$$100 = x^2$$

$$10 = x$$

Testing the value of $x = 9$ reveals that the function is decreasing and testing the value of $x = 11$ reveals that the function is increasing, confirming that $x = 10$ is a minimum value.

Find the y value by plugging in $x = 10$ into the rewritten product function.

$$\frac{100}{x} = y$$

$$\frac{100}{10} = y$$

$$10 = y$$

So, the two numbers are 10 and 10.

25. **B** For optimization problems, you must find two equations to relate to one another. Establish your equations for product and sum, keeping in mind that the sum is provided to you.

$$23 = x + y \qquad P = xy$$

Take the sum equation and isolate one of the variables. Solving for y yields:

$$23 - x = y$$

Plug the expression from the above into the product formula to gain the new expression in terms of x.

$$P = x(23 - x)$$
$$P = 23x - x^2$$

Take the derivative and set it equal to zero to determine the critical point.

$$P = 23x - x^2$$
$$0 = 23 - 2x$$
$$2x = 23$$
$$x = 11.5$$

Testing the value of $x = 10$ reveals that the function is increasing and testing the value of $x = 12$ reveals that the function is decreasing, confirming that $x = 11.5$ is a maximum value.

Find the y value by plugging $x = 11.5$ into the rewritten sum function.

$$23 - x = y$$
$$23 - 11.5 = y$$
$$11.5 = y$$

So, the numbers are 11.5 and 11.5.

26. **D** Take the derivative and set it equal to zero to determine the critical points.

$$y = 4x^3 - 9x^2 + 6x$$
$$y' = 12x^2 - 18x + 6 = 0$$
$$6(2x^2 - 3x + 1) = 0$$
$$6(2x - 1)(x - 1) = 0$$
$$x = \frac{1}{2} \ ; \ x = 1$$
$$y'(0) = + \ ; \ y'\left(\frac{3}{4}\right) = - \ ; \ y'(2) = +$$

By testing values around the determined critical points, it can be concluded that $x = 1$ is a relative minimum. To find the value, simply plug $x = 1$ into the original function.

$$y(1) = 4(1)^3 - 9(1)^2 + 6(1)$$
$$= 4 - 9 + 6 = 1$$

Chapter 17
General and Partial Fraction Integration Drill

GENERAL AND PARTIAL FRACTION INTEGRATION DRILL

1. Find $f(x)$ if $f(0) = 8$ and $f'(x) = 1 - 6x$.

   (A) $8 + x + 3x^2$
   (B) $8 + x - 3x^2$
   (C) $6 - x + 3x^2$
   (D) $-8 + x + 3x^2$
   (E) $1 - x - 3x^2$

2. If $f'(x) = 8x^3 + 12x + 3$, find $f(x)$ if $f(1) = 6$.

   (A) $2x^4 + 6x^2 + 3x - 5$
   (B) $5x^4 + 3x^2 + 2x + 5$
   (C) $-4x^4 + 6x^2 + 3x - 5$
   (D) $5x^4 + 6x^2 + 3x + 5$
   (E) $2x^4 - 6x^2 - 3x - 5$

3. If $f\left(\dfrac{\pi}{3}\right) = 4$, and $f'(x) = 2\cos x + \sec^2 x$, then find $f(x)$.

   (A) $-2\cos x + \tan x + 4$

   (B) $2\sin x - \tan x + 4$

   (C) $2\sin x + \tan x + 4 - 2\sqrt{3}$

   (D) $-2\sin x + 2\sec x + 4 + 2\sqrt{3}$

   (E) $2\sin x + 2\tan x + 4 + 2\sqrt{3}$

4. If $f''(x) = 24x^2 + 2x + 10$, $f(1) = 5$, and $f'(1) = -3$, then $f(x) =$

   (A) $2x^4 + x^3 + 5x^2 - 22x - \dfrac{59}{3}$

   (B) $2x^4 - \dfrac{x^3}{3} - 5x^2 - 22x + \dfrac{59}{3}$

   (C) $-2x^4 + \dfrac{x^3}{3} + 5x^2 - 22x + \dfrac{59}{3}$

   (D) $2x^4 - 4x^3 + 5x^2 - 22x + \dfrac{59}{3}$

   (E) $2x^4 + \dfrac{x^3}{3} + 5x^2 - 22x + \dfrac{59}{3}$

5. Given $f(0) = 2$, $f'(0) = 1$, $f''(x) = 4 - 6x - 40x^3$, what is $f(x)$?

   (A) $2 - x - 2x^2 - x^3 + 2x^5$
   (B) $2 + 2x + 3x^2 - x^3 - 6x^5$
   (C) $-2 + x + 2x^2 - x^3 - 2x^5$
   (D) $2 + x + 2x^2 - x^3 - 2x^5$
   (E) $2 + x + 2x^2 + x^3 + 6x^5$

6. Given $f''(x) = \sin x + \cos x$, $f(0) = 3$, and $f'(0) = 4$, then what is $f(x)$?

   (A) $\sin x + \cos x + 5x + 4$
   (B) $\cos x - \sin x + 5x + 4$
   (C) $\sin x - \cos x - 5x - 4$
   (D) $\sin x - \cos x + 5x + 4$
   (E) $-\sin x - \cos x + 5x + 4$

7. If $f''(x) = 2 - 12x$, $f(0) = 9$, and $f(2) = 15$, then find $f(x)$.

   (A) $2x^3 - x^2 + 9x + 9$
   (B) $-2x^3 + x^2 - 9x + 9$
   (C) $2x^3 + x^2 + 9x + 9$
   (D) $-2x^3 - x^2 + 9x - 9$
   (E) $-2x^3 + x^2 + 9x + 9$

8. Find $f(x)$ if $f''(x) = 20x^3 + 12x^2 + 4$, $f(0) = 8$, and $f(1) = 5$.

   (A) $-x^5 + x^4 + 2x^2 - 5x + 2$
   (B) $x^5 + x^4 + 2x^2 - 7x + 8$
   (C) $6x^5 + 5x^4 + 2x^2 - 7x + 8$
   (D) $-x^5 + x^4 + 2x^2 - 7x + 8$
   (E) $x^5 + x^4 + 2x^2 - 5x + 2$

9. Find $f(x)$ if $f'(0) = 2, f(1) = 1$, and $f''(x) = 20x^3 + 12x^2 + 4$.

   (A) $x^5 + x^4 + 2x^2 - 5x + 2$
   (B) $6x^5 + x^4 + 2x^2 - 5x + 2$
   (C) $x^5 - x^4 - 2x^2 - 5x - 2$
   (D) $-x^5 + x^4 + 2x^2 - 5x + 2$
   (E) $x^5 + 5x^4 + 3x^2 - 5x + 2$

10. Find $f(x)$ if $f''(x) = 48x^2 - 6x + 1, f(0) = 1$, and $f'(0) = 2$.

   (A) $x^4 - 4x^3 + \dfrac{1}{2}x^2 + 2x + 1$

   (B) $x^4 - \dfrac{1}{2}x^3 + x^2 + 2x + 1$

   (C) $4x^4 - x^3 + \dfrac{1}{2}x^2 + 2x + 1$

   (D) $-4x^4 + x^3 + \dfrac{1}{2}x^2 + 2x + 1$

   (E) $4x^4 + x^3 + 2x^2 + \dfrac{1}{2}x + 1$

11. $\displaystyle\int_1^4 (5 - 2x + 3x^2)\, dx =$

   (A) -63
   (B) -14
   (C) 2
   (D) 14
   (E) 63

12. $\displaystyle\int_0^2 x(2 + x^5)\, dx =$

   (A) -33

   (B) $-\dfrac{156}{7}$

   (C) 0

   (D) $\dfrac{156}{7}$

   (E) 33

13. $\displaystyle\int \dfrac{x^3 - 2\sqrt{x}}{x}\, dx =$

   (A) $x^4 - x^2 + C$

   (B) $x^{\frac{3}{2}} - x + C$

   (C) $\dfrac{2}{3}x^{\frac{1}{3}} - 4\sqrt{x} + C$

   (D) $\dfrac{1}{3}x^{\frac{1}{3}} - 4\sqrt{x} + C$

   (E) $x^{\frac{1}{3}} - 4\sqrt{x} + C$

14. $\displaystyle\int (3x^2 + 2x)(x^3 + x^2)^5\, dx =$

   (A) $\dfrac{1}{6}(x^3 + x^2)^6 + C$

   (B) $\dfrac{1}{6}(3x^2 + 2x)^6 + C$

   (C) $(x^3 + x^2)^6 + C$

   (D) $(3x^2 + 2x)^6 + C$

   (E) $-\dfrac{1}{6}(x^3 + x^2)^6 + C$

15. $\dfrac{1}{2}\displaystyle\int\left(\dfrac{dx}{\sqrt{x}}\right)-3\int x^{2}\,dx=$

(A) $x-x^{3}+C$

(B) $x^{2}-x^{3}+C$

(C) $\sqrt{x}-x^{3}+C$

(D) $2\sqrt{x}-x^{3}+C$

(E) $\dfrac{1}{2}\sqrt{x}-x^{3}+C$

16. $\displaystyle\int(x^{2}+x-x^{-1}+2x^{-2})\,dx=$

(A) $2x+1+x^{2}-4x^{3}+C$

(B) $-\dfrac{1}{3}x^{3}-\dfrac{1}{2}x^{2}+\ln x+2x^{1}+C$

(C) $\dfrac{1}{3}x^{3}+\dfrac{1}{2}x^{2}-\ln x-2x^{1}+C$

(D) $2x-1-x^{2}+4x^{3}+C$

(E) $3x+C$

17. $\displaystyle\int(2x^{2}+3)\,dx=$

(A) $2x^{3}+3x+C$

(B) $x^{3}+3x+C$

(C) $\dfrac{2}{3}x^{3}+3x+C$

(D) $4x+C$

(E) $4x^{3}+3+C$

18. $\displaystyle\int x\left(2x^{2}+7\right)^{5}dx=$

(A) $\dfrac{\left(2x^{2}+7\right)^{4}}{4}+C$

(B) $\dfrac{\left(2x^{2}+7\right)^{6}}{24}+C$

(C) $\left(2x^{2}+7\right)^{6}+C$

(D) $\dfrac{\left(2x^{2}+7\right)^{6}}{6}+C$

(E) $\left(2x^{2}+7\right)^{4}+C$

19. $\displaystyle\int_{0}^{3}\left(x^{2}-x\right)\left(6x^{3}-9x^{2}\right)dx=$

(A) $\dfrac{725}{4}$

(B) $\dfrac{727}{4}$

(C) $\dfrac{729}{4}$

(D) $\dfrac{731}{4}$

(E) $\dfrac{733}{4}$

20. Find $\dfrac{d}{dx}\displaystyle\int_{7}^{x^{3}}\left(2t-3t^{3}\right)dt=$

(A) $-x^{3}$

(B) $6x^{5}-9x^{11}$

(C) $2x^{3}-3x^{6}$

(D) $2x^{3}-3x^{9}$

(E) $6x^{6}-3x^{18}$

21. $\int_{-2}^{2} \dfrac{1}{x^4} dx =$

(A) 0

(B) $\dfrac{1}{24}$

(C) $\dfrac{1}{12}$

(D) $\dfrac{1}{8}$

(E) The integral diverges.

22. $\int \dfrac{x-9}{(x+5)(x-2)} dx =$

(A) $-2\int \dfrac{dx}{(x+5)} + \int \dfrac{dx}{(x-2)}$

(B) $\int \dfrac{dx}{(x+5)} - 2\int \dfrac{dx}{(x-2)}$

(C) $2\int \dfrac{dx}{(x+5)} + 2\int \dfrac{dx}{(x-2)}$

(D) $2\int \dfrac{dx}{(x+5)} - \int \dfrac{dx}{(x-2)}$

(E) $\int \dfrac{dx}{(x+5)} - \int \dfrac{dx}{(x-2)}$

23. $\int \dfrac{1}{(x+4)(x-1)} dx =$

(A) $\dfrac{1}{5}\int \dfrac{dx}{(x+4)} - \dfrac{1}{5}\int \dfrac{dx}{(x-1)}$

(B) $-\dfrac{1}{5}\int \dfrac{dx}{(x+4)} + \dfrac{1}{5}\int \dfrac{dx}{(x-1)}$

(C) $-\dfrac{4}{5}\int \dfrac{dx}{(x+4)} + \dfrac{4}{5}\int \dfrac{dx}{(x-1)}$

(D) $\dfrac{4}{5}\int \dfrac{dx}{(x+4)} - \dfrac{4}{5}\int \dfrac{dx}{(x-1)}$

(E) $\dfrac{1}{5}\int \dfrac{dx}{(x+4)} + \dfrac{1}{5}\int \dfrac{dx}{(x-1)}$

24. $\int \dfrac{2}{x^2-1} dx =$

(A) $-\ln|x-1| + \ln|x+1| + C$

(B) $2|\ln x-1| - \ln|x+1| + C$

(C) $\ln|x-1| - \ln|x+1| + C$

(D) $\ln|x-1| - 2\ln|x+1| + C$

(E) $2\ln|x-1| - 2\ln|x+1| + C$

25. $\int \dfrac{3}{x^2+x-2} dx =$

(A) $-\int \dfrac{dx}{(x+2)} + \int \dfrac{dx}{(x-1)}$

(B) $\int \dfrac{dx}{(x+2)} - \int \dfrac{dx}{(x-1)}$

(C) $-3\int \dfrac{dx}{(x+2)} + \int \dfrac{dx}{(x-1)}$

(D) $3\int \dfrac{dx}{(x+2)} - \int \dfrac{dx}{(x-1)}$

(E) $\int \dfrac{dx}{(x+2)} + \int \dfrac{dx}{(x-1)}$

26. $\int \dfrac{5-x}{2x^2+x-1} dx =$

(A) $-3\int \dfrac{dx}{(2x-1)} + 2\int \dfrac{dx}{(x+1)}$

(B) $5\int \dfrac{dx}{(2x-1)} - \int \dfrac{dx}{(x+1)}$

(C) $2\int \dfrac{dx}{(2x-1)} - 3\int \dfrac{dx}{(x+1)}$

(D) $-2\int \dfrac{dx}{(2x-1)} - 3\int \dfrac{dx}{(x+1)}$

(E) $3\int \dfrac{dx}{(2x-1)} - 2\int \dfrac{dx}{(x+1)}$

27. $\int \dfrac{x^2 + 12x + 12}{x^3 - 4x}\, dx =$

(A) $-3\int \dfrac{dx}{x} - \int \dfrac{dx}{(x+2)} + 5\int \dfrac{dx}{(x-2)}$

(B) $-5\int \dfrac{dx}{x} - 3\int \dfrac{dx}{(x+2)} + \int \dfrac{dx}{(x-2)}$

(C) $3\int \dfrac{dx}{x} - \int \dfrac{dx}{(x+2)} - 5\int \dfrac{dx}{(x-2)}$

(D) $\int \dfrac{dx}{x} - 3\int \dfrac{dx}{(x+2)} + 5\int \dfrac{dx}{(x-2)}$

(E) $-3\int \dfrac{dx}{x} + \int \dfrac{dx}{(x+2)} - 5\int \dfrac{dx}{(x-2)}$

28. $\int \dfrac{4x^2 + 2x - 1}{x^3 + x^2}\, dx =$

(A) $-3\int \dfrac{dx}{x} + \int \dfrac{dx}{x^2} - \int \dfrac{dx}{(x+1)}$

(B) $\int \dfrac{dx}{x} - 3\int \dfrac{dx}{x^2} + \int \dfrac{dx}{(x+1)}$

(C) $-\int \dfrac{dx}{x} - \int \dfrac{dx}{x^2} + 3\int \dfrac{dx}{(x+1)}$

(D) $\int \dfrac{dx}{x} + 3\int \dfrac{dx}{x^2} - \int \dfrac{dx}{(x+1)}$

(E) $3\int \dfrac{dx}{x} - \int \dfrac{dx}{x^2} + \int \dfrac{dx}{(x+1)}$

29. $\int \dfrac{x^2 - 1}{x^3 + x}\, dx =$

(A) $\int \dfrac{dx}{x} - \int \dfrac{2x}{(x^2+1)}$

(B) $-\int \dfrac{dx}{x} + \int \dfrac{2x}{(x^2+1)}$

(C) $2\int \dfrac{dx}{x} + \int \dfrac{2x}{(x^2+1)}$

(D) $-2\int \dfrac{dx}{x} - \int \dfrac{2x}{(x^2+1)}$

(E) $-\int \dfrac{dx}{x} - \int \dfrac{2x}{(x^2+1)}$

30. $\int \dfrac{1}{x^2 + x}\, dx =$

(A) $\ln x + \ln |x+1| + C$
(B) $-\ln x + \ln |x+1| + C$
(C) $\ln x - \ln |x+1| + C$
(D) $-\ln x - \ln |x+1| + C$
(E) $\ln x - \ln |x-1| + C$

31. $\int \dfrac{1}{2x^2 + x}\, dx =$

(A) $-\ln x - \ln |2x+1| + C$
(B) $\ln x + \ln |2x+1| + C$
(C) $-\ln x + \ln |2x+1| + C$
(D) $\ln x - \ln |2x+1| + C$
(E) $\ln x - \ln |2x-1| + C$

32. $\int y(y^2 + 1)^5 \, dy =$

(A) $(y^2 + 1)^6 + C$

(B) $\dfrac{1}{4}(y^2 + 1)^4 + C$

(C) $\dfrac{1}{5}(y^2 + 1)^5 + C$

(D) $\dfrac{1}{6}(y^2 + 1)^6 + C$

(E) $\dfrac{1}{12}(y^2 + 1)^6 + C$

33. $\int \dfrac{\sqrt{x} - 2x^2}{x} \, dx =$

(A) $\sqrt{x} - x^2 + C$

(B) $\dfrac{1}{2}\sqrt{x} - x^2 + C$

(C) $\dfrac{1}{3}\sqrt{x} - x^3 + C$

(D) $2\sqrt{x} - x^2 + C$

(E) $3\sqrt{x} - x^3 + C$

34. $\int_{-4}^{-2} \left(x^3 + 5x^2 - 7\right) dx =$

(A) 19.333
(B) 24.667
(C) 33
(D) 38.333
(E) 46

35. If the series $\sum_{n=1}^{\infty} \dfrac{6}{4^n}$ converges, then which of the following series will not converge?

(A) $\sum_{n=1}^{\infty} \dfrac{1}{2 + 4^n}$

(B) $\sum_{n=1}^{\infty} \dfrac{6}{4n}$

(C) $\sum_{n=1}^{\infty} \dfrac{1}{4^n}$

(D) $\sum_{n=1}^{\infty} \dfrac{6n}{4^n}$

(E) $\sum_{n=1}^{\infty} \dfrac{6}{2 + 4^n}$

36. To what value does the series $\sum_{n=1}^{\infty} (n+1)2^n$ converge?

(A) 0

(B) $\dfrac{1}{2}$

(C) 1

(D) 2

(E) The series diverges.

37. A particle's acceleration is given by $a(t) = 6t^2 - 4$. Its initial position is 1 and its velocity at $t = 2$ is 9. What is the position of the particle at $t = 4$?

(A) 113
(B) 110
(C) 101
(D) 100
(E) 92

38. Find the average value of $f(x) = x^3 - 2$ from $x = 1$ to $x = 3$.

(A) 2
(B) 4
(C) 8
(D) 16
(E) 32

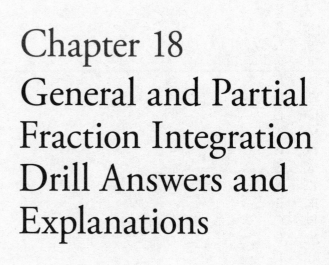

Chapter 18
General and Partial Fraction Integration Drill Answers and Explanations

ANSWER KEY

1. B
2. A
3. C
4. E
5. D
6. D
7. E
8. B
9. A
10. C
11. E
12. D
13. D
14. A
15. C
16. C
17. A
18. B
19. C
20. B
21. E
22. D
23. B
24. C
25. A
26. E
27. A
28. E
29. B
30. C
31. D
32. E
33. D
34. A
35. B
36. E
37. C
38. C

EXPLANATIONS

1. **B** To find $f(x)$, you must integrate to find the general antiderivative.

$$\int (1 - 6x)\, dx = x - 3x^2 + C$$

To find the value of C, you must use the given point $f(0) = 8$.

$f(0) = (0) - 3(0)^2 + C = 8$; so, $C = 8$

$f(x) = 8 + x - 3x^2$

2. **A** To find $f(x)$, you must integrate to find the general antiderivative.

$$\int (8x^3 + 12x + 3)\, dx = 2x^4 + 6x^2 + 3x + C$$

To find the value of C, you must use the given point $f(1) = 6$.

$f(1) = 2(1)^4 + 6(1)^2 + 3(1) + C = 6$; so $C = -5$

$f(x) = 2x^4 + 6x^2 + 3x - 5$

3. **C** To find $f(x)$, you must integrate to find the general antiderivative.

$$\int (2 \cos x + \sec^2 x)\, dx = 2 \sin x + \tan x + C$$

To find the value of C, you must use the given point $f\left(\dfrac{\pi}{3}\right) = 4$.

$f\left(\dfrac{\pi}{3}\right) = 2\sin\left(\dfrac{\pi}{3}\right) + \tan\left(\dfrac{\pi}{3}\right) = 4;$ so $C = 4 - 2\sqrt{3}$

$f(x) = 2 \sin x + \tan x + 4 - 2\sqrt{3}$

4. **E** To find $f(x)$, you must integrate twice. Integrate once to find the first general antiderivative.

$$\int (24x^2 + 2x + 10)\, dx = 8x^3 + x^2 + 10x + C$$

To find the value of C, you must first use the coordinate affecting the first derivative, $f'(1) = -3$.

$f'(1) = 8(1)^3 + (1)^2 + 10(1) + C = -3$; so $C = -22$

Now, you must integrate again to find the general antiderivative f.

$$\int (8x^3 + x^2 + 10x - 22)\, dx = 2x^4 + \frac{x^3}{3} + 5x^2 - 22x + C$$

Use the coordinate $f(1) = 5$ to find the value of the constant.

$$f(1) = 2(1)^4 + \frac{(1)^3}{3} + 5(1)^2 - 22(1) + C = 5 \; ; \text{so } C = \frac{59}{3}$$
$$f(x) = 2x^4 + \frac{x^3}{3} + 5x^2 - 22x + \frac{59}{3}$$

5. **D** To find $f(x)$, you must integrate twice. Integrate once to find the first antiderivative.

$$\int (4 - 6x - 40x^3)\, dx = 4x - 3x^2 - 10x^4 + C$$

Use the coordinate involving the first derivative to find the value of C.

$f'(0) = 4(0) - 3(0)^2 - 10(0)^4 + C = 1 \; ;$ so $C = 1$

Now integrate once again to find f.

$$\int (4x - 3x^2 - 10x^4 + 1)\, dx = 2x^2 - x^3 - 2x^5 + x + C$$

Use the other coordinate to find the value of the constant of integration, C.

$f(0) = 2(0)^2 - (0)^3 - 2(0)^5 + (0) + C = 2 \; ;$ so $C = 2$

$f(x) = 2 + x + 2x^2 - x^3 - 2x^5$

6. **D** To find $f(x)$, you must integrate twice. Integrate once to find the first antiderivative.

$$\int (\sin x + \cos x)\, dx = -\cos x + \sin x + C$$

To find the value of C, you must use the coordinate that affects the first derivative.

$f'(0) = -\cos (0) + \sin (0) + C = 4 \; ;$ so $C = 5$

Now integrate again to find the general function f.

$$\int (-\cos x + \sin x + 5)\, dx = -\sin x - \cos x + 5x + C$$

To find the value of C, you must use the other coordinate given affecting the function.

$f(0) = -\sin(0) - \cos(0) + 5(0) + C = 3$; so $C = 4$

$f(x) = -\sin x - \cos x + 5x + 4$

7. **E** To find $f(x)$, you must integrate twice.

$$\int (2 - 12x)\, dx = 2x - 6x^2 + C$$

$$\int (2x - 6x^2 + C)\, dx = x^2 - 2x^3 + Cx + D$$

Use the coordinates given to find the values of the constants.

$f(0) = (0)^2 - 2(0)^3 + C(0) + D = 9$; so $D = 9$

$f(2) = (2)^2 - 2(2)^3 + C(2) + 9 = 15$; so $C = 9$

$f(x) = -2x^3 + x^2 + 9x + 9$

8. **B** To find $f(x)$, you must integrate twice.

$$\int (20x^3 + 12x^2 + 4)\, dx = 5x^4 + 4x^3 + 4x + C$$

$$\int (5x^4 + 4x^3 + 4x + C)\, dx = x^5 + x^4 + 2x^2 + Cx + D$$

Use the coordinates given to find the values of the constants.

$f(0) = (0)^5 + (0)^4 + 2(0)^2 + C(0) + D = 8$; so $D = 8$

$f(1) = (1)^5 + (1)^4 + 2(1)^2 + C(1) + 8 = 5$; so $C = -7$

$f(x) = x^5 + x^4 + 2x^2 - 7x + 8$

9. **A** To find $f(x)$, you must integrate twice.

$$\int (20x^3 + 12x^2 + 4)\, dx = 5x^4 + 4x^3 + 4x + C$$

$$\int (5x^4 + 4x^3 + 4x + C)\, dx = x^5 + x^4 + 2x^2 + Cx + D$$

Use the coordinates given to find the values of the constants.

$f(0) = (0)^5 + (0)^4 + 2(0)^2 + C(0) + D = 2$; so $D = 2$

$f(1) = (1)^5 + (1)^4 + 2(1)^2 + C(1) + 2 = 1$; so $C = -5$

$f(x) = x^5 + x^4 + 2x^2 - 5x + 2$

10.   **C**   To find $f(x)$, you must integrate the function.

$$\int (48x^2 - 6x + 1)\, dx = 16x^3 - 3x^2 + x + C$$

Use the coordinate given that affects the first derivative.

$f(0) = 16(0)^3 - 3(0)^2 + (0) + C = 2$; so $C = 2$

Integrate once again to find the general antiderivative function.

$$\int (16x^3 - 3x^2 + x + 2)\, dx = 4x^4 - x^3 + \frac{1}{2}x^2 + 2x + C$$

Now, plug the other coordinate into the function to determine the value of C.

$f(0) = 4(0)^4 - (0)^3 + \dfrac{1}{2}(0)^2 + 2(0) + C = 1$; so $C = 1$

$f(x) = 4x^4 - x^3 + \dfrac{1}{2}x^2 + 2x + 1$

11.   **E**   Calculate the anti-derivative.

$$\int_{1}^{4} (5 - 2x + 3x^2)\, dx = \left[5x - x^2 + x^3 \right]_{1}^{4}$$

Evaluate the function at the endpoints.

$[5(4) - (4)^2 + (4)^3] - [5(1) - (1)^2 + (1)^3]$

$[20 - 16 + 64] - [5 - 1 + 1]$

$[68] - [5] = 63$

12.   **D**   Calculate the anti-derivative.

$$\int_{0}^{2} x(2 + x^5)\, dx = \int_{0}^{2} (2x + x^6)\, dx = \left[x^2 + \frac{1}{7}x^7 \right]_{0}^{2}$$

Evaluate the function at the endpoints.

$$\left[(2)^2 + \left(\frac{1}{7} \right)(2)^7 \right] - \left[(0)^2 + \left(\frac{1}{7} \right)(0)^7 \right] =$$

$$\left[4 + \frac{128}{7} \right] = \frac{156}{7}$$

13. **D** Evaluate the integral first by dividing x into each term in the numerator.

$$\int \frac{x^3 - 2\sqrt{x}}{x}\, dx = \int x^2 - 2x^{-\frac{1}{2}}\, dx =$$

$$\frac{1}{3}x^3 - 4\sqrt{x} + C$$

14. **A** Evaluate the integral using the substitution $u = x^3 + x^2$, then $du = 3x^2 + 2x\, dx$

$$\int (3x^2 + 2x)(x^3 + x^2)^5\, dx = \int u^5\, du =$$

$$\frac{1}{6}u^6 + C = \frac{1}{6}(x^3 + x^2)^6 + C$$

15. **C** This is truly a friendly problem if you identify what is actually given to you. The coefficients should be moved into the integrand to see that the integrands are perfect derivatives. Utilizing this fact, we have:

$$\frac{1}{2}\int \left(\frac{dx}{\sqrt{x}} \right) - 3\int x^2\, dx = \int \left(\frac{1}{2}x^{-\frac{1}{2}} - 3x^2 \right) dx$$

Which yields:

$$x^{\frac{1}{2}} - x^3 + C = \sqrt{x} - x^3 + C$$

16. **C** Evaluate the integral using the power rule for integration, paying attention to the x^{-1} term, which will turn out to be the natural logarithm.

$$\int (x^2 + x - x^{-1} + 2x^{-2})\, dx = \frac{1}{3}x^3 + \frac{1}{2}x^2 - \ln x - 2x^{-1} + C$$

17. **A** Use the addition and power rules of integration: $\int (2x^2 + 3)\, dx = \frac{2}{3}x^3 + 3x + C.$

18. **B** Use u-substitution. $u = (2x^2 + 7)$ and $du = 4x\, dx$. Plug this back into the integral:

$$\frac{1}{4}\int u^5\, du = \frac{1}{4}\left(\frac{u^6}{6} \right) + C = \frac{(2x^2 + 7)^6}{24} + C.$$

19. **C** Use u-substitution and the Fundamental Theorem of Calculus to evaluate this integral.

$u = 6x^3 - 9x^2$ and $du = 18x^2 - 18x$. Thus,

$$\int_0^3 (x^2 - x)(6x^3 - 9x^2)\,dx = \frac{1}{18}\int_0^3 u\,du = \frac{(6x^3 - 9x^2)^2}{36}\Big|_0^3 = \frac{729}{4}.$$

20. **B** From the Second Fundamental Theorem of Calculus,

$$\frac{d}{dx}\int_7^{x^3}(2t - 3t^3)\,dt = \left(2x^3 - 3(x^3)^3\right)(3x^2) = 6x^5 - 9x^{11}.$$

21. **E** Since $\dfrac{1}{x^4}$ is undefined at $x = 0$, this is an improper integral and we must evaluate it in two parts:

$$\int_{-2}^2 \frac{1}{x^4}\,dx = \lim_{a\to 0-}\int_{-2}^a \frac{1}{x^4}\,dx + \lim_{b\to 0+}\int_b^2 \frac{1}{x^4}\,dx = \infty.$$ Thus, the integral diverges.

22. **D** You must use the method of partial fractions to evaluate this integral. First begin by separating the function to solve for the individual numerators.

$$\frac{x-9}{(x+5)(x-2)} = \frac{A}{x+5} + \frac{B}{x-2}$$

$x - 9 = A(x - 2) + B(x + 5)$

$x - 9 = Ax - 2A + Bx + 5B$

$x - 9 = (A + B)x - 2A + 5B$

So, it follows that :

(1) $A + B = 1$ and   (2) $-2A + 5B = -9$

Multiply the first equation by 2 and then stack and add them to start solving simultaneously.

$$\begin{array}{r} 2A + 2B = 2 \\ -2A + 5B = -9 \\ \hline 7B = -7 \\ B = -1 \end{array}$$

If $B = -1$, using equation (1) means that A must equal 2. So, the partial fraction decomposition must be:

$$\int \frac{x-9}{(x+5)(x-2)}\,dx = 2\int \frac{dx}{(x+5)} - \int \frac{dx}{(x-2)}$$

23. **B** To solve this integral, you must use the method of partial fractions. First, start by breaking down the function into its individual components.

$$\frac{1}{(x+4)(x-1)} = \frac{A}{x+4} + \frac{B}{x-1}$$

$1 = A(x-1) + B(x+4)$
$1 = Ax - A + Bx + 4B$
$1 = (A+B)x - A + 4B$

So, it follows that:

$A + B = 0$
$-A + 4B = 1$

Add the two equations together to start solving for the individual values of the constants. This yields that $B = \frac{1}{5}$ and A equals $-\frac{1}{5}$. So, the partial fraction decomposition is:

$$-\frac{1}{5}\int \frac{dx}{(x+4)} + \frac{1}{5}\int \frac{dx}{(x-1)}$$

24. **C** To solve this integral, you must use the method of partial fractions. First, start by breaking down the function into its individual components.

$$\frac{2}{x^2-1} = \frac{A}{x+1} + \frac{B}{x-1}$$

$2 = A(x-1) + B(x+1)$
$2 = Ax - A + Bx + B$
$2 = (A+B)x - A + B$

So, it follows that:

$A + B = 0$
$-A + B = 2$

Add the two equations together to start solving for the individual values of the constants. This yields that $B = 1$ and $A = -1$. So, the partial fraction decomposition is:

$$-\int \frac{dx}{(x+1)} + \int \frac{dx}{(x-1)} =$$

$$-\ln\left|x+1\right| + \ln\left|x-1\right| + C =$$
$$\ln\left|x-1\right| - \ln\left|x+1\right| + C$$

25. **A** To solve this integral, you must use the method of partial fractions. First, start by breaking down the function into its individual components.

$$\frac{3}{x^2 + x - 2} = \frac{A}{x + 2} + \frac{B}{x - 1}$$

$3 = A(x - 1) + B(x + 2)$

$3 = Ax - A + Bx + 2B$

$3 = (A + B)x - A + 2B$

So, it follows that:

$A + B = 0$

$-A + 2B = 3$

Add the two equations together to start solving for the individual values of the constants. This yields that $B = 1$ and $A = -1$. So, the partial fraction decomposition is:

$$-\int \frac{dx}{(x + 2)} + \int \frac{dx}{(x - 1)}$$

26. **E** To solve this integral, you must use the method of partial fractions. First, start by breaking down the function into its individual components.

$$\frac{5 - x}{2x^2 + x - 1} = \frac{A}{2x - 1} + \frac{B}{x + 1}$$

$5 - x = A(x + 1) + B(2x - 1)$

$5 - x = Ax + A + 2Bx - B$

$5 - x = (A + 2B)x + A - B$

So, it follows that:

$A + 2B = -1$

$A - B = 5$

Subtract the two equations to start solving for the individual values of the constants. This yields that $B = -2$ and $A = 3$. So, the partial fraction decomposition is:

$$3\int \frac{dx}{(2x - 1)} - 2\int \frac{dx}{(x + 1)}$$

27.   **A**   To solve this integral, you must use the method of partial fractions. First, start by breaking down the function into its individual components.

$$\frac{x^2 + 12x + 12}{x^3 - 4x} = \frac{A}{x} + \frac{B}{x+2} + \frac{C}{x-2}$$

$x^2 + 12x + 12 = A(x^2 - 4) + Bx(x - 2) + Cx(x + 2)$
$x^2 + 12x + 12 = Ax^2 - 4A + Bx^2 - 2Bx + Cx^2 + 2Cx$
$x^2 + 12x + 12 = (A + B + C)x^2 + (-2B + 2C)x - 4A$

So, it follows that:

$A + B + C = 1$
$-2B + 2C = 12$
$-4A = 12$

You must start solving the equations simultaneously. Start with the third one since it only has the A in it. A must equal -3. Plugging that value into the first equation now means that $B + C = 4$. Multiply this equation by 2 and add it to the remaining equation.

$2B + 2C = 8$
$-2B + 2C = 12$

This yields that $C = 5$ and $B = -1$. So, the partial fraction decomposition is:

$$-3\int \frac{dx}{x} - \int \frac{dx}{(x+2)} + 5\int \frac{dx}{(x-2)}$$

28.   **E**   To solve this integral, you must use the method of partial fractions. First, start by breaking down the function into its individual components.

$$\frac{4x^2 + 2x - 1}{x^3 + x^2} = \frac{A}{x} + \frac{B}{x^2} + \frac{C}{x+1}$$

$4x^2 + 2x - 1 = Ax(x + 1) + B(x + 1) + Cx^2$
$4x^2 + 2x - 1 = Ax^2 + Ax + Bx + B + Cx^2$
$4x^2 + 2x - 1 = (A + C)x^2 + (A + B)x + B$

So, it follows that:

$A + C = 4$
$A + B = 2$
$B = -1$

The value of B is given immediately, so use that to determine the values of A and C which are 3 and 1, respectively. So, the partial fraction decomposition is:

$$3\int \frac{dx}{x} - \int \frac{dx}{x^2} + 5\int \frac{dx}{(x+1)}$$

29.　**B**　To solve this integral, you must use the method of partial fractions. First, start by breaking down the function into its individual components.

$$\frac{x^2 - 1}{x^3 + x} = \frac{A}{x} + \frac{Bx + C}{x^2 + 1}$$

(* A quadratic denominator requires a linear numerator)

$$x^2 - 1 = A(x^2 + 1) + (Bx + C)x$$
$$x^2 - 1 = Ax^2 + A + Bx^2 + Cx$$
$$x^2 - 1 = (A + B)x^2 + Cx + A$$

So, it follows that:

$A + B = 1$
$C = 0$
$A = -1$

$A = -1$, $B = 2$, and $C = 0$

Now that you know the values of the constants, the partial fraction decomposition becomes:

$$-\int \frac{dx}{x} + \int \frac{2x}{\left(x^2 + 1\right)}$$

30.　**C**　To solve this integral, you must use the method of partial fractions. First, start by breaking down the function into its individual components.

$$\frac{1}{x^2 + x} = \frac{A}{x} + \frac{B}{x + 1}$$

$$1 = A(x + 1) + Bx$$
$$1 = Ax + A + Bx$$
$$1 = (A + B)x + A$$

So, it follows that:

$A + B = 0$
$A = 1$
So, $A = 1$ and $B = -1$.

Now that you know the values of the constants, the partial fraction decomposition becomes:

$$\int \frac{dx}{x} - \int \frac{x}{(x+1)} = \ln x - \ln|x+1| + C$$

31. **D** To solve this integral, you must use the method of partial fractions. First, start by breaking down the function into its individual components.

$$\frac{1}{2x^2 + x} = \frac{A}{x} + \frac{B}{2x+1}$$

$1 = A(2x + 1) + Bx$
$1 = 2Ax + A + Bx$
$1 = (2A + B)x + A$

So, it follows that

$2A + B = 0$ and $A = 1$; so B must equal -2.

Now that you know the values of the constants, the partial fraction decomposition becomes:

$$\int \frac{dx}{x} - 2\int \frac{dx}{(2x+1)} = \ln x - \ln|2x+1| + C$$

32. **E** Evaluate the integral using the substitution $u = y^2 + 1$, then $\frac{1}{2} du = y\, dy$.

$$\int y(y^2 + 1)^5 \, dy = \frac{1}{2}\int u^5 \, du =$$

$$\frac{1}{12} u^6 + C = \frac{1}{12}(y^2 + 1)^6 + C$$

33. **D** First, divide the numerator by x to begin solving the integral.

$$\int \frac{\sqrt{x} - 2x^2}{x} \, dx = \int x^{-\frac{1}{2}} - 2x \, dx =$$

$$2\sqrt{x} - x^2 + C$$

34. **A** From the First Fundamental Theorem of Calculus, $\int_{-4}^{-2}(x^3 + 5x^2 - 7)dx = \frac{x^4}{4} + \frac{5x^3}{3} - 7x\Big|_{-4}^{-2} = 19.333$

Answer is B.

35. **B** First, recognize that the series $\sum_{n=1}^{\infty} \frac{6}{4^n}$ is a geometric series with $a = 6$ and $r = \frac{1}{4}$. Since geometric series with $r < 1$, always converge, look through the answer choices for any other geometric series. Notice, answer choice C is also a geometric series with $a = 1$ and $r = \frac{1}{4}$. The other four answer choices are not geometric series. Therefore, we need to use other tests to determine if these series converge or not. Although you may choose any test you like, look for indicators that one test may be better suited than the others. For instance, answers A and E are good candidates for the Comparison Test. Recall the Comparison Test says let $0, \leq a_n \leq b$, if $\sum_{n=1}^{\infty} b_n$ converges, then $\sum_{n=1}^{\infty} a_n$ converges. In this case, the question stem gives $b_n = \frac{6}{4^n}$, and the answer choices give a_n. In both answer choices A and E, $a_n < b_n$ for all values of n, so both A and E converge. For answer choice D, the Ratio Test is a good option to use. In the Ratio Test, $\rho = \lim_{n \to \infty} \frac{a_{n+1}}{a_n}$, where $\sum a_n$. If $\rho < 1$, the series converges. As $\rho < 1$, in D, that series converges. If you use the Ratio Test for answer choice B, you will find that $\rho = 1$, the test is insufficient and we don't know whether the series converges or diverges. To determine with certainty if the series in B will converge or not, you will need to use another test, such as the Integral Test or the P-Series Test. If you use the Integral Test, remember $a_n = f(n)$ where f is positive, continuous and decreasing for $x \geq 1$. If $\int_1^{\infty} f(x)\,dx$ converges, then $\sum_{n=1}^{\infty} a_n$ converges. In B, the integral diverges, so the series diverges and the answer is B. The P-Series Test is even easier; recognize that any series in the form $\sum_{n=1}^{\infty} \frac{1}{n^p}$, where $p > 0$, converges if $p > 1$ and diverges if $0 < p \leq 1$, so B diverges.

36. **E** In order to determine to what value the series converges, we must first determine if the series converges. You may use whichever test you please. Here, we will use the Ratio Test. In the Ratio Test, $\rho = \lim_{n \to \infty} \frac{a_{n+1}}{a_n}$, where $\sum_{n=1}^{\infty} a_n$. If $\rho < 1$, the series converges and if $\rho < 1$, the series diverges. In this case, $\rho = 2$, so the series diverges and cannot converge to a single value.

37. **C** First, integrate, $a(t) = 6t^2 - 4$, to determine $v(t)$. Thus, $v(t) = 2t^3 - 4t + C$. Determine C by plugging in (2,9), so $v(t) = 2t^3 - 4t + 1$. Next, integrate $v(t)$ to determine the position function, $x(t)$: $x(t) = \frac{1}{2}t^4 - 2t^2 + t + C$. At the point, (0,1), $x(t) = \frac{1}{2}t^4 - 2t^2 + t + 1$. Now, evaluate $x(4)$ to determine the position of the particle. $x(4) = 101$.

38. **C** $f(c) = \frac{1}{b-a}\int_a^b f(x)\,dx$. For this problem $f(c) = \frac{1}{3-1}\int_1^3 (x^3 - 2)\,dx = 8$.

Chapter 19
Trigonometric
Integration Drill

TRIGONOMETRIC INTEGRATION DRILL

1. $\int (\csc 5x \cot 5x)\,dx =$

   [handwritten: $\frac{1}{\sin}$ $\frac{\sin\cos - \cos 1}{\sin^2}$; $\frac{-\cos 1}{\sin^2} = -\cot 5x$]

   (A) $\dfrac{\sec 5x}{5} + C$

   (B) $-\dfrac{\csc 5x}{5} + C$

   (C) $-\dfrac{\cot 5x}{5} + C$

   (D) $\dfrac{\csc 5x}{5} + C$

   (E) $\dfrac{\cot 5x}{5} + C$

2. $\int (2\sin x + 3\cos x)\,dx =$ *[handwritten: $-2\cos x + 3\sin x$]*

   (A) $3\sin x + 2\cos x + C$

   (B) $3\sin x - 2\cos x + C$

   (C) $3\cos x - 2\sin x + C$

   (D) $2\cos x - 3\sin x + C$

   (E) $-2\cos x - 3\sin x + C$

3. $\dfrac{d}{dx}\left(\sin^{-1}\left(x^3 + x^2\right)\right) =$

   [handwritten: $\frac{1}{\sqrt{1-(x^3+x^2)^2}}(3x^2+2x)$]

   (A) $\dfrac{3x^2 + 2x}{\sqrt{1 + (x^2 + x^2)^2}}$

   [handwritten: $\frac{3x^2+2x}{\sqrt{1-(x^3+x^2)^2}}$]

   (B) $\dfrac{-\left(3x^2 + 2x\right)}{\sqrt{1 - (x^2 + x^2)^2}}$

   (C) $\dfrac{3x^2 + 2x}{\sqrt{1 - (x^2 + x^2)^2}}$ *[handwritten: — thats wrong]*

   (D) $\dfrac{3x^2 + 2x}{\sqrt{1 + \left(x^3 + x^2\right)}}$

   (E) $\dfrac{3x^2 + 2x}{1 + (x^2 + x^2)^2}$

4. $\int \sin^3 x \cos x\,dx =$ *[handwritten: $v = \sin x$; $dv = \cos x\,dx$]*

   (A) $\dfrac{1}{4}\sin^4 x + C$ *[circled]* *[handwritten: $\int v^3\,dv$]*

   (B) $\sin^4 x + C$

   (C) $\cos^4 x + C$ *[handwritten: $\frac{v^4}{4}+C$]*

   (D) $\dfrac{1}{4}\cos^4 x + C$

   (E) $4\sin^4 x + C$ *[handwritten: $\frac{\sin^4 x}{4}+C$]*

5. $\int \left(3\sec^2(3x) + \left(x^3 - 2\right)\csc^2\left(\dfrac{x^4}{4} - 2x\right)\right)dx =$

   [handwritten: $\tan 3x + \cot(\frac{x^4}{4}-2x)+C$]

   (A) $\cot(3x) - \tan\left(\dfrac{x^4}{4} - 2x\right) + C$

   (B) $\tan(3x) - \cot\left(\dfrac{x^4}{4} - 2x\right) + C$ *[circled]*

   (C) $3\tan(3x) - \cot\left(\dfrac{x^4}{4} - 2x\right) + C$

   (D) $\tan(3x) + \cot\left(\dfrac{x^4}{4} - 2x\right) + C$

   (E) $\cot\left(\dfrac{x^4}{4} - 2x\right) - \tan(3x) + C$

6. $\int \sin^2 x \cos x \, dx =$

$u = \sin x$
$du = \cos dx$

$\int u^2 \, du$

$\dfrac{u^3}{3}$

$\dfrac{\sin^3 x}{3} + C$

(A) $\dfrac{\sin^2 x}{2} + C$

(B) $\cos^3 x + C$

(C) $\sin^3 x + C$

(D) $\dfrac{\cos^3 x}{3} + C$

(E) $\dfrac{\sin^3 x}{3} + C$

7. Find $\int_0^{\frac{\pi}{4}} (3\cos x - 2\sin x) \, dx$.

$\int -3\sin x + 2\cos x \Big|_0^{\pi}$

$3\sin\left(\frac{\pi}{4}\right) + 2\cos\frac{\pi}{4} - (0 + 2)$

$\dfrac{3\sqrt{2}}{2} + \dfrac{3\sqrt{2}}{2}$

$\dfrac{5\sqrt{2}}{2} + 2$

(A) $\dfrac{5\sqrt{2}}{2} + 2$

(B) $\dfrac{5\sqrt{2}}{2} - 2$

(C) $5\sqrt{2} - 2$

(D) $\dfrac{\sqrt{2}}{2} + 2$

(E) $\dfrac{3\sqrt{2}}{2} + 2$

8. $\int \csc(8x)\cot(8x) \, dx =$

$\dfrac{-\csc(8x)}{8} + C$

(A) $-\dfrac{\csc(8x)}{8} + C$

(B) $-\dfrac{\cos(8x)}{8} + C$

(C) $\dfrac{\sin(8x)}{8} + C$

(D) $\dfrac{\sec(8x)}{8} + C$

(E) $-\dfrac{\cot(8x)}{8} + C$

9. $\int (\cos 3x - \csc^2 3x) \, dx =$ $\dfrac{\sin(3x) + \cot(3x)}{3} + C$

(A) $\sin 3x + \cot 3x + C$

(B) $\dfrac{1}{3}(\sin 3x + \cot 3x) + C$

(C) $3(\sin 3x + \cot 3x) + C$

(D) $\sin 3x - \cot 3x + C$

(E) $\dfrac{1}{3}(\sin 3x - \cot 3x) + C$

10. $\int (3\sin x - 2\cos x) \, dx =$ $-3\cos x - 2\sin x$

(A) $-3\cos x - 2\sin x + C$

(B) $3\cos x + 2\sin x + C$

(C) $2\sin x - 3\cos x + C$

(D) $3\cos x - 2\sin x + C$

(E) $2\cos x + 3\sin x + C$

11. $\int (8\sin^2 x + 8\cos^2 x - 8x^2) \, dx =$ $\int 8 - 8x^2 \, dx$

$8\int 1 - x^2 \, dx$

$8\left(x - \dfrac{x^3}{3} + C\right)$

$8x - \dfrac{8x^3}{3} + C$

(A) $8x - \dfrac{8}{3}x^3 + C$

(B) $8x + \dfrac{8}{3}x^3 + C$

(C) $16x + \sin x - \cos x + C$

(D) $16x + C$

(E) $\sin^2 x - \cos^2 x + \dfrac{8}{3}x^3 + C$

12. $\int 3 \csc 2x \, dx =$ $3\int \csc 2x\, dx$

(A) $-\dfrac{3}{2} \ln |\csc 3x - \cot 3x| + C$

(B) $\dfrac{3}{2} \ln |\csc 3x + \cot 3x| + C$

(C) $\dfrac{3}{2} \ln |\csc 3x - \cot 3x| + C$

(D) $-\dfrac{3}{2} \ln |\csc 3x + \cot 3x| + C$

(E) $\ln |\csc 3x - \cot 3x| + C$

13. $\int x^2 \cos x \, dx =$

(A) $x^2 \sin x + 2x \cos x - 2\sin x + C$

(B) $-2x \sin x + C$

(C) $\dfrac{1}{3} x^3 \sin x + C$

(D) $x^2 \sin x - 2x \cos x + 2\sin x + C$

(E) $-x^2 \sin x - 2x \cos x + 2\sin x + C$

14. $\int x \sec^2 x \, dx =$

(A) $2 \sec^2 x \tan x + C$

(B) $x \tan x + \ln |\cos x| + C$

(C) $\dfrac{1}{2} x^2 \tan x + C$

(D) $x \tan x - \ln |\cos x| + C$

(E) $\ln |\sec x| + C$

15. $\int e^{2x} \sin x \, dx =$

(A) $-\dfrac{1}{2} e^{2x} \cos x + C$

(B) $-\dfrac{1}{2} e^{2x} \cos x + \dfrac{1}{2} \int e^{2x} \sin x \, dx$

(C) $-2 e^{2x} \cos x - 2 \int e^{2x} \cos x \, dx$

(D) $-e^{2x} \cos x + 2 \int e^{2x} \cos x \, dx$

(E) $e^{2x} \cos x - 2 \int e^{2x} \cos x \, dx$

16. $\int \arctan x \, dx =$

(A) $x \arctan x + \int \dfrac{x}{\sqrt{(1 + x^2)}} \, dx$

(B) $-x \arctan x + \int \dfrac{x}{(1 + x^2)} \, dx$

(C) $x \arctan x - \int \dfrac{x}{(1 + x^2)} \, dx$

(D) $-x \arctan x - \int \dfrac{x}{\sqrt{(1 + x^2)}} \, dx$

(E) $-x \arctan x + \int \dfrac{x}{\sqrt{(1 + x^2)}} \, dx$

17. $\int x \cos x \, dx =$

(A) $x \sin x + \cos x + C$
(B) $x \cos x + \sin x + C$
(C) $(x + 1) \cos x + C$
(D) $(x + 1) \sin x + C$
(E) $x \sin x - \cos x + C$

18. $\int \theta \cos 5\theta \, d\theta =$

   (A) $\frac{1}{5} \theta^2 \sin 5\theta + \frac{1}{25} \cos 5\theta + C$

   (B) $\frac{1}{25} \theta^2 \sin 5\theta + \frac{1}{5} \cos 5\theta + C$

   (C) $\frac{1}{5} \theta \sin 5\theta + \frac{1}{25} \cos 5\theta + C$

   (D) $\frac{1}{5} \theta \cos 5\theta + \frac{1}{25} \sin 5\theta + C$

   (E) $\frac{1}{5} \theta \sin 5\theta - \frac{1}{25} \cos 5\theta + C$

19. $\int x \sin 2x \, dx =$

   (A) $\frac{1}{2} x \sin 2x + \frac{1}{4} \cos 2x + C$

   (B) $\frac{1}{2} x \cos 2x + \frac{1}{4} \sin 2x + C$

   (C) $-\frac{1}{2} x \sin 2x + \frac{1}{4} \cos 2x + C$

   (D) $-\frac{1}{2} x \cos 2x + \frac{1}{4} \sin 2x + C$

   (E) $\frac{1}{2} x \cos 2x - \frac{1}{4} \sin 2x + C$

20. $\int_0^\pi x \sin 3x \, dx =$

   (A) $-\frac{\pi}{3}$

   (B) $-\frac{\pi}{6}$

   (C) 0

   (D) $\frac{\pi}{6}$

   (E) $\frac{\pi}{3}$

21. $\int x \sec x \tan x \, dx =$

   (A) $x \sec x - \ln |\sec x + \tan x| + C$

   (B) $x \sec x - \ln |\sec x \tan x| + C$

   (C) $x \sec x + C$

   (D) $\frac{1}{2} x^2 \sec x + C$

   (E) $x \sec x + \ln |\sec x + \tan x| + C$

22. $\int \sec^3 x \tan x \, dx =$

   (A) $\frac{1}{3} \sec^3 x + C$

   (B) $\frac{1}{9} \sec^3 x + C$

   (C) $3 \sec^3 x + C$

   (D) $\frac{1}{3} \tan^2 x + C$

   (E) $\frac{1}{3} \sec x \tan x + C$

23. $\int \sqrt{(\cot x)} \csc^2 x \, dx =$

   (A) $-\frac{1}{3} \cot x + C$

   (B) $-\frac{2}{3} (\cot x)^{\frac{3}{2}} + C$

   (C) $-\frac{1}{3} (\cot x)^{\frac{3}{2}} + C$

   (D) $\frac{1}{3} (\csc x)^{\frac{3}{2}} + C$

   (E) $\frac{1}{9} (\cot x)^{\frac{3}{2}} + C$

24. $\int e^{\tan x} \sec^2 x \, dx =$

   (A) $e^{\sec x} + C$

   (B) $e^{\tan x} + C$

   (C) $e^{\sec x \tan x} + C$

   (D) $e^{\csc x \cot x} + C$

   (E) $e^{\cot x} + C$

25. $\int_0^{\frac{\pi}{4}} \dfrac{1+\cos^2\theta}{\cos^2\theta}\, d\theta =$

(A) $1 - \dfrac{\pi}{4}$

(B) 0

(C) $1 + \dfrac{\pi}{4}$

(D) π

(E) $\dfrac{3\pi}{4}$

26. $\int \dfrac{\sin 2x}{1+\cos^2 x}\, dx =$

(A) $\ln(1+\cos^2 x) + C$
(B) $\ln(\sin^2 x) + C$
(C) $\ln(\sec^2 x) + C$
(D) $\ln(1-\cos^2 x) + C$
(E) $-\ln(1+\cos^2 x) + C$

27. $\int \dfrac{\tan^{-1} x}{1+x^2}\, dx =$

(A) $(\tan^{-1} x)^2 + C$

(B) $\dfrac{1}{3}(\tan^{-1} x)^2 + C$

(C) $\dfrac{1}{2}(\tan^{-1} x)^2 + C$

(D) $\dfrac{1}{2}(\tan^{-1} x) + C$

(E) $2\tan^{-1} x + C$

28. $\int x^2 \cos(x^3)\, dx =$

(A) $\dfrac{1}{3}\sin(x^3) + C$

(B) $\dfrac{1}{3}\sin(x^2) + C$

(C) $\dfrac{1}{2}\sin(x^3) + C$

(D) $\dfrac{1}{6}\sin(x^3) + C$

(E) $\dfrac{2}{3}\sin(x^3) + C$

29. $\int \sin x \sec^2(\cos x)\, dx =$

(A) $\tan(\cos x) + C$
(B) $-\tan(\cos x) + C$
(C) $-\cos(\cos x) + C$
(D) $-\sin(\cos x) + C$
(E) $\sin(\cos x) + C$

30. $\int \cot x\, dx =$

(A) $\ln(\sin x) + C$
(B) $\ln(\cos x) + C$
(C) $\ln(\tan x) + C$
(D) $\ln(\csc^2 x) + C$
(E) $-\ln(\sin x) + C$

31. $\int \sec 2\theta \tan 2\theta\, d\theta =$

(A) $\dfrac{1}{3}\sec 2\theta + C$

(B) $\dfrac{1}{6}\sec 2\theta + C$

(C) $\dfrac{1}{2}\sec 2\theta + C$

(D) $\dfrac{2}{3}\sec 2\theta + C$

(E) $-\dfrac{1}{2}\sec 2\theta + C$

32. $\int \tan x \, dx =$

(A) $\ln (\cos x) + C$
(B) $\ln (\sin x) + C$
(C) $\ln (\tan x) + C$
(D) $\ln (\sec x) + C$
(E) $\ln (\cot x) + C$

33. $\int \dfrac{1+x}{1+x^2} \, dx =$

(A) $\sin^{-1} x + \dfrac{1}{2} \ln (1 + x^2) + C$
(B) $\sec^{-1} x + \dfrac{1}{2} \ln (1 + x^2) + C$
(C) $\tan x + \dfrac{1}{2} \ln (1 + x^2) + C$
(D) $\sin x + \dfrac{1}{2} \ln (1 + x^2) + C$
(E) $\tan^{-1} x + \dfrac{1}{2} \ln (1 + x^2) + C$

34. $\int \dfrac{dx}{\sqrt{1-x^2} \, \sin^{-1} x} =$

(A) $\ln (\sin^{-1} x) + C$
(B) $\ln (\cos^{-1} x) + C$
(C) $\ln (\tan^{-1} x) + C$
(D) $\ln (\csc^{-1} x) + C$
(E) $\ln (\cot^{-1} x) + C$

35. $\int (1 - \cos^2 x) \cos x \, dx =$

(A) $\cos^3 x + C$
(B) $\dfrac{1}{3} \cos^3 x + C$
(C) $\sin^3 x + C$
(D) $\dfrac{1}{3} \sin^3 x + C$
(E) $\dfrac{1}{2} (1 - \cos^2 x)^2 + C$

36. $\int (\tan^2 x + 1) \, dx =$

(A) $\dfrac{1}{3} \tan^3 x + C$
(B) $\dfrac{1}{3} \tan^3 x + x + C$
(C) $\cos x + C$
(D) $\sec^2 x + C$
(E) $\tan x + C$

37. $\int x^2 \cos (x^3) \, dx =$

(A) $\dfrac{1}{3} x^3 \sin (x^3) + C$
(B) $\dfrac{1}{3} x^3 + \dfrac{1}{6} \sin (2x^3) + C$
(C) $\dfrac{1}{6} x^3 - \dfrac{1}{12} \sin (2x^3) + C$
(D) $\dfrac{1}{6} x^3 + \dfrac{1}{12} \sin (2x^3) + C$
(E) $2x \cos (x^3) - 3x^5 \sin (x^3) + C$

38. $\int \sin^2 (3x) \, dx =$

(A) $2x - 12 \sin (6x) + C$
(B) $\dfrac{1}{2} x - \dfrac{1}{12} \sin (6x) + C$
(C) $\dfrac{1}{3} \sin^3 (3x) + C$
(D) $\dfrac{1}{2} x + \dfrac{1}{12} \sin (6x) + C$
(E) $2x + 12 \sin (6x) + C$

39. $\int (4 \sec^2 x + \csc x \cot x)\, dx =$

   (A) $4 \tan x - \csc x + C$
   (B) $4 \tan x + \csc x + C$
   (C) $8 \sec x \tan x - \csc x + C$
   (D) $8 \sec x - \csc x + C$
   (E) $4 \tan x - \csc^2 x + C$

40. $\int \sec x (\sec x + \tan x)\, dx =$

   (A) $\tan x - \sec x + C$
   (B) $2 \sec x \tan x + \sec x + C$
   (C) $\sec^2 x + \sec x \tan x + C$
   (D) $2 \sec x \tan x - \sec x + C$
   (E) $\tan x + \sec x + C$

41. $\int \dfrac{1}{1 + \sin x}\, dx =$

   (A) $1 - \cos x + C$
   (B) $\tan x - \sec x + C$
   (C) $\tan x + \sec x + C$
   (D) $x - \csc x \cot x + C$
   (E) $\sec x - \tan x + C$

42. $\int \tan^2 x\, dx =$

   (A) $x - \tan x + C$
   (B) $\sec^2 x - 1 + C$
   (C) $\tan x - x + C$
   (D) $2\tan x \sec^2 x + C$
   (E) $\tan x + x + C$

43. $\int \sec x (\tan x + \cos x)\, dx =$

   (A) $\sec x - x + C$
   (B) $\sec x + \sin x + C$
   (C) $x - \sec x + C$
   (D) $\sec x \tan x - \sin x + C$
   (E) $\sec x + x + C$

44. $\int \dfrac{1}{1 + 4x^2}\, dx =$

   (A) $\dfrac{1}{2} \arctan (2x) + C$

   (B) $2 \arctan (2x) + C$

   (C) $\dfrac{1}{2} \arcsin (2x) + C$

   (D) $2 \arcsin (2x) + C$

   (E) $\dfrac{1}{2} \arccos (2x) + C$

45. $\int \dfrac{x + 2}{\sqrt{\left(x^2 + 4x\right)}}\, dx =$

   (A) $\dfrac{1}{2} \arctan (2x) + C$

   (B) $\dfrac{1}{2} \sqrt{\left(x^2 + 4x\right)} + C$

   (C) $2\sqrt{\left(x^2 + 4x\right)} + C$

   (D) $\sqrt{\left(x^2 + 4x\right)} + C$

   (E) $\dfrac{1}{2} \arcsin (2x) + C$

46. $\int \sin x\, e^{\cos x}\, dx =$

   (A) $-e^{\sin x} + C$
   (B) $e^{\cos x} + C$
   (C) $e^{\sin x} + C$
   (D) $-e^{\sec x} + C$
   (E) $-e^{\cos x} + C$

47. $\int \dfrac{\sin (\ln x)}{x}\, dx =$

 (A) $-\csc (\ln x) + C$
 (B) $-\cos (\ln x) + C$
 (C) $\cos (\ln x) + C$
 (D) $\sin (\ln x) + C$
 (E) $-\sin (\ln x) + C$

48. $\int_{0}^{\frac{\pi}{2}} \cos^3 x \sin 2x\, dx =$

 (A) $\dfrac{1}{5}$

 (B) $\dfrac{2}{5}$

 (C) $\dfrac{3}{5}$

 (D) $\dfrac{4}{5}$

 (E) 1

49. $\int \dfrac{\sin^{-1} x}{\sqrt{(1-x^2)}}\, dx =$

 (A) $\dfrac{1}{2} (\sin^{-1} x)^2 + C$

 (B) $\dfrac{1}{2} (\tan^{-1} x) + C$

 (C) $\dfrac{1}{2} (\tan^{-1} x)^2 + C$

 (D) $\dfrac{1}{2} (\sin^{-1} x) + C$

 (E) $-2\sqrt{(1-x^2)} \cos^{-1} x + C$

Chapter 20
Trigonometric Integration Drill Answers and Explanations

ANSWER KEY

1.	B		26.	E
2.	B		27.	C
3.	C		28.	A
4.	A		29.	B
5.	B		30.	A
6.	E		31.	C
7.	B		32.	D
8.	A		33.	E
9.	B		34.	A
10.	A		35.	D
11.	A		36.	E
12.	D		37.	D
13.	A		38.	B
14.	B		39.	A
15.	D		40.	E
16.	C		41.	B
17.	A		42.	C
18.	C		43.	E
19.	D		44.	A
20.	E		45.	D
21.	A		46.	E
22.	A		47.	B
23.	B		48.	B
24.	B		49.	A
25.	C			

EXPLANATIONS

1. **B** Recall $\int \csc u \cot u \, du = -\csc u + C$, so you need to use u-substitution. Here, $u = 5x$ and $du = 5 \, dx$.

   When these are replaced into the integral, we get: $\int \csc 5x \cot 5x \, dx = \frac{1}{5} \int \csc u \cot u \, du = -\frac{1}{5} \csc u + C$.

   Replacing $5x$ back in for u, the solution is $-\dfrac{\csc 5x}{5} + C$.

2. **B** Recall $\int \cos u \, du = \sin u + C$ and $\int \sin u \, du = -\cos u + C$. So the integral becomes:

   $$\int (2 \sin x + 3 \cos x) \, dx = -2 \cos x + 3 \sin x + C.$$

3. **C** Recall $\dfrac{d}{dx}\left(\sin^{-1} u\right) = \dfrac{1}{\sqrt{1 - u^1}} \dfrac{du}{dx}$. In this case, $u = x^3 + x^2$ and $du = \left(3x^2 + 2x\right) dx$. Thus,

   $$\frac{d}{dx}\left(\sin^{-1}\left(x^3 + x^2\right)\right) = \frac{3x^2 + 2x}{\sqrt{1 - (x^2 + x^2)^2}}.$$
   this should be x^3

4. **A** Use u-substitution: $u = \sin x$ and $du = \cos x \, dx$. Thus, $\int \sin^3 x \cos x \, dx = \int u^3 \, du = \frac{1}{4} \sin^4 x + C$.

5. **B** Treat this as two separate integrals added together and then use u-substitution on each part.

   For the first integral, $\int 3 \sec^2 (3x) \, dx$, $u = 3x$ and $du = 3 \, dx$. Then, $\int 3 \sec^2 (3x) \, dx = \tan(3x) + C$.

   For the second integral, $\int \left(x^3 - 2\right) \csc^2 \left(\frac{x^4}{4} - 2x\right) dx$, $u = \frac{x^4}{4} - 2x$ and $du = \left(x^3 - 2\right) dx$. So,

   $$\int \left(x^3 - 2\right) \csc^2 \left(\frac{x^4}{4} - 2x\right) dx = -\cot\left(\frac{x^4}{4} - 2x\right) + C.$$

   Thus, the final solution is $\int \left(3 \sec^2 (3x) + \left(x^3 - 2\right) \csc^2 \left(\frac{x^4}{4} - 2x\right)\right) dx = \tan(3x) - \cot\left(\frac{x^4}{4} - 2x\right) + C$.

6. **E** Use u-substitution where $u = \sin x$ and $du = \cos x \, dx$. Therefore, $\int \sin^2 x \cos x \, dx = \dfrac{\sin^3 x}{3} + C$.

7. **B** Use the first fundamental theorem of calculus:

   $$\int_0^{\frac{\pi}{4}} (3 \cos x - 2 \sin x) \, dx = (3 \sin x + 2 \cos x)\Big|_0^{\frac{\pi}{4}} = \frac{5\sqrt{2}}{2} - 2.$$

8. **A** Remember the integrals of trig functions and use u-substitution:

   $$\int \csc(8x) \cot(8x) \, dx = -\frac{\csc(8x)}{8} + C.$$

9. **B** Use the addition rule, *u*-substitution, and the integrals of trig functions:

$$\int (\cos 3x - \csc^2 3x)dx = \frac{\sin 3x}{3} + \frac{\cot 3x}{3} + C$$

10. **A** Remember coefficients do not change a derivative. $\int (3\sin x - 2\cos x)dx = -3\cos x - 2\sin x + C$.

11. **A** Remember the trig identities. In this case, notice $\sin^2 x + \cos^2 x = 1$. Thus, you can rewrite the integral as $\int (8(1) - 8x^2)dx$. Now, using the power rule, you can integrate: $8x - \frac{8}{3}x^3 + C$.

12. **D** Using *u*-substitution and the integral of cosecant, $\int 3\csc 2x\, dx = -\frac{3}{2}\ln|\csc 3x + \cot 3x| + C$.

13. **A** Evaluate the integral using Integration by Parts. Make the following substitutions:

$u = x^2$ $\qquad\qquad\qquad$ $dv = \cos x\, dx$

Then,

$du = 2x\, dx$ $\qquad\qquad$ $v = \sin x$

Recall the formula for Integration by Parts is $uv - \int v\, du$. So,

$$\int x^2 \cos x\, dx = x^2 \sin x - 2\int x \sin x\, dx$$

Integration by Parts is required again for this new integral, so make the following substitutions:

$u = x$ $\qquad\qquad\qquad$ $dv = \sin x\, dx$

Then,

$du = dx$ $\qquad\qquad\quad$ $v = -\cos x$

Proceed with Integration by Parts once again.

$$\int x^2 \cos x\, dx = x^2 \sin x - 2\left[-x \cos x + \int \cos x\, dx \right]$$
$$= x^2 \sin x + 2x \cos x - 2\sin x + C$$

14. **B** Evaluate the integral using Integration by Parts. Make the following substitutions:

$u = x$ $\qquad\qquad\qquad$ $dv = \sec^2 x\, dx$

Then,

$du = dx$ $\qquad\qquad\quad$ $v = \tan x$

Recall the formula for Integration by Parts is $uv - \int v\, du$. So,

$$\int x \sec^2 x\, dx = x \tan x - \int \tan x\, dx$$
$$= x \tan x + \ln|\cos x| + C$$

15. **D**   Integration by parts is required to evaluate this integral, but looking at the answers, you do not have to solve it out entirely. So, proceed with the following substitutions:

$$u = e^{2x} \qquad\qquad\qquad dv = \sin x \, dx$$

Then,

$$du = 2e^{2x} \, dx \qquad\qquad\qquad v = -\cos x$$

Recall the formula for Integration by parts is $uv - \int v \, du$. So,

$$\int e^{2x} \sin x \, dx = -e^{2x} \cos x + 2 \int e^{2x} \cos x \, dx$$

16. **C**   Evaluate the integral using Integration by Parts. Looking at the answers reveals that you are not required to solve out the integral entirely, so proceed using the following substitutions:

$$u = \arctan x \qquad\qquad\qquad dv = dx$$

Then,

$$du = \frac{1}{(1 + x^2)} \qquad\qquad\qquad v = x$$

Recall the formula for Integration by Parts is $uv - \int v \, du$. So,

$$\int \arctan x \, dx = x \arctan x - \int \frac{x}{(1 + x^2)} \, dx$$

17. **A**   Evaluate the integral by using the Integration by Parts method.

$$u = x \qquad\qquad\qquad dv = \cos x \, dx$$
$$du = dx \qquad\qquad\qquad v = \sin x$$

Recall, the proper integration by parts format is $uv - \int v \, du$. So,

$$\int x \cos x \, dx = x \sin x - \int \sin x \, dx$$
$$= x \sin x + \cos x + C$$

18. **C**   Evaluate the integral by using the Integration by Parts method.

$$u = \theta \qquad\qquad\qquad dv = \cos 5\theta \, dx$$
$$du = d\theta \qquad\qquad\qquad v = \frac{1}{5} \sin 5\theta$$

Recall, the proper integration by parts format is $uv - \int v \, du$. So,

$$\int \theta \cos 5\theta \, d\theta = \frac{1}{5} \theta \sin 5\theta - \frac{1}{5} \int \sin 5\theta \, d\theta$$

$$= \frac{1}{5} \theta \sin 5\theta + \frac{1}{25} \cos 5\theta + C$$

19. **D** Evaluate the integral by using the Integration by Parts method.

$$u = x \qquad\qquad dv = \sin 2x \, dx$$

$$du = dx \qquad\qquad v = -\frac{1}{2}\cos 2x$$

Recall, the proper integration by parts format is $uv - \int v \, du$. So,

$$\int x \sin 2x \, dx = -\frac{1}{2}x \cos 2x + \frac{1}{2}\int \cos 2x \, dx$$

$$= -\frac{1}{2}x \cos 2x + \frac{1}{4}\sin 2x + C$$

20. **E** Evaluate the integral by using the Integration by Parts method.

$$u = x \qquad\qquad dv = \sin 3x \, dx$$

$$du = dx \qquad\qquad v = -\frac{1}{3}\cos 3x$$

Recall, the proper integration by parts format is $uv\Big|_a^b - \int_a^b v \, du$. So,

$$\int_0^\pi x \sin 3x \, dx = -\frac{1}{3}x \cos 3x \,\Big|_0^\pi + \frac{1}{3}\int_0^\pi \cos 3x \, dx$$

$$= -\frac{1}{3}x \cos 3x \,\Big|_0^\pi + \frac{1}{9}\sin 3x \,\Big|_0^\pi$$

$$= -\frac{1}{3}\Big[\pi \cos 3\pi - (0)\cos(0)\Big] + \frac{1}{9}\Big[\sin 3\pi - \sin(0)\Big]$$

$$= -\frac{1}{3}\big[-\pi\big] = \frac{\pi}{3}$$

21. **A** Evaluate the integral by using the Integration by Parts method.

$$u = x \qquad\qquad dv = \sec x \tan x \, dx$$

$$du = dx \qquad\qquad v = \sec x$$

Recall, the proper integration by parts format is $uv - \int v \, du$. So,

$$\int x \sec x \tan x \, dx = x \sec x - \int \sec x \, dx$$

$$= x \sec x - \ln|\sec x + \tan x| + C$$

Note: $\int \sec x \, dx$ can be found by multiplying the top and the bottom by $\sec x + \tan x$ and performing a u-substitution.

22. **A** Rewrite the integral to make integration easier.

$$\int \sec^3 x \tan x \, dx = \int \sec^2 x \sec x \tan x \, dx =$$

Now integrate with u-substitution, allowing u to equal sec x, since the derivative, du, shows up in the integrand.

Let $u = \sec x$, so $du = \sec x \tan x \, dx$.

$$\int \sec^2 x \sec x \tan x \, dx = \int u^2 \, du =$$

$$\frac{1}{3}u^3 = \frac{1}{3}\sec^3 x + C$$

23. **B** Evaluate the integral substituting $u = \cot x$, then $-du = \csc^2 x \, dx$.

$$\int \sqrt{(\cot x)} \csc^2 x \, dx = -\int \sqrt{u} \, du =$$

$$-\frac{2}{3}u^{\frac{3}{2}} + C = -\frac{2}{3}(\cot x)^{\frac{3}{2}} + C$$

24. **B** Evaluate the integral using the substitution $u = \tan x$, then $du = \sec^2 x \, dx$.

$$\int e^{\tan x} \sec^2 x \, dx = \int e^u \, du =$$

$$e^u + C = e^{\tan x} + C$$

25. **C** Evaluate the integral first by dividing each term in the numerator by $\cos^2 \theta$.

$$\int_0^{\frac{\pi}{4}} \frac{1 + \cos^2 \theta}{\cos^2 \theta} \, d\theta = \int_0^{\frac{\pi}{4}} \sec^2 \theta + 1 \, d\theta =$$

$$\left[\tan \theta + \theta\right]_0^{\frac{\pi}{4}}$$

Calculate the value at the endpoints.

$$\left[\tan\left(\frac{\pi}{4}\right) + \left(\frac{\pi}{4}\right)\right] - [\tan(0) + (0)] =$$

$$\left[1 + \frac{\pi}{4}\right] - 0 = 1 + \frac{\pi}{4}$$

26. **E** Rewrite the integral using the identity $\sin 2x = 2 \sin x \cos x$

$$\int \frac{\sin 2x}{1 + \cos^2 x} \, dx = \int \frac{2 \sin x \cos x}{1 + \cos^2 x} \, dx =$$

Evaluate the integral using the substitution $u = 1 + \cos^2 x$, because then $-du = 2\sin x \cos x \, dx$.

$$\int \frac{2 \sin x \cos x}{1 + \cos^2 x} \, dx = \int \frac{du}{u} =$$

$-\ln (u) = -\ln (1 + \cos^2 x) + C.$

27. **C** Evaluate the integral using the substitution $u = \tan^{-1} x$, then $du = \dfrac{dx}{1 + x^2}$.

$$\int \frac{\tan^{-1} x}{1 + x^2} \, dx = \int u \, du =$$

$\dfrac{1}{2} u^2 + C = \dfrac{1}{2} (\tan^{-1} x)^2 + C.$

28. **A** Evaluate the integral by using the substitution $u = x^3$, then $\dfrac{1}{3} du = x^2 \, dx$.

$$\int x^2 \cos(x^3) \, dx = \frac{1}{3} \int \cos (u) \, du =$$

$\dfrac{1}{3} \sin u + C = \dfrac{1}{3} \sin (x^3) + C$

29. **B** Evaluate the integral using the substitution $u = \cos x$, then $-du = \sin x \, dx$.

$$\int \sin x \sec^2 (\cos x) \, dx = -\int \sec^2 u \, du =$$

$-\tan u + C = -\tan (\cos x) + C$

30. **A** Rewrite the integral to make integration easier:

$$\int \cot x \, dx = \int \frac{\cos x}{\sin x} \, dx$$

Evaluate the integral using the substitution $u = \sin x$, then $du = \cos x \, dx$.

$$\int \frac{\cos x}{\sin x} \, dx = \int \left(\frac{du}{u} \right) =$$

$\ln (u) + C = \ln (\sin x) + C.$

31. **C** Evaluate the integral using the substitution $u = 2\theta$, then $\frac{1}{2} du = d\theta$.

$$\int \sec 2\theta \tan 2\theta \, d\theta = \frac{1}{2} \int \sec u \tan u \, du =$$

$$\frac{1}{2} \sec u + C = \frac{1}{2} \sec 2\theta + C$$

32. **D** Rewrite the integral to make it easier to integrate.

$$\int \tan x \, dx = \int \frac{\sin x}{\cos x} \, dx$$

Evaluate the integral using the substitution $u = \cos x$, then $-du = \sin x \, dx$.

$$\int \frac{\sin x}{\cos x} \, dx = -\int \frac{du}{u} =$$

$$-\ln u + C = -\ln (\cos x) + C = \ln (\sec x) + C$$

33. **E** Separate the integral into the sum of 2 integrals:

$$\int \frac{1}{(1 + x^2)} \, dx + \int \frac{x}{(1 + x^2)} \, dx$$

The first integral is the derivative of the $\tan^{-1} x$. The second integral requires the substitution of $u = 1 + x^2$, which allows $\frac{1}{2} du = x \, dx$.

$$\int \frac{1}{(1 + x^2)} \, dx + \int \frac{x}{(1 + x^2)} \, dx =$$

$$\tan^{-1} x + \frac{1}{2} \ln (1 + x^2) + C$$

34. **A** Evaluate the integral using the substitution $u = \sin^{-1} x$, then $du = \dfrac{dx}{\sqrt{(1 - x^2)}}$.

$$\int \frac{dx}{\sqrt{(1 - x^2)} \sin^{-1} x} = \int \frac{du}{u} =$$

$$\ln (u) + C = \ln (\sin^{-1} x) + C$$

35. **D** Evaluate the integral by first rewriting it using the Pythagorean identity $\sin^2 x + \cos^2 x = 1$.

$$\int (1 - \cos^2 x) \cos x \, dx = \int \sin^2 x \cos x \, dx$$

Evaluate the integral now by using the substitution $u = \sin x$, then $du = \cos x \, dx$

$$\int \sin^2 x \cos x \, dx = \int u^2 \, du =$$

$$\frac{1}{3} u^3 + C = \frac{1}{3} \sin^3 x + C$$

36. **E** Evaluate the integral by first rewriting it using the Pythagorean identity $\tan^2 x + 1 = \sec^2 x$.

$$\int (\tan^2 x + 1) \, dx = \int \sec^2 x \, dx = \tan x + C$$

37. **D** First, to evaluate the integral, you must make the substitution $u = x^3$, which makes $\frac{1}{3} du = x^2 \, dx$.

$$\int x^2 \cos^2 (x^3) \, dx = \frac{1}{3} \int \cos^2 u \, du =$$

$$\frac{1}{3} \int \frac{1}{2} (1 + \cos 2u) \, du =$$

$$\frac{1}{6} \int du = \frac{1}{6} \int \cos 2u \, du =$$

$$\frac{1}{6} u + \frac{1}{12} \sin 2u + C \qquad \left[{}^* \cos^2 u = \frac{1}{2}(1 + \cos 2u) \right]$$

Make the substitution back of $u = x^3$ to get the final answer.

$$\frac{1}{6} u + \frac{1}{12} \sin 2u + C = \frac{1}{6} x^3 + \frac{1}{12} \sin (2x^3) + C$$

38. **B** First, make a u-substitution to evaluate this integral. Let $u = 3x$, which makes $\frac{1}{3} du = dx$.

$$\int \sin^2 (3x) \, dx = \frac{1}{3} \int \sin^2 u \, du =$$

$$\frac{1}{3} \int \frac{1}{2} (1 - \cos 2u) \, du =$$

$$\frac{1}{6} \int du - \frac{1}{6} \int \cos 2u \, du =$$

$$\frac{1}{6} u - \frac{1}{12} \sin 2u + C \qquad \left[{}^* \sin^2 u = \frac{1}{2}(1 - \cos 2u) \right]$$

Make the substitution back of $u = 3x$ to get the final answer.

$$\frac{1}{6}u - \frac{1}{12}\sin 2u + C = \frac{1}{2}x - \frac{1}{12}\sin (6x) + C$$

39. **A** Evaluate the integral using the trigonometric integration rules for the $\sec^2 x$ function and the $\csc x \cot x$ function.

$$\int (4\sec^2 x + \csc x \cot x)\, dx = 4\tan x - \csc x + C$$

40. **E** Evaluate the integral by first rewriting it applying a distribution of $\sec x$ throughout the integrand. Then, use the trigonometric integration rules for the $\sec^2 x$ function and the $\sec x \tan x$ function.

$$\int \sec x\,(\sec x + \tan x)\, dx = \int (\sec^2 x + \sec x \tan x)\, dx =$$
$$\tan x + \sec x + C$$

41. **B** To tackle this integral, you must first perform a little algebraic manipulation. Multiply both the top and the bottom by $(1 - \sin x)$.

$$\int \frac{1}{1 + \sin x}\, dx = \int \frac{1}{1 + \sin x} \cdot \frac{1 - \sin x}{1 - \sin x}\, dx =$$

$$\int \frac{1 - \sin x}{1 - \sin^2 x}\, dx =$$

$$\int \frac{1 - \sin x}{\cos^2 x}\, dx$$

The resulting integrand can be split up into two integrals now. $\dfrac{1}{\cos^2 x}$ will now become $\sec^2 x$, and $\dfrac{-\sin x}{\cos^2 x}$ will now become $-\sec x \tan x$.

$$\int \frac{1 - \sin x}{\cos^2 x}\, dx = \int \sec^2 x\, dx - \int \sec x \tan x\, dx = \tan x - \sec x + C$$

42. **C** Evaluate the integral by first using the Pythagorean identity $1 + \tan^2 x = \sec^2 x$.

$$\int \tan^2 x\, dx = \int (\sec^2 x - 1)\, dx = \tan x - x + C$$

43.   **E**   Evaluate the integral first by rewriting it after an application of distribution of the sec x term. Then, evaluate using the trigonometric integration rule for the sec x tan x function.

$$\int \sec x \, (\tan x + \cos x) \, dx = \int (\sec x \tan x + 1) \, dx = \sec x + x + C$$

44.   **A**   This integral takes on the form of the inverse tangent function, but the denominator must be rewritten as $1 + (2x)^2$ to be able to apply a u-substitution.

$$\int \frac{1}{1 + 4x^2} \, dx = \int \frac{1}{1 + (2x)^2} \, dx$$

Now, let $u = 2x$, which makes $\frac{1}{2} \, du = dx$.

$$\int \frac{1}{1 + (2x)^2} \, dx = \frac{1}{2} \int \frac{1}{1 + u^2} \, du =$$

$$\frac{1}{2} \arctan u + C = \frac{1}{2} \arctan (2x) + C$$

45.   **D**   Evaluate the integral using the substitution $u = x^2 + 4x$, which makes $\frac{1}{2} \, du = x + 2 \, dx$.

$$\int \frac{x + 2}{\sqrt{(x^2 + 4x)}} \, dx = \frac{1}{2} \int u^{-\frac{1}{2}} \, du =$$

$$\sqrt{(x^2 + 4x)} + C$$

46.   **E**   Evaluate the integral making the substitution $u = \cos x$, then $-du = \sin x \, dx$.

$$\int \sin x \, e^{\cos x} \, dx = - \int e^u \, du =$$

$$-e^{\cos x} + C$$

47.   **B**   Evaluate the integral using the substitution $u = \ln x$, then $du = \frac{dx}{x}$.

$$\int \frac{\sin (\ln x)}{x} \, dx = \int \sin u \, du =$$

$$-\cos u + C =$$
$$-\cos (\ln x) + C$$

48.   **B**   First, rewrite the integral making the substitution

$$\int_0^{\frac{\pi}{2}} \cos^3 x \sin 2x \, dx = 2\int_0^{\frac{\pi}{2}} \cos^4 x \sin x \, dx$$

Evaluate the integral making the substitution $u = \cos x$, making $-du = \sin x \, dx$. The new limits of integration, when $x = 0$ and $\frac{\pi}{2}$ respectively, become 1 and 0.

$$2\int_0^{\frac{\pi}{2}} \cos^4 x \sin x \, dx = -2\int_1^0 u^4 \, du =$$

$$-\frac{2}{5} u^5 \Big|_0^{\frac{\pi}{2}} = -\frac{2}{5}(\cos x)^5 \Big|_0^{\frac{\pi}{2}}$$

$$-\frac{2}{5}(0 - 1) = \frac{2}{5}$$

49.   **A**   Evaluate the integral making the substitution $u = \sin^{-1} x$, which makes $du = \dfrac{dx}{\sqrt{\left(1 - x^2\right)}}$.

$$\int \frac{\sin^{-1} x}{\sqrt{\left(1 - x^2\right)}} \, dx = \int u \, du =$$

$$\frac{1}{2} u^2 = \frac{1}{2}(\sin^{-1} x)^2 + C$$

Chapter 21
Exponential and Logarithmic Integration Drill

EXPONENTIAL AND LOGARITHMIC INTEGRATION DRILL

1. $\int \dfrac{(\ln x)^2}{x}\, dx =$

   (A) $\dfrac{1}{3}\, (\ln x)^3 + C$

   (B) $3x\, (\ln x)^3 + C$

   (C) $3\, (\ln x)^3 + C$

   (D) $\dfrac{2}{3}\, (\ln x)^3 + C$

   (E) $(\ln x)^3 + C$

2. $\int_0^1 \dfrac{dx}{x\sqrt{\ln x}} =$

   (A) -4
   (B) -2
   (C) 0
   (D) 2
   (E) 4

3. $\int_0^1 \dfrac{e^z + 1}{e^z + z}\, dz =$

   (A) $\ln (e + 1)$
   (B) $\ln 2$
   (C) 0
   (D) $-\ln (e + 1)$
   (E) $-\ln 2$

4. $\int e^{5x}\, dx =$

   (A) $5e^{5x} + C$

   (B) $\dfrac{1}{5}\, e^{5x} + C$

   (C) $e^{5x} + C$

   (D) $\dfrac{1}{5}\, e^{x} + C$

   (E) $(5e)^{5x} + C$

5. $\int e^{-3x}\, dx =$

   (A) $-\dfrac{1}{3}\, e^{-\frac{1}{3}x} + C$

   (B) $-\dfrac{1}{3}\, e^{-3x} + C$

   (C) $\dfrac{1}{3}\, e^{-3x} + C$

   (D) $-3\, e^{-3x} + C$

   (E) $-3\, e^{-\frac{1}{3}x} + C$

6. $\int e^x \sqrt{(1 + e^x)}\, dx =$

   (A) $(1 + e^x)^{\frac{3}{2}} + C$

   (B) $\dfrac{3}{2}\, (1 + e^x)^{\frac{3}{2}} + C$

   (C) $\dfrac{2}{3}\, (1 + e^x)^{\frac{3}{2}} + C$

   (D) $\dfrac{1}{3}\, (1 + e^x)^{\frac{3}{2}} + C$

   (E) $3\, (1 + e^x)^{\frac{3}{2}} + C$

7. $\int (e^x + e^{-x})^2 \, dx =$

(A) $\dfrac{1}{2} e^{2x} + 2x - \dfrac{1}{2} e^{-2x} + C$

(B) $2e^{2x} + 2x - 2e^{-2x} + C$

(C) $\dfrac{1}{2} e^{2x} + 2x - 2e^{-2x} + C$

(D) $\dfrac{1}{2} e^{2x} + \dfrac{1}{2} x - \dfrac{1}{2} e^{-2x} + C$

(E) $\dfrac{1}{2} e^{2x} + 2x + 2e^{-2x} + C$

8. $\int e^x (4 + e^x)^4 \, dx =$

(A) $\dfrac{2}{5} (4 + e^x)^5 + C$

(B) $\dfrac{3}{5} (4 + e^x)^5 + C$

(C) $\dfrac{4}{5} (4 + e^x)^5 + C$

(D) $\dfrac{1}{5} (4 + e^x)^5 + C$

(E) $e^x (4 + e^x)^5 + C$

9. $\int e^x \sin (e^x) \, dx =$

(A) $-\cos (e^x) + C$
(B) $\cos (e^x) + C$
(C) $\sin (e^x) + C$
(D) $-\sin (e^x) + C$
(E) $-\csc (e^x) + C$

10. $\int \dfrac{(1 + e^x)^2}{e^x} \, dx =$

(A) $-e^{-x} - 2x + e^x + C$
(B) $2x + e^x + C$
(C) $2e^x + 2x + C$
(D) $-e^{-x} + 2x + C$
(E) $-e^{-x} + 2x + e^x + C$

11. $\int_1^2 \dfrac{4 + x^2}{x^3} \, dx =$

(A) $\dfrac{1}{2} + \ln 2$

(B) $-\dfrac{3}{2} + \ln 2$

(C) $\dfrac{5}{2} + \ln 2$

(D) $\dfrac{3}{2} + \ln 2$

(E) $\dfrac{3}{2} - \ln 2$

12. $\int_2^4 \dfrac{3}{x} \, dx =$

(A) $\ln 3$
(B) $\ln 4$
(C) $\ln 8$
(D) $\ln 16$
(E) $\ln 24$

13. $\int_1^2 \dfrac{dx}{8 - 3x} =$

(A) $\dfrac{1}{3} \ln \left(\dfrac{2}{5} \right)$

(B) $3 \ln \left(\dfrac{5}{2} \right)$

(C) $3 \ln \left(\dfrac{2}{5} \right)$

(D) $\dfrac{1}{3} \ln \left(\dfrac{5}{2} \right)$

(E) $\dfrac{1}{3} \ln (5)$

14. $\int_0^1 xe^{-(x^2)}\, dx =$

(A) $-\dfrac{1}{2}[1 - e^{-1}]$

(B) $\dfrac{1}{2}[1 + e^{-1}]$

(C) $-\dfrac{1}{2}[1 + e^{-1}]$

(D) $\dfrac{1}{2}[e^{-1} - 1]$

(E) $\dfrac{1}{2}[1 - e^{-1}]$

17. $\int_1^2 10^x\, dx =$

(A) $10^x \ln 10$

(B) $\dfrac{10^x}{\ln 10}$

(C) $\dfrac{\ln 10}{90}$

(D) $\dfrac{90}{\ln 10}$

(E) $\dfrac{10}{\ln 10}$

15. $\int \dfrac{e^{\frac{1}{x}}}{x^2}\, dx =$

(A) $-e^{\frac{1}{x}} + C$

(B) $-e^{\frac{2}{x}} + C$

(C) $e^{\frac{1}{x}} + C$

(D) $e^{-\frac{1}{x}} + C$

(E) $-e^{-\frac{1}{x}} + C$

18. $\int \dfrac{e^x}{e^x + 1}\, dx =$

(A) $\ln (e^x - 1) + C$
(B) $(e^x + 1)^2 + C$
(C) $\ln (e^{2x} + 1) + C$
(D) $e^x \ln (e^x + 1) + C$
(E) $\ln (e^x + 1) + C$

16. $\int \dfrac{e^{\sqrt{x}}}{\sqrt{x}}\, dx =$

(A) $\dfrac{1}{2} e^{\sqrt{x}} + C$

(B) $2e^{\sqrt{2x}} + C$

(C) $2e^{\sqrt{x}} + C$

(D) $-2e^{\sqrt{x}} + C$

(E) $2e^{-\sqrt{x}} + C$

19. $\int \dfrac{x}{x - 6}\, dx =$

(A) $x - 6 \ln |x - 6| + C$
(B) $x - 6 \ln |x + 6| + C$
(C) $x + 6 \ln |x + 6| + C$
(D) $x + 6 \ln |x - 6| + C$
(E) $x - 6 \ln |x + 6| + C$

20. $\int \dfrac{e^x}{1 + e^{2x}}\, dx =$

(A) $\dfrac{1}{2} (1 + e^{2x}) + C$

(B) $\dfrac{1}{2} e^{2x} + C$

(C) $\tan^{-1}(e^x) + C$

(D) $\sin^{-1}(e^x) + C$

(E) $\sqrt{(1 + e^{2x})} + C$

21. $\int e^{2x} \cos x \, dx =$

(A) $\dfrac{2}{5}e^{2x}\cos x + \dfrac{1}{5}e^{2x}\sin x + C$

(B) $\dfrac{1}{2}e^{2x}\cos x + \dfrac{1}{4}e^{2x}\sin x + C$

(C) $\dfrac{2}{5}e^{2x}\cos x - \dfrac{1}{5}e^{2x}\sin x + C$

(D) $\dfrac{1}{2}e^{2x}\cos x - \dfrac{1}{4}e^{2x}\sin x + C$

(E) $\dfrac{1}{5}e^{2x}\cos x + \dfrac{2}{5}e^{2x}\sin x + C$

22. $\int x^2 \ln^2 x \, dx =$

(A) $\dfrac{x^3}{27}\left(9\ln^2 x + 6\ln x + 2\right) + C$

(B) $\dfrac{x^3}{27}\left(9\ln^2 x - 6\ln x + 2\right) + C$

(C) $\dfrac{x^3}{27}\left(9\ln^2 x - 6\ln x - 2\right) + C$

(D) $\dfrac{x^3}{27}\left(9\ln^2 x + 6\ln x - 2\right) + C$

(E) $-\dfrac{x^3}{27}\left(9\ln^2 x - 6\ln x + 2\right) + C$

23. $\int x 2^{x^2+7} \, dx =$

(A) $\dfrac{2^{x^2+7}}{\ln 4}$

(B) $-\dfrac{2^{x^2+7}}{2\ln 2}$

(C) $\dfrac{2^{2x}}{2\ln 2}$

(D) $-\dfrac{2^{2x}}{\ln 4}$

(E) $\dfrac{2^{x^2+7}}{2}$

24. $\int 3\left(4^{6x}\right) dx =$

(A) $\dfrac{12^{6x}}{\ln 4} + C$

(B) $\dfrac{12^{6x}}{6\ln 4} + C$

(C) $\dfrac{2^{12x}}{\ln 4} + C$

(D) $\dfrac{4^{6x}}{\ln 4} + C$

(E) $\dfrac{4^{6x}}{\ln 16} + C$

25. $\int \dfrac{2}{x^2 - x - 6} \, dx =$

(A) $\ln|x-3| + \ln|x+2| + C$

(B) $\ln|x-3| - \ln|x+2| + C$

(C) $\dfrac{2}{5}\ln|x-3| + \dfrac{2}{5}\ln|x+2| + C$

(D) $\dfrac{2}{5}\ln|x-3| - \dfrac{2}{5}\ln|x+2| + C$

(E) $\dfrac{2}{5}\ln|x+2| - \dfrac{2}{5}\ln|x-3| + C$

26. $\int x e^{2x} \, dx =$

(A) $\dfrac{1}{2}xe^{2x} - e^{2x} + C$

(B) $2xe^{2x} - 4e^{2x} + C$

(C) $2xe^{2x} - e^{2x} + C$

(D) $\dfrac{1}{2}xe^{2x} - 4e^{2x} + C$

(E) $\dfrac{1}{2}xe^{2x} + e^{2x} + C$

27. $\int x^2 e^{2x}\, dx =$

(A) $2x^2 e^{2x} - 2xe^{2x} + 4e^{2x} + C$

(B) $\dfrac{1}{2} x^2 e^{2x} + \dfrac{1}{2} xe^{2x} - e^{2x} + C$

(C) $-\dfrac{1}{2} x^2 e^{2x} + xe^{2x} - 4e^{2x} + C$

(D) $\dfrac{1}{2} x^2 e^{2x} - \dfrac{1}{2} xe^{2x} + \dfrac{1}{4} e^{2x} + C$

(E) $2\, x^2 e^{2x} - xe^{2x} + e^{2x} + C$

28. $\int xe^{-2x}\, dx =$

(A) $\dfrac{1}{2} xe^{-2x} - 4e^{-2x} + C$

(B) $-\dfrac{1}{2} xe^{-2x} - e^{-2x} + C$

(C) $\dfrac{1}{2} xe^{-2x} + e^{-2x} + C$

(D) $-2xe^{-2x} - 4e^{-2x} + C$

(E) $\dfrac{1}{2} xe^{-2x} - \dfrac{1}{4} e^{-2x} + C$

29. $\int x^3 e^x\, dx =$

(A) $\dfrac{1}{4} x^4 e^x + C$

(B) $3x^2 e^x + x^3 e^x + C$

(C) $x^3 e^x + 3x^2 e^x + 6xe^x + 6e^x + C$

(D) $-x^3 e^x + 3x^2 e^x - 6xe^x + 6e^x + C$

(E) $x^3 e^x - 3x^2 e^x + 6xe^x - 6e^x + C$

30. $\int x^3 \ln x\, dx =$

(A) $3x + C$

(B) $\dfrac{1}{4} x^4 \ln x + C$

(C) $\dfrac{1}{4} x^4 \ln x - \dfrac{1}{16} x^4 + C$

(D) $-\dfrac{1}{4} x^4 \ln x + \dfrac{1}{16} x^4 + C$

(E) $4x^4 \ln x - 16x^4 + C$

31. $\int \ln (3x)\, dx =$

(A) $\dfrac{1}{x} + C$

(B) $\dfrac{3}{x} + C$

(C) $3x \ln (3x) + C$

(D) $x \ln (3x) + x + C$

(E) $x \ln (3x) - x + C$

32. $\int x^2 \ln x\, dx =$

(A) $\dfrac{1}{9} x^3 \ln x - \dfrac{1}{3} x^3 + C$

(B) $\dfrac{1}{3} x^3 \ln x - \dfrac{1}{9} x^3 + C$

(C) $\dfrac{1}{9} x^3 (-1 + \ln x) + C$

(D) $\dfrac{1}{3} \ln x\, (x^3 - 1) + C$

(E) $3x^3 \ln x - \dfrac{1}{3} x^3 + C$

33. $\int x e^{-x}\,dx =$

(A) $e^{-x}(x+1)+C$
(B) $e^{x}(x+1)+C$
(C) $-e^{x}(x-1)+C$
(D) $e^{-x}(x-1)+C$
(E) $-e^{-x}(x+1)+C$

34. $\int (\ln x)^2\,dx =$

(A) $x^2(\ln x)^2 - 2x\ln x + 2x + C$
(B) $x(\ln x)^2 + 2x\ln x + 2x + C$
(C) $x(\ln x)^2 - 2x\ln x + 2x + C$
(D) $x(\ln x)^2 - 2x\ln x - 2x + C$
(E) $-x(\ln x)^3 - 2x\ln x + 2x + C$

35. $\int \ln x\,dx =$

(A) $x\ln x + x + C$
(B) $x - x\ln x + C$
(C) $\left(\dfrac{1}{x}\right) + C$
(D) $x\ln x - x + C$
(E) $x - \ln x + C$

36. $\int x^5 \ln x\,dx =$

(A) $\dfrac{1}{6}x^6\ln x + \dfrac{1}{36}x^6 + C$

(B) $\dfrac{1}{6}x^6\ln x - \dfrac{1}{36}x^6 + C$

(C) $\dfrac{1}{36}x^6 - \dfrac{1}{6}x^6\ln x + C$

(D) $5x^4\ln x + x^4 + C$

(E) $\dfrac{1}{36}x^6\ln x - \dfrac{1}{6}x^6 + C$

37. $\int_1^e \dfrac{x^2 + x + 1}{x}\,dx =$

(A) $\left(\dfrac{e^2}{2}\right) + e - \dfrac{1}{2}.$

(B) $\left(\dfrac{e^3}{3}\right) + e - \dfrac{1}{2}.$

(C) $\left(\dfrac{e^4}{2}\right) + e + \dfrac{1}{2}.$

(D) $\left(\dfrac{e^2}{2}\right) + e + \dfrac{1}{2}.$

(E) $\left(\dfrac{e^{-2}}{2}\right) + e - \dfrac{1}{2}.$

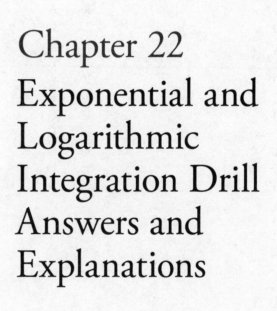

Chapter 22
Exponential and Logarithmic Integration Drill Answers and Explanations

ANSWER KEY

1.   A
2.   B
3.   A
4.   B
5.   B
6.   C
7.   A
8.   D
9.   A
10. E
11. D
12. C
13. D
14. E
15. A
16. C
17. D
18. E
19. D

20. C
21. A
22. D
23. A
24. E
25. D
26. A
27. D
28. B
29. E
30. C
31. E
32. B
33. E
34. C
35. D
36. B
37. A

EXPLANATIONS

1.   **A**   Evaluate the integral using the substitution $u = \ln x$, then $du = \dfrac{dx}{x}$.

$$\int \frac{(\ln x)^2}{x}\, dx = \int u^2\, du =$$

$$\frac{1}{3}u^3 + C = \frac{1}{3}(\ln x)^3 + C$$

2.   **B**   Evaluate the integral using the substitution $u = \ln x$, then $du = \dfrac{dx}{x}$. The new endpoints of the integral would be from 1 to 0.

$$\int_0^1 \frac{dx}{x\sqrt{\ln x}} = \int_1^0 \frac{du}{\sqrt{u}} = \int_1^0 u^{-\frac{1}{2}}\, du =$$

$$\left[2u^{\frac{1}{2}} \right]_1^0 = 2\left[\sqrt{0} - \sqrt{1} \right] = 2(-1) = -2$$

3.   **A**   Evaluate the integral using the substitution $u = e^z + z$, then $du = e^z + 1\ dz$.

$$\int_0^1 \frac{e^z + 1}{e^z + z}\, dz = \int_0^1 \frac{du}{u} - \ln u = \ln(e^z + z)$$

Calculate the function at the endpoints.

$\ln(e^1 + 1) - \ln(e^0 + 0) = \ln(e + 1)$.

4.   **B**   Evaluate the integral using the substitution $u = 5x$, then $\dfrac{1}{5}du = dx$.

$$\int e^{5x}\, dx = \frac{1}{5}\int e^u\, du =$$

$$\frac{1}{5}e^u + C = \frac{1}{5}e^{5x} + C$$

5. **B** Evaluate the integral making the substitution $u = -3x$, then $-\dfrac{1}{3}\,du = dx$.

$$\int e^{-3x}\,dx = -\frac{1}{3}\int e^u\,du =$$

$$-\frac{1}{3}e^u + C =$$

$$-\frac{1}{3}e^{-3x} + C$$

6. **C** Evaluate the integral making the substitution $u = 1 + e^x$, making $du = e^x\,dx$.

$$\int e^x \sqrt{(1+e^x)}\,dx = \int u^{\frac{1}{2}}\,du =$$

$$\frac{2}{3}u^{\frac{3}{2}} + C =$$

$$\frac{2}{3}(1+e^x)^{\frac{3}{2}} + C$$

7. **A** Expand out the integrand by squaring the terms in parentheses.

$$(e^x + e^{-x})^2 = e^{2x} + 2 + e^{-2x}$$

Integrate each piece of the integrand separately to find the antiderivative.

$$\int (e^x + e^{-x})^2\,dx = \int e^{2x}\,dx + 2\int dx + \int e^{-2x}\,dx =$$

$$\frac{1}{2}e^{2x} + 2x - \frac{1}{2}e^{-2x} + C$$

8. **D** Evaluate the integral making the substitution $u = 4 + e^x$, then $du = e^x\,dx$.

$$\int e^x (4 + e^x)^4\,dx = \int u^4\,du =$$

$$\frac{1}{5}u^5 + C =$$

$$\frac{1}{5}(4+e^x)^5 + C$$

9.   **A**   Evaluate the integral using the substitution $u = e^x$, then $du = e^x\, dx$.

$$\int e^x \sin(e^x)\, dx = \int \sin u\, dx =$$
$$-\cos u + C =$$
$$-\cos(e^x) + C$$

10.   **E**   Expand out the integrand by squaring the numerator.

$$(1 + e^x)^2 = 1 + 2e^x + e^{2x}$$

Divide the denominator into the numerator.

$$\frac{1 + 2e^x + e^{2x}}{e^x} = e^{-x} + 2 + e^x$$

Perform the integration on each part of the reduced integrand.

$$\int e^{-x}\, dx + 2\int dx + \int e^x\, dx =$$
$$-e^{-x} + 2x + e^x + C$$

11.   **D**   Simplify the integrand by dividing the denominator into the numerator.

$$\frac{4 + x^2}{x^3} = 4x^{-3} + x^{-1}$$

Perform the integration on each part of the reduced integrand.

$$4\int_{1}^{2} x^{-3}\, dx + \int_{1}^{2} x^{-1}\, dx =$$

$$4\left[-\frac{1}{2}x^{-2} \right]_{1}^{2} + \left[\ln x \right]_{1}^{2} =$$

$$-2\left[\frac{1}{4} - 1 \right] + [\ln 2 - \ln 1] = \frac{3}{2} + \ln 2$$

12. **C** Evaluate the integral and plug in the endpoints immediately.

$$\int_2^4 \frac{3}{x}\, dx = 3\int_2^4 \frac{dx}{x} = 3[\ln x]_2^4 =$$

$$3[\ln 4 - \ln 2]$$

Use the subtraction and exponent properties of natural logarithms to simplify the answer.

$$3[\ln 4 - \ln 2] = 3[\ln 2] = \ln 8$$

13. **D** Evaluate the integral by using the substitution $u = 8 - 3x$, then $-\frac{1}{3}\, du = dx$. The new limits of integration then become, when x is 1 and 2 respectively, 5 and 2.

$$\int_1^2 \frac{dx}{8-3x} = -\frac{1}{3}\int_5^2 \frac{du}{u} =$$

$$-\frac{1}{3}[\ln u]_5^2 =$$

$$-\frac{1}{3}[\ln 2 - \ln 5]$$

Use the subtraction and exponent properties of natural logarithms to simplify the answer.

$$-\frac{1}{3}[\ln 2 - \ln 5] = -\frac{1}{3}\left[\ln \frac{2}{5}\right] = \frac{1}{3}\ln\left(\frac{5}{2}\right)$$

14. **E** Evaluate the integral making the substitution $u = -x^2$, the $-\frac{1}{2}\, du = x\, dx$. The new limits of integration, when $x = 0$ and 1 respectively, become 0 and –1.

$$\int_0^1 xe^{-(x^2)}\, dx = -\frac{1}{2}\int_0^{-1} e^u\, du =$$

$$-\frac{1}{2}\left[e^u\right]_0^{-1} =$$

$$-\frac{1}{2}\left[e^{-1} - e^0\right] =$$

$$-\frac{1}{2}\left[e^{-1} - 1\right] = \frac{1}{2}\left[1 - e^{-1}\right]$$

15.   **A**   Evaluate the integral making the substitution $u = \dfrac{1}{x}$, making $-du = \dfrac{dx}{x^2}$.

$$\int \frac{e^{\frac{1}{x}}}{x^2}\,dx = -\int e^u\,du =$$

$$-e^u + C =$$

$$-e^{\frac{1}{x}} + C$$

16.   **C**   Evaluate the integral making the substitution $u = \sqrt{x}$, making $2\,du = \dfrac{dx}{\sqrt{x}}$.

$$\int \frac{e^{\sqrt{x}}}{\sqrt{x}}\,dx = 2\int e^u\,du =$$

$$2e^u + C = 2e^{\sqrt{x}} + C$$

17.   **D**   Recall that $\int A^x\,dx = \dfrac{A^x}{\ln A}$, then plug in the limits immediately.

$$\int_1^2 10^x\,dx = \left[\frac{10^x}{\ln 10}\right]_1^2 =$$

$$\left[\frac{10^2 - 10^1}{\ln 10}\right] = \frac{90}{\ln 10}$$

18.   **E**   Evaluate the integral making the substitution $u = e^x + 1$, making $du = e^x$.

$$\int \frac{e^x}{e^x + 1}\,dx = \int \frac{du}{u} =$$
$$\ln u + C =$$
$$\ln (e^x + 1) + C$$

19. **D** Evaluate the integral making the substitution $u = x - 6$. This makes $du = dx$. To tackle the x in the numerator, you must add 6 to u in the substitution, so $x = u + 6$.

$$\int \frac{x}{x-6}\, dx = \int \frac{u+6}{u\, du} =$$

$$\int du + 6\int \frac{du}{u} =$$

$$u + 6 \ln u =$$
$$x - 6 + 6 \ln |x - 6| + C$$

The final simplification is to have the general constant C absorb the -6 to look like the answer choice.

$$x - 6 + 6 \ln |x - 6| + C = x + 6 \ln |x - 6| + C$$

20. **C** Evaluate the integral by making the substitution $u = e^x$, which makes $du = e^x\, dx$.

$$\int \frac{e^x}{1 + e^{2x}}\, dx = \int \frac{du}{(1 + u^2)} =$$

$$\tan^{-1} x + C =$$
$$\tan^{-1}(e^x)\ C$$

21. **A** Since u-substitution will not work, we need to use integration by parts. Set $u = \cos x$ and $dv = e^{2x}\, dx$, then $du = -\sin x\, dx$ and $v = \frac{1}{2}e^{2x}$. The integral then becomes: $\int e^{2x} \cos x\, dx = \frac{1}{2}e^{2x}\cos x + \frac{1}{2}\int e^{2x} \sin x\, dx$. We need to use integration by parts again to evaluate the resulting integral. Set $u = \sin x$ and $dv = e^{2x}\, dx$, then $du = \cos x\, dx$ and $v = \frac{1}{2}e^{2x}$. So the full solution is: $\int e^{2x} \cos x\, dx = \frac{1}{2}e^{2x}\cos x + \frac{1}{2}\left(\frac{1}{2}e^{2x}\sin x - \frac{1}{2}\int e^{2x}\cos x\, dx\right)$. With some algebra, the final solution is: $\int e^{2x} \cos x\, dx = \frac{2}{5}e^{2x}\cos x + \frac{1}{5}e^{2x}\sin x + C$.

22. **D** Since u-substitution will not work, we need to use integration by parts. Set

$u = \ln^2 x$ and $dv = x^2\,dx$, then $du = -\dfrac{2\ln x}{x}\,dx$ and $v = \dfrac{x^3}{3}$. The integral then becomes:

$\int x^2 \ln^2 x\,dx = \dfrac{x^3}{3}\ln^2 x + \dfrac{2}{3}\int x^2 \ln x\,dx$. We need to use integration by parts again to evaluate the

resulting integral. Set $u = \ln x$ and $dv = x^2\,dx$, then $du = \dfrac{1}{x}\,dx$ and $v = \dfrac{x^3}{3}$. So the full solution is:

$\int x^2 \ln^2 x\,dx = \dfrac{x^3}{3}\ln^2 x + \dfrac{2}{3}\left(\dfrac{x^3}{3}\ln x - \dfrac{1}{3}\int x^2\,dx\right)$. With some calculus and algebra, the final solution

is: $\int x^2 \ln^2 x\,dx = \dfrac{x^3}{27}\left(9\ln^2 x + 6\ln x + 2\right) + C$.

23. **A** Recall, $\int a^u\,du = \dfrac{1}{\ln a}a^u + C$. In this problem, $u = x^2 + 7$ and $du = 2x\,dx$. Thus,

$\int x\,2^{x^2+7}\,dx = \dfrac{1}{2}\int 2^u\,du = \dfrac{2^{x^2+7}}{2\ln 2} = \dfrac{2^{x^2+7}}{\ln 4}$.

24. **E** $\int a^u\,du = \dfrac{1}{\ln a}a^u + C$, $u = 6x$, and $du = \dfrac{1}{6}\,dx$. $\int 3\left(4^{6x}\right)dx = \dfrac{4^{6x}}{2\ln 4} + C = \dfrac{4^{6x}}{\ln 16} + C$.

25. **D** To solve this integral, we must use the method of partial fractions. Set up the frac-

tion as an equation with two parts: $\dfrac{2}{(x-3)(x+2)} = \dfrac{A}{x-3} + \dfrac{B}{x+2}$. Solve for A and B:

$A = \dfrac{2}{5}$ and $B = -\dfrac{2}{5}$. Plug in those values as coefficients into the re-written integral and solve:

$\int \dfrac{2}{x^2 - x - 6}\,dx = \dfrac{2}{5}\int \dfrac{1}{x-3}\,dx - \dfrac{2}{5}\int \dfrac{1}{x+2}\,dx = \dfrac{2}{5}\ln|x-3| - \dfrac{2}{5}\ln|x+2| + C$.

26. **A** You must evaluate this integral by parts using the following substitutions:

$u = x$ $dv = e^{2x}\,dx$

Then,

$du = dx$ $v = \dfrac{1}{2}e^{2x}$

Recall the Integration by Parts formula is $uv - \int v\,du$, so,

$\int xe^{2x}\,dx = \dfrac{1}{2}xe^{2x} - \dfrac{1}{2}\int e^{2x}\,dx = \dfrac{1}{2}xe^{2x} - \dfrac{1}{4}e^{2x} + C$

27.   **D**   You must evaluate this integral by parts using the following substitutions:

$$u = x^2 \qquad\qquad dv = e^{2x}\,dx$$

Then,

$$du = 2x\,dx \qquad\qquad v = \frac{1}{2}e^{2x}$$

Recall the Integration by Parts formula is $uv - \int v\,du$, so,

$$\int x^2 e^{2x}\,dx = \frac{1}{2}x^2 e^{2x} - \int x e^{2x}\,dx$$

You must use Integration by parts once again to evaluate the integral.

$$u = x \qquad\qquad dv = e^{2x}\,dx$$

Then,

$$du = dx \qquad\qquad v = \frac{1}{2}e^{2x}$$

$$\int x^2 e^{2x}\,dx = \frac{1}{2}x^2 e^{2x} - \int x e^{2x}\,dx =$$

$$\frac{1}{2}x^2 e^{2x} - \left[\frac{1}{2}x e^{2x} - \frac{1}{2}\int e^{2x}\,dx \right] =$$

$$\frac{1}{2}x^2 e^{2x} - \frac{1}{2}x e^{2x} + \frac{1}{4}e^{2x} + C$$

28.   **B**   You must evaluate this integral by parts using the following substitutions:

$$u = x \qquad\qquad dv = e^{-2x}\,dx$$

Then,

$$du = dx \qquad\qquad v = -\frac{1}{2}e^{-2x}$$

Recall the Integration by Parts formula is $uv - \int v\,du$, so,

$$\int x e^{-2x}\,dx = -\frac{1}{2}x e^{-2x} + \frac{1}{2}\int e^{-2x}\,dx =$$

$$-\frac{1}{2}x e^{-2x} - \frac{1}{4}e^{-2x} + C$$

29.   **E**   You must evaluate the integral using Integration by Parts. Make the following substitutions:

$$u = x^3 \qquad\qquad dv = e^x \, dx$$

Then,

$$du = 3x^2 \, dx \qquad\qquad v = e^x$$

Recall the Integration by Parts formula is $uv - \int v \, du$, so,

$$\int x^3 e^x \, dx = x^3 e^x - 3 \int x^2 e^x \, dx$$

Integration by parts is required again for this new integral.

$$u = x^2 \qquad\qquad dv = e^x \, dx$$
$$du = 2x \, dx \qquad\qquad v = e^x$$

Set up the formula again, recalling the first step of integration.

$$\int x^3 e^x \, dx = x^3 e^x - 3 \left[x^2 e^x - 2 \int x e^x \, dx \right]$$

Integration by parts is required once again for the new integral.

$$u = x \qquad\qquad dv = e^x \, dx$$
$$du = dx \qquad\qquad v = e^x$$

Set up the formula once again, recalling the previous steps.

$$\int x^3 e^x \, dx = x^3 e^x - 3 \left[x^2 e^x - 2 \left[x e^x - \int e^x \, dx \right] \right] =$$

$$x^3 e^x - 3x^2 e^x + 6x e^x - 6e^x + C$$

30.   **C**   Evaluate the integral using Integration by Parts. Make the following substitutions:

$$u = \ln x \qquad\qquad dv = x^3 \, dx$$

Then,

$$du = \frac{1}{x} \, dx \qquad\qquad v = \frac{1}{4} x^4$$

Recall the Integration by Parts formula is $uv - \int v \, du$. So,

$$\int x^3 \ln x \, dx = \frac{1}{4} x^4 \ln x - \frac{1}{4} \int x^3 \, dx$$

$$= \frac{1}{4} x^4 \ln x - \frac{1}{16} x^4 + C$$

31. **E** You must evaluate this using the Integration by Parts format. Make the following substitutions:

$u = \ln(3x)$ $\qquad\qquad\qquad$ $dv = dx$

Then,

$du = \dfrac{1}{x}\,dx$ $\qquad\qquad\qquad$ $v = x$

Recall the formula for Integration by Parts is $uv - \int v\,du$. So,

$$\int \ln(3x)\,dx = x\ln(3x) - \int dx$$
$$= x\ln(3x) - x + C$$

32. **B** Evaluate the integral by using the Integration by Parts method.

$u = \ln x$ $\qquad\qquad\qquad$ $dv = x^2\,dx$

$du = \dfrac{dx}{x}$ $\qquad\qquad\qquad$ $v = \dfrac{1}{3}x^3$

Recall, the proper integration by parts format is $uv - \int v\,du$. So,

$$\int x^2 \ln x\,dx = \frac{1}{3}x^3 \ln x - \frac{1}{3}\int x^2\,dx$$

$$= \frac{1}{3}x^3 \ln x - \frac{1}{9}x^3 + C$$

33. **E** Evaluate the integral by using the Integration by Parts method.

$u = x$ $\qquad\qquad\qquad$ $dv = e^{-x}\,dx$

$du = dx$ $\qquad\qquad\qquad$ $v = -e^{-x}$

Recall, the proper integration by parts format is $uv - \int v\,du$. So,

$$\int xe^{-x}\,dx = -xe^{-x} + \int e^{-x}\,dx$$
$$= -xe^{-x} - e^{-x} + C$$
$$= -e^{-x}(x+1) + C$$

34. **C** Evaluate the integral by using the Integration by Parts method.

$u = (\ln x)^2$ $\qquad\qquad\qquad$ $dv = dx$

$du = 2(\ln x)\left(\dfrac{1}{x}\right)dx$ $\qquad\qquad$ $v = x$

Recall, the proper integration by parts format is $uv - \int v\,du$. So,

$$\int (\ln x)^2\,dx = x(\ln x)^2 - 2\int \ln x\,dx$$

Integration by parts is required again to complete the solution.

$$u = \ln x \qquad\qquad dv = dx$$

$$du = \frac{dx}{x} \qquad\qquad v = x$$

$$\int (\ln x)^2 \, dx = x (\ln x)^2 - 2 \int \ln x \, dx$$
$$= x (\ln x)^2 - 2x \ln x - \int dx$$
$$= x (\ln x)^2 - 2x \ln x + 2x + C$$

35.   **D**   Evaluate the integral by using the Integration by Parts method.

$$u = \ln x \qquad\qquad dv = dx$$

$$du = \frac{dx}{x} \qquad\qquad v = x$$

Recall, the proper integration by parts format is $uv - \int v \, du$. So,

$$\int \ln x \, dx = x \ln x - \int dx$$
$$= x \ln x - x + C$$

36.   **B**   Evaluate the integral by using the Integration by Parts method.

$$u = \ln x \qquad\qquad dv = x^5 \, dx$$

$$du = \frac{dx}{x} \qquad\qquad v = \frac{1}{6} x^6$$

Recall, the proper integration by parts format is $uv - \int v \, du$. So,

$$\int x^5 \ln x \, dx = \frac{1}{6} x^6 \ln x - \frac{1}{6} \int x^5 \, dx$$

$$= \frac{1}{6} x^6 \ln x - \frac{1}{36} x^6 + C$$

37. **A** First, divide x into each term in the numerator.

$$\int_1^e \frac{x^2 + x + 1}{x} \, dx = \int_1^e \left(x + 1 + \frac{1}{x} \right) dx$$

Evaluate the integral with the power rule, then plug in the endpoints.

$$\int_1^e \left(x + 1 + \frac{1}{x} \right) dx = \frac{1}{2} \left[x^2 + x + \ln x \right]_1^e =$$

$$\left(\frac{1}{2} e^2 + e + \ln e \right) - \left(\frac{1}{2} (1)^2 + 1 + \ln(1) \right) =$$

$$\frac{e^2}{2} + e + 1 - \frac{1}{2} - 1 + 0 = \frac{e^2}{2} + e - \frac{1}{2}$$

Chapter 23
Areas, Volumes, and Average Values Drill

AREAS, VOLUMES, AND AVERAGE VALUES DRILL

1. What is the area between the curve $y = x^3 - 8$ and the x-axis from $x = 0$ to $x = 2$.

   (A) 0
   (B) 4
   (C) 8
   (D) 12
   (E) 16

2. What is the area enclosed by the curve $x = y^2 - y - 2$ and the y-axis?

   (A) 3
   (B) 3.5
   (C) 4
   (D) 4.5
   (E) 5

3. What is the volume of the solid formed by revolving the curve $y = 2x^2 - 8$ about the x-axis?

   (A)   21.333
   (B)   67.021
   (C) 136.533
   (D) 221.867
   (E) 428.932

4. What is the volume of the solid formed by the curves $y = \frac{3}{2}x^2$ and $y = 3x$ revolved around the line $y = 7$?

   (A) $\frac{87}{4}\pi$

   (B) $\frac{92}{4}\pi$

   (C) $\frac{87}{5}\pi$

   (D) $\frac{92}{5}\pi$

   (E) $\frac{97}{5}\pi$

5. Find the area of the region in the plane enclosed by the cardioid $r = 2 + 2\sin\theta$.

   (A) π
   (B) 2π
   (C) 3π
   (D) 6π
   (E) 12π

6. Find the volume of the solid formed by revolving $y = x^2$ from $x = 1$ to $x = 3$ over the x-axis.

   (A) 20π

   (B) $\frac{124}{5}\pi$

   (C) $\frac{240}{5}\pi$

   (D) $\frac{242}{5}\pi$

   (E) 50π

7. Find the area between the curves $y = x^4$ and $y = x^2$ from $x = 0$ to $x = 1$.

(A) $\dfrac{1}{15}$

(B) $\dfrac{2}{15}$

(C) $\dfrac{1}{5}$

(D) $\dfrac{1}{3}$

(E) 1

8. Approximate the area under the curve $f(x) = x^3 + 4$ from $x = 0$ to $x = 2$ using four inscribed trapezoids.

(A) $\dfrac{33}{4}$

(B) 10

(C) $\dfrac{59}{4}$

(D) 12

(E) $\dfrac{49}{4}$

9. Given the following table of values for x and y:

x	0	1	3	4	5	7	10	13	15
$f(x)$	2	7	10	9	6	8	12	15	20

Use a left-hand Riemann sum with eight subintervals to approximate $\int_0^{15} f(x)\,dx$.

(A) 110
(B) 121
(C) 123
(D) 126
(E) 137

10. What is the area between the curves

$y = 6x^2 - x$ and $y = x^2 - 6x$?

(A) 4

(B) $\dfrac{25}{6}$

(C) $\dfrac{9}{2}$

(D) $\dfrac{14}{3}$

(E) $\dfrac{29}{6}$

11. Which of the following would yield the area between the curves $y = x^2$ and $y = 2x - x^2$?

(A) $\displaystyle\int_0^1 (2x^2 + 2x)\,dx$

(B) $\displaystyle\int_0^1 (2x - 2x^2)\,dx$

(C) $\displaystyle\int_0^1 (2x^2 - 2x)\,dx$

(D) $\displaystyle\int_0^1 (x^2 - 2x)\,dx$

(E) $\displaystyle\int_0^1 (x - x^2)\,dx$

12. Which of the following would yield the area between the equations $y = 5x - x^2$ and $y = x$?

(A) $\displaystyle\int_0^1 (4x - x^2)\,dx$

(B) $\displaystyle\int_1^4 (4x - x^2)\,dx$

(C) $\displaystyle\int_0^2 (4x - x^2)\,dx$

(D) $\displaystyle\int_2^4 (4x - x^2)\,dx$

(E) $\displaystyle\int_0^4 (4x - x^2)\,dx$

13. Which of the following would yield the area between $y = x$ and $y = x^2$?

(A) $\int_0^4 (x - x^2)\, dx$

(B) $\int_0^1 (x^2 - x)\, dx$

(C) $\int_0^1 (x - x^2)\, dx$

(D) $\int_0^4 (x^2 - x)\, dx$

(E) $\int_0^1 (x - 2x^2)\, dx$

14. Find the volume of the solid obtained by rotating about the x-axis the region under the curve $y = \sqrt{x}$ from 0 to 1.

(A) $\pi \int_0^1 x^3\, dx$

(B) $\pi \int_0^1 x\, dx$

(C) $\pi \int_0^1 x^2\, dx$

(D) $2\pi \int_0^1 x^2\, dx$

(E) $2\pi \int_0^1 x\, dx$

15. Which of the following would calculate the volume of the solid obtained by rotating the region bounded by $y = x^3$, $y = 8$, and $x = 0$ about the y-axis?

(A) $\pi \int_0^8 x^6\, dx$

(B) $2\pi \int_0^8 y^{\frac{1}{3}}\, dy$

(C) $\pi \int_0^8 y^{\frac{2}{3}}\, dy$

(D) $2\pi \int_0^8 y^{\frac{4}{3}}\, dy$

(E) $2\pi \int_0^8 x^{\frac{2}{3}}\, dx$

16. What is the average value of the function $y = 4x - x^2$ on the interval $[0,4]$?

(A) 6

(B) $\dfrac{19}{3}$

(C) $\dfrac{20}{3}$

(D) 7

(E) $\dfrac{22}{3}$

17. Find the average value of $f(x) = 2\sin x - \sin 2x$ from 0 to π.

(A) $\dfrac{4}{\pi}$

(B) $\dfrac{3}{\pi}$

(C) $\dfrac{2}{\pi}$

(D) $\dfrac{1}{\pi}$

(E) $-\dfrac{1}{\pi}$

18. Find the average value of $f(x) = x\sqrt{1 + x^2}$ from 0 to 5.

(A) $\dfrac{2}{3} \int_0^5 \left[x\sqrt{1 + x^2} \right]\, dx$

(B) $\dfrac{1}{3} \int_0^5 \left[x\sqrt{1 + x^2} \right]\, dx$

(C) $\dfrac{1}{6} \int_0^5 \left[x\sqrt{1 + x^2} \right]\, dx$

(D) $\dfrac{1}{5} \int_0^5 \left[x\sqrt{1 + x^2} \right]\, dx$

(E) $\dfrac{1}{10} \int_0^5 \left[x\sqrt{1 + x^2} \right]\, dx$

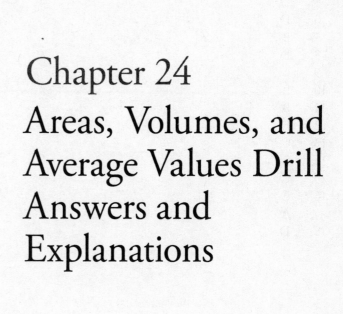

Chapter 24
Areas, Volumes, and Average Values Drill Answers and Explanations

ANSWER KEY

1. D
2. D
3. E
4. D
5. D
6. D
7. B
8. E
9. E
10. B
11. B
12. E
13. C
14. B
15. C
16. E
17. A
18. D

EXPLANATIONS

1. **D** Notice, over this interval, the curve is below the x-axis, so set up your integral with the x-axis "on top." $\int_0^2 \left(0-\left(x^3-8\right)\right) dx = \int_0^2 \left(-x^3+8\right) dx = 12$.

2. **D** Notice, over this interval, the curve is left of the y-axis, so set up your integral with the y-axis "on top." Also, set the two curves equal to each other to solve for the bounds of the integral: $0 = y^2 - y - 2$, so $y = -1$ and $y = 2$. Then, set up the integral and solve $\int_{-1}^2 \left(0-\left(y^2-y-2\right)\right) dy = \int_{-1}^2 \left(-y^2+y+2\right) dy = \frac{9}{2} = 4.5$.

3. **E** It is probably easier to solve this problem via the washer method. First, determine where the curve and the x-axis intersect: $0 = 2x^2 - 8$, $x = -2$ and $x = 2$. Next, set up your integral and solve: $\pi \int_{-2}^2 \left(2x^2-8\right)^2 dx = 428.932$.

4. **D** First set the two curves equal to each other to determine the bounds for integration: $\frac{3}{2}x^2 = 3x$, $x = 0$ and $x = 2$. Using the washer method, since $y = 7$ is more positive than the two curves, subtract the curves from 7 in your integral and solve: $\pi \int_0^2 \left(7-\frac{3}{2}x^2\right)^2 - \left(7-3x\right)^2 dx = \frac{92}{5}\pi$.

5. **D** Area in polar coordinates is found by the formula $Area = \int_a^b \frac{1}{2} r^2 d\theta$. In this problem, r sweeps the region from 0 to 2π. $A = \int_0^{2\pi} \frac{1}{2}(2+2\sin\theta)^2 d\theta = 6\pi$. Note, in order to solve this, you must use the trig identity, $\sin^2\theta = \frac{1-\cos 2\theta}{2}$.

6. **D** Using the washer method, $\pi \int_1^3 (x^2)^2 dx = \frac{242}{5}\pi$.

7. **B** Note, that $y = x^2$ is the more positive curve over that region, so $\int_0^1 \left(x^2-x^4\right) dx = \frac{2}{15}$.

8. **E** The formula for the area under a curve using trapezoids is:

    $A = \frac{1}{2}\left(\frac{b-a}{n}\right)\left(y_0 + 2y_1 + 2y_2 + \ldots + 2y_{n-2} + 2y_{n-1} + y_n\right)$. For this question $n = 4$, $b = 2$, and $a = 0$.

The required $f(x)$ values are $f(0) = 4$, $f\left(\dfrac{1}{2}\right) = \dfrac{33}{8}$, $f(1) = 5$, $f\left(\dfrac{3}{2}\right) = \dfrac{59}{8}$, and $f(2) = 12$. Plugging everything into the equation for area:

$$A = \frac{1}{2}\left(\frac{2-0}{4}\right)\left(4 + 2\left(\frac{33}{8}\right) + 2(5) + 2\left(\frac{59}{8}\right) + 12\right) = \frac{49}{4}.$$

9. **E** The widths of the subintervals are the differences between the x-values in the table. Since the Riemann sum is a left-handed one, start using $f(x)$ values from the left side of the table over.

$$\int_0^{15} f(x)\,dx = 1(2) + 2(7) + 1(10) + 1(9) + 2(6) + 3(8) + 3(12) + 2(15) = 137.$$

10. **B** First, determine where to two curves intersect. Set them equal to each other and solve for x. Thus, $x = 0$ and $x = 1$ at the points of intersection that bind the area. Next, integrate from $x = 0$ to $x = 1$. Determine which curve is "on top" in order to solve properly: $\displaystyle\int_0^1 6x^2 - x - \left(x^2 - 6x\right)dx = \dfrac{25}{6}$.

11. **B** To figure out an area integral, you must know which function is on top, as well as the limits of integration. A quick sketch of the equations will reveal that $2x - x^2$ is the equation on top. The limits of integration are:

$x^2 = 2x - x^2$
$2x^2 - 2x = 0$
$2x(x - 1) = 0$
$x = 0 \,;\, x = 1$

Set up the integral without solving.

$$\int_0^1 (2x - x^2) - (x^2)\,dx = \int_0^1 (2x - 2x^2)\,dx$$

12. **E** To figure out an area integral, you must know which function is on top, as well as the limits of integration. A quick sketch of the equations will reveal that $5x - x^2$ is the equation on top. The limits of integration are:

$5x - x^2 = x$
$0 = x^2 - 4x$
$0 = x(x - 4)$
$x = 0 \,;\, x = 4$

Set up the integral without solving.

$$\int_0^4 (5x - x^2) - (x)\,dx = \int_0^4 (4x - x^2)\,dx$$

13. **C** To figure out an area integral, you must know which function is on top, as well as the limits of integration. A quick sketch of the equations will reveal that x is the equation on top. The limits of integration are:

$x = x^2$
$0 = x^2 - x$
$0 = x(x - 1)$
$x = 0 \; ; x = 1$

Set up the integral without solving.

$$\int_0^1 (x) - (x^2) \, dx = \int_0^1 (x - x^2) \, dx$$

14. **B** Recall the general formula for calculating volume with integrals:

$$V = \pi \int_a^b \left[f(x) \right]^2 dx$$

Plug in to the formula to gain the answer.

$$V = \pi \int_0^1 \left(\sqrt{x} \right)^2 dx = \pi \int_0^1 x \, dx$$

15. **C** Recall the general formula for calculating volume with integrals:

$$V = \pi \int_c^d \left[g(y) \right]^2 dy$$

Plug in to the formula to gain the answer.

$$V = \pi \int_0^8 \left(\sqrt[3]{y} \right)^2 dy = \pi \int_0^8 y^{\frac{2}{3}} \, dy$$

16. **E** Recall the formula for calculating average value.

$$f_{ave} = \frac{1}{b - a} \int_a^b f(x) \, dx$$

Plug in and solve out the integral.

$$f_{ave} = \frac{1}{b-a} \int_a^b f(x)\,dx = \frac{1}{4} \int_0^4 (4x - x^2)\,dx =$$

$$\frac{1}{4} \left[2x^2 - \frac{1}{3}x^3 \right]_0^4 =$$

$$\frac{1}{4} \left[2(4)^2 - \frac{1}{3}(2)^3 - (0) \right] =$$

$$\frac{1}{4} \left[32 - \frac{8}{3} \right] = \frac{22}{3}$$

17.   **A**   Find the average value of $f(x) = 2\sin x - \sin 2x$ from 0 to π.

Recall the formula for calculating average value.

$$f_{ave} = \frac{1}{b-a} \int_a^b f(x)\,dx$$

Plug in and solve out the integral.

$$f_{ave} = \frac{1}{b-a} \int_a^b f(x)\,dx = \frac{1}{\pi} \int_0^\pi (2\sin x - \sin 2x)\,dx =$$

$$\frac{1}{\pi} \left[-2\cos x + \frac{1}{2}\cos 2x \right]_0^\pi =$$

$$\frac{1}{\pi} \left[-2(-1) + \frac{1}{2}(1) - \left(-2(1) + \frac{1}{2}(1) \right) \right] =$$

$$\frac{1}{\pi} \left[\frac{5}{2} - \left(-\frac{3}{2} \right) \right] = \frac{4}{\pi}$$

18.   **D**   Recall the formula for calculating average value.

$$f_{ave} = \frac{1}{b-a} \int_a^b f(x)\,dx$$

Plug in and set up the integral.

$$f_{ave} = \frac{1}{b-a} \int_a^b f(x)\,dx = \frac{1}{5} \int_0^5 \left[x\sqrt{(1+x^2)} \right] dx$$

Chapter 25
AB & BC Calculus
Free Response Drill

AB & BC CALCULUS FREE RESPONSE DRILL

1. Let f be a function defined by $f(x) = \dfrac{1}{(x^2 - 9)}$.

   (a) What is the domain of f? Justify your answer.

   (b) Discuss the symmetry of f. Justify your answer.

   (c) For what interval(s) is f increasing? Justify your answer.

   (d) For what interval(s) is f concave down?

2. Let f be the function defined by $f(x) = 2 - 15x + 9x^2 - x^3$.

   (a) Find the x- and y-coordinates of the relative maxima and relative minima. Justify your answer.

   (b) Find an equation for the line normal to f at $(2, 1)$. Justify your answer.

   (c) Find the x- and y-coordinates of any points of inflection. Justify your answer.

3. The velocity of a particle is given by $v(t) = 3t^2 - 12t + 9$, where t is measured in seconds and v is measured in meters/second.

   (a) Find the position function if $s(3) = 0$.

   (b) When is the particle moving forward?

   (c) Find the total distance traveled by the particle during the first five seconds.

4. Let f be defined by the function $f(x) = 4x - x^2$.

   (a) Find the average value of the function on the interval $[0,4]$.

   (b) Let R be the region bounded by the x-axis and the graph of $f(x) = 4x - x^2$. Find the area of the region R.

   (c) Let R be the region bounded by the x-axis and the graph of $f(x) = 4x - x^2$. Find the volume of the solid formed by revolving the region R around the x-axis.

   (d) Find the x- and y-coordinates of the absolute maximum of f from $[0,4]$.

5. Let a curve be defined as $x^2 + 4xy + y^2 = 13$.

   (a) Find the equation of the line tangent to the curve at the point (2,1).

   (b) Find the equation of the line normal to the curve at the point (1,2).

   (c) Find $\dfrac{d^2y}{dx^2}$ at (2,1).

6. Let $y = x^4 + 4x^3$.

   (a) Discuss the domain and symmetry of y. Justify your answer.

   (b) Find the x- and y-intercepts of y. Justify your answer.

   (c) Find the intervals on which y is increasing or decreasing and state any relative extrema. Justify your answer.

   (d) Find the intervals of concavity and the point(s) of inflection of y. Justify your answer.

7. A particle moves according to the function $f(t) = t^3 - 12t^2 + 36t$, where t is measured in seconds and f in feet.

   (a) Find the velocity and acceleration at time t. Justify your answer.

   (b) What is the velocity after 3 seconds? The acceleration after 3 seconds? Is the particle speeding up or slowing down?

   (c) When is the particle at rest?

   (d) Find the total distance traveled by the particle during the first 8 seconds.

8. Consider the equation $f(x) = 2\cos x + \cos^2 x$ on the interval $[0, 2\pi]$.

   (a) Find the intervals where the function is increasing or decreasing. Justify your answer.

   (b) Find the intervals of concavity of $f(x) = 2\cos x + \cos^2 x$. Justify your answer.

   (c) State the x- and y-coordinates for any relative extrema and point(s) of inflection. Justify your answer.

9. Consider the equation $y = x\sqrt{(x+3)}$.

    (a)   What is the domain of y? Justify your answer.

    (b)   Find the relative extrema of y. Justify your answer.

    (c)   Find the intervals of concavity and points of inflection, if any. Justify your answer.

10. Water is leaking out of an inverted conical tank at a rate of $10,000 \text{ cm}^3/\text{min}$ at the same time that water is being pumped into the tank at a constant rate. The tank has a height of 6 m and the diameter at the top is 4 m.

    (a)   Find an expression for the volume in terms of the height, h.

    (b)   Find an expression for the volume in terms of the radius, r.

    (c)   If the water level is rising at a rate of 20 cm/min when the height of the water is 2 m, find the rate at which water is being pumped into the tank.

11. Bacteria grows in a petri dish. The rate of growth of the bacteria is $\dfrac{dB}{dt} = kB$, where k is a constant.

    (a)   Find an expression for B, the number of cells in the dish (in thousands), in terms of t, the number of minutes passed, if the number of cells is 30 thousand initially and 60 thousand after 1 minute.

    (b)   In how many minutes will the number of cells be 300 thousand?

12. If the velocity of the particle traveling along the x-axis is given by $v(t) = \dfrac{2t-5}{t^2+10t+24}$:

    (a)   Find the distance the particle travels from $t = 0$ to $t = 5$.

    (b)   What is the formula for the acceleration of the particle? What is the acceleration at $t = 3$?

    (c)   At what time(s) is the particle's speed decreasing?

13. Consider the parametric functions $x = 3t^3 - 3t$ and $y = 2t^2 + 6t - 4$ that describes the curve of a particle.

   (a) Find $\dfrac{dx}{dt}$ and $\dfrac{dy}{dt}$.

   (b) What is the slope of the curve at $t = 3$?

   (c) Find the equation of the normal line to the curve at $t = 3$.

   (d) Find $\dfrac{d^2y}{dx^2}$ at $t = 3$.

14. Let $F(x) = \displaystyle\int_0^x \left[\sin 2t + t^2\right] dt$ on the closed interval $[0, 2\pi]$.

   (a) Approximate $F(\pi)$ using six inscribed trapezoids.

   (b) Find $F'(2\pi)$.

   (c) Find the average value of $F'(x)$ on the interval $[0, 2\pi]$.

15. If the acceleration of a train is given by $a(t) = 24t \, \text{m/sec}^2$. The velocity of the train is 60 m/sec at $t = 0$. If the train has traveled 72 m after 2 sec, find:

   (a) The equation for the train's velocity at time t.

   (b) The speed of the train at $t = 10$.

   (c) The distance the train travels from $t = 0$ to $t = 10$.

16.

x	$f(x)$	$f'(x)$	$f''(x)$	$f'''(x)$	$f^{(4)}(x)$
–1	3	–2	–16	72	–168
0	0	0	12	24	72
1	15	46	112	216	312

Let f be a function that is differentiable on all orders for $x > 0$. Selected values of f and its first four derivatives are given in the table above. The function and first two derivatives are increasing on the interval $-1 \le x \le 1$.

(a) Write the second-degree Taylor polynomial for f about $x = -1$ and use it to approximate $f(-0.8)$. Is the approximation greater than or less than the true value?

(b) Write the fourth-degree Taylor polynomial for f about $x = -1$ and use it to approximate $f(-0.8)$.

(c) Use the Lagrange error bound to show that the fourth-degree Taylor polynomial for f about $x = -1$ approximates $f(-0.8)$ with an error less than –0.01.

Chapter 26
AB & BC Calculus
Free Response Drill
Answers and
Explanations

EXPLANATIONS

1. Let f be a function defined by $f(x) = \dfrac{1}{(x^2 - 9)}$.

    (a) What is the domain of f? Justify your answer.

    (a) Anytime there is a function in the denominator of the expression, you must figure out where that denominator equals zero. The value(s) calculated will turn out to be where x cannot exist due to being undefined. So, set the denominator equal to zero and solve for x.

    $$x^2 - 9 = 0$$
    $$x^2 = 9$$
    $$x = \pm 3$$

    So, the domain must be $\{ x \mid x \neq \pm 3 \}$.

    (b) Discuss the symmetry of f. Justify your answer.

    (b) To figure out symmetry of a function, you must determine whether it is even or odd. If f is even, then that means $f(-x) = f(x)$. If f is odd, then that means $f(-x) = -f(x)$. Plug $-x$ into the function to see what happens.

    $$f(-x) = \frac{1}{\left((-x)^2 - 9\right)} = \frac{1}{\left(x^2 - 9\right)} = f(x)$$

    Since $f(-x) = f(x)$, the function f is even. Thus, it is symmetric about the x-axis.

    (c) For what interval(s) is f increasing? Justify your answer.

    (c) To find the interval(s) on which f is increasing, you must take the derivative. First, make things a little easier for yourself by rewriting the expression with a negative exponent and use the chain rule.

    $$f(x) = \frac{1}{\left(x^2 - 9\right)} = (x^2 - 9)^{-1}$$
    $$f'(x) = \frac{1}{\left(x^2 - 9\right)^{-2}}(2x)$$
    $$= \frac{-2x}{\left(x^2 - 9\right)^2}$$

To find the intervals, you must set the expression equal to zero to find the critical points. Since you have discontinuities at $x = \pm 3$, they are a part of your critical values, so you only need to set the numerator equal to zero.

$$-2x = 0$$
$$x = 0$$

Test values around your critical points to determine the behavior of f. Since the denominator will always remain positive, the only real focus must be at the numerator.

$$f'(-4) = + \ ; \ \ f'(-1) = + \ ; \ \ f'(1) = - \ ; \ \ f'(4) = -$$

So, f is increasing on $(-\infty, -3)$ and $(-3, 0)$.

(d)   For what interval(s) is f concave down?

(d)   To tackle this part, you must take the second derivative. You can use the first derivative you already found in part (c) to start this question. You may use either the quotient rule, or you may rewrite the derivative with a negative exponent and use the product rule in conjunction with the chain rule. (Both are shown)

Quotient Rule:

$$f'(x) = \frac{-2x}{\left(x^2 - 9\right)^2}$$

$$f''(x) = \frac{(-2)(x^2-9)^2 - (-2x)[2(x^2-9)^1(2x)]}{\left[\left(x^2-9\right)^2\right]^2}$$

$$f''(x) = \frac{(x^2-9)[-2(x^2-9)+8x^2]}{\left(x^2-9\right)^4}$$

$$f''(x) = \frac{6x^2+18}{\left(x^2-9\right)^3}$$

Product and Chain Rule:

$$f'(x) = \frac{2x}{\left(x^2-9\right)^2} = 2x(x^2-9)^{-2}$$

$$f''(x) = (2)(x^2-9)^2 + (2x)[-2(x^2-9)^{-3}(2x)]$$

$$f''(x) = (x^2-9)^{-3}[2(x^2-9)-8x]$$

$$f''(x) = \frac{6x^2+18}{\left(x^2-9\right)^2}$$

To find the intervals of concavity, you must set the second derivative equal to zero. When this is done, there are no non-imaginary points of inflection to be solved for, so you must use the discontinuities at $x = \pm\, 3$ to test for concavity of f. Since the numerator now will always remain positive no matter what is plugged in for x, your focus must be with the denominator to determine whether f is concave up or concave down.

$$f''(-4) = +\;\;;\;\;f''(0) = \;-\;\;;\;\;f''(4) = +$$

So, f is concave down on $(-3,3)$.

2.   Let f be the function defined by $f(x) = 2 - 15x + 9x^2 - x^3$.

(a)   Find the x- and y-coordinates of the relative maxima and relative minima. Justify your answer.

(a)   To find the relative maxima and relative minima, you must take the first derivative and set it equal to zero to solve for x.

$$f(x) = 2 - 15x + 9x^2 - x^3$$
$$f'(x) = -15 + 18x - 3x^2$$
$$f'(x) = -3(x^2 - 6x + 5) = 0$$
$$= -3(x - 5)(x - 1) = 0$$
$$x = 5\;\;;x = 1$$

To determine whether your x-coordinate is a maximum or a minimum, you must test values around your critical points to see the behavior of f.

$$f'(0) = -3(-)(-) = -\;\;;\;\;f'(3) = -3(-)(+) = +\;\;;\;\;f'(6) = -3(+)(+) = -$$

From the testing of random x values into the derivative, you can conclude that $x = 1$ is a relative minimum, and that 5 is a relative maximum. To find the y-coordinates, simply plug the x-coordinate into the original function.

$$f(1) = 2 - 15(1) + 9(1)^2 - (1)^3 = -5$$
$$f(5) = 2 - 15(5) + 9(5)^2 - (5)^3 = 27$$

So the relative maximum occurs at $(5,27)$ and the relative minimum occurs at $(1,-5)$.

(b)   Find an equation for the line normal to f at $(2,0)$. Justify your answer.

(b)   To find an equation for a normal line at a given point, you must take the first derivative and plug in the coordinate to find the slope. For a normal line, you must take the negative reciprocal of the calculated slope. You can use the derivative found in part (a) already (pending it's correctly calculated).

$$f'(x) = -15 + 18x - 3x^2$$
$$f'(2) = -15 + 18(2) - 3(2)^2 = 9.$$

Since 9 is the calculated slope, the normal slope must be $\left(-\dfrac{1}{9}\right)$.

To find the equation, you must use the point-slope form of a line equation.

$$y - y_1 = m\,(x - x_1)$$
$$y - (0) = \left(-\frac{1}{9}\right)[x - (2)]$$
$$-9y = x - 2$$
$$2 = x + 9y$$

(c)   Find the x- and y-coordinates of any points of inflection of f. Justify your answer.

(c)   To find the point(s) of inflection, you must take the second derivative and set it equal to zero, so go ahead and grab that first derivative calculated in the earlier parts yet again!

$$f'(x) = -15 + 18x - 3x^2$$
$$f''(x) = 18 - 6x = 0$$
$$18 = 6x$$
$$3 = x$$

To find the y-coordinate, simply take the x-value calculated and plug it into the original function.

$$f(3) = 2 - 15(3) + 9(3)^2 - (3)^3 = 11$$

So the point of inflection occurs at (3, 11).

3.   The velocity of a particle is given by $v(t) = 3t^2 - 12t + 9$, where t is measured in seconds and v is measured in meters/second.

(a)   Find the position function knowing $s(3) = 0$.

(a)   You must integrate the velocity function to find the position function.

$$s(t) = \int v(t)\, dt$$
$$= \int (3t^2 - 12t + 9)\, dt$$
$$= t^3 - 6t^2 + 9t + C$$

Use the initial condition of $s(3) = 0$ to find the value of the constant C.

$s(3) = (3)^3 - 6(3)^2 + 9(3) + C = 0$
$27 - 54 + 27 + C = 0$
$C = 0$

So, the position function is $s(t) = t^3 - 6t^2 + 9t$.

(b)   When is the particle moving forward?

(b)   To find this, you must find where the derivative (the velocity) is equal to zero and test points around those values.

$v(t) = 0$
$3t^2 - 12t + 9 = 0$
$3(t^2 - 4t + 3) = 0$
$3(t - 3)(t - 1) = 0$
$t = 3 \ ; \ t = 1$

Test values of $t = 0$, $t = 2$, and $t = 4$ to determine the sign of the velocity.

$v(0) = + \ ; \ v(2) = - \ ; \ v(4) = +$

Since the velocity is positive at 2 of the areas, the particle is moving forward for values $t < 1$ and $t > 3$.

(c)   Find the total distance traveled by the particle during the first five seconds.

(c)   Since the signs change in the velocity, you must calculate the distance separately for each interval, [0,1], [1,3], and [3,5].

$|s(1) - s(0)| = |4 - 0| = 4$ m
$|s(3) - s(1)| = |0 - 4| = 4$ m
$|s(5) - s(3)| = |20 - 0| = 20$ m

The total distance traveled is $20 + 4 + 4 = 28$ m.

4.   Let f be defined by the function $f(x) = 4x - x^2$.

(a)   Find the average value of the function on the interval [0,4].

(a)   To find the average value of a function on a closed interval, you must use the formula:

$$f_{ave} = \frac{1}{(b-a)} \int f(x)\, dx$$

So you only need to plug in to calculate it.

$$f_{ave} = \frac{1}{(4-0)} \int (4x - x^2)\, dx$$

$$= \frac{1}{4}\left[2x^2 - \frac{1}{3}x^3 \right]_0^4$$

$$= \frac{1}{4}\left[2(4)^2 - \frac{1}{3}(4)^3 \right]$$

$$= \frac{1}{4}\left[32 - \frac{64}{3} \right]$$

$$= \frac{1}{4}\left[\frac{32}{3} \right]$$

$$= \frac{8}{3}$$

(b)   Let R be the region bounded by the graph of $f(x) = 4x - x^2$ and the x-axis. Find the area of R.

(b)   To calculate the area of the region in question, you must integrate the function with respect to x. To find the endpoints of integration, you must set the function equal to zero and solve for x.

$4x - x^2 = 0$

$4x(1 - x) = 0$

$x = 0 \;;\; x = 1$

Now, integrate.

$$A = \int_0^1 (4x - x^2)\, dx$$

$$= \left[2x^2 - \frac{1}{3}x^3 \right]_0^1$$

$$= 2(1)^2 - \frac{1}{3}(1)^3$$

$$= \frac{5}{3}$$

(c) Let R be the region bounded by the x-axis and the graph of $f(x) = 4x - x^2$. Find the volume of the solid formed by revolving the region R around the x-axis.

(c) To find the volume of the region in question, you must integrate the function with respect to x. You can use the endpoints of integration calculated in part (b) for the integral here. Proceed to integration.

$$V = \pi \int_a^b f(x)\, dx$$
$$= \pi \int_0^1 (4x - x^2)^2\, dx$$
$$= \pi \int_0^1 (16x^2 - 8x^3 + x^4)\, dx$$
$$= \pi \left(\frac{16x^3}{3} - 2x^4 + \frac{x^5}{5} \right) \Bigg|_0^1$$
$$= \pi \left[\frac{16}{3} - 2 + \frac{1}{5} \right]$$
$$= \frac{53\pi}{15}$$

(d) Find the x- and y-coordinates of the absolute maximum of f from [0,4].

(d) You first must take the derivative of the function and set it equal to zero to find the critical points on the interval.

$$f(x) = 4x - x^2$$
$$f'(x) = 4 - 2x = 0$$
$$4 = 2x$$
$$2 = x$$

Now test values around the critical point to determine behavior of f.

$$f'(1) = + \quad ; \quad f'(3) = -$$

So, x = 2 is a relative maximum.

To determine the absolute maximum, you must evaluate the critical point and the endpoints of the interval in the original function.

$$f(0) = 4(0) - (0)^2 = 0$$
$$f(2) = 4(2) - (2)^2 = 4$$
$$f(4) = 4(4) - (4)^2 = 0$$

So, the absolute maximum occurs (2,4).

5.   Let a curve be defined as $x^2 + 4xy + y^2 = 13$.

(a) Find the equation of the line tangent to the curve at the point (2,1).

(a) Take the derivative implicitly with respect to x.

$x^2 + 4xy + y^2 = 13$
$2x + 4(y + x\,y') + 2y\,y' = 0$

Do not simplify! Plug the coordinate in immediately to find the slope.

$2(2) + 4[(1) + (2)\,y'] + 2(1)\,y' = 0$

$4 + 4 + 8\,y' + 2\,y' = 0$

$10\,y' = -8$

$y' = -\dfrac{4}{5}$

Use the point-slope formula to find the equation of the tangent line.

$y - y_1 = m(x - x_1)$

$y - 1 = -\dfrac{4}{5}(x - 2)$

$5y - 5 = -4x + 8$

$4x + 5y = 13$

(b) Find the equation of the line normal to the curve at the point (1,2).

(b) Use the derivative found in part (a) and plug the coordinate into it to find the slope. Since that would be the tangent slope, the normal slope would be the negative reciprocal.

$2(1) + 4[(2) + (1)\,y'] + 2(2)\,y' = 0$
$2 + 8 + 4\,y' + 4\,y' = 0$

$8\,y' = -10$

$y' = -\dfrac{5}{4}$

So, the normal slope is $\dfrac{4}{5}$.

Use the point-slope formula to find the equation of the normal line.

$y - y_1 = m(x - x_1)$

$y - 2 = \dfrac{4}{5}(x - 1)$

$5y - 10 = 4x - 4$

$-6 = 4x - 5y$

(c)   Find $\dfrac{d^2 y}{dx^2}$ at (2,1).

(c)   Recall that you've found the derivative already so now you need to solve for y'.

$x^2 + 4xy + y^2 = 13$

$2x + 4(y + x\,y') + 2y\,y' = 0$

$2x + 4y + 4x\,y' + 2y\,y' = 0$

$(4x + 2y)\,y' = -(2x + 4y)$

$y' = \dfrac{-(2x + 4y)}{4x + 2y}$

Take the second derivative implicitly with respect to x using the quotient rule for derivatives.

$$y'' = \dfrac{-(2 + 4y')(4x + 2y) - [-(2x + 4y)(4 + 2y')]}{\left(4x + 2y\right)^2}$$

Do not simplify! Plug in the coordinate immediately. Now, in part (a), you figured out the value of y' at (2, 1), which is $-\dfrac{4}{5}$, which must be plugged in as well.

$$y'' = \dfrac{-\left(2 + 4\left(-\dfrac{4}{5}\right)\right)(4(2) + 2(1)) + (2(2) + 4(1))\left(4 + 2\left(-\dfrac{4}{5}\right)\right)}{\left(4(2) + 2(1)\right)^2}$$

$$= \dfrac{\left(-\dfrac{6}{5}\right)(10) + (8)\left(\dfrac{12}{5}\right)}{100}$$

$$= \dfrac{156}{500} = \dfrac{39}{125}$$

6.   Let $y = x^4 + 4x^3$.

(a)   Discuss the domain and symmetry of y. Justify your answer.

(a)   When looking to the domain of a function, it's strictly asking you to figure out all of the potential values that x can take on in the function. Since y has no undefined values or imaginary values, it is continuous everywhere.

Domain: No restrictions; no vertical or horizontal asymptotes, so $x \, \varepsilon \, \mathrm{R}$.

To determine the symmetry of y, you must find $f(-x)$. If $f(-x) = f(x)$, then the function is even and symmetric about the y-axis. If $f(-x) = -f(x)$, then the function is odd and symmetric about the origin $(0,0)$.

$$f(-x) = (-x)^4 + 4(-x)^3 = x^4 - 4x \neq f(x)$$

$$f(-x) = (-x)^4 + 4(-x)^3 = x^4 - 4x \neq -f(x)$$

Thus, y has no symmetry.

(b) Find the x- and y-intercepts of y. Justify your answer.

(b) To find the intercepts, you will need to make $x = 0$ and solve for y, then make $y = 0$ and solve for x.

$$0 = x^4 + 4x^3 \qquad\qquad y = (0)^4 + 4(0)^3$$
$$0 = x^3(x + 4) \qquad\qquad y = 0$$
$$x = 0 \;\; ; \;\; x = -4$$

So, the intercepts are $(0,0)$ and $(-4,0)$

(c) Find the intervals on which y is increasing or decreasing and state any relative extrema. Justify your answer.

(c) You must take the derivative and set it equal to zero to find the critical points.

$$y = x^4 + 4x^3$$
$$y' = 4x^3 + 12x^2$$
$$4x^2(x + 3) = 0$$
$$x = 0 \;\; ; \;\; x = -3$$

Test values around the critical points to determine the behavior of y.

$$y'(-4) = - \;\; ; \;\; y'(-1) = + \;\; ; \;\; y'(1) = +$$

So, y is increasing on $(-3,\infty)$ and decreasing on $(-\infty,-3)$ and the relative minimum occurs at $y(-3) = (-3)^4 + 4(-3)^3 = -27$.

(d) Find the intervals of concavity and the point(s) of inflection of y. Justify your answer.

(d) From part (c), you determined the first derivative, so keep it going and find the second derivative. Then set it equal to zero and find the inflection points.

$y' = 4x^3 + 12x^2$
$y'' = 12x^2 + 24x = 0$
$12x(x + 2) = 0$
$x = 0 \; ; \; x = -2$

Test values around the inflection points to determine behavior of y.

$y''(-3) = + \; ; \quad y''(-1) = - \; ; \quad y''(1) = +$

So, y is concave up on $(-\infty, -2)$ and $(0, \infty)$, concave down on $(-2, 0)$, and has points of inflection at $y(0) = 0$ and $y(-2) = -16$.

7. A particle moves according to the function $f(t) = t^3 - 12t^2 + 36t$, where t is measured in seconds and f in feet.

(a) Find the velocity and acceleration at time t.

(a) To find the velocity and acceleration functions, you will need to take the first and second derivatives.

$f(t) = t^3 - 12t^2 + 36t$
$f'(t) = v(t) = 3t^2 - 24t + 36$
$f''(t) = v'(t) = a(t) = 6t - 24$

So, the velocity and acceleration at time t, respectively, are:

$v(t) = 3t^2 - 24t + 36$
$a(t) = 6t - 24$

(b) What is the velocity after 3 seconds? What is the acceleration after 3 seconds? Is the particle speeding up or slowing down?

(b) To calculate the velocity and acceleration at 3 seconds, simply plug 3 into each of their respective formulae.

$v(3) = 3(3)^2 - 24(3) + 36 = -9$ ft/s
$a(3) = 6(3) - 24 = -6$ ft/s^2

When figuring out if the particle is speeding up or slowing down, you simply need to look to the signs of each of the velocity and acceleration at the specific time. When the signs match, the particle is speeding up, when the signs are opposite, the particle slows down.

In this case, at $t = 3$ seconds, the particle is speeding up.

(c)   When is the particle at rest?

(c)   To find this, you must set the derivative equal to zero to find the time values. Take your velocity function found in part (a) and set it equal to zero.

$v(t) = 3t^2 - 24t + 36 = 0$
$3(t^2 - 8t + 12) = 0$
$3(t - 6)(t - 2) = 0$
$t = 6 \; ; \; t = 2$

So, the particle is at rest when $t = 2$ seconds and when $t = 6$ seconds.

(d)   Find the total distance traveled during the first 8 seconds.

(d)   To determine the total distance traveled, you must first check the behavior of the velocity function by testing values around the values of t calculated when you set the velocity equal to zero.

$v(t) = 3(t - 6)(t - 2)$
$v(t) = 0$ at $t = 2 \; ; \; 6$
$v(1) = + \; ; \; v(4) = - \; ; \; v(7) = +$

Since there are sign changes when testing the intervals of the velocity, you must evaluate the position for each critical point.

$|f(2) - f(0)| = |32 - 0| = 32$
$|f(6) - f(2)| = |0 - 32| = 32$
$|f(8) - f(6)| = |32 - 0| = 32$

So, the total distance traveled is $32 + 32 + 32 = 96$ ft.

8.   Consider the equation $f(x) = 2 \cos x + \cos^2 x$ on the interval $[0, 2\pi]$.

(a)   Find the intervals where the function is increasing or decreasing. Justify your answer.

(a)   To calculate the intervals, you must take the derivative and set it equal to zero to find any critical points. The chain rule is required to take the derivative for the squared term.

$$f(x) = 2 \cos x + \cos^2 x = 2 \cos x + (\cos x)^2$$
$$f'(x) = -2 \sin x - 2(\cos x)(\sin x) = 0$$
$$= -2 \sin x \, (1 + \cos x) = 0$$
$$= -2 \sin x = 0 \quad ; \quad 1 + \cos x = 0$$
$$\sin x = 0 \quad ; \quad \cos x = -1$$
$$x = 0, \pi, 2\pi \; ; \; x = \pi$$

Since two of the critical points occur at the endpoints, you need only test values around π to determine the behavior.

$$f'\left(\frac{\pi}{2}\right) = - \quad ; \quad f'\left(\frac{3\pi}{2}\right) = +$$

So, f is decreasing on $[0,\pi)$ and decreasing on $(\pi,2\pi]$.

(b)   Find the intervals of concavity of $f(x) = 2 \cos x + \cos^2 x$. Justify your answer.

(b)   Take the second derivative using your first derivative from part (a). The product rule is necessary for this calculation.

$$f'(x) = -2 \sin x(1 + \cos x)$$
$$f''(x) = (-2 \cos x)(1 + \cos x) + (-2\sin x)(-\sin x)$$
$$= -2 \cos x - 2 \cos^2 x + 2 \sin 2x$$
$$= -2 \cos x - 2 \cos^2 x + 2(1 - \cos^2 x) \qquad (* \sin^2 x + \cos^2 x = 1)$$
$$= -2 \cos x - 2 \cos^2 x + 2 - 2 \cos^2 x$$
$$= -2(2 \cos^2 x + \cos x - 1) = 0$$
$$= -2(2 \cos x - 1)(\cos x + 1) = 0$$
$$2 \cos x - 1 = 0 \quad ; \quad \cos x + 1 = 0$$
$$\cos x = \frac{1}{2} \quad ; \quad \cos x = -1$$
$$x = \frac{\pi}{3}, \frac{5\pi}{3} \quad ; \quad x = \pi$$

Now test values around the inflection points to determine the concavity of f.

$$f''\left(\frac{\pi}{4}\right) = - \quad ; \quad f''\left(\frac{\pi}{2}\right) = + \quad ; \quad f''\left(\frac{5\pi}{4}\right) = + \quad ; \quad f''\left(\frac{11\pi}{6}\right) = -$$

So, f is concave up on $\left(\frac{\pi}{3}, \frac{5\pi}{3}\right)$ and concave down on $\left[0, \frac{\pi}{3}\right)$ and $\left(\frac{5\pi}{3}, 2\pi\right]$.

(c)   State the x- and y-coordinates for any relative extrema and point(s) of inflection. Justify your answer.

(c)   The bulk of the work has already been completed for this part; you just have to take your critical points determined in part (a), and your inflection points determined in part (b), and now plug them into the original function to determine the y-coordinates.

$$f(\pi) = 2 \cos(\pi) + \cos^2(\pi) = 2(-1) + (1) = -1$$

$$f\left(\frac{\pi}{3}\right) = 2 \cos\left(\frac{\pi}{3}\right) + \cos^2\left(\frac{\pi}{3}\right) = 2\left(\frac{1}{2}\right) + \left(\frac{1}{4}\right) = \frac{5}{4}$$

$$f\left(\frac{5\pi}{3}\right) = 2 \cos\left(\frac{5\pi}{3}\right) + \cos^2\left(\frac{5\pi}{3}\right) = 2\left(\frac{1}{2}\right) + \left(\frac{1}{4}\right) = \frac{5}{4}$$

So, f has a relative minimum at $(\pi, -1)$ and points of inflection at $\left(\frac{\pi}{3}, \frac{5}{4}\right)$ and $\left(\frac{5\pi}{3}, \frac{5}{4}\right)$.

9.   Consider the equation $y = x\sqrt{(x+3)}$.

(a)   What is the domain of y? Justify your answer.

(a)   To find the domain of a function with a radical, you must determine the domain by setting what is under the radical greater than or equal to zero and solving for x. When the radical is in the numerator, the radicand CAN equal zero. It's when it is in the denominator that it cannot.

$$x + 3 \geq 0$$
$$x \geq -3$$

So, the domain is $\{x \, \varepsilon \, \mathrm{R} \mid x \geq -3\}$, or simply $\{x \geq -3\}$.

(b)   Find the relative extrema of y. Justify your answer.

(b)   To find the relative extrema, you must take the first derivative and set it equal to zero. The product rule and the chain rule will be required to take the derivative.

$$y = x\sqrt{(x+3)}$$

$$y' = 1(x+3)^{\frac{1}{2}} + x\left[\frac{1}{2}(x+3)^{-\frac{1}{2}}(1)\right] = 0$$

$$\sqrt{(x+3)} = -\frac{x}{2\sqrt{(x+3)}}$$

$$= 2(x+3) = -x$$

$$2x + 6 = -x$$

$$6 = -3x$$

$$-2 = x$$

$$x = -3 \quad ; \quad x = -2$$

Though x can't equal -3, since it's in the denominator, it must be considered as a critical number due to a discontinuity in the derivative.

Test values around the critical numbers to determine the behavior of y.

$$y'\left(-\frac{5}{2}\right) = - \quad ; \quad y'(0) = +$$

So, y has a relative minimum at $y(-2) = -2$.

(c) Find the intervals of concavity and points of inflection, if any. Justify your answer.

(c) Find the second derivative using the first derivative you gathered in part (b). The product rule and the chain rule will be required to take the derivative.

$$y' = (x+3)^{\frac{1}{2}} + \frac{x}{2}(x+3)^{-\frac{1}{2}}$$

$$y'' = \frac{1}{2}(x+3)^{-\frac{1}{2}} + \frac{x}{2}\left(-\frac{1}{2}\right)(x+3)^{-\frac{3}{2}} + (x+3)^{-\frac{1}{2}}\left(\frac{1}{2}\right)$$

$$y'' = (x+3)^{-\frac{1}{2}} - \frac{x}{4}(x+3)^{-\frac{3}{2}}$$

$$(x+3)^{-\frac{1}{2}} = \frac{x}{4}(x+3)^{-\frac{3}{2}}$$

$$x+3 = \frac{x}{4}$$

$$4x+12 = x$$

$$3x = -12$$

$$x = -4 \leftarrow (Out\ of\ domain)$$

Another point of inflection exists at $x = -3$, where the denominator of the second derivative is discontinuous.

Since any value greater than -3 will make y'' positive, the function y is concave up everywhere and will not have any points of inflection.

So, y is concave up from $(-3, \infty)$.

10. Water is leaking out of an inverted conical tank at a rate of 10,000 cm³/min at the same time that water is being pumped into the tank at a constant rate. The tank has a height of 6 m and the diameter at the top is 4 m.

(a) Find an expression for the volume in terms of the height, h.

(a) First, recall the formula for volume of a cone. It is:

$$V = \frac{1}{3}\pi r^2 h$$

Next, since the equation must be in terms of the single variable h, you need to see how the radius, r, relates to h. You are given the following:

Height = 6 m   Diameter = 4 m (which means Radius = 2 m)

So you can now find a fractional relationship relating the radius and the height.

Since $r = 2$ m and $h = 6$ m, r must be $\dfrac{1}{3}$ of h.

Rewrite the volume equation explicitly in terms of h.

$$V = \frac{1}{3}\pi\left(\frac{h}{3}\right)^2 h$$
$$= \frac{1}{3}\pi\left(\frac{h^2}{9}\right)h$$
$$= \frac{\pi}{27}h^3$$

(b)   Find an expression for the volume in terms of the radius, r.

(b)   Use the information gathered in part (a) to aid you here. The only difference is you are now keeping the equation in terms of r. Since r is $\dfrac{1}{3}$ of h, it follows that h would be equal to $3r$. The formula will now be:

$$V = \frac{1}{3}\pi r^2(3r)$$
$$= 3 \times \frac{1}{3}\pi r^3$$
$$= \pi r^3$$

(c)   If the water level is rising at a rate of 20 cm/min when the height of the water is 2 m, find the rate at which water is being pumped into the tank.

(c)   In any related rates question, it is imperative to identify what is given to you and what you must solve for.

$$\frac{dh}{dt} = 20 \text{ cm/min} \quad ; \quad h = 2\text{m} \quad ; \quad \frac{dV}{dt} = ?$$

Note the difference in units for $\dfrac{dh}{dt}$ and h. Convert $h = 2$ m into cm by multiplying by 100. So, h now equals 200 cm.

In part (a), you gathered a formula for volume explicitly in terms of h. This is the formula you need to use since all given information is in terms of either the height or the height differential. So now you must take the derivative, with respect to time, and plug in what you know.

$$V = \frac{\pi}{27} h^3$$

$$\frac{dV}{dt} = \left(\frac{\pi}{9}\right) h^2 \frac{dh}{dt}$$

$$\frac{dV}{dt} = \left(\frac{\pi}{9}\right)(200 \text{ cm})^2 (20 \text{ cm} / \text{min})$$

$$\frac{dV}{dt} = \frac{800,000 \, \pi}{9} \frac{\text{cm}^3}{\text{min}}$$

Recall, in the given information, the rate of 10,000 cm³/min, so the rate is:

$$\frac{800,000 \, \pi}{9} - 10,000 \frac{\text{cm}^3}{\text{min}}$$

11.   Bacteria grows in a petri dish. The rate of growth of the bacteria is $\frac{dB}{dt} = kB$, where k is a constant.

(a)   Find an expression for B, the number of cells in the dish (in thousands), in terms of t, the number of minutes passed, if the number of cells is 30 thousand initially and 60 thousand after 1 minute.

(a)   Solve the differential equation for B: $\int \frac{dB}{B} = k \int dt$, so $B = Ce^{kt}$. Use the initial condition to solve for C: $30 = Ce^{k(0)}$, so $C = 30$. Then, use the second point to solve for k: $60 = 30e^{k}$, thus, $k = \ln 2$. The final equation for B is: $B = 30e^{(\ln 2)t}$.

(b)   In how many minutes will the number of cells be 300 thousand?

(b)   To determine the time it takes to reach 300 thousand cells, set the equation to 300 and solve for t: $300 = 30e^{(\ln 2)t}$, so $t = \frac{\ln 10}{\ln 2} \approx 3.32193$ minutes.

12.   If the velocity of the particle traveling along the *x*-axis is given by $v(t) = \dfrac{2t-5}{t^2+10t+24}$.

(a)   Find the distance the particle travels from *t* = 0 to *t* = 5.

(a)   First, determine whether the particle changes direction or not. In order to do that, set $v(t)=0$. $v(t) = \dfrac{2t-5}{t^2+10t+24} = 0$. The velocity changes direction at $t = \dfrac{5}{2}$. In order to find the distance travels, you must take the absolute value of the distance traveled from *t* = 0 to $t = \dfrac{5}{2}$ and add it to the absolute value of the distance traveled from $t = \dfrac{5}{2}$ to *t* = 5. The absolute values are required to have total distance, regardless of direction.

The distance will be found by integrating *v(t)*, but first the method of partial fractions is re-

quired. $\int v(t)\,dt = d(t)$. $\dfrac{2t-5}{t^2+10t+24} = \dfrac{2t-5}{(t+6)(t+4)} = \dfrac{A}{t+6} + \dfrac{B}{t+4}$. Solving for *A* and *B*,

$A = \dfrac{17}{2}$ and $B = -\dfrac{13}{2}$. Thus, $d(t) = \left| \int_{0}^{\frac{5}{2}} \left(\dfrac{\frac{17}{2}}{t+6} - \dfrac{\frac{13}{2}}{t+4} \right) dt \right| + \left| \int_{\frac{5}{2}}^{5} \left(\dfrac{\frac{17}{2}}{t+6} - \dfrac{\frac{13}{2}}{t+4} \right) dt \right| = 0.271496$.

(b)   What is the formula for the acceleration of the particle? What is the acceleration at *t* = 3?

(b)   The acceleration is the derivative of the velocity, so $\dfrac{d}{dt}v(t) = a(t) = \dfrac{2(t^2+10t+24) - (2t-5)(2t+10)}{(t^2+10t+24)^2}$. At *t* = 5, $a(t) = 0.027715$.

(c)   At what time(s) is the particle's speed decreasing?

(c)   The particle's speed decreases when the acceleration and velocity have opposite signs. The signs of both of these functions change when they equal zero. We already know when *v(t)* = 0, so take *a(t)* from part be, set it equal to zero and solve. $a(t) = 0$ at $t = 9.93$. Now, make a chart:

Time	Velocity	Acceleration
$0 < t < \dfrac{5}{2}$	$-$	$+$
$\dfrac{5}{2} < t < 9.93$	$+$	$+$
$t > 9.93$	$+$	$-$

Thus, the speed is decreasing from $0 < t < \dfrac{5}{2}$ and $t > 9.93$.

13.   Consider the parametric functions $x = 3t^3 - 3t$ and $y = 2t^2 + 6t - 4$ that describes the curve of a particle.

(a)   Find $\dfrac{dx}{dt}$ and $\dfrac{dy}{dt}$.

(a) $\dfrac{dx}{dt} = 9t^2 - 3$

$\dfrac{dy}{dt} = 4t + 6$

(b)   What is the slope of the curve at $t = 3$?

(b) $\dfrac{dy}{dx} = \dfrac{\dfrac{dy}{dt}}{\dfrac{dx}{dt}} = \dfrac{4t + 6}{9t^2 - 3}$

At $t = 3$, $\dfrac{dy}{dx} = \dfrac{4(3) + 6}{9(3)^2 - 3} = \dfrac{18}{78} = \dfrac{3}{13}$

(c)   Find the equation of the normal line to the curve at $t = 3$.

(c)   Since the slope of the curve at $t = 3$ is $\dfrac{3}{13}$, the slope of the normal line is $-\dfrac{13}{3}$. Determine the coordinates at $t = 3$ by plugging it into both parametric functions: $x = 72$ and $y = 32$. Thus, the equation of the normal line is $y - 32 = -\dfrac{13}{3}(x - 72)$.

(d) Find $\dfrac{d^2 y}{dx^2}$ at $t = 3$.

(d) $\dfrac{d^2 x}{dt^2} = 18t$ and $\dfrac{d^2 y}{dt^2} = 4$. From there, $\dfrac{d^2 y}{dx^2} = \dfrac{\dfrac{d^2 y}{dt^2}}{\dfrac{d^2 x}{dt^2}} = \dfrac{4}{18t}$. At $t = 3$, $\dfrac{d^2 y}{dx^2} = \dfrac{2}{27}$.

14   Let $F(x) = \displaystyle\int_0^x \left[\sin 2t + t^2 \right] dt$ on the closed interval $[0, 2\pi]$.

(a) Approximate $F(\pi)$ using six inscribed trapezoids.

(a) The area under the curve using trapezoids is found from the formula:
$A = \dfrac{1}{2}\left(\dfrac{b-a}{n}\right)\left(y_0 + 2y_1 + 2y_2 + \ldots + 2y_{n-2} + 2y_{n-1} + y_n\right)$, where n is the number of sub intervals

and a and b are the limits of integration.

$$A = \dfrac{1}{2}\left(\dfrac{\pi - 0}{6}\right)\begin{pmatrix} \sin 0 + 0 + 2\left(\sin\dfrac{\pi}{3} + \dfrac{\pi^2}{36}\right) + 2\left(\sin\dfrac{2\pi}{3} + \dfrac{\pi^2}{9}\right) + 2\left(\sin\pi + \dfrac{\pi^2}{4}\right) + \\ 2\left(\sin\dfrac{4\pi}{3} + \dfrac{4\pi^2}{9}\right) + 2\left(\sin\dfrac{5\pi}{3} + \dfrac{25\pi^2}{36}\right) + \sin 2\pi + \pi^2 \end{pmatrix} = 10.479$$

(b) Find $F'(2\pi)$.

(b) The Second Fundamental Theorem of Calculus states $\dfrac{d}{dx}\displaystyle\int_0^x f(t)\,dt = f(x)$. Thus, $F'(x) = f(x)$ or $\sin 2x + x^2$. At 2π, $F'(x) = 4\pi^2 = 39.478$.

(c) Find the average value of $F'(x)$ on the interval $[0, 2\pi]$.

(c) Use the MVTI, which states $\dfrac{1}{b-a}\displaystyle\int_a^b f(x)\,dx$. Thus, for $F(x)$, the average value is 13.1595.

15. If the acceleration of a train is given by $a(t) = 24t$ m/sec^2. The velocity of the train is 60 m/sec at $t = 0$. If the train has traveled 72 m after 2 sec, find:

(a) The equation for the train's velocity at time t

(a) As $a(t) = \dfrac{dv}{dt}$, you can separate the variables to solve for v: $dv = 24t\,dt$ so $v = 12t^2 + C$. Plug in the condition given, 60 m/sec at $t = 0$, to solve for C. The final equation is $v(t) = 12t^2 + 60$.

(b) The speed of the train at $t = 10$

(b) The speed of the train is the absolute value of the velocity. Use the equation for velocity from part (a) and plug in 10. Take the absolute value to find the speed: $\left|v(10)\right| = \left|12(10^2) + 60\right| = 1260$ m/sec.

(c) The distance the train travels from $t = 0$ to $t = 10$

(c) Since the velocity does not equal zero anywhere on the interval, [0, 10], to determine the distance traveled, integrate the equation for velocity from $t = 0$ to $t = 10$. First, separate the variables: $v(t) = \dfrac{dx}{dt} = 12t^2 + 60$, so $dx = (12t^2 + 60)dt$. Integrate both sides, with the right side integrated from $t = 0$ to $t = 10$: $\int dx = \int_0^{10} (12t^2 + 60)dt$. The total distance traveled is 4600 m.

16.

x	$f(x)$	$f'(x)$	$f''(x)$	$f'''(x)$	$f^{(4)}(x)$
−1	3	−2	−16	72	−168
0	0	0	12	24	72
1	15	46	112	216	312

Let f be a function that is differentiable on all orders for $x > 0$. Selected values of f and its first four derivatives are given in the table above. The function and first two derivatives are increasing on the interval $-1 \le x \le 1$.

(a) Write the second-degree Taylor polynomial for f about $x = -1$ and use it to approximate $f(-0.8)$. Is the approximation greater than or less than the true value?

(a) $T_2(x) = f(-1) + f'(-1)(x+1) + \dfrac{f''(-1)}{2}(x+1)^2 = -8x^2 - 18x - 7$

$T_2(-0.8) = -8(-0.8)^2 - 18(-0.8) - 7 = 2.28$

$T_2(-0.8) < f(-0.8)$ because $f'(x)$ and $f''(x)$ are increasing on the interval $-1 \le x \le 1$.

(b) Write the fourth-degree Taylor polynomial for f about $x = -1$ and use it to approximate $f(-0.8)$.

(b)

$T_4(x) = f(-1) + f'(-1)(x+1) + \dfrac{f''(-1)}{2}(x+1)^2 + \dfrac{f'''(-1)}{3!}(x+1)^3$

$+ \dfrac{f^4(-1)}{4!}(x+1)^4 = 3 - 2(x+1) - 8(x+1)^2 + 12(x+1)^3 - 7(x+1)^4$

$T_4(-0.8) = 3 - 2(-0.8+1) - 8(-0.8+1)^2 + 12(-0.8+1)^3 - 7(-0.8+1)^4 = 2.3648$

(c) Use the Lagrange error bound to show that the fourth-degree Taylor polynomial for f about $x = -1$ approximates $f(-0.8)$ with an error less than -0.01.

(c) $\max\limits_{-1 \le x \le -0.8} \left| f^4(x) \right| = -168$ because the fourth derivative of f is increasing on the interval $-1 \le x \le 1$.

Thus, $\left| T_4(-0.8) - f(-0.8) \right| \le -168 \left(\dfrac{\left| -1 - (-0.8)^4 \right|}{4!} \right)$. The maximum error would then be -0.0112

which is less than -0.01.

Part V
Practice Exams

Chapter 27
AB Calculus
Practice Test

AP® Calculus AB Exam

SECTION I: Multiple-Choice Questions

DO NOT OPEN THIS BOOKLET UNTIL YOU ARE TOLD TO DO SO.

At a Glance

Total Time
1 hour and 45 minutes
Number of Questions
45
Percent of Total Grade
50%
Writing Instrument
Pencil required

Instructions

Section I of this examination contains 45 multiple-choice questions. Fill in only the ovals for numbers 1 through 45 on your answer sheet.

CALCULATORS MAY NOT BE USED IN THIS PART OF THE EXAMINATION.

Indicate all of your answers to the multiple-choice questions on the answer sheet. No credit will be given for anything written in this exam booklet, but you may use the booklet for notes or scratch work. After you have decided which of the suggested answers is best, completely fill in the corresponding oval on the answer sheet. Give only one answer to each question. If you change an answer, be sure that the previous mark is erased completely. Here is a sample question and answer.

Sample Question   Sample Answer

Chicago is a
(A) state
(B) city
(C) country
(D) continent
(E) village

Use your time effectively, working as quickly as you can without losing accuracy. Do not spend too much time on any one question. Go on to other questions and come back to the ones you have not answered if you have time. It is not expected that everyone will know the answers to all the multiple-choice questions.

About Guessing

Many candidates wonder whether or not to guess the answers to questions about which they are not certain. Multiple choice scores are based on the number of questions answered correctly. Points are not deducted for incorrect answers, and no points are awarded for unanswered questions. Because points are not deducted for incorrect answers, you are encouraged to answer all multiple-choice questions. On any questions you do not know the answer to, you should eliminate as many choices as you can, and then select the best answer among the remaining choices.

THIS PAGE INTENTIONALLY LEFT BLANK.

CALCULUS AB

SECTION I, Part A

Time—55 Minutes

Number of questions—28

A CALCULATOR MAY NOT BE USED ON THIS PART OF THE EXAMINATION

<u>Directions</u>: Solve each of the following problems, using the available space for scratchwork. After examining the form of the choices, decide which is the best of the choices given and fill in the corresponding oval on the answer sheet. No credit will be given for anything written in the test book. Do not spend too much time on any one problem.

<u>In this test</u>: Unless otherwise specified, the domain of a function f is assumed to be the set of all real numbers x for which $f(x)$ is a real number.

1. Find the second derivative of $x^2 y = 2$.

   (A) $\dfrac{6y}{x^2}$

   (B) $\dfrac{x^2}{y}$

   (C) $\dfrac{y}{x^2}$

   (D) $-\dfrac{6y}{x^2}$

   (E) $-\dfrac{x^2}{6y}$

GO ON TO THE NEXT PAGE.

2. If $y = \ln\left(6x^3 - 2x^2\right)$, then $f'(x) =$

   (A) $\dfrac{9x + 2}{3x^2 - x}$

   (B) $\dfrac{9x + 2}{3x^2 + x}$

   (C) $\dfrac{9x - 2}{3x^2 - x}$

   (D) $\dfrac{9x + 2}{3x^2 + x}$

   (E) $\dfrac{18x^2 + 4x}{6x^3 - 2x^2}$

3. Find $\lim\limits_{x \to \infty} 3xe^{-3x}$.

   (A) $\dfrac{1}{3}$

   (B) 3

   (C) -1

   (D) 1

   (E) 0

4. The radius of a sphere is measured to be 5 cm with an error of ± 0.1 cm. Use differentials to approximate the error in the volume.

   (A) $\pm \pi \, \text{cm}^3$

   (B) $\pm 100\pi \, \text{cm}^3$

   (C) $\pm 10\pi \, \text{cm}^3$

   (D) $\pm 4\pi \, \text{cm}^3$

   (E) $\pm 40\pi \, \text{cm}^3$

GO ON TO THE NEXT PAGE.

5. A side of a cube is measured to be 10 cm. Estimate the change in surface area of the cube when the side shrinks to 9.8 cm.

(A) $+2.4\,\text{cm}^2$

(B) $-2.4\,\text{cm}^2$

(C) $-120\,\text{cm}^2$

(D) $+24\,\text{cm}^2$

(E) $-24\,\text{cm}^2$

6. Find the derivative of y, when $y^2 = (x^2 + 2)(x+3)^2(2x+7)^{\frac{1}{2}}$ at $(1,12)$?

(A) $\dfrac{20}{3}$

(B) 7

(C) $\dfrac{22}{3}$

(D) $\dfrac{23}{3}$

(E) 8

7. $\displaystyle\int \frac{x^3}{2}\,dx =$

(A) $\dfrac{x^4}{8} + C$

(B) $\dfrac{x^4}{2} + C$

(C) $2x^4 + C$

(D) $\dfrac{3}{2}x^2 + C$

(E) $8x^4 + C$

GO ON TO THE NEXT PAGE.

8. $\int x^2 \sin(3x^3 + 2)\,dx =$

(A) $-9\cos(3x^3 + 2) + C$

(B) $-\cos(3x^3 + 2) + C$

(C) $\dfrac{-\cos(3x^3 + 2)}{9} + C$

(D) $\dfrac{\cos(3x^3 + 2)}{9} + C$

(E) $9\cos(3x^3 + 2) + C$

---

9. If $f(x) = \begin{cases} 2ax^2 + bx + 6, & x \le -1 \\ 3ax^3 - 2bx^2 + 4x, & x > -1 \end{cases}$ and is differentiable for all real values, then $b = ?$

(A) -13
(B) $\quad 0$
(C) $\quad 45$
(D) $\quad 55$
(E) $\quad 110$

---

10. $\dfrac{d}{dx}\left(\dfrac{x^3 - 4x^2 + 3x}{x^2 + 4x - 21}\right) =$

(A) $\dfrac{x^2 - x}{x + 7}$

(B) $\dfrac{x - 1}{x - 7}$

(C) $\dfrac{x^2 - 14x + 7}{(x - 7)^2}$

(D) $\dfrac{2x^2 + 13x - 7}{(x + 7)^2}$

(E) $\dfrac{x^2 + 14x - 7}{(x + 7)^2}$

GO ON TO THE NEXT PAGE.

AB Calculus Practice Test | 351

11. $\lim_{h \to 0} \dfrac{2x^2 + 4xh + 2h^2 - 2x^2}{h}$

   (A) 4

   (B) $3x^2$

   (C) $2x^2$

   (D) $4x$

   (E) $6x$

12. Find the point on the curve $x^2 + y^2 = 9$ that is a minimum distance from the point (1,2).

   (A) $\left(\sqrt{5}, 2\right)$

   (B) $\left(-\sqrt{5}, -2\right)$

   (C) $\left(\sqrt{5}, -2\right)$

   (D) $\left(-\sqrt{5}, 2\right)$

   (E) $(5, 2)$

GO ON TO THE NEXT PAGE.

13. Find $\dfrac{dy}{dx}$ if $y = \log_3\left(2x^3 + 4x^2\right)$.

(A) $\dfrac{6x^2 + 8x}{\left(x^2 + 2x\right)\ln 3}$

(B) $\dfrac{3x + 4}{\left(2x^3 + 4x^2\right)\ln 3}$

(C) $\dfrac{3x + 4}{\left(x^2 + 2x\right)\ln 3}$

(D) $\dfrac{3x + 4}{3\ln\left(x^2 + 2x\right)}$

(E) $\dfrac{6x^2 + 8x}{\left(3x^3 + 2x^2\right)\ln 3}$

14. What curve is represented by $x = 2t^3$ and $y = 4t^9$?

(A) $y = 2x^2$

(B) $y = x^2$

(C) $y = 3x^2$

(D) $y = x^3$

(E) $y = 2x^3$

GO ON TO THE NEXT PAGE.

15. Find $\lim\limits_{x\to 0}\dfrac{2x^3-3\sin x}{x^4}$.

    (A) -1

    (B) $-\dfrac{1}{2}$

    (C) 0

    (D) $\dfrac{1}{2}$

    (E) 1

16. $\int 18x^2\sec^2\left(3x^3\right)dx =$

    (A) $2\tan^2\left(3x^3\right)+C$

    (B) $2\cot^2\left(3x^3\right)+C$

    (C) $\cot\left(3x^3\right)+C$

    (D) $\tan\left(3x^3\right)+C$

    (E) $2\tan\left(3x^3\right)+C$

17. What is the equation of the line normal to the curve $y = x^3 + 2x^2 - 5x + 7$ at $x = 1$?

    (A) $y = -\dfrac{1}{2}x + \dfrac{11}{2}$

    (B) $y = 2x + 3$

    (C) $y = -\dfrac{1}{2}x - \dfrac{11}{2}$

    (D) $y = -2x + 3$

    (E) $y = -2x - \dfrac{11}{2}$

GO ON TO THE NEXT PAGE.

18. Find the value of c that satisfies Rolle's Theorem for $f(x) = \dfrac{x^2 + 4x - 12}{x^2 + 2x - 3}$ on the interval $[-6, 2]$.

    (A) -6
    (B) -3
    (C) 1
    (D) 2
    (E) No such value exists.

19. If $\cos^2 x + \sin^2 y = y$, then $\dfrac{dy}{dx}$.

    (A) $\dfrac{2\cos x \sin x}{2\cos y \sin y + 1}$

    (B) $\dfrac{\cos x \sin x}{\cos y \sin y}$

    (C) $\dfrac{2\cos x \sin x}{2\cos y \sin y - 1}$

    (D) $\dfrac{\sin y \cos y}{1 - \cos x \sin x}$

    (E) $\dfrac{2\cos y \sin y}{2\cos x \sin x - 1}$

20. If $f(x) = e^{3x}$, then $f''(\ln 3) =$

    (A) 9
    (B) 27
    (C) 81
    (D) 243
    (E) 729

GO ON TO THE NEXT PAGE.

21. Find $\dfrac{dy}{dx}$ if $2y^2 - 6y = x^4 + 2x^3 - 2x - 5$ at $(1,1)$.

   (A) -1
   (B) -2
   (C) -3
   (D) -4
   (E) -5

22. Find $\dfrac{dy}{dx}$ if $2\sin^3 y + 2\cos^3 x = 2\cos^3 y - 4\sin^3 x$.

   (A) $-\dfrac{\sin 2x(\cos x + 2\sin x)}{\sin 2y(\sin y + \cos y)}$

   (B) $\dfrac{\sin 2x(\cos x + 2\sin x)}{\sin 2y(\sin y + \cos y)}$

   (C) $\dfrac{\sin x \cos x(\cos x + 2\sin x)}{\sin y \cos y(\sin y + \cos y)}$

   (D) $-\dfrac{\sin 2x}{\sin 2y}$

   (E) $\dfrac{\cos 2x(\cos x + 2\sin x)}{\cos 2y(\sin y + \cos y)}$

GO ON TO THE NEXT PAGE.

23. $\displaystyle\int \frac{\ln^3 x}{x}\,dx =$

    (A) $\dfrac{\ln^3 x}{3} + C$

    (B) $\dfrac{\ln^4 x}{4} + C$

    (C) $\dfrac{\ln^5 x}{5} + C$

    (D) $\ln^3 x + C$

    (E) $\ln^4 x + C$

---

24. Find the volume of the region formed by the curve $y = x^2$, the x-axis, and the line $x = 3$ when revolved around the y-axis.

    (A) $\dfrac{3}{2}\pi$

    (B) $\dfrac{9}{2}\pi$

    (C) $\dfrac{27}{2}\pi$

    (D) $\dfrac{81}{2}\pi$

    (E) $\dfrac{243}{2}\pi$

GO ON TO THE NEXT PAGE.

25. $\int_0^4 x^3 dx =$

(A) 16
(B) 32
(C) 48
(D) 56
(E) 64

26. Is the function $f(x) = \begin{cases} x^3 - 3, & x < 3 \\ 2x + 7, & x \geq 3 \end{cases}$ continuous at $x = 3$? If not, what is the discontinuity?

(A) The function is continuous.
(B) Point
(C) Essential
(D) Jump
(E) Removable

27. Where does the curve $y = 5 - (x - 2)^{\frac{2}{3}}$ have a cusp?

(A) $(0,5)$
(B) $(5,2)$
(C) $(2,5)$
(D) $(5,0)$
(E) There is no cusp.

GO ON TO THE NEXT PAGE.

28. $\int \left(x^2 + 2x\right)\cos\left(x^3 + 3x^2\right)dx =$

(A) $\sin\left(3x^2 + 6x\right) + C$

(B) $-\dfrac{1}{3}\sin\left(x^3 + 3x^2\right) + C$

(C) $-\sin\left(x^3 + 3x^2\right) + C$

(D) $\sin\left(x^3 + 3x^2\right) + C$

(E) $\dfrac{1}{3}\sin\left(x^3 + 3x^2\right) + C$

END OF PART A, SECTION I

**IF YOU FINISH BEFORE TIME IS CALLED, YOU MAY CHECK
YOUR WORK ON PART A ONLY.**

DO NOT GO ON TO PART B UNTIL YOU ARE TOLD TO DO SO.

CALCULUS AB

SECTION I, Part B

Time—50 Minutes

Number of questions—17

A GRAPHING CALCULATOR IS REQUIRED FOR SOME QUESTIONS ON THIS PART OF THE EXAMINATION

Directions: Solve each of the following problems, using the available space for scratchwork. After examining the form of the choices, decide which is the best of the choices given and fill in the corresponding oval on the answer sheet. No credit will be given for anything written in the test book. Do not spend too much time on any one problem.

In this test:

1. The **exact** numerical value of the correct answer does not always appear among the choices given. When this happens, select from among the choices the number that best approximates the exact numerical value.

2. Unless otherwise specified, the domain of a function f is assumed to be the set of all real numbers x for which $f(x)$ is a real number.

---

29. An open top cylinder has a volume of $125\pi \text{ in}^3$. Find the radius required to minimize the amount of material to make the cylinder.

    (A) 2
    (B) 3
    (C) 4
    (D) 5
    (E) 6

GO ON TO THE NEXT PAGE.

30. If the position of a particle is given by $x(t) = 2t^3 - 5t^2 + 4t + 6$, where $t > 0$. What is the distance traveled by the particle from $t = 0$ to $t = 3$?

(A) $\dfrac{1}{27}$

(B) $\dfrac{28}{27}$

(C) 20

(D) 21

(E) $\dfrac{569}{27}$

31. At what times, t, are the x- and y-components of the particle's velocity equal if the curve is represented by $x = 2t^3 + 3t^2 - 5$ and $y = t^4 - 4t^3 + 7t^2$?

(A) $t = 0$

(B) $t = \dfrac{1}{2}$

(C) $t = 4$

(D) $t = 0$ and $t = \dfrac{1}{2}$

(E) $t = 0$, $t = \dfrac{1}{2}$, and $t = 4$

GO ON TO THE NEXT PAGE.

32. Find the equation of the line tangent to the graph of $y = 2x - 3x^{-\frac{2}{3}} + 5$ at $x = 8$.

   (A) $y = \dfrac{33}{16}x + \dfrac{15}{4}$

   (B) $y = \dfrac{15}{4}x + \dfrac{33}{16}$

   (C) $y = \dfrac{16}{33}x + \dfrac{4}{15}$

   (D) $y = \dfrac{16}{33}x + \dfrac{15}{4}$

   (E) $y = \dfrac{33}{16}x + \dfrac{4}{15}$

---

33. Which point on the curve $y = 5x^3 - 12x^2 - 12x + 64$ has a tangent that is parallel to $y = 3$?

   (A) $(0, -2)$

   (B) $(2, 32)$

   (C) $\left(\dfrac{2}{5}, 12\right)$

   (D) $\left(-2, \dfrac{288}{25}\right)$

   (E) $\left(\dfrac{2}{5}, \dfrac{256}{25}\right)$

GO ON TO THE NEXT PAGE.

34. A 50 foot ladder is leaning against a building and being pulled to the ground, so the top is sliding down the building. If the rate the bottom of the ladder is being pulled across the ground is 12 ft/sec, what is the rate of the top of the ladder sliding down the building when the top is 30 ft from the ground?

(A) 12 ft/sec
(B) 9 ft/sec
(C) 20 ft/sec
(D) 9.6 ft/sec
(E) 16 ft/sec

35. What is the distance traveled from $t = 0$ to $t = 4$ given the position function, $x(t) = 2t^3 - 9t^2 + 12t + 13$?

(A) 30 units
(B) 32 units
(C) 33 units
(D) 34 units
(E) 35 units

36. The tangent to a curve described by $x = 3t^3 - 5t + 2$ and $y = 7t^2 - 16$ is what at $t = 1$?

(A) $-7x + 2y = -18$
(B) $2x - 7y = 18$
(C) $7x + 2y = 18$
(D) $2x + 7y = -18$
(E) $7x - 2y = -18$

GO ON TO THE NEXT PAGE.

37. Approximate $\sqrt{16.04}$.

    (A) 4.005
    (B) 4.04
    (C) 4.02
    (D) 4.002
    (E) 4.05

38. Approximate the area under the curve $y = x^2 + 2$ from $x = 1$ to $x = 2$ using four midpoint rectangles.

    (A) 4.333
    (B) 3.969
    (C) 4.719
    (D) 4.344
    (E) 4.328

39. Find the area under the curve $y = x^2 + 2$ from $x = 1$ to $x = 2$.

    (A) 4.333
    (B) 3.969
    (C) 4.719
    (D) 4.344
    (E) 4.328

GO ON TO THE NEXT PAGE.

40. $\int \dfrac{3x-2}{(x+2)^2}\,dx =$

   (A) $\ln|x+2| + \dfrac{1}{x+2} + C$

   (B) $3\ln|x+2| + \dfrac{4}{x+2} + C$

   (C) $3\ln|x+2| - \dfrac{4}{x+2} + C$

   (D) $-3\ln|x+2| - \dfrac{4}{x+2} + C$

   (E) $-3\ln|x+2| + \dfrac{4}{x+2} + C$

41. The side of a cube is increasing at a rate of 3 inches per second. At the instant when the side of the cube is 6 inches long. What is the rate of change (in inches/second) of the surface area of the cube?

   (A) 108
   (B) 216
   (C) 324
   (D) 648
   (E) 1296

42. If the position of a particle is given by $x(t) = 3t^3 - 2t^2 - 16$ where $t > 0$. When does the particle change direction?

   (A) $\dfrac{2}{3}$

   (B) $\dfrac{4}{3}$

   (C) $\dfrac{9}{4}$

   (D) 2

   (E) 3

GO ON TO THE NEXT PAGE.

43. The radius of a sphere is increased from 9 cm to 9.05 cm. Estimate the change in volume.

   (A) $1.25 \times 10^{-4} \, \text{cm}^3$

   (B) $11.3097 \, \text{cm}^3$

   (C) $16.965 \, \text{cm}^3$

   (D) $50.894 \, \text{cm}^3$

   (E) $152.681 \, \text{cm}^2$

44. Find an equation of the line tangent to the curve represented by $x = 4\cos t + 2$ and $y = 2\sin t$ at $t = \dfrac{\pi}{3}$.

   (A) $y = \dfrac{\sqrt{3}}{6} x + \dfrac{5\sqrt{3}}{3}$

   (B) $y = -\dfrac{\sqrt{3}}{6} x + \dfrac{2\sqrt{3}}{3}$

   (C) $y = \dfrac{\sqrt{3}}{6} x + \sqrt{3}$

   (D) $y = -\dfrac{\sqrt{3}}{6} x + \dfrac{5\sqrt{3}}{3}$

   (E) $y = -\dfrac{\sqrt{3}}{6} x - \dfrac{\sqrt{3}}{3}$

45. Use differentials to approximate $\sqrt{4.002}$.

   (A) 2
   (B) 2.0005
   (C) 2.005
   (D) 2.05
   (E) 2.5

STOP

END OF PART B, SECTION I

IF YOU FINISH BEFORE TIME IS CALLED, YOU MAY CHECK YOUR WORK ON PART B ONLY.

DO NOT GO ON TO SECTION II UNTIL YOU ARE TOLD TO DO SO.

SECTION II
GENERAL INSTRUCTIONS

You may wish to look over the problems before starting to work on them, since it is not expected that everyone will be able to complete all parts of all problems. All problems are given equal weight, but the parts of a particular problem are not necessarily given equal weight.

A GRAPHING CALCULATOR IS REQUIRED FOR SOME PROBLEMS OR PARTS OF PROBLEMS ON THIS SECTION OF THE EXAMINATION.

- You should write all work for each part of each problem in the space provided for that part in the booklet. Be sure to write clearly and legibly. If you make an error, you may save time by crossing it out rather than trying to erase it. Erased or crossed-out work will not be graded.

- Show all your work. You will be graded on the correctness and completeness of your methods as well as your answers. Correct answers without supporting work may not receive credit.

- Justifications require that you give mathematical (noncalculator) reasons and that you clearly identify functions, graphs, tables, or other objects you use.

- You are permitted to use your calculator to solve an equation, find the derivative of a function at a point, or calculate the value of a definite integral. However, you must clearly indicate the setup of your problem, namely the equation, function, or integral you are using. If you use other built-in features or programs, you must show the mathematical steps necessary to produce your results.

- Your work must be expressed in standard mathematical notation rather than calculator syntax. For example, $\int_{1}^{5} x^2 \, dx$ may not be written as fnInt $(X^2, X, 1, 5)$.

- Unless otherwise specified, answers (numeric or algebraic) need not be simplified. If your answer is given as a decimal approximation, it should be correct to three places after the decimal point.

- Unless otherwise specified, the domain of a function f is assumed to be the set of all real numbers x for which $f(x)$ is a real number.

GO ON TO THE NEXT PAGE.

SECTION II, PART A
Time—30 minutes
Number of problems—2

A graphing calculator is required for some problems or parts of problems.

During the timed portion for Part A, you may work only on the problems in Part A.

On Part A, you are permitted to use your calculator to solve an equation, find the derivative of a function at a point, or calculate the value of a definite integral. However, you must clearly indicate the setup of your problem, namely the equation, function, or integral you are using. If you use other built-in features or programs, you must show the mathematical steps necessary to produce your results.

---

1. Water is dripping from a pipe into a container whose volume increases at a rate of $150\,\text{cm}^3/\text{min}$. The water takes the shape of a cone with both its radius and height changing with time.

   (a) What is the rate of change of the radius of the water at the instant the height is 2 cm and the radius is 5 cm? At this instant the height is changing at a rate of $0.5\,\text{cm/min}$.

   (b) The water begins to be extracted from the container at a rate of $E(t) = 75t^{0.25}$. Water continues to drip from the pipe at the same rate as before. When is the water at its maximum volume? Justify your reasoning.

   (c) By the time water began to be extracted, $3000\,\text{cm}^3$ of water had already leaked from the pipe. Write, but do not evaluate, an expression with an integral that gives the volume of water in the container at the time in part (b).

---

2. The temperature in a room increases at a rate of $\dfrac{dT}{dt} = kT$, where k is a constant.

   (a) Find an equation for T, the temperature (in °F), in terms of t, the number of hours passed, if the temperature is 65 °F initially and 70 °F after one hour.

   (b) How many hours will it take for the temperature to reach 85 °F?

   (c) After the temperature reaches 85 °F, a fan is turned on and cools the room at a consistent rate of 7 °F/hour. How long will it take for the room to reach 0 °F?

GO ON TO THE NEXT PAGE.

SECTION II, PART B
Time—1 hour
Number of problems—4

No calculator is allowed for these problems.

During the timed portion for Part B, you may continue to work on the problems in Part A without the use of any calculator.

---

3. Let R be the region enclosed by the graphs of $y = \dfrac{2}{x+1}, y = x^2$, and the lines $x = 0$ and $x = 1$.

   (a) Find the area of R.

   (b) Find the volume of the solid generated when R is revolved about the x-axis.

   (c) Set up, but do not evaluate, the expression for the volume of the solid generated when R is revolved around the line $x = 2$.

---

4. Consider the equation $x^3 + 2x^2y + 4y^2 = 12$.

   (a) Write an equation for the slope of the curve at any point (x,y).

   (b) Find the equation of the tangent line to the curve at $x = 0$.

   (c) If the equation given for the curve is the path a car travels in feet over t seconds, find $\dfrac{d^2y}{dx^2}$ at $\left(0, \sqrt{3}\right)$ and explain what it represents with proper units.

GO ON TO THE NEXT PAGE.

5. Water is filling at a rate of $64\pi \text{ in}^3$ into a conical tank that has a diameter of 36 in at its base and whose height is 60 in.

   (a) Find an expression for the volume of water (in in^3) in the tank in terms of its radius.
   (b) At what rate is the radius of the water expanding when the radius is 20 in.
   (c) How fast in (in/sec) is the height of the water increasing in the tank when the radius is 20 in?

---

6. If a ball is accelerating at a rate given by $a(t) = -64\dfrac{\text{ft}}{\text{sec}^2}$, the velocity of the ball is $96\dfrac{\text{ft}}{\text{sec}}$ at time $t = 1$, and the height of the ball is 100 ft at $t = 0$, what is

   (a) The equation of the ball's velocity at time t ?
   (b) The time when the ball is changing direction?
   (c) The equation of the ball's height?
   (d) The ball's maximum height?

STOP

END OF EXAM

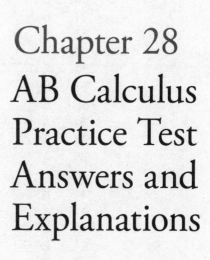

Chapter 28
AB Calculus
Practice Test
Answers and
Explanations

ANSWER KEY

Section I

1.	A	24.	D	
2.	C	25.	E	
3.	E	26.	D	
4.	C	27.	C	
5.	E	28.	E	
6.	C	29.	D	
7.	A	30.	E	
8.	C	31.	E	
9.	D	32.	A	
10.	E	33.	B	
11.	D	34.	E	
12.	A	35.	D	
13.	C	36.	A	
14.	B	37.	A	
15.	C	38.	E	
16.	E	39.	A	
17.	A	40.	B	
18.	E	41.	B	
19.	C	42.	A	
20.	D	43.	D	
21.	D	44.	D	
22.	A	45.	B	
23.	B			

EXPLANATIONS

Section I

1. **A**   First, use implicit differentiation to find $\dfrac{dy}{dx}$:

    $$x^2 \frac{dy}{dx} + 2xy = 0$$

    Isolate $\dfrac{dy}{dx}$ and simplify:

    $$\frac{dy}{dx} = \frac{-2xy}{x^2} = \frac{-2y}{x}$$

    Next, take the second derivative via implicit differentiation:

    $$\frac{d^2 y}{dx^2} = \frac{x\left(-2\dfrac{dy}{dx}\right) - (-2y)(1)}{x^2} = \frac{-2x\dfrac{dy}{dx} + 2y}{x^2}$$

    Plug in $\dfrac{dy}{dx}$ and simplify:

    $$\frac{d^2 y}{dx^2} = \frac{-2x\left(\dfrac{-2y}{x}\right) + 2y}{x^2} = \frac{4y + 2y}{x^2} = \frac{6y}{x^2}$$

2. **C**   When $y = \ln u$, $\dfrac{dy}{dx} = \dfrac{1}{u}\dfrac{du}{dx}$. For this problem, $u = 6x^3 - 2x^2$ and $\dfrac{du}{dx} = 18x^2 - 4x$. Then,
    $$\frac{dy}{dx} = \frac{18x^2 - 4x}{6x^3 - 2x^2} = \frac{9x - 2}{3x^2 - x}.$$

3. **E**   When you insert ∞ for x, the limit is $\dfrac{\infty}{\infty}$, which is indeterminate. First, rewrite the limit as $\displaystyle\lim_{x \to \infty} \frac{3x}{e^{3x}}$. Then, use L'Hôpital's Rule to evaluate the limit: $\displaystyle\lim_{x \to 0} \frac{3}{3e^{3x}}$. This limit exists and equals 0.

4. **C**   In order to approximate the error in the volume of the sphere use the approximation formula: $dy = f'(x)\,dx$. For this problem, $f(x) = V = \dfrac{4}{3}\pi r^3$, $f'(x) = \dfrac{dV}{dr} = 4\pi r^2 = 100\pi$, and $dx = dr = \pm 0.1$. When these values are input, the equation is $dy = dV = 100\pi(\pm 0.1) = \pm 10\pi \text{ cm}^3$.

5. **E** In order to approximate the change in the surface area of the cube, use the approximation formula: $dy = f'(x)dx$. For this problem, $f(x) = A = 6s^2$, $f'(x) = \dfrac{dA}{ds} = 12s = 120$, and $dx = ds = -0.2$. When these values are input, the equation is $dy = dA = 120(-0.2) = -24\,\text{cm}^2$.

6. **C** This problem can be solved with implicit differentiation, but that can get especially messy. We are going to use logarithmic differentiation to solve it. First, take the natural log of both sides: $\ln y^2 = \ln\left((x^2+2)(x+3)^2(2x+7)^{\frac{1}{2}}\right)$. Use logarithmic rules to simplify the equation:

$2\ln y = \ln(x^2+2) + 2\ln(x+3) + \dfrac{1}{2}\ln(2x+7)$. Now, differentiate both sides with respect to x:

$\dfrac{2}{y}\dfrac{dy}{dx} = \dfrac{2x}{x^2+2} + \dfrac{2}{x+3} + \dfrac{1}{4x+14}$. Next, isolate $\dfrac{dy}{dx}$: $\dfrac{dy}{dx} = \dfrac{y}{2}\left(\dfrac{2x}{x^2+2} + \dfrac{2}{x+3} + \dfrac{1}{4x+14}\right)$. Finally,

plug in the given values for x and y and solve, so $\dfrac{dy}{dx} = 88$.

7. **A** Use the Power rule to integrate: $\displaystyle\int \dfrac{x^3}{2}\,dx = \dfrac{1}{4}\left(\dfrac{x^4}{2}\right) = \dfrac{x^4}{8} + C$.

8. **C** Use u-substitution. Here, $u = 3x^3 + 2$ and $du = 9x^2\,dx$. Then,

$\displaystyle\int x^2 \sin(3x^3+2)\,dx = \dfrac{1}{9}\int \sin x\,dx = \dfrac{1}{9}(-\cos u) + C = \dfrac{-\cos u}{9} + C$. Replace u for the final solution:

$-\dfrac{\cos(3x^3+2)}{8} + C.$

9. **D** First take the derivative of $f(x)$. $f'(x) = \begin{cases} 4ax + b,\ x \le -1 \\ 9ax^2 - 4bx + 4,\ x > -1 \end{cases}$. In order for $f(x)$ to be differentiable for all real values, both pieces of $f(x)$ must be equal at $x = -1$ and both pieces of $f'(x)$ must be equal at $x = -1$. Therefore, plug $x = -1$ into both $f(x)$ and $f'(x)$. $f(-1) = \begin{cases} 2a - b + 6 \\ -3a - 2b - 4 \end{cases}$ and $f'(-1) = \begin{cases} -4a + b \\ 9a + 4b + 4 \end{cases}$. When the two parts of $f(-1)$ are set equal to each other, $10 = -5a - b$ and when the two parts of $f'(-1)$ are set equal to each other, $-4 = 13a + 3b$. When this system is solved, $a = -13$ and $b = 55$.

10. **E** $\dfrac{d}{dx}\left(\dfrac{x^3 - 4x^2 + 3x}{x^2 + 4x - 21}\right) = \dfrac{d}{dx}\left(\dfrac{x(x-3)(x-1)}{(x-3)(x+7)}\right) = \dfrac{d}{dx}\left(\dfrac{x(x-1)}{(x+7)}\right) = \dfrac{d}{dx}\left(\dfrac{x^2 - x}{(x+7)}\right)$

$= \left(\dfrac{(2x-1)(x+7)(x^2-x)}{(x+7)^2}\right)$

11. **D** Notice the limit is in the form of the definition of the derivative. You could evaluate the limit, but if you see the definition of the derivative and the main function, $f(x) = 2x^2$, it is easier to evaluate the derivative directly. Thus, the solution is $f'(x) = 4x$.

12. **A** Use the distance formula ($D^2 = (x - x_1)^2 + (y - y_1)^2$) to determine the distance between the curve and the point: $D^2 = (x - 1)^2 + (y - 2)^2 = x^2 - 2x + 1 + y^2 - 4y + 4$. From the equation of the curve, you can solve for y^2 and y: $y^2 = 9 - x^2$ and $y = \sqrt{(9 - x^2)}$. Substitute these back into the formula for distance:

$$D^2 = x^2 - 2x + 1 + 9 - x^2 - 4\sqrt{(9 - x^2)} + 4.$$

To simplify calculations, recall that the functions D^2 and D will be minimized at the same point, so instead of solving for D, continue calculations with D^2 which will now be called L: $D^2 = L$. Thus, $L = 14 - 2x - 4\sqrt{9 - x^2}$. To minimize the distance, take the first derivative of L and set it equal to zero: $\dfrac{dL}{dx} = -2 + \dfrac{4}{\sqrt{9 - x^2}} = 0$. Solve this equation for x: $x = \pm\sqrt{5}$. Find the corresponding y-values: $y = \pm 2$. The point closest to (1,2) would then be $\left(\sqrt{5}, 2\right)$. You can verify this with the second derivative test.

13. **C** If $y = \log_a u$, then $\dfrac{dy}{dx} = \dfrac{1}{u \ln a} \dfrac{du}{dx}$. In this case, $\dfrac{dy}{dx} = \dfrac{6x^2 + 8x}{(2x^3 + 4x^2)\ln 3} = \dfrac{3x + 4}{(x^2 + 2x)\ln 3}$.

14. **B** When dealing with parametric functions, your task is to eliminate t. In this case, notice $y = 4t^9 = (2t^3)^2$. Since $x = 2t^3$, $y = x^2$.

15. **C** Use l'Hôpital's Rule.

$$\lim_{x \to 0} \frac{2x^3 - 3\sin x}{x^4} = \lim_{x \to 0} \frac{6x^2 - 3\cos x}{4x^3} = \lim_{x \to 0} \frac{12x + 3\sin x}{12x^2}$$

$$= \lim_{x \to 0} \frac{12x + 3\cos x}{24x} = \lim_{x \to 0} \frac{-3\sin x}{24} = 0$$

16. **E** Use u-substitution where $u = 3x^3$ and $du = 9x^2$. Therefore,

$$\int 18x^2 \sec^2(3x^3)\,dx = 2\int \sec^2 u\,du = 2\tan u + C = 2\tan(3x^3) + C.$$

17. **A.** First, plug $x = 1$ into the equation and solve for y; $y = 5$. Next, take the first derivative of y: $\dfrac{dy}{dx} = 3x^2 + 4x - 5$. Solve for $\dfrac{dy}{dx}$ at $x = 1$: $\dfrac{dy}{dx} = 2$. The slope of the normal line is $-\dfrac{1}{2}$. Thus, the equation of the normal line is $y - 5 = -\dfrac{1}{2}(x - 1)$. The equation simplified is $y = -\dfrac{1}{2}x + \dfrac{11}{2}$.

18. **E** Factor $f(x)$ and notice there are discontinuities over the interval: $f(x) = \dfrac{(x-2)(x+6)}{(x-1)(x+3)}$. The discontinuities are located at $x = 1$ and $x = -3$. Because there are discontinuities over the integral, Rolle's Theorem cannot be applied.

19. **C** Using implicit differentiation, you can evaluate this equation: $-2\cos x \sin x + 2\sin y \cos y \dfrac{dy}{dx} = \dfrac{dy}{dx}$. After simplifying, $\dfrac{dy}{dx} = \dfrac{2\cos x \sin x}{2\cos y \sin y - 1}$.

20. **D** Via the chain rule, $f'(x) = 3e^{3x}$ and $f''(x) = 9e^{3x}$. Plugging in $\ln 3$ for x, results in $f''(\ln 3) = 9e^{3(\ln 3)} = 9e^{\ln 3^3} = 9e^{\ln 27} = 9 \bullet 27 = 243$.

21. **D** Use implicit differentiation and plug in for the point (1,1):

$$4y\frac{dy}{dx} - 6\frac{dy}{dx} = 4x^3 + 6x^2 - 2$$

$$4(1)\frac{dy}{dx} - 6\frac{dy}{dx} = 4(1)^3 + 6(1)^2 - 2$$

$$-2\frac{dy}{dx} = 8$$

$$\frac{dy}{dx} = -4$$

22. **A** Use implicit differentiation: $6\sin^2 y \cos y \dfrac{dy}{dx} - 6\sin x \cos^2 x = -6\sin y \cos^2 y \dfrac{dy}{dx} - 12\sin^2 x \cos x$. In addition, recall that $\sin 2x = 2\sin x \cos x$. When the equation is rearranged and that trig identity used, $\dfrac{dy}{dx} = -\dfrac{\sin 2x(\cos x + 2\sin x)}{\sin 2y(\sin y + \cos y)}$.

23. **B** Using u-substitution, $\displaystyle\int \dfrac{\ln^3 x}{x}\, dx = \dfrac{\ln^4 x}{4} + C$.

24. **D** Because the region is bound by three curves given in the form $y =$ and $x =$, it is likely better to use

the cylindrical shells method to solve this problem: $2\pi\int_0^3 x\left(x^2-0\right)dx = 2\pi\int_0^3 x^3\,dx = \dfrac{81\pi}{2}$.

25. **E** Follow the First Fundamental Theorem of Calculus: $\int_0^4 x^3\,dx = \dfrac{x^4}{4}\bigg|_0^4 = \dfrac{256}{4} = 64$.

26. **D** There are three conditions that must be satisfied for a function to be continuous: 1. $f(c)$ exists.
2. $\lim\limits_{x\to c} f(x)$ exists. 3. $\lim\limits_{x\to c} f(x) = f(c)$. For this function, condition 1 is met as $f(3) = 13$. Condition 2, however, is violated; from the left the limit equals 24 and from the right it equals 13. This signifies a jump discontinuity.

27. **C** If the derivative of a function approaches infinity and negative infinity from both sides of a

point and it is continuous at that point, then there is a cusp. The graph of $y = 5 - \left(x-2\right)^{\frac{2}{3}}$ is

continuous. Next, check the points where the derivative is undefined or zero. In this case,

$\dfrac{dy}{dx} = -\dfrac{2}{3}\left(x-2\right)^{-\frac{1}{3}}$ is undefined at $x = 2$, and zero nowhere. To determine whether there is

a cusp at $x = 2$, we need to check the limit of $\dfrac{dy}{dx}$ as x approaches 2 from the left and right.

$\lim\limits_{x\to 2+} -\dfrac{2}{3}\left(x-2\right)^{-\frac{1}{3}} = -\infty$ and $\lim\limits_{x\to 2-} -\dfrac{2}{3}\left(x-2\right)^{-\frac{1}{3}} = \infty$. Thus, there is a cusp at $x = 2$, when you plug in

2 to the equation for y, the location of the cusp is $(2,5)$.

28. **E** Solve the integral using u-substitution: $u = x^3 + 3x^2$ and $du = \left(3x^2 + 6x\right)dx$.

$$\int\left(x^2 + 2x\right)\cos\left(x^3 + 3x^2\right)dx = \frac{1}{3}\int\cos u\,du = \frac{1}{3}\sin u + C = \frac{1}{3}\sin\left(x^3 + 3x^2\right) + C.$$

29. **D** The amount of material required to make this cylinder corresponds with the surface area of the cyl-

inder found by $S = \pi r^2 + 2\pi rh$. As the problem gave the volume of the cylinder and only asked for

the radius, use the volume to eliminate h. $V = \pi r^2 h = 125\pi$. Thus, $h = \dfrac{125}{r^2}$. Plug this expression

for h into the equation for the surface area: $S = \pi r^2 + \dfrac{250\pi}{r}$. Next, to minimize the amount of

material, take the first derivative of S and set it equal to zero to determine the critical points for r:

$\dfrac{dS}{dr} = 2\pi r - \dfrac{250\pi}{r^2} = 0$. Thus, the critical point is at $r = 5$. To verify that this value of r minimizes the material, take the second derivative and ensure that the second derivative is positive at $r = 5$.

$\dfrac{d^2 S}{dr^2} = 2\pi + \dfrac{500\pi}{r^3}$. At $r = 5$, $\dfrac{d^2 S}{dr^2} = 6\pi$, so $r = 5$ minimizes the amount of material.

30.　E　To determine the distance traveled by the particle, we need to know the position of the particle at those two times. However, we first need to know whether the particle changes direction at any time over the interval. In other words, we need to know if the velocity is zero over the interval at all. Since the velocity is the first derivative of the position function, we take the first derivative and set it equal to zero: $x'(t) = 6t^2 - 10t + 4 = 0$. Solving for t, the particle changes direction at $t = \dfrac{2}{3}$ and $t = 1$. Now, the positions at the four times are found: $x(0) = 6$, $x\left(\dfrac{2}{3}\right) = \dfrac{190}{27}$, $x(1) = 7$, and $x(3) = 27$. To determine the distance traveled, take the absolute value of the distance traveled over the smaller time intervals and add them together.

$$\left| x\left(\dfrac{2}{3}\right) - x(0) \right| + \left| x(1) - x\left(\dfrac{2}{3}\right) \right| + \left| x(3) - x(1) \right| = \dfrac{28}{27} + \dfrac{1}{27} + 20 = \dfrac{569}{27}.$$

31.　E　Take the derivative of the x- and y-components of the position functions with respect to t:

$\dfrac{dx}{dt} = 6t^2 + 6t$ and $\dfrac{dy}{dt} = 4t^3 - 12t^2 + 14t$. Set those two derivatives equal to each other and solve for t: $6t^2 + 6t = 4t^3 - 12t^2 + 14t$ or $0 = 4t^3 - 18t^2 + 8t$. Solving for t, $t = 0$, $t = \dfrac{1}{2}$, and $t = 4$.

32.　A　First, calculate the derivative of y at $x = 8$: $\dfrac{dy}{dx} = 2 + 2x^{-\frac{5}{3}} = 2 + 2(8)^{-\frac{5}{3}} = \dfrac{33}{16}$. Then, determine y at $x = 8$: $y = 2x - 3x^{-\frac{2}{3}} + 5 = 2(8) - 3(8)^{-\frac{2}{3}} + 5 = \dfrac{81}{4}$. Finally, plug these values into the point-slope formula: $y - \dfrac{81}{4} = \dfrac{33}{16}(x - 8)$, thus, $y = \dfrac{33}{16}x + \dfrac{15}{4}$.

33.　B　Take the derivative of $y = 5x^3 - 12x^2 - 12x + 64$ and set it equal to 0, because the slope of $y = 3$ is 0. Thus, $0 = 15x^2 - 24x - 12 = (3x - 6)(5x + 2)$ and $x = 2$ or $-\dfrac{2}{5}$. Plug these values into the equation and solve for y. The two possible points are then $(2, 32)$ and $\left(-\dfrac{2}{5}, \dfrac{288}{25} \right)$.

34.　E　The ladder makes a right triangle with the building and the ground, so the relationship between the three can be found using the Pythagorean theorem, in which we will call x the distance the bottom of the ladder is from the building across the ground and y the distance the top of the ladder is from the ground up the building, so $x^2 + y^2 = 50^2$. Since we want to find the rate that the top of the ladder is sliding, we need to differentiate this equation with respect to t: $2x\dfrac{dx}{dt} + 2y\dfrac{dy}{dt} = 0$. We already know $\dfrac{dx}{dt} = 12\,\text{ft/sec}$ and our y at the time of interest is 30 ft. In order to determine x at that time, plug 30 into $x^2 + y^2 = 50^2$ and solve for x. Thus, $x = 40$ feet. Plug these values into the differentiated equation and solve for $\dfrac{dy}{dt}$: $2(40)(12) + 2(30)\dfrac{dy}{dt} = 0$, so $\dfrac{dy}{dt} = -16\,\text{ft/sec}$.

35. **D** When determining the distance traveled, first determine whether the velocity changes sign over the specified time interval. If it does, then the distance traveled will need to be found piecewise. Thus, to begin, differentiate $x(t)$ with respect to time to get $v(t)$: $v(t) = 6t^2 - 18t + 12$. Set $v(t)$ equal to zero and determine when the velocity is zero. In this case, the velocity is zero at $t = 1$ and $t = 2$. To confirm that the particle is changing directions at those times, differentiate the velocity with respect to time and determine whether the acceleration is zero at $t = 1$ and $t = 2$. $a(t) = 12t - 18$, $a(1) = -6$, and $a(2) = 6$. Since the acceleration is not zero at either of those times, the particle is changing directions. Therefore, the distance traveled must be found by adding the distance traveled from $t = 0$ to $t = 1$, $t = 1$ to $t = 2$, and $t = 2$ to $t = 4$. The equation should look like this: $\left|x(1) - x(0)\right| + \left|x(2) - x(1)\right| + \left|x(4) - x(2)\right|$ = total distance. Absolute values are used so the directions will not affect the final result, so the total distance is 34 units.

36. **A** The slope of the tangent is $\dfrac{dy}{dx}$ which is represented parametrically by $\dfrac{dy}{dx} = \dfrac{dy/dt}{dx/dt}$. $\dfrac{dy}{dt} = 14t$ and $\dfrac{dx}{dt} = 9t^2 - 5$, so $\dfrac{dy}{dx} = \dfrac{14t}{9t^2 - 5}$. At $t = 1$ the slope is $\dfrac{7}{2}$. At $t = 1$, $x = 0$ and $y = -9$. Therefore, the equation of the tangent to the curve is $y + 9 = \dfrac{7}{2}(x - 0)$ or $-7x + 2y = -18$.

37. **A** Use a differential to approximate $\sqrt{16.04}$. Recall the general formula is $f(x + \Delta x) \approx f(x) + f'(x)\Delta x$. For this problem, $f(x) = \sqrt{16} = 4$, $f'(x) = \dfrac{1}{2}(16)^{-\frac{1}{2}} = \dfrac{1}{8}$, and $\Delta x = 0.04$. When these values are input into the equation is $\sqrt{16.04} \approx 4 + \dfrac{0.04}{8} \approx 4.005$.

38. **E** The formula for the area under a curve using midpoint rectangles is: $A = \left(\dfrac{b-a}{n}\right)\left(y_{\frac{1}{2}} + y_{\frac{3}{2}} + y_{\frac{5}{2}} + \ldots + y_{\frac{2n-1}{2}}\right)$, where a and b are the x-values that bound the area and n is the number of rectangles. Since we are interested in the midpoints, the x-coordinates

are $x_\frac{1}{2} = \frac{9}{8}$, $x_\frac{3}{2} = \frac{11}{8}$, $x_\frac{5}{2} = \frac{13}{8}$, and $x_\frac{7}{2} = \frac{15}{8}$. The y-coordinates are found by plugging these values

into the equation for y, so $y_\frac{1}{2} = 3.26563$, $y_\frac{3}{2} = 3.89063$, $y_\frac{7}{2} = 4.64063$, and $y_\frac{9}{2} = 5.51563$. Then,

$$A = \left(\frac{2-1}{4}\right)(3.26563 + 3.89063 + 4.64063 + 5.51563) = 4.32813.$$

39. **A** Use the Fundamental Theorem of Calculus: $\int_a^b f(x)dx = F(b) - F(a)$. For this problem,

$\int_1^2 (x^2 + 2)dx = \frac{x^3}{3} + 2x\Big|_1^2 = \frac{8}{3} + 4 - \left(\frac{1}{3} + 2\right) = \frac{13}{3} \approx 4.333$.

40. **B** Use the Method of Partial Fractions to evaluate: $\dfrac{A}{x+2} + \dfrac{B}{(x+2)^2} = \dfrac{3x+2}{(x+2)^2}$. Then, $A = 3$ and

$B = -4$. $\int \dfrac{3x-2}{(x+2)^2} dx = \int \dfrac{3}{x+2} dx - \int \dfrac{4}{(x+2)^2} dx = 3\ln|x+2| + \dfrac{4}{x+2} + C$.

41. **B** This is a related rates problem. The surface area of the cube is given by $A = 6s^2$. If you differentiate

with respect to time, the function becomes $\dfrac{dA}{dt} = 12s\dfrac{ds}{dt}$. We are given $s = 6$ and $\dfrac{ds}{dt} = 3$. We must

solve for $\dfrac{dA}{dt}$. When everything is plugged into the equation, $\dfrac{dA}{dt} = 216$.

42. **A** Recall, a particle changes direction when its velocity equals zero but its acceleration does not,

and recall that $v(t) = x'(t)$ and $a(t) = x''(t)$. First, take the derivative of $x(t)$, set it equal to

zero, and solve for t: $x'(t) = 9t^2 - 4 = 0$ and $t = \dfrac{2}{3}$. To determine whether the particle changes

at that time, take the second derivative and determine the value of the second derivative at

$t = \dfrac{2}{3}$: $x(t) = 18t$ and $x\left(\dfrac{2}{3}\right) = 12$. Since, $x''(t)$ is not zero when $x'(t)$ is, the particle is changing

direction at $t = \dfrac{2}{3}$.

43. **D** Use this formula for differentials: $dy = f'(x)dx$. The formula for the volume of a sphere is

$f(x) = \dfrac{4}{3}\pi r^3$ and $f'(x) = 4\pi r^2$. In order to estimate the change in volume, we must evaluate

the function at $x = 9$ and $dx = 0.05$. When the equation is evaluated using the given equations and

values, $dy = 50.894$ cm^3.

44. **D** $\dfrac{dy}{dx} = \dfrac{dy/dt}{dx/dt} = \dfrac{2\cos t}{-4\sin t} = -\dfrac{\cos t}{2\sin t}$. At $t = \dfrac{\pi}{3}$, $\dfrac{dy}{dx} = -\dfrac{\sqrt{3}}{6}$. At this time, $x = 4$ and $y = \sqrt{3}$. Thus,

equation for the tangent line is $(y - \sqrt{3}) = -\dfrac{\sqrt{3}}{6}(x-4)$ or $y = -\dfrac{\sqrt{3}}{6}x + \dfrac{5\sqrt{3}}{3}$.

45. **B** Recall the equation for solving for differentials: $f(x+\Delta x)=f(x)+f'(x)\Delta x$. In this case, $f(x)=\sqrt{x}$, $f'(x)=\frac{1}{2}x^{-\frac{1}{2}}$, $x=4$, and $\Delta x=0.002$. If you plug all of those equations and values into the formula for differentials, the solution is 2.0005.

Section II

1. Water is dripping from a pipe into a container whose volume increases at a rate of $150\,\text{cm}^3/\text{min}$. The water takes the shape of a cone with both its radius and height changing with time.

(a) What is the rate of change of the radius of the container at the instant the height is 2 cm and the radius is 5 cm? At this instant the height is changing at a rate of $0.5\,\text{cm/min}$.

(a) The rate in the question stem refers to volume, so use equation for volume of a cone to relate radius and height. The volume of a cone is: $V=\frac{1}{3}\pi r^2 h$. Differentiate this equation with respect to time to determine the rate of change of the radius: $\frac{dV}{dt}=\frac{1}{3}\pi\left(r^2\frac{dh}{dt}+2rh\frac{dr}{dt}\right)$. Now, plug in the given values, $r=5\,\text{cm}, h=2\,\text{cm}, \frac{dV}{dt}=150\,\text{cm}^3/\text{min}$, and $\frac{dh}{dt}=0.5\,\text{cm/min}$, so $150=\frac{1}{3}\pi\left(5^2(0.5)+2(5)(2)\frac{dr}{dt}\right)$. Finally, solve for $\frac{dr}{dt}$: $\frac{dr}{dt}=6.53697\,\text{cm/min}$.

(b) The water begins to be extracted from the container at a rate of $E(t)=75t^{0.25}$. Water continues to drip from the pipe at the same rate as before. When is the water at its maximum volume? Justify your reasoning.

(b) The rate of the volume of water now has to be adjusted because water is being extracted, so $\frac{dV}{dt}=150-E(t)=150-75t^{0.25}$. To maximize the volume, set $\frac{dV}{dt}$ equal to 0 and solve for t: $150-75t^{0.25}=0$, thus $t=16$. To confirm this is a maximum, use the first derivative test. Since $\frac{dV}{dt}>0$ when $0<t<16$ and $\frac{dV}{dt}<0$ when $t>16$, $t=16$ is when the volume will be at a maximum. You can also go a step further and take the derivative of $\frac{dV}{dt}$ and use the second derivative test. $\frac{d^2V}{dt^2}=-\frac{75}{4}t^{-0.75}$ which is negative at $t=16$, so $t=16$ is a maximum.

(c) By the time water began to be extracted, 3000 cm³ of water had already leaked from the pipe. Write, but do not evaluate, an expression with an integral that gives the volume of water in the container at the time in part (b).

(c) The volume of water in the container can be found by integrating the new expression for $\dfrac{dV}{dt}$

from part (b): $\dfrac{dV}{dt} = 150 - 75t^{0.25}$, over the interval $t = 0$ to $t = 16$, from part (b). In this part, we

are given an initial volume that must be added to the volume found by the integral. Therefore the

expression for the total volume is $V(t) = 3000 + \displaystyle\int_0^{16} 150 - 75t^{0.25}\, dt$.

2. The temperature in a room increases at a rate of $\dfrac{dT}{dt} = kT$, where k is a constant.

(a) Find an equation for T, the temperature (in °F), in terms of t, the number of hours passed, if the temperature is 65 °F initially and 70 °F after one hour.

(a) First, solve the differential equation for the rate of the temperature increase, $\dfrac{dT}{dt} = kT$,

by separating the variables and integrating. When that is done, $T(t) = Ce^{kt}$. You are given that

$T = 65$ at $t = 0$, so insert those values into the equation for T and solve for C: $65 = Ce^{k(0)}$, $C = 65$.

Finally, you are given a second temperature and time point, $(1,70)$; use those values in the new for-

mula for T, $T(t) = 65e^{kt}$, and solve for k: $70 = 65e^{k(1)}$, $k = \ln\dfrac{14}{13} = 0.07411$. Therefore, the equation

for T is $T(t) = 65e^{0.07411t}$.

(b) How many hours will it take for the temperature to reach 85 °F?

(b) Use the formula from part (a): $T(t) = 65e^{0.07411t}$. Insert 85 for $T(t)$ and solve for t:

$85 = 65e^{0.07411t}$, thus $t = 3.6199$ hours.

(c) After the temperature reaches 85 °F, a fan is turned on and cools the room at a consistent rate of 7 °F/hour, how long will it take for the room to reach 0 °F?

(c) With the introduction of the fan cooling the room, the rate the temperature increases changes to $\dfrac{dT}{dt} = kT - 7$. Solve this differential equation by separating the variable and integrating: $T(t) = Ce^{kt} + \dfrac{7}{k}$. At $t = 0$, the temperature is 85 °F, so $C = 85 - \dfrac{7}{k}$. Use the value of k from part (a), $k = 0.07411$ and solve the equation for t when $T = 0$ °F: $0 = \left(85 - \dfrac{7}{0.07411}\right)e^{0.07411t} + \dfrac{7}{0.07411}$.

Therefore, the time to get to 0 °F is 31.0548 hours.

3. Let R be the region enclosed by the graphs of $y = \dfrac{2}{x+1}$, $y = x^2$, and the lines $x = 0$ and $x = 1$.

(a) Find the area of R.

(a) First, determine which curve is more positive ($f(x)$), and set up your integral for area between curves: $A = \int_a^b (f(x) - g(x))\,dx$. For this problem, $f(x) = \dfrac{2}{x+1}$, so the integral is: $A = \int_0^1 \left(\dfrac{2}{x+1} - x^2\right)dx = 2\ln|2| - \dfrac{1}{3} \approx 1.05296$.

(b) Find the volume of the solid generated when R is revolved about the x-axis.

(b) You can use the washer method to find the volume: $V = \pi \int_a^b \left[(f(x))^2 - (g(x))^2\right]dx$. Thus, $V = \pi \int_0^1 \left[\left(\dfrac{2}{x+1}\right)^2 - (x^2)^2\right]dx = 1.8\pi$.

(c) Set up, but do not evaluate, the expression for the volume of the solid generated when R is revolved around the line $x = 2$.

(c) Here, use the cylindrical shells method: $V = 2\pi \int_a^b x(f(x) - g(x))\,dx$. Adjust the axis of rotation since we are revolving around the line $x = 2$. Because, $x = 2$ is more positive than the x-axis, we set up the integral with $(2 - x)$, not x. Thus, the integral is: $V = 2\pi \int_0^1 (2 - x)\left(\dfrac{2}{x+1} - x^2\right)dx$.

4. Consider the equation $x^3 + 2x^2 y + 4y^2 = 12$.

(a) Write an equation for the slope of the curve at any point (x,y).

(a) Use implicit differentiation to find the first derivative which is the slope of the curve at any point (x,y):

$$x^3 + 2x^2 y + 4y^2 = 12$$

$$3x^2 + 2\left(x^2 \frac{dy}{dx} + 2xy\right) + 8y\frac{dy}{dx} = 0$$

$$3x^2 + 2x^2 \frac{dy}{dx} + 4xy + 8y\frac{dy}{dx} = 0$$

$$\frac{dy}{dx}\left(2x^2 + 8y\right) = -3x^2 - 4xy$$

$$\frac{dy}{dx} = \frac{-3x^2 - 4xy}{2x^2 + 8y}$$

(b) Find the equation of the tangent line to the curve at $x = 0$.

(b) First, plug in $x = 0$ to the original equation to solve for y: $0^3 + 2(0)^2 y + 4y^2 = 12$, so $y = \sqrt{3}$.

Now, plug $x = 0$ and $y = \sqrt{3}$ into the equation for slope from part (a): $\frac{dy}{dx} = \frac{-3(0)^2 - 4(0)\left(\sqrt{3}\right)}{2(0)^2 + 8\left(\sqrt{3}\right)} = 0$.

Use the point-slope form of a line to get your equation for the tangent line to point $(0, \sqrt{3})$:

$$y - \sqrt{3} = 0(x - 0), \text{ so } y = \sqrt{3}.$$

(c) If the equation given for the curve is the path a car travels in feet over t seconds, find $\frac{d^2 y}{dx^2}$ at $\left(0, \sqrt{3}\right)$ and explain what it represents with proper units.

(c) Use $\frac{dy}{dx}$ from part (a) to find $\frac{d^2 y}{dx^2}$ via implicit differentiation. Do not simplify; immediately plug in 0 for x, $\sqrt{3}$ for y, and 0 for $\frac{dy}{dx}$, from part (b): $\frac{d^2 y}{dx^2}$ represents the car's acceleration. At the position $(0, \sqrt{3})$, the acceleration is $-\dfrac{1}{16}$ ft/sec^2.

5.   Water is filling at a rate of 64π in^3 into a conical tank that has a diameter of 36 in at its base and whose height is 60 in.

(a) Find an expression for the volume of water (in in^3) in the tank in terms of its radius.

(a) The volume of a cone is $V = \dfrac{1}{3}\pi r^2 h$. The height and radius of a cone are constantly proportionate at any point, so given the values for the height and diameter, we can write: $\dfrac{h}{r} = \dfrac{60}{18}$, so $h = \dfrac{10}{3}r$. Thus, in terms of r, the volume of the water in the tank will be found from evaluating:

$V = \dfrac{10}{9}\pi r^3$.

(b) At what rate is the radius of the water expanding when the radius is 20 in.

(b) We can differentiate the formula for volume from part (a) with respect to time. Then we can plug in the rate the volume is changing, $\dfrac{dV}{dt} = 64\pi$, and the radius given, 20 in. $\dfrac{dV}{dt} = \dfrac{10}{3}\pi r^2 \dfrac{dr}{dt}$, so $64\pi = \dfrac{10}{3}\pi\left(20^2\right)\dfrac{dr}{dt}$. Then, $\dfrac{dr}{dt} = \dfrac{6}{125}\dfrac{\text{in}}{\text{sec}}$.

(c) How fast in (in/sec) is the height of the water increasing in the tank when the radius is 20 in?

(c) In order to find how fast the height is changing, we must go back to the relationship between height and radius in part (a) and rewrite the formula for volume with respect to height, not radius. Thus, $r = \dfrac{3}{10}h$ and $V = \dfrac{3}{100}\pi h^3$. If we differentiate this equation with respect to time, as in part (b), the rate will be found from the equation $\dfrac{dV}{dt} = \dfrac{9}{100}\pi h^2 \dfrac{dh}{dt}$. We can use the relationship between radius and height to solve for the height when the radius is 20 in, so the height is $\dfrac{200}{3}$ in. Plugging in this value for h and the given value of $\dfrac{dV}{dt} = (64\pi)$. The equation to evaluate is $64\pi = \dfrac{9}{100}\pi\left(\dfrac{200}{3}\right)^2 \dfrac{dh}{dt}$. From this, $\dfrac{dh}{dt} = \dfrac{4}{25}$ in/sec.

6.   If a ball is accelerating at a rate given by $a(t) = -64 \dfrac{\text{ft}}{\text{sec}^2}$, the velocity of the ball is $96 \dfrac{\text{ft}}{\text{sec}}$ at time $t = 1$, and the height of the ball is 100 ft at $t = 0$, what is

(a)   The equation of the ball's velocity at time t?

(a)   The velocity of the ball can be found by integrating the acceleration function. $a(t) = \dfrac{dv}{dt} = -64$. So, $\int dv = \int -64 \, dt$ or $v = -64t + C$. Plug in the condition that the velocity is 96 at $t = 1$ to solve for C: $C = 160$, so $v(t) = -64t + 160$.

(b)   The time when the ball is changing direction?

(b)   The ball changes direction when the velocity is zero, but the acceleration is not. Set $v(t)$ equal to zero and solve for such times, t. $v(t) = -64t + 160 = 0$ when $t = \dfrac{5}{2}$. Since $a(t)$ is a constant, (-64), the ball is changing direction at 2.5 sec.

(c)   The equation of the ball's height?

(c)   To determine the equation of the ball's height, repeat the procedure in part (a), but integrate the velocity function to get the position function: $v(t) = \dfrac{dh}{dt} = -64t + 160$. So, $\int dh = \int (-64t + 160) \, dt$ or $h(t) = -32t^2 + 160t + C$. To find C, plug in the ball's height at time $t = 0$, 100 ft, and $C = 100$. Thus $h(t) = -32t^2 + 160t + 100$.

(d)   The ball's maximum height?

(d)   The maximum height occurs when the velocity of the ball is zero, i.e. when it is changing direction from rising to falling. In part (b), we found that time to be $t = 2.5$ sec. Plug 2.5 into the position function to solve for the maximum height: $h(2.5) = -32(2.5)^2 + 160(2.5) + 100 = 300 \, \text{ft}$.

Chapter 29
BC Calculus
Practice Test

AP® Calculus BC Exam

SECTION I: Multiple-Choice Questions

DO NOT OPEN THIS BOOKLET UNTIL YOU ARE TOLD TO DO SO.

At a Glance

Total Time
1 hour and 45 minutes
Number of Questions
45
Percent of Total Grade
50%
Writing Instrument
Pencil required

Instructions

Section I of this examination contains 45 multiple-choice questions. Fill in only the ovals for numbers 1 through 45 on your answer sheet.

CALCULATORS MAY NOT BE USED IN THIS PART OF THE EXAMINATION.

Indicate all of your answers to the multiple-choice questions on the answer sheet. No credit will be given for anything written in this exam booklet, but you may use the booklet for notes or scratch work. After you have decided which of the suggested answers is best, completely fill in the corresponding oval on the answer sheet. Give only one answer to each question. If you change an answer, be sure that the previous mark is erased completely. Here is a sample question and answer.

Sample Question   Sample Answer

Chicago is a
(A) state
(B) city
(C) country
(D) continent
(E) village

Use your time effectively, working as quickly as you can without losing accuracy. Do not spend too much time on any one question. Go on to other questions and come back to the ones you have not answered if you have time. It is not expected that everyone will know the answers to all the multiple-choice questions.

About Guessing

Many candidates wonder whether or not to guess the answers to questions about which they are not certain. Multiple choice scores are based on the number of questions answered correctly. Points are not deducted for incorrect answers, and no points are awarded for unanswered questions. Because points are not deducted for incorrect answers, you are encouraged to answer all multiple-choice questions. On any questions you do not know the answer to, you should eliminate as many choices as you can, and then select the best answer among the remaining choices.

THIS PAGE INTENTIONALLY LEFT BLANK.

CALCULUS BC

SECTION I, Part A

Time—55 Minutes

Number of questions—28

A CALCULATOR MAY NOT BE USED ON THIS PART OF THE EXAMINATION

Directions: Solve each of the following problems, using the available space for scratchwork. After examining the form of the choices, decide which is the best of the choices given and fill in the corresponding oval on the answer sheet. No credit will be given for anything written in the test book. Do not spend too much time on any one problem.

In this test: Unless otherwise specified, the domain of a function f is assumed to be the set of all real numbers x for which $f(x)$ is a real number.

1. Which of the following is a y-coordinate for the equation $y = \frac{1}{2}x^4 + \frac{2}{3}x^3 - 2x^2 + 6$ when the tangents to the curve equal zero?

    (A) $-\frac{35}{6}$

    (B) -6

    (C) 0

    (D) $\frac{34}{3}$

    (E) 36

2. What is the sum of the series $\sqrt{5} - \frac{5}{2} + \frac{5\sqrt{5}}{3} - \frac{25}{4} + \ldots + (-1)^n \frac{\sqrt{5}^{n+1}}{n+1} + \ldots?$

    (A) $\ln\left(1+\sqrt{5}\right)$
    (B) $e^{\sqrt{5}}$
    (C) $\ln(\sqrt{5})$
    (D) $\sqrt{5}$
    (E) The series diverges.

GO ON TO THE NEXT PAGE.

3. $\displaystyle\lim_{x \to 0}\frac{\sqrt{x+2}+2x-4}{x^3}$

(A) 0

(B) $\dfrac{3\sqrt{2}}{64}$

(C) $\dfrac{\sqrt{2}}{24}$

(D) $\dfrac{\sqrt{2}}{18}$

(E) Undefined

---

4. Find $\dfrac{d^2y}{dx^2}$ at $x = 1$ for $y^2 - y = 2x^3 - 3x^2 - 4x + 7$.

(A) $-\dfrac{26}{9}$

(B) $-\dfrac{22}{27}$

(C) $-\dfrac{22}{25}$

(D) $-\dfrac{10}{9}$

(E) $\dfrac{26}{9}$

GO ON TO THE NEXT PAGE.

5. $\lim\limits_{h \to 0} \dfrac{\left(2x^2 + 4xh + 2h^2\right) - 2x^2}{h} =$

(A) $2x^2$

(B) $-2x^2$

(C) $4x$

(D) 4

(E) Undefined

6. $\displaystyle\int \dfrac{dx}{4x^2 - 20x + 26} =$

(A) $\tan^{-1}(2x - 5) + C$

(B) $\sin^{-1}(x - 5) + C$

(C) $\tan^{-1}(x - 5) + C$

(D) $\dfrac{1}{2}\tan^{-1}(2x - 5) + C$

(E) $\dfrac{1}{2}\sin^{-1}(2x - 5) + C$

7. $\displaystyle\int \dfrac{14x - 12}{(x^2 + 9)(x + 3)}\,dx =$

(A) $\left(\dfrac{3}{2}\right)\ln|x^2 + 9| + \left(\dfrac{5}{3}\right)\tan^{-1}\dfrac{x}{3} + 3\ln|x + 3| + C$

(B) $\left(\dfrac{3}{2}\right)\ln|x^2 + 9| + \left(\dfrac{5}{3}\right)\tan^{-1}\dfrac{x}{3} - 3\ln|x + 3| + C$

(C) $\left(\dfrac{3}{2}\right)\ln|x^2 + 9| - \left(\dfrac{5}{3}\right)\tan^{-1}\dfrac{x}{3} - 3\ln|x + 3| + C$

(D) $\left(\dfrac{3}{2}\right)\ln|x^2 + 9| - \left(\dfrac{5}{3}\right)\tan^{-1}\dfrac{x}{3} + 3\ln|x + 3| + C$

(E) $-\left(\dfrac{3}{2}\right)\ln|x^2 + 9| + \left(\dfrac{5}{3}\right)\tan^{-1}\dfrac{x}{3} - 3\ln|x + 3| + C$

GO ON TO THE NEXT PAGE.

8. If $\dfrac{dy}{dx} = 2x^3 y$ and $y(0) = 4$, find an equation for y in terms of x.

(A) $y = e^{2x^4}$

(B) $y = 4e^{2x^4}$

(C) $y = 4e^{x^4}$

(D) $y = e^{\frac{x^4}{2}}$

(E) $y = 4e^{\frac{x^4}{2}}$

9. Find the derivative of $y^3 = (x+2)^2 (2x-3)^3$

(A) $\dfrac{y}{3}\left(\dfrac{2}{x+2} + \dfrac{3}{2x-3}\right)$

(B) $\dfrac{y}{3}\left(\dfrac{2}{x+2} + \dfrac{6}{2x-3}\right)$

(C) $\dfrac{3}{y}\left(\dfrac{2}{x+2} + \dfrac{3}{2x-3}\right)$

(D) $\dfrac{3}{y}\left(\dfrac{2}{x+2} + \dfrac{6}{2x-3}\right)$

(E) $\dfrac{y}{3}\left(\dfrac{2}{x+2} - \dfrac{6}{2x-3}\right)$

GO ON TO THE NEXT PAGE.

10. $\dfrac{dy}{dx} = \left(x^3 - 3\right)y^2$ and $f(2) = \dfrac{1}{2}$. Find an equation for y in terms of x.

(A) $y = \dfrac{4}{12x - x^4}$

(B) $y = \dfrac{4}{x^4 - 12x}$

(C) $y = \dfrac{1}{3x - x^4} - \dfrac{1}{2}$

(D) $y = \dfrac{1}{x^4 - 3x}$

(E) $y = \dfrac{4}{12x - x^4} + 2$

11. Find the derivative of $y = \cos^{-1}\left(x^2 + 2x\right)$.

(A) $\dfrac{-2x - 2}{\sqrt{1 - \left(x^2 + 2x\right)^2}}$

(B) $\dfrac{2x + 2}{\sqrt{1 - \left(x^2 + 2x\right)^2}}$

(C) $\dfrac{-1}{\sqrt{1 - \left(2x + 2\right)^2}}$

(D) $\dfrac{1}{\sqrt{1 - \left(2x + 2\right)^2}}$

(E) $\dfrac{-1}{\sqrt{1 - \left(x^2 + 2x\right)^2}}$

GO ON TO THE NEXT PAGE.

12. $\lim\limits_{x \to 2}\left(x^3 - 5x + 3\right) =$

    (A)   1
    (B)   3
    (C)   8
    (D) 10
    (E) 18

---

13. $\dfrac{d}{dx}\left(\csc x \sec x\right) =$

    (A) $\sec^2 x - \csc^2 x$

    (B) $\sec x - \csc x$

    (C) $\csc^2 x - \sec^2 x$

    (D) $\sec^2 x + \csc^2 x$

    (E) $\csc x + \sec x$

---

14. $\dfrac{d}{dx}\left(\tan\left(\dfrac{x^3}{x+1}\right)\right) =$

    (A) $\dfrac{3x^3 + 2x^2}{\left(x+1\right)^2}\sec^2\left(\dfrac{x^3}{x+1}\right)$

    (B) $\dfrac{2x^3 + 3x^2}{\left(x+1\right)^2}\sec^2\left(\dfrac{x^3}{x+1}\right)$

    (C) $\dfrac{2x^3 - 3x^2}{x+1}\sec^2\left(\dfrac{x^3}{x+1}\right)$

    (D) $\dfrac{2x^3 - 3x}{\left(x+1\right)^2}\sec^2\left(\dfrac{x^3}{x+1}\right)$

    (E) $\dfrac{2x^3 + 3x^2}{x+1}\sec^2\left(\dfrac{x^3}{x+1}\right)$

GO ON TO THE NEXT PAGE.

15. $\lim\limits_{x\to\infty}\dfrac{2x^3+4x^2-6x+7}{12x^3+2x^2+4x-9}=$

    (A) 0

    (B) $\dfrac{1}{6}$

    (C) $\dfrac{1}{3}$

    (D) $\dfrac{1}{2}$

    (E) The limit is undefined.

---

16. Where is the tangent line perpendicular to the y-axis for the curve $y=2x^4-4x^2+7$ located?

    (A) $y=5$
    (B) $y=-7$
    (C) $x=5$
    (D) $y=1$
    (E) $x=7$

---

17. If f is continuous on the interval $[-3,3]$ and differentiable everywhere on $(-3,3)$, find $x=c$, where $f(c)$ is the mean value of $f(x)=x^3-3x^2+x-4$.

    (A) -2
    (B) -1
    (C)   0
    (D)   1
    (E)   2

GO ON TO THE NEXT PAGE.

18. A toy manufacturer has determined the total profit for a month can be determined by the equation $P = -3x^2 + 30x + 150$, where x is the number of thousands of toys sold. How many thousands of toys should be sold to maximize the profit that month?

    (A) 2
    (B) 3
    (C) 4
    (D) 5
    (E) 6

19. Find the derivative of $f(x) = x^{x^2}$.

    (A) $x^{(2x^2)}(1 + 2\ln x)$

    (B) $e^{x^2 \ln x}(1 + 2\ln x)$

    (C) $x^{x^2}(x + 2x\ln x)$

    (D) $x^{x^2}(x^2 + 2x\ln x)$

    (E) $e^{x^2 \ln x}(x + 2x\ln x)$

20. If $f(x) = x^2\left(\sqrt[3]{x-4}\right)$, $f'(x) =$

    (A) $y\left(\dfrac{2}{x} + \dfrac{1}{3x-12}\right)$

    (B) $\dfrac{2}{x} + \dfrac{1}{3x-12}$

    (C) $y\left(\dfrac{2}{x} + \dfrac{1}{x-4}\right)$

    (D) $y\left(\dfrac{2}{x} - \dfrac{1}{3(x-4)}\right)$

    (E) $\dfrac{2}{x} - \dfrac{1}{x-4}$

GO ON TO THE NEXT PAGE.

21. Find the equation of the line normal to the graph of $y = \dfrac{3x^2 + 6}{x+1}$ at $(2,6)$.

(A) $y = -\dfrac{1}{2}x + 5$

(B) $y = 2x - 7$

(C) $y = \dfrac{1}{2}x + 5$

(D) $y = -\dfrac{1}{2}x + 7$

(E) $y = -2x + 2$

22. Find the value of C that satisfies the MVTD for $f(x) = 2x^{\frac{3}{2}} + 5x - 2$ on the interval $[0,4]$.

(A) $\dfrac{16}{9}$

(B) 1

(C) $\dfrac{4}{3}$

(D) 9

(E) 8

GO ON TO THE NEXT PAGE.

23. If $y = 7^{2x\cos^2 x}$, then $\dfrac{dy}{dx} =$

(A) $7^{2x\cos^2 x}\left(2\cos^2 x + 4x\cos x\sin x\right)$

(B) $7^{2x\cos^2 x}\left(2\cos^2 x - 4x\cos x\sin x\right)$

(C) $7^{2x\cos^2 x}\left(\ln 7\right)\left(2\cos^2 x + 4x\cos x\sin x\right)$

(D) $49^{x\cos^2 x}\left(\ln 7\right)\left(2\cos^2 x + 4x\cos x\sin x\right)$

(E) $49^{x\cos^2 x}\left(\ln 7\right)\left(2\cos^2 x - 4x\cos x\sin x\right)$

24. Find the derivative of the inverse of $y = x^3 - 3x + 5$ when $y = 7$.

(A) $\dfrac{1}{9}$

(B) 0

(C) 9

(D) 144

(E) $\dfrac{1}{144}$

25. Find the derivative of the inverse of $f(x) = \sin^2(6\pi - x)$ at $f(x) = \dfrac{1}{2}$ for $0 \le x \le \dfrac{\pi}{2}$.

(A) -1

(B) $-\dfrac{\sqrt{2}}{2}$

(C) $\dfrac{1}{2}$

(D) $\dfrac{\sqrt{2}}{2}$

(E) 1

GO ON TO THE NEXT PAGE.

26. $\int \left(3x^3 - 2x^2 + x - 7\right) dx =$

(A) $12x^4 - 6x^3 + 2x^2 + 7x + C$

(B) $x^2 - x + C$

(C) $12x^4 - 6x^3 + 2x^2 - 7x + C$

(D) $\dfrac{3}{4}x^4 - \dfrac{2}{3}x^3 + \dfrac{x^2}{2} - 7x + C$

(E) $\dfrac{3}{4}x^4 + \dfrac{2}{3}x^3 - \dfrac{x^2}{2} + 7x + C$

27. Find the derivative of $y = \sqrt{\dfrac{1+x}{3x-1}}\left(\dfrac{x+2}{x-1}\right)^2$?

(A) $\dfrac{y}{2}\left(\dfrac{1}{x+1} - \dfrac{1}{3x+1}\right) + 2y\left(\dfrac{1}{x+2} - \dfrac{1}{x-1}\right)$

(B) $\dfrac{y}{2}\left(\dfrac{1}{1+x} - \dfrac{3}{3x-1}\right) + \dfrac{1}{x+2} - \dfrac{1}{x-1}$

(C) $2y\left(\dfrac{1}{x+1} - \dfrac{1}{3x+1}\right) + \dfrac{y}{2}\left(\dfrac{1}{x+2} - \dfrac{1}{x-1}\right)$

(D) $\dfrac{y}{2}\left(\dfrac{1}{x+1} - \dfrac{3}{3x-1}\right) + 2y\left(\dfrac{1}{x+2} - \dfrac{1}{x-1}\right)$

(E) $2y\left(\dfrac{1}{1+x} - \dfrac{3}{3x-1}\right) + \dfrac{y}{2}\left(\dfrac{1}{x+2} - \dfrac{1}{x-1}\right)$

GO ON TO THE NEXT PAGE.

28. Find $\lim\limits_{x\to\frac{\pi}{2}}\dfrac{3x}{2\cos x}$.

(A) $\dfrac{3}{2}$

(B) $-\dfrac{3}{2}$

(C) $\dfrac{2}{3}$

(D) 3

(E) 0

END OF PART A, SECTION I

IF YOU FINISH BEFORE TIME IS CALLED, YOU MAY CHECK YOUR WORK ON PART A ONLY.

DO NOT GO ON TO PART B UNTIL YOU ARE TOLD TO DO SO.

CALCULUS BC

SECTION I, Part B

Time—50 Minutes

Number of questions—17

A GRAPHING CALCULATOR IS REQUIRED FOR SOME QUESTIONS ON THIS PART OF THE EXAMINATION

Directions: Solve each of the following problems, using the available space for scratchwork. After examining the form of the choices, decide which is the best of the choices given and fill in the corresponding oval on the answer sheet. No credit will be given for anything written in the test book. Do not spend too much time on any one problem.

In this test:

1. The **exact** numerical value of the correct answer does not always appear among the choices given. When this happens, select from among the choices the number that best approximates the exact numerical value.

2. Unless otherwise specified, the domain of a function f is assumed to be the set of all real numbers x for which $f(x)$ is a real number.

29. $\int x^2 e^{4x^3+7} dx =$

(A) $12e^{4x^3+7} + C$

(B) $e^{4x^3+7} + C$

(C) $\dfrac{1}{12}e^{4x^3+7} + C$

(D) $\dfrac{1}{2}e^{4x^3+7} + C$

(E) $2e^{4x^3+7} + C$

GO ON TO THE NEXT PAGE.

30. $\int \dfrac{x+7}{(2x-3)(x+6)}\,dx =$

    (A) $\dfrac{17}{30}\ln|2x-3| - \dfrac{1}{15}\ln|x+6| + C$

    (B) $\dfrac{1}{15}\ln|2x-3| - \dfrac{17}{30}\ln|x+6| + C$

    (C) $\dfrac{17}{30}\ln|2x-3| + \dfrac{1}{15}\ln|x+6| + C$

    (D) $\dfrac{17}{15}\ln|2x-3| - \dfrac{1}{15}\ln|x+6| + C$

    (E) $\dfrac{17}{15}\ln|2x-3| + \dfrac{1}{15}\ln|x+6| + C$

---

31. Find b where $y = x^2 - ax + b$ and $y = x^2 + cx$ have a common tangent at $(2,1)$.

    (A) $-\dfrac{3}{2}$

    (B) $\dfrac{3}{2}$

    (C) -8

    (D) 8

    (E) 0

---

32. Car A and car B leave a town at the same time. Car A drives due north at a rate of 60 km/hr and car B goes east at a rate of 80 km/hr. How fast is the distance between them increasing after 2 hours?

    (A) 120 km/hr
    (B) 160 km/hr
    (C) 100 km/hr
    (D) 200 km/hr
    (E) 70 km/hr

GO ON TO THE NEXT PAGE.

33. Approximate cos 91°.

(A) $-\dfrac{179\pi}{180}$

(B) $\dfrac{179\pi}{180}$

(C) $\dfrac{\pi}{180}$

(D) $-\dfrac{\pi}{180}$

(E) 0

34. A 30-foot ladder leaning against a wall is pushed up the wall at a rate of 3 ft/sec. How fast is the ladder sliding across the ground towards the wall when it is 18 feet up the wall from the ground?

(A) $-\dfrac{9}{4}$ ft/sec

(B) $-\dfrac{4}{9}$ ft/sec

(C) $-\dfrac{3}{2}$ ft/sec

(D) -4 ft/sec

(E) -3 ft/sec

35. Approximate the area under the curve $y = x^2 + 2$ from $x = 1$ to $x = 2$ using four left-endpoint rectangles.

(A) 4.333
(B) 3.969
(C) 4.719
(D) 4.344
(E) 4.328

GO ON TO THE NEXT PAGE.

36. What is the mean value of $f(x) = \dfrac{\cos x + 1}{2x^2}$ over the interval $(-1,1)$?

(A) −196
(B)   −1
(C)   1
(D)   196
(E) There is no such value.

---

37. Find the second derivative of $y = x^5 - 2x^2 + 7$ at $x = 1$.

(A) 0
(B) 1
(C) 12
(D) 16
(E) 20

---

38. What is $\dfrac{dy}{dx}$ if $y = 3^{x^2}$?

(A) $2x \ln 3 \left(3^{x^2} \right)$

(B) $2x \ln 3$

(C) 3^{x^2}

(D) $2x 3^{x^2}$

(E) $\ln 3 \left(3^{x^2} \right)$

GO ON TO THE NEXT PAGE.

39. $\displaystyle\int_{\ln 2}^{2} \frac{x^3 + x^2 - 2x}{x^2 + x - 2}\,dx$

(A) $\dfrac{(\ln 2)^2 - 4}{2}$

(B) $\dfrac{4 - (\ln 2)^2}{2}$

(C) $\dfrac{\ln 4 - 4}{2}$

(D) $\dfrac{4 - \ln 4}{2}$

(E) $2 - (\ln 2)^2$

---

40. Find the derivative of the inverse of $y = 2x^2 - 8x + 9$ at $y = 3$.

(A) $\dfrac{1}{4}$

(B) $\dfrac{1}{2}$

(C) 1

(D) 3

(E) 4

GO ON TO THE NEXT PAGE.

41. A frame is bought for a photo that is 144 in². The artist would like to have a mat that is 3 in on the top and bottom and 6 in on each side. Find the dimensions of the frame that will minimize its area.

(A) $\left(12\sqrt{2}+12\right)$ in $\times\left(6\sqrt{2}+6\right)$ in

(B) $\left(12\sqrt{2}+6\right)$ in $\times\left(6\sqrt{2}+12\right)$ in

(C) $\left(12\sqrt{2}\right)$ in $\times\left(6\sqrt{2}\right)$ in

(D) $\left(12\sqrt{2}+6\right)$ in $\times\left(6\sqrt{2}+3\right)$ in

(E) $\left(12\sqrt{2}+3\right)$ in $\times\left(6\sqrt{2}+6\right)$ in

---

42. What is the length of the curve $y=\dfrac{2}{3}x^{\frac{3}{2}}$ from $x=1$ to $x=6$.

(A) $\dfrac{4}{3}\sqrt{7}-\dfrac{14}{3}\sqrt{2}$

(B) $\dfrac{14}{3}\sqrt{7}+\dfrac{4}{3}\sqrt{2}$

(C) $\dfrac{14}{3}\sqrt{7}-\dfrac{4}{3}\sqrt{2}$

(D) $\dfrac{4}{3}\sqrt{2}-\dfrac{14}{3}\sqrt{7}$

(E) $\dfrac{14}{3}\sqrt{2}+\dfrac{4}{3}\sqrt{7}$

---

43. Find the length of the curve defined by $x=\left(\dfrac{1}{2}\right)t^{2}+7$ and $y=\left(\dfrac{8}{3}\right)(t+4)^{\frac{3}{2}}$ from $t=0$ to $t=8$.

(A) 36
(B) 64
(C) 80
(D) 96
(E) 100

GO ON TO THE NEXT PAGE.

44. Use Euler's method with $h = 0.2$ to estimate $y = 1$ if $y' = \dfrac{y^2 - 1}{2}$ and $y(0) = 0$.

    (A) 7.690

    (B) 12.730

    (C) 13.504

    (D) 29.069

    (E) 90.676

45. Which of the following series converges?

    (A) $\displaystyle\sum_{n=1}^{\infty} \left(\frac{2}{3}\right)^n$

    (B) $\displaystyle\sum_{n=1}^{\infty} \frac{1}{n}$

    (C) $\displaystyle\sum_{n=1}^{\infty} \frac{1}{n-1}$

    (D) $\displaystyle\sum_{n=1}^{\infty} \frac{4^n}{n^2}$

    (E) $\displaystyle\sum_{n=1}^{\infty} 3^n$

STOP

END OF PART B, SECTION I

IF YOU FINISH BEFORE TIME IS CALLED, YOU MAY CHECK YOUR WORK ON PART B ONLY.

DO NOT GO ON TO SECTION II UNTIL YOU ARE TOLD TO DO SO.

SECTION II
GENERAL INSTRUCTIONS

You may wish to look over the problems before starting to work on them, since it is not expected that everyone will be able to complete all parts of all problems. All problems are given equal weight, but the parts of a particular problem are not necessarily given equal weight.

A GRAPHING CALCULATOR IS REQUIRED FOR SOME PROBLEMS OR PARTS OF PROBLEMS ON THIS SECTION OF THE EXAMINATION.

- You should write all work for each part of each problem in the space provided for that part in the booklet. Be sure to write clearly and legibly. If you make an error, you may save time by crossing it out rather than trying to erase it. Erased or crossed-out work will not be graded.

- Show all your work. You will be graded on the correctness and completeness of your methods as well as your answers. Correct answers without supporting work may not receive credit.

- Justifications require that you give mathematical (noncalculator) reasons and that you clearly identify functions, graphs, tables, or other objects you use.

- You are permitted to use your calculator to solve an equation, find the derivative of a function at a point, or calculate the value of a definite integral. However, you must clearly indicate the setup of your problem, namely the equation, function, or integral you are using. If you use other built-in features or programs, you must show the mathematical steps necessary to produce your results.

- Your work must be expressed in standard mathematical notation rather than calculator syntax. For example, $\int_{1}^{5} x^2\,dx$ may not be written as fnInt (X^2, X, 1, 5).

- Unless otherwise specified, answers (numeric or algebraic) need not be simplified. If your answer is given as a decimal approximation, it should be correct to three places after the decimal point.

- Unless otherwise specified, the domain of a function f is assumed to be the set of all real numbers x for which $f(x)$ is a real number.

GO ON TO THE NEXT PAGE.

SECTION II, PART A
Time—30 minutes
Number of problems—2

A graphing calculator is required for some problems or parts of problems.

During the timed portion for Part A, you may work only on the problems in Part A.

On Part A, you are permitted to use your calculator to solve an equation, find the derivative of a function at a point, or calculate the value of a definite integral. However, you must clearly indicate the setup of your problem, namely the equation, function, or integral you are using. If you use other built-in features or programs, you must show the mathematical steps necessary to produce your results.

1.

x	2	2.2	2.4	2.6	2.8	3
$\dfrac{dy}{dx}$	6	5	4	2.5	1	0.5

The equation for y is thrice differentiable for $x > 0$ with $y = 3$ at $x = 2$, the second derivative is equal to 2 at $x = 2$, and the third derivative is 4 at $x = 2$. Values of the first derivative are given for select values of x above.

(a) Write an equation for the tangent line of y at $x = 3$. Use this line to approximate y at $x = 3$.

(b) Use a right endpoint Riemann sum with five subintervals of equal length and values from the table to approximate $\int_2^3 \dfrac{dy}{dx}\,dx$. Use this approximation to estimate y at $x = 3$. Show your work.

(c) Use Euler's Method, starting at $x = 2$ with five steps of equal size, to approximate y at $x = 3$. Show your work.

(d) Write a third degree Taylor polynomial for y about $x = 2$. Use it to approximate y at $x = 3$.

---

2. Let R be the region bound by $y_1 = 2x^3 - 4x^2 - 8$ and $y_2 = 2x^2 + 8x - 8$.

(a) Find the area of R.
(b) Find the volume of the solid generated when R is revolved about the x-axis for $0 \le x \le 4$.
(c) Find the volume of the solid generated when R is revolved about the line $x = 2$ when $-1 \le x \le 0$.

GO ON TO THE NEXT PAGE.

SECTION II, PART B
Time—1 hour
Number of problems—4

No calculator is allowed for these problems.

During the timed portion for Part B, you may continue to work on the problems in Part A without the use of any calculator.

---

3. Consider the graph of the polar curve $r = 1 + 2\sin\theta$ for $0 \le \theta \le 2\pi$. Let S be the region bound between the inner and outer loops.

    (a) Write an integral expression for the area of S.

    (b) Write expressions for $\dfrac{dx}{d\theta}$ and $\dfrac{dy}{d\theta}$ in terms of θ.

    (c) Write an equation in terms of x and y for the line normal to the graph of the polar curve at the point where $\theta = \dfrac{3\pi}{2}$. Show your work.

---

4. For $t \ge 0$, a particle is moving along a curve so that its position at time t is $(x(t), y(t))$. At time $t = 3$, the particle is at position $(3,1)$. It is known that $\dfrac{dx}{dt} = e^{-2t}(t+1)^2$ and $\dfrac{dy}{dt} = \cos^2 t$.

    (a) Is the horizontal movement to the left or to the right at time $t = 3$? Find the slope of the particle's path at $t = 3$.

    (b) Find the y-coordinate of the particle's position at time $t = 6$.

    (c) Find the speed and acceleration of the particle at $t = 6$.

    (d) Find the distance traveled by the particle from time $t = 3$ to $t = 6$.

GO ON TO THE NEXT PAGE.

5. A particle's position in the xy-plane at any time t is given by $x = 3t^3 - 4$ and $y = 2t^5 - 3t^3$. Find:

   (a) The x and y components of the particle's velocity.

   (b) $\dfrac{dy}{dx}$ at $t = 3$.

   (c) The acceleration of the particle at $t = 3$.

   (d) The time(s) when the particle is changing direction.

---

6. Let $y_1' = \dfrac{3x^2}{y_1^2}$ and $y_2' = 2x^3 y_2 - xy_2$.

   (a) If $x = 0$ and $y = 6$, find y_1.

   (b) If $x = -2$ and $y = e^2$, find y_2.

   (c) Use Euler's method to approximate y_1 when $x = 3$. Start at $x = 0$ using three steps. Check your answer against the real value of y_1 at $x = 3$. Is this a reasonable approximation?

STOP

END OF EXAM

Chapter 30
BC Calculus
Practice Test
Answers and
Explanations

ANSWER KEY

Section I

1.	D	24.	C
2.	A	25.	E
3.	B	26.	D
4.	B	27.	D
5.	C	28.	B
6.	D	29.	C
7.	B	30.	A
8.	E	31.	E
9.	B	32.	C
10.	A	33.	D
11.	A	34.	A
12.	A	35.	B
13.	A	36.	E
14.	B	37.	D
15.	B	38.	A
16.	A	39.	B
17.	A	40.	A
18.	D	41.	A
19.	C	42.	C
20.	A	43.	D
21.	D	44.	C
22.	A	45.	A
23.	E		

EXPLANATIONS

Section I

1. **D**   Take the derivative of y and set it equal to zero. $\dfrac{dy}{dx} = 2x^3 - 2x^2 - 4x = 0$. When the equation is solved, $x = 0$, $x = -1$, and $x = 2$. Then, plug these values into the original equation for y. When this is done, y at $x = 0$ is 6, y at $x = -1$ is $\dfrac{23}{6}$ and y at $x = 2$ is $\dfrac{34}{3}$. The only answer choice of these three that is available is $\dfrac{34}{3}$.

2. **A**   The series is the Taylor series expansion of $\ln(1+x)$, in which $x = \sqrt{5}$.

3. **B**   Use L'Hôpital's Rule to differentiate the top and bottom. Repeat when necessary: Since the limit will exist now, do not differentiate anymore; evaluate the limit at $x = 0$. $\displaystyle\lim_{x \to 0} \dfrac{1}{16}(x+2)^{-\frac{5}{2}} = \dfrac{\sqrt{2}}{128}$.

4. **B**   First, find the corresponding y value for $x = 1$ by plugging $x = 1$ into $y^2 - y = 2x^3 - 3x^2 - 4x + 7$.

    Thus, $y = -1$ or $y = 2$. Next, use implicit differentiation to find the first derivative with respect to x:

    $\dfrac{dy}{dx} = \dfrac{6x^2 - 6x - 4}{2y - 1}$. Then, take the second derivative, but do not simplify; plug in the x and y-values found above to solve for the second derivative. $\dfrac{d^2y}{dx^2} = \dfrac{(2y-1)(12x-6) - (6x^2 - 6x - 4)(2)\frac{dy}{dx}}{(2y-1)^2}$

    At $(1,-1)$, $\dfrac{d^2y}{dx^2} = -\dfrac{22}{27}$ and at $(1, 2)$, $\dfrac{d^2y}{dx^2} = \dfrac{22}{27}$, so the answer is B.

5. **C**   This limit is just the definition of the derivative, so rather than deal with the limit, simply take the derivative of the function. In this case, $f(x) = 2x^2$ and $f'(x) = 4x$.

6. **D**   Although it does not appear so right away, the solution will be an inverse tangent function. Start by completing the square: $\displaystyle\int \dfrac{dx}{4x^2 - 20x + 26} = \int \dfrac{dx}{4x^2 - 20x + 25 + 1} = \int \dfrac{dx}{(2x-5)^2 + 1}$. Use u-substitution to solve from here. Thus, the final solution is $\dfrac{1}{2}\tan^{-1}(2x - 5) + C$.

7. **B**   Use the Method of Partial Fractions to evaluate: $\dfrac{Ax + B}{x^2 + 9} + \dfrac{C}{x + 3} = \dfrac{14x - 12}{(x^2 + 9)(x + 3)}$. Then, $A = 3$, $B = 5$, and $C = -3$.

$$\int \frac{3x-2}{(x+2)^2}\,dx = \int \frac{3x}{x^2+9}\,dx + \int \frac{5}{x^2+9}\,dx - \int \frac{3}{x+3}\,dx$$

$$= \left(\frac{3}{2}\right)\ln\left|x^2+9\right| + \left(\frac{5}{3}\right)\tan^{-1}\frac{x}{3} - 3\ln\left|x+3\right| + C.$$

8. **E** Separate the variables to solve the differential equation. $\int \frac{dy}{y} = \int 2x^3\,dx$. Then, $\ln|y| = \frac{1}{2}x^4 + C$.

$y = Ce^{\frac{x^4}{2}}$. When the initial point, (0, 4), is plugged in, $C = 4$ and the final answer is $y = 4e^{\frac{x^4}{2}}$.

9. **B** Use logarithms and implicit differentiation to find the derivative. The steps are as follows:

$$\ln y^3 = \ln\left[(x+2)^2(2x-3)^3\right]$$

$$3\ln y = 2\ln(x+2) + 3\ln(2x-3)$$

$$\frac{3}{y}\frac{dy}{dx} = \frac{2}{x+2} + \frac{6}{2x-3}$$

$$\frac{dy}{dx} = \frac{y}{3}\left(\frac{2}{x+2} + \frac{6}{2x-3}\right)$$

10. **A** Separate the variables to solve the differential equation: $\int \frac{dy}{y^2} = \int (x^3-3)\,dx$. Then, $y = \dfrac{1}{3x - \dfrac{x^4}{4}} + C$.

Plug in the initial condition $(2, \frac{1}{2})$ to find $C = 0$, then the final equation is $y = \dfrac{1}{3x - \dfrac{x^4}{4}} = \dfrac{4}{12x - x^4}$.

11. **A** Remember the derivative of the inverse cosine function is just negative the derivative of the inverse

sine function, so $\frac{d}{dx}\left(\cos^{-1} u\right) = \frac{-1}{\sqrt{1-u^2}}\frac{du}{dx}$. In this case, $\frac{dy}{dx} = \frac{-2x-2}{\sqrt{1-\left(x^2+2x\right)^2}}$.

12. **A** Since the function is continuous over $x = 2$, evaluate the limit by plugging in 2 for x. $\lim\limits_{x\to 2}\left(x^3 - 5x + 3\right) = \lim\limits_{x\to 2}\left(2^3 - 5(2) + 3\right) = 1$.

13. **A**   Use the product rule and remember your derivatives of trig functions. $\dfrac{d}{dx}(\csc x \sec x) = \csc x(\sec x \tan x) + \sec x(-\csc x \cot x)$. Simplify by separating each of the trig functions into sine and cosine functions:

$$\left(\frac{1}{\sin x}\right)\left(\frac{1}{\cos x}\right)\left(\frac{\sin x}{\cos x}\right) - \left(\frac{1}{\cos x}\right)\left(\frac{1}{\sin x}\right)\left(\frac{\cos x}{\sin x}\right)$$

$$= \left(\frac{1}{\cos^2 x}\right) - \left(\frac{1}{\sin^2 x}\right) = \sec^2 x - \csc^2 x$$

14. **B**   Use u-substitution, the quotient rule, and remember your derivatives of trig functions. $\dfrac{d}{dx}\left(\tan\left(\dfrac{x^3}{x+1}\right)\right) = \dfrac{(x+1)(3x^2) - x^3}{(x+1)^2}\sec^2\left(\dfrac{x^3}{x+1}\right) = \dfrac{2x^3 + 3x^2}{(x+1)^2}\sec^2\left(\dfrac{x^3}{x+1}\right)$.

15. **B**   Use l'Hôpital's Rule.

$$\lim_{x\to\infty}\frac{2x^3 + 4x^2 - 6x + 7}{12x^3 + 2x^2 + 4x - 9} = \lim_{x\to\infty}\frac{6x^2 + 8x - 6}{36x^2 + 4x + 4} = \lim_{x\to\infty}\frac{12x + 8}{72x + 4}$$

$$= \lim_{x\to\infty}\frac{12}{72} = \frac{12}{72} = \frac{1}{6}$$

16. **A**   First, notice the question asks for the tangent line that is perpendicular to the y-axis, or parallel to the x-axis. Any line that is parallel to the x-axis will have an equation in the form "$y =$" and the slope of that line will be 0. Eliminate answer choices C and E. Next, take the first derivative of the equation and set it equal to zero: $\dfrac{dy}{dx} = 8x^3 - 8x = 0$. Solving the resulting equation, the slope will be zero at $x = -1$, $x = 0$, and $x = 1$. To determine the equation of the tangent lines, plug each value of x into the original equation to solve for the corresponding y-values. At $x = -1$ and $x = 1$, $y = 5$ and at $x = 0$, $y = 7$. Thus, the answer is A.

17. **A**   Use the MVTD! $f'(c) = 3c^2 - 6c + 1$, $f(3) = -1$, and $f(-3) = -61$. The MVTD states $f'(c) = \dfrac{f(a) - f(b)}{a - b}$, where a and b are the endpoints of the interval over which $f(x)$ is continuous and differentiable everywhere and c is the mean value over that interval. For this problem, $3c^2 - 6c + 1 = \dfrac{-1 + 61}{3 + 3}$. When simplified, $c = -1$ or $c = 3$.

18. **D** In order to maximize the profit, the first derivative of P must be found and set equal to zero. When the first derivative is set equal to zero or does not exist, the maximum or minimum of a function exists. The first derivative, $\frac{dP}{dx} = -6x + 30 = 0$, is solved for x. The critical value is $x = 5$. To ensure that $x = 5$ maximizes the profit, the second derivative is found. If the second derivative is negative at $x = 5$, that critical value corresponds to a relative maximum value. The second derivative is $\frac{d^2P}{dx^2} = -6$. Thus, $x = 5$ is at a relative maximum.

19. **C** Recall $a^x = e^{x\ln a}$, and, if $y = e^u$, then $\frac{dy}{dx} = e^u \frac{du}{dx}$. To simplify the calculations, re-write $f(x) = x^{x^2}$ as $f(x) = e^{x^2 \ln x}$. Now, take the derivative of $f(x)$: $f'(x) = e^{x^2 \ln x}(x + 2x\ln x) = x^{x^2}(x + 2x\ln x)$.

20. **A** Rather than using the product rule and chain rule, use logarithmic differentiation. Take the natural log of both sides of the equation and simplify: $\ln y = \ln\left(x^2\left(\sqrt[3]{x-4}\right)\right) = 2\ln x + \frac{1}{3}\ln(x-4)$.

Next, use implicit differentiation to find the derivative: $\frac{1}{y}\frac{dy}{dx} = \frac{2}{x} + \frac{1}{3(x-4)}$. Simplify and solve for $\frac{dy}{dx}$: $\frac{dy}{dx} = y\left(\frac{2}{x} + \frac{1}{3(x-4)}\right)$.

21. **D** First, calculate the derivative of y at $(2,6)$:

$$\frac{dy}{dx} = \frac{(x+1)(6x) - (3x^2+6)}{(x+1)^2} = \frac{(2+1)(6\cdot 2) - (3(2)^2+6)}{(2+1)^2} = 2.$$

Recall that the slope of a normal line is the opposite reciprocal of the slope of a tangent line, so the slope of the normal is $-\frac{1}{2}$. From there, plug these values into the point-slope formula:

$y - 6 = -\frac{1}{2}(x-2)$, thus, $y = -\frac{1}{2}x + 7$.

22. **A** The MVTD states if $y = f(x)$ is continuous on the interval $[a,b]$, and is differentiable everywhere on the interval (a,b), then there is at least one number c between a and b such that: $f'(c) = \frac{f(b) - f(a)}{b-a}$. As $f(x)$ is continuous, determine $f(0)$ and $f(4)$. $F(0) = -2$ and $f(4) = 34$.

Thus, when these values are plugged into the formula, $f'(c) = 9$. Finally, to determine c, set this value equal to the derivative of $f(x)$, $3x^{\frac{1}{2}} + 5 = 9$. $c = \dfrac{16}{9}$.

23. **E** When $y = a^u$, $\dfrac{dy}{dx} = a^u (\ln a) \dfrac{du}{dx}$. For this problem, $u = 2x \cos^2 x$ and $\dfrac{du}{dx} = 2\cos^2 x - 4x \sin x \cos x$.

Then, $\dfrac{dy}{dx} = 7^{2x \cos^2 x} (\ln 7)(2\cos^2 x - 4x \sin x \cos x) = 49^{x \cos^2 x} (\ln 7)(2\cos^2 x - 4x \sin x \cos x)$.

24. **C** At $y = 7$, $x = 2$ or $x = -1$. (Remember, if the equation is not easy to solve, try easy values.) Further,

the derivative of the inverse of a function is found by $\dfrac{d}{dx} f^{-1}(x)\Big|_{x=c} = \dfrac{1}{\left[\dfrac{d}{dy} f(y)\right]_{y=a}}$. Then, take

the derivative of y, $\dfrac{dy}{dx} = 3x^2 - 3$. At $x = 2$, $\dfrac{dy}{dx} = 9$ and at $x = -1$, $\dfrac{dy}{dx} = 0$. Finally, the derivative

of the inverse is $\dfrac{1}{\dfrac{dy}{dx}}$, which for these values of x are $\dfrac{1}{9}$ and undefined. Since, undefined is not an

answer choice, the answer is A.

25. **E** Since the domain is limited, you don't have to work too hard to find x when $f(x) = \dfrac{1}{2}$. Test a

couple values or solve algebraically and you will find $x = \dfrac{\pi}{4}$. (Make sure you memorize the sines,

cosines, and tangents of $0, \dfrac{\pi}{6}, \dfrac{\pi}{4}, \dfrac{\pi}{3}, \dfrac{\pi}{2}$, and π. Know how to use the unit circle, too!) Further, the

derivative of the inverse of a function is found by $\dfrac{d}{dx} f^{-1}(x)\Big|_{x=c} = \dfrac{1}{\left[\dfrac{d}{dy} f(y)\right]_{y=a}}$. Then, take the

derivative of y, $f'(x) = -2\sin(6\pi - x)\cos(6\pi - x)$. At $x = \dfrac{\pi}{4}$, $\dfrac{dy}{dx} = 1$. Finally, the derivative of

the inverse is $\dfrac{1}{\dfrac{dy}{dx}}$, which equals 1.

26. **D** Use the Power and Addition rules to integrate:

$$\int\left(3x^3-2x^2+x-7\right)dx=3\left(\frac{1}{4}x^4\right)-2\left(\frac{1}{3}x^3\right)+\frac{1}{2}x^2-7x+C=\frac{3}{4}x^4-\frac{2}{3}x^3+\frac{x^2}{2}-7x+C.$$

27. **D** Since this function is very complicated, it will probably be easiest to differentiate using logarithmic differentiation, instead of the Quotient, Product, and Chain Rules. First, take the natural log of both sides: $\ln y=\ln\left(\sqrt{\frac{1+x}{3x-1}}\left(\frac{x+2}{x-1}\right)^2\right)$. Use logarithmic rules to simplify the equation: $\ln y=\frac{1}{2}\left[\ln(1+x)-\ln(3x-1)\right]+2\left[\ln(x+2)-\ln(x-1)\right]$. Now, differentiate both sides with respect to x: $\frac{1}{y}\frac{dy}{dx}=\frac{1}{2}\left(\frac{1}{x+1}-\frac{3}{3x-1}\right)+2\left(\frac{1}{x+2}-\frac{1}{x-1}\right)$. Finally, isolate $\frac{dy}{dx}$: $\frac{dy}{dx}=\frac{y}{2}\left(\frac{1}{x+1}-\frac{3}{3x-1}\right)+2y\left(\frac{1}{x+2}-\frac{1}{x-1}\right)$.

28. **B** When you insert $\frac{\pi}{2}$ for x, the limit is $\dfrac{3\pi/2}{0}$, which is indeterminate. Use L'Hôpital's Rule to evaluate the limit: $\lim\limits_{x\to\frac{\pi}{2}}\dfrac{3}{-2\sin x}$. This limit exists and equals $-\dfrac{3}{2}$.

29. **C** Recall, $\int e^u\,du=e^u+C$. In this problem, $u=4x^3+7$ and $du=12x^2dx$. Thus, $\frac{1}{12}\int e^u\,du=\frac{1}{12}e^u+C=\frac{1}{12}e^{4x^3+7}+C.$

30. **A** Use the method of partial fractions to solve this integral. First, split the fraction into parts in equation form $\dfrac{A}{2x-3}+\dfrac{B}{x+6}=\dfrac{x+7}{(2x-3)(x+6)}$. Then, solve for A and B; $A=\dfrac{17}{15}$ and $B=-\dfrac{1}{15}$.

Now, you can rewrite the fraction as the sum of two fractions and integrate those separately:

$$\int\frac{x+7}{(2x-3)(x+6)}dx=\frac{17}{15}\int\frac{dx}{2x-3}-\frac{1}{15}\int\frac{dx}{x+6}.$$ Use u-substitution to integrate both parts and simplify to get the final solution: $\int\dfrac{x+7}{(2x-3)(x+6)}dx=\dfrac{17}{30}\ln|2x-3|-\dfrac{1}{15}\ln|x+6|+C.$

31. **E** Take the derivative of both equations and set them equal to each other: $2x - a = 2x + c$, thus $-a = c$. Next, plug in the point, (2,1), into the equations for both curves and simplify. Therefore, $-3 = -2a + b$ and $1 = 4 + 2c$. When these equations are solved $c = -\dfrac{3}{2}$, $a = \dfrac{3}{2}$, and $b = 0$.

32. **C** Since the cars are going in two directions that are orthogonal to each other, the distances they travel and the distance between them form a right triangle, in which A is the distance car A travels, B is the distance car B travels, and D is the distance between them: $A^2 + B^2 = D^2$. Because this equation is relating distances, and we were given a point in time, the distances the two cars traveled at that point (2 hours) must be determined. Using the rate formula, distance = rate • time, the speed the cars are traveling multiplied by the time will give us their distances. Car A then traveled 120 km in 2 hours and Car B traveled 160 km. Use these values to determine D: 200 km. Next, differentiate the equation relating their distances with respect to time: $2A\dfrac{dA}{dt} + 2B\dfrac{dB}{dt} = 2D\dfrac{dD}{dt}$. Plug in the values for A, $\dfrac{dA}{dt}$, B, $\dfrac{dB}{dt}$, and D into the equation and solve for $\dfrac{dD}{dt}$: $\dfrac{dD}{dt} = 100\,\text{km/hr}$.

33. **D** Use a differential to approximate cos 91°, but be careful! First, you must convert from degrees to radians, so you will be approximating $\cos\dfrac{91\pi}{180}$ since $1° = \dfrac{\pi}{180}$. Then, recall the general formula is $f(x + \Delta x) \approx f(x) + f'(x)\Delta x$. For this problem, $f(x) = \cos\dfrac{\pi}{2} = 0$, $f'(x) = -\sin\dfrac{\pi}{2} = -1$, and $\Delta x = \dfrac{\pi}{180}$. When these values are input, the equation is $\cos\dfrac{91\pi}{180} \approx 0 - 1\left(\dfrac{\pi}{180}\right) \approx -\dfrac{\pi}{180}$.

34. **A** The ladder makes a right triangle with the wall and the ground, so the relationship between the three can be found using the Pythagorean theorem, in which we will call x the distance the bottom of the ladder is from the building across the ground and y the distance the top of the ladder is from the ground up the building, so $x^2 + y^2 = 30^2$. Since we want to find the rate that the top of the ladder is sliding, we need to differentiate this equation with respect to t: $2x\dfrac{dx}{dt} + 2y\dfrac{dy}{dt} = 0$. We already know $\dfrac{dy}{dt} = 3\,\text{ft/sec}$ and our y at the time of interest is 18 ft. In order to determine x at

that time, plug 18 into $x^2 + y^2 = 30^2$ and solve for x. Thus, $x = 24$ feet. Plug these values into the differentiated equation and solve for $\dfrac{dx}{dt}$: $2(24)\left(\dfrac{dx}{dt}\right) + 2(18)(3) = 0$, so $\dfrac{dy}{dt} = -\dfrac{9}{4}$ ft/sec.

35. **B** The formula for the area under a curve using left-endpoint rectangles is: $A = \left(\dfrac{b-a}{n}\right)(y_0 + y_1 + y_2 + y_3 + \ldots + y_n)$, where a and b are the x-values that bound the area and n is the number of rectangles. Since we are interested in the left-endpoints, the x-coordinates are $x_0 = 1, x_1 = \dfrac{5}{4}, x_2 = \dfrac{3}{2}$, and $x_3 = \dfrac{7}{4}$. The y-coordinates are found by plugging these values into the equation for y, so $y_0 = 3$, $y_1 = 3.5625$, $y_2 = 4.25$, and $y_3 = 5.0625$. Then, $A = \left(\dfrac{2-1}{4}\right)(3 + 3.5625 + 4.25 + 5.0625) = 3.96875$.

36. **E** Whether you use the MVTD or the MVTI, the requirement is that the function be continuous over the interval in question. $f(x)$ is not continuous over the interval $(-1, 1)$; therefore, there is no mean value.

37. **D** $\dfrac{dy}{dx} = 5x^4 - 4x; \dfrac{d^2y}{dx^2} = 20x - 4$. Plug in $x = 1$ to evaluate the second derivative, so $\dfrac{d^2y}{dx^2} = 16$.

38. **A** Recall, $\dfrac{dy}{dx} = a^u \ln a \left(\dfrac{du}{dx}\right)$. In this problem, $u = x^2$ and $du = 2x\,dx$. Thus, $\dfrac{dy}{dx} = 3^{x^2} \ln 3 (2x)$.

39. **B** $\displaystyle\int_{\ln 2}^{2} \dfrac{x^3 + x^2 - 2x}{x^2 + x - 2}\,dx = \int_{\ln 2}^{2} \dfrac{x(x^2 + x - 2)}{x^2 + x - 2}\,dx = \int_{\ln 2}^{2} x\,dx = \dfrac{x^2}{2}\Big|_{\ln 2}^{2} = 2 - \dfrac{(\ln 2)^2}{2}$

40. **A** Recall, the derivative of the inverse is given by $\dfrac{d}{dx}f^{-1}(x)\Big|_{x=c} = \dfrac{1}{\left[\dfrac{d}{dy}f(y)\right]_{y=a}}$. First, take the derivative of y, $\dfrac{dy}{dx} = 4x - 8$. Next, use the given y value, $y = 3$ and solve for their corresponding x values, so $x = 1$ or $x = 3$. Now, following the formula above, solve for the derivative of the inverse using the x values: $\dfrac{1}{4(1) - 8} = -\dfrac{1}{4}$ and $\dfrac{1}{4(3) - 8} = \dfrac{1}{4}$. Thus, the answer is A.

41.　**A**　The area of the photo, mat, and frame is found by the equation $A = (x+12)(y+6)$, where x is the width (side-side) of the photo and y the length (top-bottom). If the equation is expanded out, the area is $A = xy + 6x + 12y + 72$, where $xy = 144$ and $y = 144/x$. The final equation, in one variable, is $A = 6x + \dfrac{1728}{x} + 216$. In order to minimize the area, we take the derivative, set it equal to zero and solve for x: $\dfrac{dA}{dx} = 6 - \dfrac{1728}{x^2} = 0$, and $x = 12\sqrt{2}$. To confirm that will minimize the area, take the second derivative of A and confirm that it is greater than zero at $x = 12\sqrt{2}$: $\dfrac{d^2A}{dx^2} = \dfrac{3456}{x^3} > 0$, so $x = 12\sqrt{2}$ will minimize the area of the frame. Use x to solve for y: $y = \dfrac{144}{12\sqrt{2}} = 6\sqrt{2}$. Recall, x and y are the dimensions of the photo, so the dimensions of the frame will be these values plus the mat, so the dimensions of the frame are $\left(12\sqrt{2} + 12\right)$ in $\times \left(6\sqrt{2} + 6\right)$ in.

42.　**C**　$L = \displaystyle\int_a^b \sqrt{1 + \left(\dfrac{dy}{dx}\right)^2}\, dx$. For this question, $\dfrac{dy}{dx} = x^{\frac{1}{2}}$ from $a = 1$ to $b = 6$. Then, using u-substitution, evaluate: $L = \displaystyle\int_1^6 \sqrt{1 + \left(x^{\frac{1}{2}}\right)^2}\, dx = \dfrac{14}{3}\sqrt{7} - \dfrac{4}{3}\sqrt{2}$

43.　**D**　$L = \displaystyle\int_a^b \sqrt{\left(\dfrac{dx}{dt}\right)^2 + \left(\dfrac{dy}{dt}\right)^2}\, dt$. For this question, $\dfrac{dx}{dt} = t$ and $\dfrac{dy}{dt} = 4\sqrt{t+4}$ from $a = 0$ to $b = 8$. Then, using u-substitution, evaluate: $L = \displaystyle\int_0^8 \sqrt{t^2 + \left(4(t+4)^{\frac{1}{2}}\right)^2}\, dt = \displaystyle\int_0^8 \sqrt{(t+8)^2}\, dt = 96$.

44.　**C**　Remember, for Euler's Method, $x_n = x_{n-1} + h$ and $y_n = y_{n-1} + h\left(y_{n-1}'\right)$. In this case,

$x_0 = 0,\ y_0 = 2,\ y_0' = 5;\ x_1 = 0.2,\ y_1 = 3,\ y_1' = 4;\ x_2 = 0.4,\ y_2 = 3.8,\ y_2' = 6.72;\ x_3 = 0.6,$

$y_3 = 5.144,\ y_3' = 12.730;\ x_4 = 0.8,\ y_4 = 7.69,\ y_4' = 29.069;\ x_5 = 1.0,\ y_5 = 13.504$

45.　**A**　A is a geometric series with $r < 1$, so it converges. B is a harmonic series, so it diverges (verify this with the integral test). C diverges by the comparison test (compare it to the harmonic series). D diverges by the ratio test. Finally, E is a geometric series and diverges because $r > 1$.

Section II

1.

x	2	2.2	2.4	2.6	2.8	3
$\dfrac{dy}{dx}$	6	5	4	2.5	1	0.5

The equation for y is thrice differentiable for $x > 0$ with $y = 3$ at $x = 2$, the second derivative is equal to 2 at $x = 2$, and the third derivative is 4 at $x = 2$. Values of the first derivative are given for select values of x above.

(a)   Write an equation for the tangent line of y at $x = 3$. Use this line to approximate y at $x = 3$.

(a)   Since the first derivative of y at $x = 2$ is 6 and y at $x = 2$ is 3, we can write the equation of the tangent line: $y - 3 = 6(x - 2)$. When you insert 3 for x into this equation, $y = 9$.

(b)   Use a right endpoint Riemann sum with five subintervals of equal length and values from the table to approximate $\int_2^3 \dfrac{dy}{dx}\,dx$. Use this approximation to estimate y at $x = 3$. Show your work.

(b)   The right endpoint Riemann sum will look like this:

$\int_2^3 \dfrac{dy}{dx}\,dx = (0.2)(5) + (0.2)(4) + (0.2)(4) + (0.2)(2.5) + (0.2)(1) + (0.2)(0.5) = 2.6$. To approximate y at $x = 3$, add this value to y at $x = 2$: $y\big|_{x=3} = y\big|_{x=2} + \int_2^3 \dfrac{dy}{dx}\,dx$. So, y at $x = 3$ is 5.6.

(c)   Use Euler's Method, starting at $x = 2$ with five steps of equal size to approximate y at $x = 3$. Show your work.

(c)   Following Euler's Method:

$x_0 = 2$, $y_0 = 3$, $y_0' = 6$; $x_1 = 2.2$, $y_1 = 4.2$, $y_1' = 5$; $x_2 = 2.4$, $y_2 = 5.2$, $y_2' = 4$; $x_3 = 2.6$,

$y_3 = 6$, $y_3' = 2.5$; $x_4 = 2.8$, $y_4 = 6.5$, $y_4' = 1$; $x_5 = 3$, $y_5 = 6.7$

Thus, by Euler's Method, $y = 6.7$ at $x = 3$.

(d) Write a third degree Taylor polynomial for y about $x = 2$. Use it to approximate y at $x = 3$.

(d) A Taylor polynomial has the general form:

$$\sum_{k=0}^{\infty} \frac{f^{(k)}(a)}{k!}(x-a)^k = f(a) + f'(a)(k-a) + \frac{f''(a)}{2!}(x-a)^2 + \ldots + \frac{f^{(n)}(a)}{n!}(x-a)^k + \ldots. \quad \text{Given}$$

the derivative and initial conditions in the problem, the third degree Taylor polynomial for y would

be: $T_3(x) = 3 + 6(x-2) + \frac{2}{2!}(x-2)^2 + \frac{4}{3!}(x-2)^3$. At $x = 3$, y would then equal 10.667.

2.   Let R be the region bound by $y_1 = 2x^3 - 4x^2 - 8$ and $y_2 = 2x^2 + 8x - 8$.

(a) Find the area of R.

(a) First, set the two equations equal to each other to determine the bounds of R. The two curves intersect at $x = -1$, $x = 0$ and $x = 4$. Notice, that the "top" curve switches at $x = 0$, so be sure to write two separate integrals and add them together to determine the area:

$$\int_{-1}^{0} (2x^3 - 4x^2 - 8 - 2x^2 - 8x + 8)dx + \int_{0}^{4} (2x^2 + 8x - 8 - 2x^3 + 4x^2 + 8)dx = 62.5.$$

(b) Find the volume of the solid generated when R is revolved about the x-axis for $0 \le x \le 4$.

(b) Since the two curves and the axis of rotation are in the same form "$y =$", the washer method is the best way to solve for the volume of the solid: $\pi \int_{0}^{4} \left((2x^2 + 8x - 8)^2 - (2x^3 - 4x^2 - 8)^2 \right) dx = 1492.11$.

(c) Find the volume of the solid generated when R is revolved about the line $x = 2$ when $-1 \le x \le 0$.

(c) Now, because the two curves and the axis of rotation are in different forms "$y =$" and "$x =$", cylindrical shells is the best way to solve for the volume. Notice the axis of rotation is not at $x = 2$, so the "radius" of the cylinder must be adjusted. Remember that when adjusting for the axis of rotation, always subtract the less positive from the more positive. In the original equation x is the radius of the cylinder and represents $x = 0$. $x = 2$ is more positive, so the new radius is $2 - x$. The formula is $2\pi \int_{-1}^{0} (2-x)(2x^3 - 4x^2 - 8 - 2x^2 - 8x + 8)\, dx = \dfrac{113\pi}{15}$.

3. Consider the graph of the polar curve $r = 1 + 2\sin\theta$ for $0 \le \theta \le 2\pi$. Let S be the region bound between the inner and outer loops.

(a) Write an integral expression for the area of S.

(a) First determine the limits of the two loops. The inner loop spans $0 \le \theta \le \pi$ and the outer loop spans $\pi \le \theta \le 2\pi$. The area under a single polar curve is found from the equation $A = \int_{a}^{b} \dfrac{1}{2} r^2 \, d\theta$. To determine the area of S, you must take the area under the outer loop and subtract the area under the inner loop. $S = \dfrac{1}{2}\left(\int_{0}^{\pi} (1 + 2\sin\theta)^2 \, d\theta - \int_{\pi}^{2\pi} (1 + 2\sin\theta)^2 \, d\theta \right)$.

(b) Write expressions for $\dfrac{dx}{d\theta}$ and $\dfrac{dy}{d\theta}$ in terms of θ.

(b) You will need to convert between polar and Cartesian coordinates using the equations $x = r\cos\theta$ and $y = r\sin\theta$. Also, the derivative in polar coordinates of the curve is $\dfrac{dr}{d\theta} = 2\cos\theta$. Use the product rule to integrate the equations for x and y in terms of θ: $\dfrac{dx}{d\theta} = \dfrac{dr}{d\theta}\cos\theta - r\sin\theta$ and $\dfrac{dy}{d\theta} = \dfrac{dr}{d\theta}\sin\theta + r\cos\theta$. Plug in the value of $\dfrac{dr}{d\theta}$ into both equations to get $\dfrac{dx}{d\theta} = 2\cos^2\theta - \sin\theta - 2\sin^2\theta$ and $\dfrac{dy}{d\theta} = \cos\theta(1 + 4\sin\theta)$.

(c) Write an equation in terms of x and y for the line normal to the graph of the polar curve at the point where $\theta = \dfrac{3\pi}{2}$. Show your work.

(c) At $\theta = \dfrac{3\pi}{2}$, $x = 0$ and $y = 1$. The slope of the tangent $\dfrac{dy}{dx} = \dfrac{\frac{dy}{d\theta}}{\frac{dx}{d\theta}} = \dfrac{\cos\theta(1 + 4\sin\theta)}{2 - \sin\theta}$. At $\theta = \dfrac{3\pi}{2}$, $\dfrac{dy}{dx} = 0$. Thus, the slope of the normal line is undefined, so the normal is parallel to the y-axis and the equation is $y = 1$.

4.   For $t \geq 0$, a particle is moving along a curve so that its position at time t is $(x(t), y(t))$. At time $t = 3$, the particle is at position $(3,1)$. It is known that $\frac{dx}{dt} = e^{-2t}(t+1)^2$ and $\frac{dy}{dt} = \cos^2 t$.

(a) Is the horizontal movement to the left or to the right at time $t = 3$? Find the slope of the particle's path at $t = 3$.

(a) If $\frac{dx}{dt} < 0$, the particle is moving to the left. If $\frac{dx}{dt} > 0$, the particle is moving to the right. At

$t = 3$, $\frac{dx}{dt} = e^{(-2)(3)}(1+3)^2 = \frac{16}{e^6}$, so $\frac{dx}{dt} > 0$. The particle is moving to the right.

The slope of the particle's path is $\frac{dy}{dx} = \dfrac{\frac{dy}{dt}}{\frac{dx}{dt}}$. So, at $t = 3$, $\frac{dy}{dx} = \dfrac{\cos^2 3}{e^{(-2)(3)}(1+3)^2} \approx 43.9327$.

(b) Find the y-coordinate of the particle's position at time $t = 6$.

(b) We know the y-coordinate at $t = 3$ is 1, so to find the y-coordinate at $t = 6$, we must integrate from $t = 3$ to $t = 6$ and add that to the y-coordinate at $t = 3$: $y(6) = 1 + \int_3^6 \cos^2 t \, dt \approx 2.43571$.

(c) Find the speed and acceleration of the particle at $t = 6$.

(c) $\frac{dx}{dt}$ and $\frac{dy}{dt}$ represent the components of the velocity vector with respect to time. To determine the speed, we need to find the magnitude of the velocity vector: $s = \sqrt{(x'(t))^2 + +(y'(t))^2}$. At $t = 6$, the speed would be: $s = \sqrt{\left(3^{(-2)(6)}(1+6)^2\right)^2 + \left(\cos^2 6\right)^2} \approx 0.967822$.

The acceleration, however, is the first derivative of the velocity vector, so it will be a vector, too: $(x''(t), y''(t))$. For this problem, the acceleration vector is: $\left(-2t(t+1)e^{-2t}, -2t\sin t \cos t\right)$. At $t = 6$, the acceleration vector is $\left(-2(6)(6+1)e^{-2(6)}, -2(6)\sin 6 \cos 6\right)$, so $\left(-5.16 \times 10^{-4}, 0.536573\right)$.

(d) Find the distance traveled by the particle from time $t = 3$ to $t = 6$.

(d) The distance traveled will be the length of the curve the particle travels, so the distance is found by evaluating: $D = \int_a^b \sqrt{\left(\frac{dx}{dt}\right)^2 + \left(\frac{dy}{dt}\right)^2}\, dt$. For this problem, the integral will be set up like this: $D = \int_3^6 \sqrt{\left(e^{-2t}(t+1)^2\right)^2 + \left(\cos^2 t\right)^2}\, dt$. Use your calculator to evaluate this integral and the distance is 1.43634.

5. A particle's position in the *xy*-plane at any time t is given by $x = 3t^3 - 4$ and $y = 2t^5 - 3t^3$. Find:

(a) The x and y components of the particle's velocity.

(a) The velocity is just the first derivative of the position functions, so the x and y components are:

$$\frac{dx}{dt} = 9t^2 \text{ and } \frac{dy}{dt} = 10t^4 - 9t^2 \text{ or } \left(9t^2, 10t^4 - 9t^2\right).$$

(b) $\frac{dy}{dx}$ at $t = 3$.

(b) $\frac{dy}{dx} = \frac{\frac{dy}{dt}}{\frac{dx}{dt}} = \frac{10t^4 - 9t^2}{9t^2} = \frac{10}{9}t^2 - 1$. At $t = 3$, $\frac{dy}{dx} = \frac{10}{9}(3)^2 - 1 = 9$.

(c) The acceleration of the particle at $t = 3$.

(c) The acceleration is the second derivative of the position function or the first derivative of the velocity function. $\frac{d^2 x}{dt^2} = 18t$ and $\frac{d^2 y}{dt^2} = 40t^3 - 18t$. Since we are asked for the acceleration of the particle, not the components, we must find $\frac{d^2 y}{dx^2} = \frac{\frac{d^2 y}{dt^2}}{\frac{d^2 x}{dt^2}} = \frac{40t^3 - 18t}{18t} = \frac{20}{9}t^2 - 1$. At $t = 3$, the acceleration is then $\frac{d^2 y}{dx^2} = \frac{20}{9}3^2 - 1 = 19$.

(d)   The time(s) when the particle is changing direction.

(d)   The particle will change direction when the velocity is zero, but the acceleration is not. Therefore, set the velocity function equal to zero and solve for t, and see if the acceleration is zero or not
at that time. $\dfrac{dy}{dx} = \dfrac{10}{9}t^2 - 1 = 0$ when $t = \pm\dfrac{3\sqrt{10}}{10}$. Since we are only dealing with positive values
of time, ignore the negative solution when checking the acceleration. $\dfrac{d^2y}{dx^2} = \dfrac{20}{9}\left(\dfrac{3\sqrt{10}}{10}\right)^2 - 1 = 1$.
Since the velocity is zero and the acceleration is 1 at time $t = \dfrac{3\sqrt{10}}{10}$, the particle is chaning direction at that time.

6.   Let $y_1' = \dfrac{3x^2}{y_1^2}$ and $y_2' = 2x^3y_2 - xy_2$.

(a)   If $x = 0$ and $y = 6$, find y_1.

(a)   To find y_1, separate the variables in the derivative and plug in the given point to solve for the
equation.

$\dfrac{dy_1}{dx} = \dfrac{3x^2}{y_1^2}$ becomes $y_1^2 dy = 3x^2 dx$, so $y_1^3 = 3x^3 + C$

With the initial condition, $y_1^3 = 3x^3 + 216$.

(b)   If $x = -2$ and $y = e^2$, find y_2.

(b)   Repeat the same process in part (a) for the second equation and the new initial condition. The
final solution will be $\ln|y_2| = \dfrac{x^4}{2} - \dfrac{x^2}{2} - 4$.

(c)   Use Euler's method to approximate y_1 when $x = 3$. Start at $x = 0$ using three steps. Check your answer against the real value of y_1 at $x = 3$. Is this a reasonable approximation?

(c)   Using Euler's method, $y_n = y_{n-1} + h\left(y'_{n-1}\right)$. At $x = 0$, $y_1 = 6$, $y'_1 = 0$; at $x = 1$, $y_1 = 6$, $y'_1 = \dfrac{1}{12}$; at $x = 2$, $y_1 = \dfrac{73}{12}$, $y'_1 = \dfrac{1728}{5329}$; and at $x = 3$, $y_1 = 6.4076$.

The actual value for $y_1(3) = 6.67194$. The difference is 3.96%, so this is a reasonable approximation.

Completely darken bubbles with a No. 2 pencil. If you make a mistake, be sure to erase mark completely. Erase all stray marks.

1.

YOUR NAME: _____
(Print)
       Last   First   M.I.

SIGNATURE: _____   DATE: ___ / ___ / ___

HOME ADDRESS: _____
(Print)
       Number and Street

    City   State   Zip Code

PHONE NO.: _____

IMPORTANT: Please fill in these boxes exactly as shown on the back cover of your test book.

2. TEST FORM

3. TEST CODE

4. REGISTRATION NUMBER

5. YOUR NAME

First 4 letters of last name | FIRST INIT | MID INIT

6. DATE OF BIRTH

Month	Day	Year
JAN		
FEB	0 0	0 0
MAR	1 1	1 1
APR	2 2	2 2
MAY	3 3	3 3
JUN	4 4	4
JUL	5 5	5
AUG	6 6	6
SEP	7 7	7
OCT	8 8	8
NOV	9 9	9
DEC		

7. GENDER
- MALE
- FEMALE

The Princeton Review®

1. Ⓐ Ⓑ Ⓒ Ⓓ Ⓔ
2. Ⓐ Ⓑ Ⓒ Ⓓ Ⓔ
3. Ⓐ Ⓑ Ⓒ Ⓓ Ⓔ
4. Ⓐ Ⓑ Ⓒ Ⓓ Ⓔ
5. Ⓐ Ⓑ Ⓒ Ⓓ Ⓔ
6. Ⓐ Ⓑ Ⓒ Ⓓ Ⓔ
7. Ⓐ Ⓑ Ⓒ Ⓓ Ⓔ
8. Ⓐ Ⓑ Ⓒ Ⓓ Ⓔ
9. Ⓐ Ⓑ Ⓒ Ⓓ Ⓔ
10. Ⓐ Ⓑ Ⓒ Ⓓ Ⓔ
11. Ⓐ Ⓑ Ⓒ Ⓓ Ⓔ
12. Ⓐ Ⓑ Ⓒ Ⓓ Ⓔ
13. Ⓐ Ⓑ Ⓒ Ⓓ Ⓔ
14. Ⓐ Ⓑ Ⓒ Ⓓ Ⓔ
15. Ⓐ Ⓑ Ⓒ Ⓓ Ⓔ
16. Ⓐ Ⓑ Ⓒ Ⓓ Ⓔ
17. Ⓐ Ⓑ Ⓒ Ⓓ Ⓔ
18. Ⓐ Ⓑ Ⓒ Ⓓ Ⓔ
19. Ⓐ Ⓑ Ⓒ Ⓓ Ⓔ
20. Ⓐ Ⓑ Ⓒ Ⓓ Ⓔ
21. Ⓐ Ⓑ Ⓒ Ⓓ Ⓔ
22. Ⓐ Ⓑ Ⓒ Ⓓ Ⓔ
23. Ⓐ Ⓑ Ⓒ Ⓓ Ⓔ

24. Ⓐ Ⓑ Ⓒ Ⓓ Ⓔ
25. Ⓐ Ⓑ Ⓒ Ⓓ Ⓔ
26. Ⓐ Ⓑ Ⓒ Ⓓ Ⓔ
27. Ⓐ Ⓑ Ⓒ Ⓓ Ⓔ
28. Ⓐ Ⓑ Ⓒ Ⓓ Ⓔ
29. Ⓐ Ⓑ Ⓒ Ⓓ Ⓔ
30. Ⓐ Ⓑ Ⓒ Ⓓ Ⓔ
31. Ⓐ Ⓑ Ⓒ Ⓓ Ⓔ
32. Ⓐ Ⓑ Ⓒ Ⓓ Ⓔ
33. Ⓐ Ⓑ Ⓒ Ⓓ Ⓔ
34. Ⓐ Ⓑ Ⓒ Ⓓ Ⓔ
35. Ⓐ Ⓑ Ⓒ Ⓓ Ⓔ
36. Ⓐ Ⓑ Ⓒ Ⓓ Ⓔ
37. Ⓐ Ⓑ Ⓒ Ⓓ Ⓔ
38. Ⓐ Ⓑ Ⓒ Ⓓ Ⓔ
39. Ⓐ Ⓑ Ⓒ Ⓓ Ⓔ
40. Ⓐ Ⓑ Ⓒ Ⓓ Ⓔ
41. Ⓐ Ⓑ Ⓒ Ⓓ Ⓔ
42. Ⓐ Ⓑ Ⓒ Ⓓ Ⓔ
43. Ⓐ Ⓑ Ⓒ Ⓓ Ⓔ
44. Ⓐ Ⓑ Ⓒ Ⓓ Ⓔ
45. Ⓐ Ⓑ Ⓒ Ⓓ Ⓔ

Completely darken bubbles with a No. 2 pencil. If you make a mistake, be sure to erase mark completely. Erase all stray marks.

1.

YOUR NAME: _____
(Print)   Last   First   M.I.

SIGNATURE: _____ DATE: ___ / ___ / ___

HOME ADDRESS: _____
(Print)   Number and Street

_____
        City   State   Zip Code

PHONE NO.: _____

IMPORTANT: Please fill in these boxes exactly as shown on the back cover of your test book.

2. TEST FORM

_____

3. TEST CODE

⓪	Ⓐ	Ⓙ	⓪	⓪
①	Ⓑ	Ⓚ	①	①
②	Ⓒ	Ⓛ	②	②
③	Ⓓ	Ⓜ	③	③
④	Ⓔ	Ⓝ	④	④
⑤	Ⓕ	Ⓞ	⑤	⑤
⑥	Ⓖ	Ⓟ	⑥	⑥
⑦	Ⓗ	Ⓠ	⑦	⑦
⑧	Ⓘ	Ⓡ	⑧	⑧
⑨			⑨	⑨

4. REGISTRATION NUMBER

⓪	⓪	⓪	⓪	⓪	⓪	⓪
①	①	①	①	①	①	①
②	②	②	②	②	②	②
③	③	③	③	③	③	③
④	④	④	④	④	④	④
⑤	⑤	⑤	⑤	⑤	⑤	⑤
⑥	⑥	⑥	⑥	⑥	⑥	⑥
⑦	⑦	⑦	⑦	⑦	⑦	⑦
⑧	⑧	⑧	⑧	⑧	⑧	⑧
⑨	⑨	⑨	⑨	⑨	⑨	⑨

6. DATE OF BIRTH

Month		Day		Year	
◯ JAN					
◯ FEB	⓪	⓪		⓪	⓪
◯ MAR	①	①		①	①
◯ APR	②	②		②	②
◯ MAY	③	③		③	③
◯ JUN		④		④	④
◯ JUL		⑤		⑤	⑤
◯ AUG		⑥		⑥	⑥
◯ SEP		⑦		⑦	⑦
◯ OCT		⑧		⑧	⑧
◯ NOV		⑨		⑨	⑨
◯ DEC					

7. GENDER
◯ MALE
◯ FEMALE

5. YOUR NAME

First 4 letters of last name				FIRST INIT	MID INIT
Ⓐ	Ⓐ	Ⓐ	Ⓐ	Ⓐ	Ⓐ
Ⓑ	Ⓑ	Ⓑ	Ⓑ	Ⓑ	Ⓑ
Ⓒ	Ⓒ	Ⓒ	Ⓒ	Ⓒ	Ⓒ
Ⓓ	Ⓓ	Ⓓ	Ⓓ	Ⓓ	Ⓓ
Ⓔ	Ⓔ	Ⓔ	Ⓔ	Ⓔ	Ⓔ
Ⓕ	Ⓕ	Ⓕ	Ⓕ	Ⓕ	Ⓕ
Ⓖ	Ⓖ	Ⓖ	Ⓖ	Ⓖ	Ⓖ
Ⓗ	Ⓗ	Ⓗ	Ⓗ	Ⓗ	Ⓗ
Ⓘ	Ⓘ	Ⓘ	Ⓘ	Ⓘ	Ⓘ
Ⓙ	Ⓙ	Ⓙ	Ⓙ	Ⓙ	Ⓙ
Ⓚ	Ⓚ	Ⓚ	Ⓚ	Ⓚ	Ⓚ
Ⓛ	Ⓛ	Ⓛ	Ⓛ	Ⓛ	Ⓛ
Ⓜ	Ⓜ	Ⓜ	Ⓜ	Ⓜ	Ⓜ
Ⓝ	Ⓝ	Ⓝ	Ⓝ	Ⓝ	Ⓝ
Ⓞ	Ⓞ	Ⓞ	Ⓞ	Ⓞ	Ⓞ
Ⓟ	Ⓟ	Ⓟ	Ⓟ	Ⓟ	Ⓟ
Ⓠ	Ⓠ	Ⓠ	Ⓠ	Ⓠ	Ⓠ
Ⓡ	Ⓡ	Ⓡ	Ⓡ	Ⓡ	Ⓡ
Ⓢ	Ⓢ	Ⓢ	Ⓢ	Ⓢ	Ⓢ
Ⓣ	Ⓣ	Ⓣ	Ⓣ	Ⓣ	Ⓣ
Ⓤ	Ⓤ	Ⓤ	Ⓤ	Ⓤ	Ⓤ
Ⓥ	Ⓥ	Ⓥ	Ⓥ	Ⓥ	Ⓥ
Ⓦ	Ⓦ	Ⓦ	Ⓦ	Ⓦ	Ⓦ
Ⓧ	Ⓧ	Ⓧ	Ⓧ	Ⓧ	Ⓧ
Ⓨ	Ⓨ	Ⓨ	Ⓨ	Ⓨ	Ⓨ
Ⓩ	Ⓩ	Ⓩ	Ⓩ	Ⓩ	Ⓩ

1. Ⓐ Ⓑ Ⓒ Ⓓ Ⓔ
2. Ⓐ Ⓑ Ⓒ Ⓓ Ⓔ
3. Ⓐ Ⓑ Ⓒ Ⓓ Ⓔ
4. Ⓐ Ⓑ Ⓒ Ⓓ Ⓔ
5. Ⓐ Ⓑ Ⓒ Ⓓ Ⓔ
6. Ⓐ Ⓑ Ⓒ Ⓓ Ⓔ
7. Ⓐ Ⓑ Ⓒ Ⓓ Ⓔ
8. Ⓐ Ⓑ Ⓒ Ⓓ Ⓔ
9. Ⓐ Ⓑ Ⓒ Ⓓ Ⓔ
10. Ⓐ Ⓑ Ⓒ Ⓓ Ⓔ
11. Ⓐ Ⓑ Ⓒ Ⓓ Ⓔ
12. Ⓐ Ⓑ Ⓒ Ⓓ Ⓔ
13. Ⓐ Ⓑ Ⓒ Ⓓ Ⓔ
14. Ⓐ Ⓑ Ⓒ Ⓓ Ⓔ
15. Ⓐ Ⓑ Ⓒ Ⓓ Ⓔ
16. Ⓐ Ⓑ Ⓒ Ⓓ Ⓔ
17. Ⓐ Ⓑ Ⓒ Ⓓ Ⓔ
18. Ⓐ Ⓑ Ⓒ Ⓓ Ⓔ
19. Ⓐ Ⓑ Ⓒ Ⓓ Ⓔ
20. Ⓐ Ⓑ Ⓒ Ⓓ Ⓔ
21. Ⓐ Ⓑ Ⓒ Ⓓ Ⓔ
22. Ⓐ Ⓑ Ⓒ Ⓓ Ⓔ
23. Ⓐ Ⓑ Ⓒ Ⓓ Ⓔ

24. Ⓐ Ⓑ Ⓒ Ⓓ Ⓔ
25. Ⓐ Ⓑ Ⓒ Ⓓ Ⓔ
26. Ⓐ Ⓑ Ⓒ Ⓓ Ⓔ
27. Ⓐ Ⓑ Ⓒ Ⓓ Ⓔ
28. Ⓐ Ⓑ Ⓒ Ⓓ Ⓔ
29. Ⓐ Ⓑ Ⓒ Ⓓ Ⓔ
30. Ⓐ Ⓑ Ⓒ Ⓓ Ⓔ
31. Ⓐ Ⓑ Ⓒ Ⓓ Ⓔ
32. Ⓐ Ⓑ Ⓒ Ⓓ Ⓔ
33. Ⓐ Ⓑ Ⓒ Ⓓ Ⓔ
34. Ⓐ Ⓑ Ⓒ Ⓓ Ⓔ
35. Ⓐ Ⓑ Ⓒ Ⓓ Ⓔ
36. Ⓐ Ⓑ Ⓒ Ⓓ Ⓔ
37. Ⓐ Ⓑ Ⓒ Ⓓ Ⓔ
38. Ⓐ Ⓑ Ⓒ Ⓓ Ⓔ
39. Ⓐ Ⓑ Ⓒ Ⓓ Ⓔ
40. Ⓐ Ⓑ Ⓒ Ⓓ Ⓔ
41. Ⓐ Ⓑ Ⓒ Ⓓ Ⓔ
42. Ⓐ Ⓑ Ⓒ Ⓓ Ⓔ
43. Ⓐ Ⓑ Ⓒ Ⓓ Ⓔ
44. Ⓐ Ⓑ Ⓒ Ⓓ Ⓔ
45. Ⓐ Ⓑ Ⓒ Ⓓ Ⓔ

Completely darken bubbles with a No. 2 pencil. If you make a mistake, be sure to erase mark completely. Erase all stray marks.

1.

YOUR NAME: _____
(Print)
　　　　　Last　　　　　　　First　　　　　　M.I.

SIGNATURE: _____　　　DATE: __/__/__

HOME ADDRESS: _____
(Print)
　　　　　Number and Street

_____
　　City　　　　　State　　　　Zip Code

PHONE NO.: _____

IMPORTANT: Please fill in these boxes exactly as shown on the back cover of your test book.

2. TEST FORM

_____

3. TEST CODE

⓪	Ⓐ	Ⓙ	⓪	⓪	
①	Ⓑ	Ⓚ	①	①	
②	Ⓒ	Ⓛ	②	②	
③	Ⓓ	Ⓜ	③	③	
④	Ⓔ	Ⓝ	④	④	
⑤	Ⓕ	Ⓞ	⑤	⑤	
⑥	Ⓖ	Ⓟ	⑥	⑥	
⑦	Ⓗ	Ⓠ	⑦	⑦	
⑧	Ⓘ	Ⓡ	⑧	⑧	
⑨			⑨	⑨	

4. REGISTRATION NUMBER

⓪	⓪	⓪	⓪	⓪	⓪	⓪
①	①	①	①	①	①	①
②	②	②	②	②	②	②
③	③	③	③	③	③	③
④	④	④	④	④	④	④
⑤	⑤	⑤	⑤	⑤	⑤	⑤
⑥	⑥	⑥	⑥	⑥	⑥	⑥
⑦	⑦	⑦	⑦	⑦	⑦	⑦
⑧	⑧	⑧	⑧	⑧	⑧	⑧
⑨	⑨	⑨	⑨	⑨	⑨	⑨

5. YOUR NAME

First 4 letters of last name				FIRST INIT	MID INIT
Ⓐ	Ⓐ	Ⓐ	Ⓐ	Ⓐ	Ⓐ
Ⓑ	Ⓑ	Ⓑ	Ⓑ	Ⓑ	Ⓑ
Ⓒ	Ⓒ	Ⓒ	Ⓒ	Ⓒ	Ⓒ
Ⓓ	Ⓓ	Ⓓ	Ⓓ	Ⓓ	Ⓓ
Ⓔ	Ⓔ	Ⓔ	Ⓔ	Ⓔ	Ⓔ
Ⓕ	Ⓕ	Ⓕ	Ⓕ	Ⓕ	Ⓕ
Ⓖ	Ⓖ	Ⓖ	Ⓖ	Ⓖ	Ⓖ
Ⓗ	Ⓗ	Ⓗ	Ⓗ	Ⓗ	Ⓗ
Ⓘ	Ⓘ	Ⓘ	Ⓘ	Ⓘ	Ⓘ
Ⓙ	Ⓙ	Ⓙ	Ⓙ	Ⓙ	Ⓙ
Ⓚ	Ⓚ	Ⓚ	Ⓚ	Ⓚ	Ⓚ
Ⓛ	Ⓛ	Ⓛ	Ⓛ	Ⓛ	Ⓛ
Ⓜ	Ⓜ	Ⓜ	Ⓜ	Ⓜ	Ⓜ
Ⓝ	Ⓝ	Ⓝ	Ⓝ	Ⓝ	Ⓝ
Ⓞ	Ⓞ	Ⓞ	Ⓞ	Ⓞ	Ⓞ
Ⓟ	Ⓟ	Ⓟ	Ⓟ	Ⓟ	Ⓟ
Ⓠ	Ⓠ	Ⓠ	Ⓠ	Ⓠ	Ⓠ
Ⓡ	Ⓡ	Ⓡ	Ⓡ	Ⓡ	Ⓡ
Ⓢ	Ⓢ	Ⓢ	Ⓢ	Ⓢ	Ⓢ
Ⓣ	Ⓣ	Ⓣ	Ⓣ	Ⓣ	Ⓣ
Ⓤ	Ⓤ	Ⓤ	Ⓤ	Ⓤ	Ⓤ
Ⓥ	Ⓥ	Ⓥ	Ⓥ	Ⓥ	Ⓥ
Ⓦ	Ⓦ	Ⓦ	Ⓦ	Ⓦ	Ⓦ
Ⓧ	Ⓧ	Ⓧ	Ⓧ	Ⓧ	Ⓧ
Ⓨ	Ⓨ	Ⓨ	Ⓨ	Ⓨ	Ⓨ
Ⓩ	Ⓩ	Ⓩ	Ⓩ	Ⓩ	Ⓩ

6. DATE OF BIRTH

Month		Day		Year	
◯ JAN					
◯ FEB	⓪	⓪	⓪	⓪	
◯ MAR	①	①	①	①	
◯ APR	②	②	②	②	
◯ MAY	③	③	③	③	
◯ JUN		④	④	④	
◯ JUL		⑤	⑤	⑤	
◯ AUG		⑥	⑥	⑥	
◯ SEP		⑦	⑦	⑦	
◯ OCT		⑧	⑧	⑧	
◯ NOV		⑨	⑨	⑨	
◯ DEC					

7. GENDER

◯ MALE
◯ FEMALE

The Princeton Review

1. Ⓐ Ⓑ Ⓒ Ⓓ Ⓔ
2. Ⓐ Ⓑ Ⓒ Ⓓ Ⓔ
3. Ⓐ Ⓑ Ⓒ Ⓓ Ⓔ
4. Ⓐ Ⓑ Ⓒ Ⓓ Ⓔ
5. Ⓐ Ⓑ Ⓒ Ⓓ Ⓔ
6. Ⓐ Ⓑ Ⓒ Ⓓ Ⓔ
7. Ⓐ Ⓑ Ⓒ Ⓓ Ⓔ
8. Ⓐ Ⓑ Ⓒ Ⓓ Ⓔ
9. Ⓐ Ⓑ Ⓒ Ⓓ Ⓔ
10. Ⓐ Ⓑ Ⓒ Ⓓ Ⓔ
11. Ⓐ Ⓑ Ⓒ Ⓓ Ⓔ
12. Ⓐ Ⓑ Ⓒ Ⓓ Ⓔ
13. Ⓐ Ⓑ Ⓒ Ⓓ Ⓔ
14. Ⓐ Ⓑ Ⓒ Ⓓ Ⓔ
15. Ⓐ Ⓑ Ⓒ Ⓓ Ⓔ
16. Ⓐ Ⓑ Ⓒ Ⓓ Ⓔ
17. Ⓐ Ⓑ Ⓒ Ⓓ Ⓔ
18. Ⓐ Ⓑ Ⓒ Ⓓ Ⓔ
19. Ⓐ Ⓑ Ⓒ Ⓓ Ⓔ
20. Ⓐ Ⓑ Ⓒ Ⓓ Ⓔ
21. Ⓐ Ⓑ Ⓒ Ⓓ Ⓔ
22. Ⓐ Ⓑ Ⓒ Ⓓ Ⓔ
23. Ⓐ Ⓑ Ⓒ Ⓓ Ⓔ

24. Ⓐ Ⓑ Ⓒ Ⓓ Ⓔ
25. Ⓐ Ⓑ Ⓒ Ⓓ Ⓔ
26. Ⓐ Ⓑ Ⓒ Ⓓ Ⓔ
27. Ⓐ Ⓑ Ⓒ Ⓓ Ⓔ
28. Ⓐ Ⓑ Ⓒ Ⓓ Ⓔ
29. Ⓐ Ⓑ Ⓒ Ⓓ Ⓔ
30. Ⓐ Ⓑ Ⓒ Ⓓ Ⓔ
31. Ⓐ Ⓑ Ⓒ Ⓓ Ⓔ
32. Ⓐ Ⓑ Ⓒ Ⓓ Ⓔ
33. Ⓐ Ⓑ Ⓒ Ⓓ Ⓔ
34. Ⓐ Ⓑ Ⓒ Ⓓ Ⓔ
35. Ⓐ Ⓑ Ⓒ Ⓓ Ⓔ
36. Ⓐ Ⓑ Ⓒ Ⓓ Ⓔ
37. Ⓐ Ⓑ Ⓒ Ⓓ Ⓔ
38. Ⓐ Ⓑ Ⓒ Ⓓ Ⓔ
39. Ⓐ Ⓑ Ⓒ Ⓓ Ⓔ
40. Ⓐ Ⓑ Ⓒ Ⓓ Ⓔ
41. Ⓐ Ⓑ Ⓒ Ⓓ Ⓔ
42. Ⓐ Ⓑ Ⓒ Ⓓ Ⓔ
43. Ⓐ Ⓑ Ⓒ Ⓓ Ⓔ
44. Ⓐ Ⓑ Ⓒ Ⓓ Ⓔ
45. Ⓐ Ⓑ Ⓒ Ⓓ Ⓔ

Completely darken bubbles with a No. 2 pencil. If you make a mistake, be sure to erase mark completely. Erase all stray marks.

1.

YOUR NAME:
(Print)
Last   First   M.I.

SIGNATURE: _____   DATE: ___ / ___ / ___

HOME ADDRESS: _____
(Print)
Number and Street

_____
City   State   Zip Code

PHONE NO.: _____

5. YOUR NAME

First 4 letters of last name				FIRST INIT	MID INIT
Ⓐ	Ⓐ	Ⓐ	Ⓐ	Ⓐ	Ⓐ
Ⓑ	Ⓑ	Ⓑ	Ⓑ	Ⓑ	Ⓑ
Ⓒ	Ⓒ	Ⓒ	Ⓒ	Ⓒ	Ⓒ
Ⓓ	Ⓓ	Ⓓ	Ⓓ	Ⓓ	Ⓓ
Ⓔ	Ⓔ	Ⓔ	Ⓔ	Ⓔ	Ⓔ
Ⓕ	Ⓕ	Ⓕ	Ⓕ	Ⓕ	Ⓕ
Ⓖ	Ⓖ	Ⓖ	Ⓖ	Ⓖ	Ⓖ
Ⓗ	Ⓗ	Ⓗ	Ⓗ	Ⓗ	Ⓗ
Ⓘ	Ⓘ	Ⓘ	Ⓘ	Ⓘ	Ⓘ
Ⓙ	Ⓙ	Ⓙ	Ⓙ	Ⓙ	Ⓙ
Ⓚ	Ⓚ	Ⓚ	Ⓚ	Ⓚ	Ⓚ
Ⓛ	Ⓛ	Ⓛ	Ⓛ	Ⓛ	Ⓛ
Ⓜ	Ⓜ	Ⓜ	Ⓜ	Ⓜ	Ⓜ
Ⓝ	Ⓝ	Ⓝ	Ⓝ	Ⓝ	Ⓝ
Ⓞ	Ⓞ	Ⓞ	Ⓞ	Ⓞ	Ⓞ
Ⓟ	Ⓟ	Ⓟ	Ⓟ	Ⓟ	Ⓟ
Ⓠ	Ⓠ	Ⓠ	Ⓠ	Ⓠ	Ⓠ
Ⓡ	Ⓡ	Ⓡ	Ⓡ	Ⓡ	Ⓡ
Ⓢ	Ⓢ	Ⓢ	Ⓢ	Ⓢ	Ⓢ
Ⓣ	Ⓣ	Ⓣ	Ⓣ	Ⓣ	Ⓣ
Ⓤ	Ⓤ	Ⓤ	Ⓤ	Ⓤ	Ⓤ
Ⓥ	Ⓥ	Ⓥ	Ⓥ	Ⓥ	Ⓥ
Ⓦ	Ⓦ	Ⓦ	Ⓦ	Ⓦ	Ⓦ
Ⓧ	Ⓧ	Ⓧ	Ⓧ	Ⓧ	Ⓧ
Ⓨ	Ⓨ	Ⓨ	Ⓨ	Ⓨ	Ⓨ
Ⓩ	Ⓩ	Ⓩ	Ⓩ	Ⓩ	Ⓩ

IMPORTANT: Please fill in these boxes exactly as shown on the back cover of your test book.

2. TEST FORM

_____

6. DATE OF BIRTH

Month	Day		Year	
◯ JAN				
◯ FEB	⓪	⓪	⓪	⓪
◯ MAR	①	①	①	①
◯ APR	②	②	②	②
◯ MAY	③	③	③	③
◯ JUN		④	④	④
◯ JUL		⑤	⑤	⑤
◯ AUG		⑥	⑥	⑥
◯ SEP		⑦	⑦	⑦
◯ OCT		⑧	⑧	⑧
◯ NOV		⑨	⑨	⑨
◯ DEC				

3. TEST CODE

⓪	Ⓐ	Ⓙ	⓪	⓪	
①	Ⓑ	Ⓚ	①	①	
②	Ⓒ	Ⓛ	②	②	
③	Ⓓ	Ⓜ	③	③	
④	Ⓔ	Ⓝ	④	④	
⑤	Ⓕ	Ⓞ	⑤	⑤	
⑥	Ⓖ	Ⓟ	⑥	⑥	
⑦	Ⓗ	Ⓠ	⑦	⑦	
⑧	Ⓘ	Ⓡ	⑧	⑧	
⑨			⑨	⑨	

4. REGISTRATION NUMBER

⓪	⓪	⓪	⓪	⓪	⓪	⓪
①	①	①	①	①	①	①
②	②	②	②	②	②	②
③	③	③	③	③	③	③
④	④	④	④	④	④	④
⑤	⑤	⑤	⑤	⑤	⑤	⑤
⑥	⑥	⑥	⑥	⑥	⑥	⑥
⑦	⑦	⑦	⑦	⑦	⑦	⑦
⑧	⑧	⑧	⑧	⑧	⑧	⑧
⑨	⑨	⑨	⑨	⑨	⑨	⑨

7. GENDER
◯ MALE
◯ FEMALE

The Princeton Review®

1. Ⓐ Ⓑ Ⓒ Ⓓ Ⓔ
2. Ⓐ Ⓑ Ⓒ Ⓓ Ⓔ
3. Ⓐ Ⓑ Ⓒ Ⓓ Ⓔ
4. Ⓐ Ⓑ Ⓒ Ⓓ Ⓔ
5. Ⓐ Ⓑ Ⓒ Ⓓ Ⓔ
6. Ⓐ Ⓑ Ⓒ Ⓓ Ⓔ
7. Ⓐ Ⓑ Ⓒ Ⓓ Ⓔ
8. Ⓐ Ⓑ Ⓒ Ⓓ Ⓔ
9. Ⓐ Ⓑ Ⓒ Ⓓ Ⓔ
10. Ⓐ Ⓑ Ⓒ Ⓓ Ⓔ
11. Ⓐ Ⓑ Ⓒ Ⓓ Ⓔ
12. Ⓐ Ⓑ Ⓒ Ⓓ Ⓔ
13. Ⓐ Ⓑ Ⓒ Ⓓ Ⓔ
14. Ⓐ Ⓑ Ⓒ Ⓓ Ⓔ
15. Ⓐ Ⓑ Ⓒ Ⓓ Ⓔ
16. Ⓐ Ⓑ Ⓒ Ⓓ Ⓔ
17. Ⓐ Ⓑ Ⓒ Ⓓ Ⓔ
18. Ⓐ Ⓑ Ⓒ Ⓓ Ⓔ
19. Ⓐ Ⓑ Ⓒ Ⓓ Ⓔ
20. Ⓐ Ⓑ Ⓒ Ⓓ Ⓔ
21. Ⓐ Ⓑ Ⓒ Ⓓ Ⓔ
22. Ⓐ Ⓑ Ⓒ Ⓓ Ⓔ
23. Ⓐ Ⓑ Ⓒ Ⓓ Ⓔ

24. Ⓐ Ⓑ Ⓒ Ⓓ Ⓔ
25. Ⓐ Ⓑ Ⓒ Ⓓ Ⓔ
26. Ⓐ Ⓑ Ⓒ Ⓓ Ⓔ
27. Ⓐ Ⓑ Ⓒ Ⓓ Ⓔ
28. Ⓐ Ⓑ Ⓒ Ⓓ Ⓔ
29. Ⓐ Ⓑ Ⓒ Ⓓ Ⓔ
30. Ⓐ Ⓑ Ⓒ Ⓓ Ⓔ
31. Ⓐ Ⓑ Ⓒ Ⓓ Ⓔ
32. Ⓐ Ⓑ Ⓒ Ⓓ Ⓔ
33. Ⓐ Ⓑ Ⓒ Ⓓ Ⓔ
34. Ⓐ Ⓑ Ⓒ Ⓓ Ⓔ
35. Ⓐ Ⓑ Ⓒ Ⓓ Ⓔ
36. Ⓐ Ⓑ Ⓒ Ⓓ Ⓔ
37. Ⓐ Ⓑ Ⓒ Ⓓ Ⓔ
38. Ⓐ Ⓑ Ⓒ Ⓓ Ⓔ
39. Ⓐ Ⓑ Ⓒ Ⓓ Ⓔ
40. Ⓐ Ⓑ Ⓒ Ⓓ Ⓔ
41. Ⓐ Ⓑ Ⓒ Ⓓ Ⓔ
42. Ⓐ Ⓑ Ⓒ Ⓓ Ⓔ
43. Ⓐ Ⓑ Ⓒ Ⓓ Ⓔ
44. Ⓐ Ⓑ Ⓒ Ⓓ Ⓔ
45. Ⓐ Ⓑ Ⓒ Ⓓ Ⓔ

NOTES

NOTES

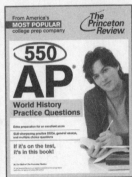
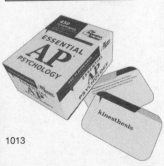